PANZERSOLDATEN!

ITALIAN BLACKSHIRT DIVISION OF THE EASTERN FRONT 1941-1943

PAOLO MORISI

FONTHILL

Fonthill Media Limited
Fonthill Media LLC
www.fonthillmedia.com
office@fonthillmedia.com

First published in the United Kingdom and the United States of America 2021

British Library Cataloguing in Publication Data:
A catalogue record for this book is available from the British Library

ISBN 978-1-78155-819-5

Typeset in 10pt on 13pt Sabon
Printed and bound in England

Acknowledgements

I would like to thank the publisher Alan Sutton, historians Giovanni Cecini, Leonardo Malatesta, Stefano Fabei, and Carlo Rastrelli for the information that they furnished me.

Contents

Introduction

'Amongst the Italian soldiers that I fought against in the Donetz region during World War Two, I admired in particular the Blackshirts. They fought heroically and I was able to ascertain, while interrogating them in the prison, the fact that they did not hate our people'.

So declared Nikita Khrushchev (1894–1971), who led the Soviet Union during the height of the Cold War, to an Italian newspaper (*Concretezza*, issue 22) on 16 November 1961. During the war, the would-be future Russian premier had been attached to the Soviet Army as a Communist Party commissar to liaison with top Soviet generals and its High Command to enforce Stalin's political and military directives. He had come across the Italian Blackshirts of the 63a *Legione CCNN Tagliamento* (63rd Blackshirt Legion Tagliamento) while the Soviet troops were fighting in the Ukraine against the Axis forces there deployed in 1941.

The Tagliamento was an Italian volunteer unit comprised overwhelmingly by older, more mature, and experienced soldiers, the majority of which had already seen action during the Spanish Civil War. The unit belonged to the *Battaglioni M* (M Battalions), the so-called Blackshirt assault units deployed by Italy during the Second World War. These units were not part of the Italian armed forces, but were deployed by the party militia, the *Milizia Volontaria per la Sicurezza Nazionale* (Voluntary Militia for National Security, or MVSN) in support of the war effort. As the later chapters will demonstrate, the MVSN had a troubled and uneven existence, and as a result, its combat units had both strengths and weaknesses that shaped their battlefield performance.

Despite the generally inadequate weapons, and while fighting against superior forces armed with heavy tanks and guns, the Blackshirts earned the respect of the Soviet enemy. There are two main reasons why the Tagliamento and the other militia units were respected by the Soviets. First, they fought with vigour and decisiveness against very unfavourable odds throughout the campaign from mid-1941 to the winter of 1942–1943. Often they fought with light weapons and ineffective anti-tank guns against both Soviet armoured and special infantry assault divisions. Second, the Blackshirts deployed on the Eastern Front performed much more effectively than other militia units that were deployed during Italy's initial campaigns of the war such as North Africa and Greece. Thus, these units turned around what up to that point had been a disappointing set of campaigns for the Blackshirt/MVSN movement. They did so while also staying clear, for the most part, and as far as the evidence is concerned, of the inhumane policies adopted by the Germans such as the killing of prisoners, or abuses against civilians.

The Tagliamento was active on the Eastern Front for almost two years. During that time, it fought in all the major engagements involving the Italian forces against the Soviet Army. In addition to the Tagliamento, three additional Blackshirt units were deployed on the Eastern Front beginning in mid-1942. These units include the *Gruppo di Battaglioni CCNN M Montebello* (Montebello Blackshirt M Battalions Group, where the M stood for Mussolini), *Gruppo di Battaglioni CCNN M Valle Scivia*, and the *Gruppo di Battaglioni CCNN M Leonessa* M Battalions. They too were made up of volunteers belonging to the party militia. What follows is the reconstruction through previously unavailable archive sources of their history while deployed on the Eastern Front. It is the first full-fledged history of these special units in English to be written. While the Walloon Legion, the Legion of French Volunteers Against Bolshevism, and the Spanish Blue Division arrived at the front in the late summer or fall of 1941, the Tagliamento Legion participated to the early advance into Ukraine along with other Axis forces almost from the start of the campaign. The former have been examined by several English language history books and journal articles often written by professional military historians. The Blackshirts, however, have been less fortunate and have only been covered in Italian language history books and articles. Often neglected or mentioned only in passing by many English written histories of the Axis campaign against the Soviet Union, the Tagliamento and the other three M Battalions fought with distinction alongside the Wehrmacht, the Romanians, the Hungarians, and the Croats. Lightly armed, lacking trucks and heavy anti-tank weapons, the Blackshirts still were deployed extensively by the Italian High Command and fought against the Soviet Army in several major engagements. After being decimated by the numerous major battles and small-scale actions, the Blackshirts were eventually withdrawn from Eastern Europe to constitute the M armoured division, a unit equipped and armed by the Germans to prop up Italy during its lowest ebb in the war in mid-1943. So what was the area of operation of the Blackshirts on the Eastern Front? How were the Blackshirts constituted? What were the tactical issues or differences between the Germans and the Italian troops, and how effective were the Blackshirts units against the Soviet Union's most powerful and well-trained infantry assault battalions? Did the German officers value the combat potential of the Blackshirts and other volunteer units? By analysing the history of the Blackshirts training and combat experiences in the Eastern Front, *Panzersoldaten!* seeks to fill a gap and provide answers to such intriguing questions.

The primary sources that are the base of this study include the war diary of the Blackshirt units, official reports from the Blackshirt units, the memoirs of common Blackshirt *legionaries* and officers, documents from the national military archive in Rome, Wehrmacht reports authored by German officers that were liaisons between the German and the Italian Army, and Italian language history studies of the Blackshirts published in the post-war era.

Mussolini hands over the battle flag of one the Blackshirt Legions to be dispatched to the frontline. (*Archivio Centrale dello stato*)

Above left: A soldier of the M Battalions recognisable by his uniform and his M red badge on his right collar. (*Archivio Centrale dello stato*)

Above right: Soldiers of the *Gruppo Battaglioni Camicie Nere* M Leonessa in Rome in 1942 prior to their trip toward the Eastern Front. They wore a black shirt (inherited from the *Squadristi*) and a red M symbol on the collar. (*Archivio Centrale dello stato*)

Left: The photo of Niccolo' Nicchiarelli, commander of the Tagliamento Legion during the Eastern Front campaign. (*Archivio Centrale dello stato*)

1

The Italian Army and Operation Barbarossa

Introduction

During the early hours of 22 June 1941, the German artillery launched a withering barrage into the Russian defensive positions of Eastern Europe, while more than 1,000 Stukas dive-bombed into them from above, dropping their lethal weapons. On that fatal day, with Operation Barbarossa, the world witnessed the opening of the most massive military campaign ever waged in history, involving millions of infantry soldiers and vast amounts of equipment such as thousands of tanks and aeroplanes. Germany's attack against the Soviet Union monolith would result in a titanic struggle that would last for five years and would see the death of hundreds of thousands of soldiers.

The campaign had been planned with the utmost secrecy by German officers, even while Hitler and Stalin were still under an alliance that had been sealed in 1939, the so-called Russo-German Pact. The German High Command had begun to plan an attack against the Soviet Union in July 1940, the original code name at the time being Operation Otto. The planning was based on extensive Luftwaffe operations, mainly numerous aerial reconnaissance missions over Soviet territory to gather intelligence on enemy strength.

Finally, in December 1940, Hitler authorised the plans for the invasion of the Soviet Union and renamed them under the code name of Operation Barbarossa; shortly thereafter, in the spring, the German Army began to slowly amass troops and equipment at the border. The aims of the operation were to defeat Communism, to occupy vast amounts of Russian territory and exploit its farms and natural resources to support the German war effort, and finally to pre-emptively defeat the Soviet Union and its military before it could attack the Axis forces.

The plan was extremely ambitious since it required occupying Leningrad, Moscow, and the Ukraine before the start of the winter of 1941–42. The

Germans assumed that they could replicate the far-reaching armoured and infantry manoeuvres that had enabled them to occupy France, albeit on a much greater scale.

When the German Army struck, the Russian forces were caught by complete surprise and forced to retreat for hundreds of miles. During the retreat, the fast-advancing Germans were able to capture record numbers of enemy soldiers and weapons. The attack was undertaken by 3.2 million German soldiers subdivided into 153 divisions, nineteen of which were armoured and fifteen were motorised. The troops were supported by 1,160 Luftwaffe planes and by twenty-seven Romanian and Hungarian infantry divisions and three Italian infantry divisions. In the North, the German Army was also supported by twelve Finnish infantry divisions that aimed to wrest back control of Finnish territory occupied by the Russians a year earlier.

The German Army and its allies advanced against three main objectives. In the North, General von Leeb's forces were directed against the city of Leningrad; in the centre, General Bock's forces aimed to lay siege to Moscow; while the Army Group South aimed to ultimately occupy the Caucasus oil fields. The main goal was to occupy the targeted positions before the start of the winter and before the Russian forces had the chance to reorganise their forces.

Despite the initial surprise that caused widespread losses within the Russian ranks and politically paralysed Stalin and his entourage, the Axis alliance still faced a formidable opponent with great strength. The Soviet Army had a massive military branch with 170 infantry divisions (and a further eighty divisions as a reserve unit in the rear), 23,200 tanks, 116,000 artillery pieces and mortars of all sizes, and 20,000 aircraft. Even though they had been extensive, German military intelligence operations had severely underestimated Soviet strength since they had failed to account for the enemy's additional soldiers and material located in the rear positions away from the European frontiers. In addition, the Soviet Army could call upon a huge reservoir of recruits and unlike its German enemy, its industrial military complex was able to produce many more weapons and at a much quicker pace. Thus, the Soviets, unlike the Axis allies, which had few reserves, could initially afford to lose a larger amount of forces and equipment because they could more easily substitute them than their opponents. In fact, the longer the campaign lasted, the more it advantaged the Soviet Red Army, which could call upon almost unlimited resources.

The Soviet Army

The Soviet Red military was composed of four main branches: infantry, air force, navy, and anti-aircraft force. The army was made of up of conscripts. At nineteen years of age, young men were recruited into the army and were expected to complete an initial two years of service. The bulk of the army was made up of peasants and factory workers. The basic unit of the Soviet Army was the rifle division, with a strength of 15,000 soldiers organised into nine battalions, two artillery regiments, a light tank battalion, and support services. At the time of the German attack, there were two major issues impacting the efficacy of the army. The first issue was that the army had left its pre-1939 defences along the Russian–Polish border in a state of disrepair. In 1941, the army was organising new defences but most of the work was still incomplete when the Germans struck. Therefore, given the unpreparedness of the Russian forces, the German armoured formations were able to move fairly quickly past the first and second lines of defence and advance against an enemy in disarray. The second issue was the lack of experienced officers and NCOs since the majority of the older, more experienced officers had been purged from the army by the Communists during the 1930s. For instance, the purges had eliminated from the army the most forward-thinking officers that had been responsible for introducing new weapons such as tanks and armoured vehicles. In other instances, well-respected career officers had been replaced by less experienced, more politically minded party appointees. Junior officers that showed even a slight allegiance to the pre-Communist regime had also been expelled, some had even been imprisoned. The purges had negatively impacted an army that had previously completed a considerable amount of work in preparing itself for modern mechanised warfare during the 1920s and early 1930s by developing 'Deep Battle' tactics. Mixed units of tanks and infantry were to take the offensive, breech enemy defences, and drive and capture key rear artillery and infantry positions. Specifically, the purges robbed the army of key tactical geniuses such as Georgy Isserson and other notable leaders and entire echelons of mid-level officers and NCOs. These mid-level officers were really the backbone of the army, while the senior career officers were its key innovators and strategists. As Glantz asserts: '... the purges and other ideological and systemic constraints convinced Red Army officers that any show of independent judgement was hazardous to their personal health'.[1]

Prior to the purges, Soviet tactics were very progressive and much further advanced than those of the German or French armies. They envisioned the use of tanks and paratroopers in deep manoeuvres against enemy defences:

> The Soviet vision was of highly mobile warfare in which massed tank forces supported by infantry, artillery and air power would conduct vast combined arms assaults on the enemy's defensive lines; a breakthrough battle would then develop seamlessly into a series of rolling sequential operations that exploited the breakthrough, with echeloned waves driving deep into the enemy's rear areas, attacking key targets and giving him no time to recover or to organise any resistance.[2]

The tactical vision of the Red Army was very advanced for the time and sought to operate tank units autonomously and not as mere support units to the infantry or under the command of an infantry officer. This vision had originally been spearheaded by some of the most forward thinkers of the post-First World War era, such as J. F. C. Fuller, who published important works on mechanisation and mechanised warfare, General Charles de Gaulle, and British military theorist Basil Liddell Hart. Its basic tenet was that armoured vehicles and tanks were going to revolutionise warfare and tactics in general, given the fact that their speed and mobility had the potential to deploy a much greater amount of fire and movement than ever before. Tanks, in particular, were seen as the key weapons to overcome the stasis of positional warfare, which had characterised much of the First World War. As a result of being one of the first armies to embrace these innovative ideas, the Soviet Army had become a leader in modern tank warfare as it formed its first mechanised unit in 1930.[3] The 1st Mechanised Brigade originally consisted of a tank regiment, a motorised infantry regiment, as well as reconnaissance and artillery battalions. Shortly thereafter, two mechanised army corps were founded to fully support the infantry during offensive operations. Each of these units consisted of three tank brigades and of motorised troops. During the decade of the 1930s, the Soviet Army, for instance, was much more advanced in terms of mechanisation than probably any other European army, and the armoured capabilities of the German Army were of much inferior quality. The Soviets were not only ahead of their time with regards to mechanisation but were also one of the first European armies that during the 1930s had already constituted large units of paratroopers to be deployed as the spearhead of combined arms attacks. The Soviet Army at the time possessed also the greatest, most potent artillery arm with exceedingly high numbers of 203-mm model 1931 (B-4) and 280-mm model 1939 (Br-5) howitzers. These units were so heavy that they had to be train mounted or required a tractor carriage to be transported to the frontline. Even more impressive was the large reservoir of foot soldiers that the military could recruit into service.

By 1938, the purges along with the large expansion of the army had taken their toll on the effectiveness of the military instrument itself, which probably had also expanded at too quick a pace. The purges robbed the army of its leadership and its mid-level officers, while tactics and strategy did not evolve in a positive fashion. In fact, from a tactical standpoint, the Red Army regressed tremendously. But the Winter War of 1939–40 against Finland, where the Soviet Army had given a very negative account of itself, had been instrumental to the Soviet leadership. That campaign had been a wake-up call. The leadership quickly realised that the Army needed deep reform. Through the experiences of that war, senior Soviet officers recognised the need for further training of the troops and for a return to the innovative tactical principles of the early 1930s. The Soviet Army during the Finnish campaign had indeed not performed very well and it was one of the reasons why Germany shortly after opted for a preventive strike in 1941. During the Winter War, for instance, Soviet tank crews had not operated well, undermined by the cold environment, by the forests which reduced manoeuvrability, and by the constant threat of the Finnish anti-tank defence. As Campbell asserts:

> A more effective use of artillery to suppress the Finnish line, and in particular better co-ordination between tanks and infantry, may well have engendered much better results. Attacks often planned rapidly and without much depth of thought, were carried out at great cost in men and material, and were blunted by conventional defensive tactics.[4]

Many tanks were lost, the infantry units deployed suffered heavy casualties and many guns were also captured by the Finns.

After the Finnish campaign came to an abrupt end, the tank units were reorganised as the Soviet High Command sought to improve their performance.

> Formed hastily in late 1940 and still forming when the war began, each mechanised corps contained two tank divisions and one motorised division. Since the former, which had strength of 10,940 men and 375 tanks, was tank heavy and lacked sufficient support, the mechanised corps also included a motorised division and various support systems.[5]

At the time, Soviet tanks did not have radios, and commanders had no way to effectively co-ordinate the movements of tank battalions while deployed in battle. Moreover, there had been little co-ordination with the infantry in the pre-war manoeuvres and it was almost like the two branches fought autonomously. Even the artillery, which was much superior in terms of firepower to its Finnish counterpart, did not fight well.

As a result of the lessons learnt during the Winter War, the Soviet Army of 1941 was in a better shape than in 1939, although it was still an army in transition and not fully organised tactically for a modern war of manoeuvre. By then, the army's senior leadership had learnt a lot about modern anti-tank gun tactics and how to conduct more determined attacks utilising different branches of the army in a more cohesive fashion. Moreover, the Soviet industry was by then fully mobilised for the war. While generally better positioned, the Soviet Army in 1941 had still not mastered how to fully integrate the mechanised units into the infantry or how to properly confront the fast paced German Panzer Divisions. Soviet offensive tactics followed a uniform pattern whereby several infantry battalions would attack with the support of few tanks. The infantry basic unit was the eleven-man platoon comprised of a squad leader, two machine gunners, two submachine gunners, and six riflemen. The riflemen and the NCO carried the SVT-40 semi-automatic rifle, while the machine gunners carried the DP-28 light machine gun and the submachine gunners carried the PPD-38/40. The infantry was well armed but initial tactics were brutish and primitive, often replicating older tactics.

In fact, their infantry units' initial tactics were not too different from those deployed by the Russian Army in the First World War:

> When the platoon had closed in and was able to make its final assault rush, the troops were ordered to ensure that weapons were fully loaded and grenades prepared. On the order, '*Na shturm marschch*!' [Assault, march!] they rose as a body and advanced at a run without bunching up or halting. Within 40-50 yards, of the enemy positions they shouted the Russian battle cry, a deep drawn out Urra!... They fired on the move and, when within range of enemy positions, threw grenades. They closed in rapidly for '*blizhnii boi*' [close combat] with point blank fire, bayonets, weapon butts, entrenching tools, and fists.[6]

An Italian officer, for example, argued the following with regards to Soviet infantry tactics:

> They always attacked us relying on the element of surprise. They moved in small groups without the accompanying mortar fire. Each soldier had a light automatic gun, a dagger and plenty of hand grenades. And since the frontline was not constituted by one continuous line of defence, they operated in the dark to infiltrate our positions. They would jump into our positions often throwing themselves to the ground to make believe they had been shot. But then at the most opportune time they would jump up and fire their weapons.[7]

The infantry and armoured units combined tactics were also still fairly primitive in 1941. An Italian intelligence report for instance argued:

> Russian tanks are deployed usually in small numbers either to support infantry attacks or to transport the troops that ride on sleds pulled by the tanks.... The standard Russian attack is preceded by the artillery preparation and then followed up by infantry supported by a few tanks. The Russians undoubtedly do not yet know how to put forth an attack involving a mass of armoured units.[8]

Another report published a few months later continued to argue that the Soviet Army did deploy tanks during offensive operations but that its tactics were still not up to par with the high degree of manoeuvrability and unit cohesion of the German tank formations: 'The enemy's infantry attacks are conducted by masses of soldiers advancing in different waves and supported by small numbers of tanks. The latter's main role appears to be the identification of our anti-tank guns in order to overtake them and put them out of action.'[9]

This initial tactic, which saw the tanks acting in a more traditional role as support for infantry, was more manageable for the Axis forces to defend against, especially because they could deploy a proper anti-tank defence with the weapons at their disposal. Then, beginning in October 1942, the Russians began to deploy larger armoured formations in what became true combined arms operations. The Russians by then based their strategy on the fact that armoured units alone could not achieve a decisive breakthrough; they must receive support from other arms, particularly from infantry and artillery. The latter must degrade ahead of time the defensive capabilities of the enemy, while the former has to fight alongside the tanks and deal with the obstacles such as the minefields and the anti-tank guns. Throughout 1941, small units of Russian tanks had been sent to fight with little or no support and had often been captured or destroyed by the enemy because they had advanced too far. The Soviet Army then evolved and refined its tactics by deploying the tanks in a much more blunt and forceful fashion. The new tactics were also aided by the fact that the tanks had been retrofitted with radios and central command could now communicate with the crews and therefore manoeuvre tank formations much more cohesively.

Accordingly, the new strategy envisaged:

> The Russians emphasise that armoured vehicles must be concentrated to attack where they can be most effective. If they are supporting infantry they must be put under command of the unit supported, but the temptation to split them up into small groups with the object of helping the infantry forward all along the front must be avoided. Tanks should not be regarded solely as a means of direct attack to overcome strong resistance which is holding up the infantry, but should aim rather at breaking in where resistance is weaker, striking strongly defended localities only in the rear, and ultimately exploiting the 'break-in' into a 'break-through'. Tank forces in the attack must be accompanied by mobile field and antitank guns, which must be well forward to deal with surprise opposition. They will also be invaluable for repulsing enemy tank counterattack. Russian tank forces rely largely on air support, particularly by dive-bombers, to extend the range of artillery preparation, to harass enemy reserves, and to break up counterattacks.[10]

During the Battle of Serafimovich in July 1942, for example, Italian commanders had reported that the Russian Army had begun to change its tactics with regards to the deployment of tanks. 'They deployed a tank brigade in a violent tank attack put forth by T-34 and BT-7 tanks and armoured vehicles. At the end of the battle 49 Russian tanks had been knocked out of action, of which 33 by the Italians, which had used anti-tank guns, howitzers and incendiary devices'.[11]

Not only had the Russians used a greater number of tanks during this battle than usual, but they had also deployed them all at once in a mass tank attack.

Also, by that time, the Russian Army was not only able to field record numbers of T-35 and T-34 tanks, but also of KV-2, and SU self-propelled assault guns, which had been developed specifically to counter the threat posed by the German Tigers and Panthers tanks. The Russian self-propelled units were used to engage enemy tanks with armour-piercing rounds and to shell the enemy infantry with high-explosive rounds. In addition to Russian-made tanks, the Soviet Army also utilised record numbers of American and British tanks. Great Britain furnished four types of tanks to the Red Army: Mk II Matilda, Mk III Valentine, Mk IV Churchill, and Mk VII Tetrarch. While the United States furnished record numbers of M3 Stuarts, M3 General Lees, M4A2 Shermans, and M10 Wolverines.

Then, during the major offensive of December 1942 against the Italian 8th Army, the Soviets would deploy an even larger amount of tank brigades to smash through the enemy lines. The tanks were deployed in mass against the weakest and most exposed sectors held by the Italians, and once they achieved the initial breakthrough, they continued to advance at a quick pace to overrun and encircle enemy defences. Their ultimate goal was to arrive at the rear defences and depots and capture or destroy the heavy artillery batteries.

As an Italian official report states:

> The great enemy offensive along the front held by the 8th Army has clearly shown that our infantry has to be better trained in fighting against armoured units in order to destroy them when possible. Moreover, it must avoid hasty or disorganised reactions to these enemy tank incursions. Once the tanks had bypassed our lines they had an easier time in reaching our rear defensive command centres, logistical hubs and weapons thereby causing disarray in our action of command and in the organisation of our reaction. Anti-tank ditches are the most proficient passive defence against enemy armour and every soldier should know that when the tanks are separated from their support troops such as the infantry they cannot occupy an enemy position for the long term.[12]

Once the positions had been overrun and the anti-tank defence had been bypassed, the Soviet tanks were free to pursue the retreating Italian infantry travelling on foot:

> In the sector held by my troops the Russians have employed masses of tanks whose objective was to rupture our defences and penetrate them. On the frontline held by the Julia Division the enemy deployed numerous tanks

> in support of the infantry. They advanced in groups and then attempted to smash their way through our lines by destroying our machine gun and anti-tank gun emplacements. Afterwards they remained in the advanced positions and sought coverage behind natural barriers in order to shell our defensive strongholds that were still holding on. Once their infantry had caught up with them they retreated back to their starting lines.... However, once our lines were broken the tanks once again took the initiative. Knowing full well that due to our lack of motorization we had to abandon our heavy weapons on the frontline, the Russian tanks, armoured units, and armoured cars began to chase our troops, often cutting them off from the main columns that were retreating in order to wreck havoc amongst our ranks. In many ways the tank formations substituted the cavalry as they continued to pursue our troops. The deployment of the tanks proved to be of uttermost importance given their speed and manoeuvrability deep into our defensive lines.[13]

The new tactics deployed by the Soviets were especially successful because the army, by effectuating those deep penetrations, forced the Italians to abandon their heavier weapons and as a result they had no way to stop the armour. The strategy, for instance, achieved its stated goal of breaking through the Axis defensive line in the sectors where the Germans and especially their Axis allies lacked more robust anti-tank defences, given the lack of adequate guns, self-propelled guns, and tanks. After the breakthrough of the enemy positions had been achieved, the Russian tanks then adopted the strategy of the cavalry by trying to cut off and isolate groups of Italian troops retreating on foot and forcing them to abandon their anti-tank weapons and their trucks on the defensive line. The Russian tanks by then had modern communication devices and were supported by motorised units carrying fuel, ammunition, and food provisions.

In short, while initially the tanks accompanied the infantry and were usually deployed in small numbers, toward the latter stages of the campaign, entire brigades of tanks and infantry were deployed together in a concerted effort to break through enemy lines. The main attacking principle being:

> Great emphasis is placed on bringing all available fire power to bear simultaneously at the point of maximum effort, thereby causing changes in the doctrine of deployment. The doctrine of deployment by echelon, which does not permit this heavy, simultaneous concentration of fire power, is being abandoned; this doctrine also leads to wastage without any positive returns for casualties suffered.[14]

Thus, while initially the mechanised tactics of the Soviet Army were not well developed, by late 1942, they had made vast advancements and in some instances they rivalled the most advanced German tactics. According to Russian sources, the Soviet Army lost approximately 20,500 tanks (most of them light units) during the first six months of the war and another 15,100 during 1942. Most of the losses in 1942 were made during the first six months of the year, which is an indication that by the latter half of the year, the tanks were performing better from a tactical perspective. During the first year of the war, half of the tank fleet of the Soviet Red Army was comprised by light tanks such as T-26, T-50, T-60, and T-70 units. These tanks were easy prey of the faster-moving German tanks, which also had greater firepower. By 1942, the Red Army was armed primarily with heavier, medium-sized tanks and self-propelled guns, which could match German Panthers and Tigers. In addition, Soviet Union mass production of weapons by 1942 such as tanks far exceeded total Axis output, thus ensuring that its frontline forces could replace at a much quicker pace any losses sustained. The Soviet Union produced approximately 100,000 tanks and self-propelled guns during the conflict, and its manufacturing capacity was a key factor in the USSR's victory over the Axis forces. The evolution of tank and combined arms tactics by the Russians was one of the primary elements that led them to ultimate victory. By 1942, even the Germans were surprised of the fighting abilities and qualities acquired by the Red Army, which had literally stolen the German combined arms tactics playbook. No longer were the Soviet armoured units easily defeated by the Axis forces or deployed in battle with obsolete tactics.

The Soviet anti-tank tactics had also seen much improvement by 1942. Initially, the anti-tank tactics were not well developed and the Soviets frequently succumbed to the deep infiltrations of the German Panzers units. The Russian troops had been originally pushed back by several hundreds of miles and as a result had lost weapons and men to the German onslaught. The latter had been facilitated by the novel tactics used by the Germans and by the lack of preparation of the Russian infantry in stopping the tanks.

By the time the Russians were defending Moscow in the fall of 1941, their tactics had much improved in large part as a result of the lesson learnt during the first months of fighting. The main tactical change came about by staggering the defensive works across large swaths of territory. This forced the Germans to advance against a system of defence that attempted to bottle them into a killing zone. The system itself was articulated into several different weapons and positions that made up the anti-tank defence. Artillery units at the back, including anti-aircraft guns were used to provide the backbone of the anti-tank screen. These weapons were used at the early stages of the enemy attack to break up enemy formations and to shell them in their assembly points with long-range artillery. During the latter stages of the enemy attack, these heavy units would be deployed to knock out tanks that had penetrated into the resistance areas. Right in front of this line, there were strong points of anti-tank units interspersed with infantry positions armed with anti-tank rifles, mortars, and hand grenades. The anti-tank defence was also aided by the Soviet air forces, which would intervene during critical stages of the battle to reconnaissance the field of battle and identify targets for the artillery. These defensive positions were often sited near or in urban areas where it was decisively more difficult for the enemy tanks to manoeuvre.

In addition, the Russians made widespread use of various tank obstacles such as mines, ditches, steel barriers, and barbed-wire works to slow down enemy tanks. Once this was achieved, the anti-tank guns, well camouflaged in small pillboxes or behind thick walls, would attempt to break up enemy attacks. Tanks that had been isolated from their squads were dealt by the antitank infantry units deploying hand grenades, rifles, and even Molotov cocktails. Russian anti-tank rifle squads were particularly successful, especially when deployed together such as when teams were armed with three or more anti-tank rifles concentrating fire on an enemy tank from different positions The Russian infantry was subsequently trained to stop the tanks with a multitude of weapons, including makeshift devices such as Molotov cocktails or bundles of hand grenades as well as more powerful weapons. When the infantry was not able to stop the tanks, it was trained to let the tanks pass by and lie low in the trenches and dugouts. After the enemy tanks had advanced, the Russian infantry would then try to stop the advance of the infantry in order to separate the latter from the tanks. The enemy armoured units were then dealt primarily by the artillery (85-mm dual-purpose gun, 76-mm, and 45-mm guns) by mobile anti-tank groups and by anti-aircraft guns, which were frequently used successfully against the tanks. As the German tanks barrelled their way through the Russian defences, the German air forces would start harassing the enemy's second line of defence. This would typically allow the more forward positioned Soviet anti-tank guns to fire at the German tanks from relatively short range and with more direct fire. By 1942, the Soviet anti-tank defence was much more elaborate. It was based on a defence in depth approach and the guns were well camouflaged and sited.

More and more frequently, the Soviet anti-tank defence began to gain the upper hand in battles against enemy tanks. A Soviet intelligence report, for instance, states that during the defence of Moscow in late 1941, a well-camouflaged single anti-tank gun destroyed five German tanks as they attempted to cross a river and forced the remainder (up to thirty-five tanks) to halt their advance. By 1942, the Red Army also had record number of self-propelled guns, including at the tail end of the year the SU-152 gun, which was called the 'Beast Hunter'.

The Red Air Force was also an organisation that was in transition in 1941. Although it could count on over 20,000 serviceable aircrafts, making it the largest air force in the world, many of its aircrafts were obsolete by Second World War standards. Stalin's crusade against the so-called traitors of the

Communist regime had been extremely fierce within the air forces and many excellent commanders, design engineers, and equipment manufacturers had been purged from the service or from supplying the air force. But by the spring of 1941, the Soviet Union was beginning to introduce into service the MiG-3 fighter jet and the Il-2 Sturmovik ground-attack aeroplane, which in many ways could fight on par with the German planes. The Red Air Force doctrine relied heavily upon the tactic of massive air bombings against enemy forces and military and non-military infrastructure. The tactics were initially rudimentary given the lack of experienced pilots, but by 1942, the Red Air Force squadrons began to fight well in combined arms operations supporting the major land counteroffensives with saturation and targeted bombing attacks of enemy positions.

As the campaign against the Soviet Union progressed into the winter of 1942–43, the Soviet Army's tactics evolved in a positive fashion with a much more modern approach that could be considered on par with the most advanced German tactics. Specifically, the Army had acquired mastery over the vast majority of weapons deployed in modern war and had become especially adept in combined arms operations. By then, its armoured units could be committed in large-scale co-ordinated operations fighting alongside special shock troops and paratroopers and capable of implementing deep penetrations and manoeuvres aimed at capturing the enemy's heavy weapons and rear command and control centres. The use of tanks to effectuate deep penetrations into the Italian lines, for instance, would result in the collapse of the 8th Army on the Don River, causing widespread havoc among the Italian ranks. Even the fiercest artillery crews and the elite infantry units of the army could do little while facing such a massive tank attack based on T-34 medium units. The Red Army also took advantage of its special knowledge of the land, of the weather conditions and of its vast industrial resources to effectuate a break through.

Glatz, for example, states that one of the main advantages that the Soviet Army enjoyed *versus* the Axis, mainly the large industrial base, allowed the Soviet Union to quickly outpace Germany in the production of heavy weapons:

> Thus, although Germany possessed clear qualitative and even quantitative advantages over the Soviet Union in a short struggle, if its first onslaught failed to knock out the Red Army, the Soviet Union was capable of overwhelming Germany in the long term. In the first place, but unrecognised by the overconfident Germans, the Soviets had sizeable forces available in the internal military districts and Far East and an immense mobilisation potential. In addition the Red Army was beginning to field a new generation of weaponry, including multiple rocket launchers (the famous katiushas and new tanks [T-34 mediums and KV heavies] that were markedly superior to all current and projected German vehicles.[15]

The Katyushas, the first self-propelled artillery mass-produced by the Soviet Union, is an example of a very effective weapon with great mobility giving the Red Army an edge over the Axis. This mobility gave the Soviet weapons the ability to concentrate firepower against the enemy and then disengage or engage somewhere else and before being located and attacked with counter-battery fire.

Katyusha weapons of the Second World War, such as the BM-13 launcher, light BM-8, and heavy BM-31, demonstrate the great technology and manufacturing capabilities that backed the Soviet Army and that no other nation, save the United States, enjoyed throughout the war. The Soviet Army's almost endless source of supply, its improvements in the technological design of its weapons and its improved tactical deployment of its troops and weapons would ultimately ensure its final victory.

The Axis Forces

The German High Command counted upon the support of Italian, Finnish, and satellite East Europeans such as the Romanian and the Hungarian forces to balance against Soviet numerical superiority. During the planning phase of Operation Barbarossa, Axis governments were notified by the Germans well in advance of the start of this massive operation. While the Finns aimed at liberating their territory, the Italian and the satellite governments shared Germany's opposition to Russia and Communism. Mussolini was one of the first leaders to pledge support to Germany's campaign in the east, even though Italy's main theatre of military operations was North Africa. Unlike Franco's Spain—token support with the dispatch of the Blue Division, whose total strength was a mere 18,000 soldiers—Mussolini from the onset wanted to send to Russia a much larger force, which was quickly assembled and hastily dispatched. On 30 May 1941, the Italian leader had met with Ugo Cavallero, the head of the Italian High Military Command (*Comando Supremo*) and told him: 'We cannot be absent in a struggle against Communism' and ordered him to assemble a force to support the German Army in anticipation of the invasion of the Soviet Union.[16] As Burgwyn asserts 'Germany and Russia were headed for an apocalyptic denouement, Mussolini prophesised, and Italy would join the attack by moving armoured and motorised divisions assembled between Ljubljana and Zagreb northward'.[17]

Then on 2 June, Mussolini had met Hitler at the Brenner Pass where, as the historian Renzo de Felice asserts, Hitler had likely revealed to his ally the date and the final plans for the attack against the Soviet Union.[18] On 5 June, the Italian ambassador in Berlin reported of widespread movements of German armed forces toward the Russian border and the shifting of weapons and tanks from France to the east. The same information was also gathered by the Italian military *attaché* in Berlin (General Efisio Marras) that was working closely with the German High Command. When Germany struck on 22 June, Mussolini was vacationing in Riccione and received a letter from Hitler stating that Operation Barbarossa had begun. Believing that the Soviet Union was bound to collapse just as France had done under the hammer of Germany's armoured divisions, Mussolini immediately wrote a letter to Hitler pledging Italian support to the Eastern Front campaign. At the time, Mussolini told General Giovanni Messe, who would later assume command of the Italian troops in Russia, that 'I must be at the side of Hitler in Russia as he was at mine in the war against Greece, and is henceforward in Africa. The destiny of Italy is intimately bound up with that of Germany.'[19, 20]

There were two motivations spurring the *Duce* to dispatch Italian troops in Russia. First, the presence of an Italian contingent would prevent Germany from consolidating overwhelming power in Europe once it had crippled the Soviet Union. Most importantly the control of the oil wells was seen as a key issue by Italy, and by contributing to the campaign, it was hoped that Russia's vast natural resources would be subdivided more equally among Axis allies. Second, revive the fortunes of the Italian military after its lacklustre performance in Greece. The army had fought the Greeks into a stalemate that was ultimately broken by the rapid intervention of the German armoured units, which in a very brief time had invaded and conquered most of Greece. The campaign against the Soviet Union was thus seen as a new opportunity to showcase the capabilities of the Italian Army. At first, Hitler politely refused Italy's pledge of support, urging Mussolini to concentrate the bulk of Italian troops in North Africa, Italy's main theatre of operations. But shortly thereafter, Hitler acceded to Italy's demands and authorised the dispatch to Russia of an Italian expeditionary force. Accordingly, on 30 June, Mussolini offered Hitler an armed corps, which was assembled in July 1941. Shortly thereafter, the troops were transferred by train to Russia, while the bulk of the heavy equipment was carried by train or by plane. Once they arrived at the train station, the troops began long marches through hundreds of kilometres of Ukrainian countryside. Finally, most troops had reached the frontline by August 1941. The initial march toward the frontline positions epitomised Italy's campaign on the Eastern Front since, due to the lack of motorised units, the troops moved primarily on foot. The initial march, although very taxing, was conducted during the summer and the soldiers for the most part had plenty of food and water. In contrast, the march conducted during the Russian winter in January 1943 would evidence the weakness of the troops and their equipment in facing such a difficult campaign with almost a complete lack of motor vehicles and of viable clothing and shoes to brave such harsh winter conditions.

The contribution of Germany's allies to the Eastern Front campaign can be subdivided into three main phases. First, the allies supported with infantry divisions and other weapons such as light tanks and aeroplanes the initial breakthrough into Russian territory during the summer of 1941. During this phase, they participated to the advance together with the German 2nd Army, which fought in Ukraine and the southern basin, pursuing the Soviet forces that at the time were in considerable disarray. During this phase they covered the German flanks and followed in the footsteps of the faster moving German units. Their role was not only to provide flanking coverage but also to overrun and mop up clusters of enemy resistance. The capture of Ukraine's major industrial hubs represented their most important contribution during these early stages of the campaign. Cities such as Stalino, Kiev, and Dinipro were strategically important since they were the backbone of Soviet industry. Also, the Ukraine was rich in coal plants. Second, as the Axis forces advance was subsequently halted by stiff Russian opposition and by the rough winter climate of 1941, the non-German Axis forces took up mostly defensive positions in order to reorganise their ranks in support of Army Group South. The harsh winter weather caused a general stasis of operations and both sides took the time to ream the troops, replenish the ranks, and dig in into prepared defensive positions. In December 1941, Italian troops fought off a major enemy counterattack during the so-called Christmas Battle. After fighting off the Soviet thrust, they then went on the attack and occupied additional frontline positions. The Christmas battle was one of the most important operations conducted by the Italians, which fought for the most part autonomously, relying on their own artillery and air force to destroy Soviet tanks and heavy artillery. Third, during the German led offensive of 1942 against the Russian city of Stalingrad and the Caucasus, Italian, Hungarian, and Romanian forces helped to lay siege to the Russian positions. Their main objective at the time was to face potential enemy counterattacks as well as to participate to localised raids and attacks against prepared enemy positions. After having reached the Don River and after having taken up defensive positions there, they took the brunt of a major enemy counterattack in the summer of 1942. In the so-called First Battle of the Don River, they were able to repel the Soviet infantry with heavy losses in both men and tanks. As the Germans continued to attack Stalingrad, the Axis allies then again took defensive positions along the Don River to cover the German flanks. Between 19 and 23 November 1942, the Russians, in order to relieve the pressure against Stalingrad, launched a major counteroffensive (Operation Uranus), which smashed through the Third and Fourth Romanian Armies and portions of the German Fourth Panzer Army. Subsequently, they attacked with a massive concentration of tanks and aircraft both the Italian and Hungarian armies deployed on the Don on 16 December 1942. This operation (code-named Little Saturn for the Russians and Second Battle of the Don River for the Italians) quickly achieved its stated goal, forcing a general retreat of Axis forces from the river. The latter, incurring the danger of being encircled by the Russians, retreated on foot for many kilometres in the dead of the Russian winter. Most soldiers died of cold and hunger during the retreat and many were also captured by the Russians. The Italians, for instance, retreated on foot with two major infantry columns and the few that survived the long strenuous journey managed to break through the siege during the battles of Cherkovo on 15 January and of Nikolayevka on 13–26 January 1943. In total, approximately 20 per cent of the 227,000 total force of Italians was able to return home, while a large majority died during the retreat and many more were captured (approximately 80,000). This was the third and final phase of the non-German Axis forces contribution to the Eastern Front campaign. After the retreat, most non-German forces were evacuated back to Europe and would no longer experience any fighting in Russian territory. Most of them had been so badly depleted that they could not be immediately reconstituted.

The non-German Axis contribution in the Eastern Front was considerable, it is estimated than at its high point in 1942, the German allies provided approximately over a quarter of the Axis soldiers deployed against the Soviet Army. The largest armies were those of Hungary, Romania, and Italy, while those of Vichy France, Franco's Spain, and the Belgian legions also participated to the campaign with a few battalions. Their deployment, however, was marred, for the most part, by the fact that they lacked the modern anti-tank guns, tanks, and aircraft available to the German and Russian armies, and as a consequence, they fought with inferior and inadequate equipment and weapons. The first three nations along with the Spanish Blue Division had their troops actually deployed in the frontline, while the Belgian and French units were for the most part used in the rear to fight the partisans because they were too weak to deploy them in combat against Russian tanks and heavy guns.

Italy's Contribution

Italy's specific contribution to the campaign against the Soviet Union was dictated by Mussolini's desire to share in the spoils and to defeat Communism. Mussolini stated that his political movement had been the first forceful opponent of Soviet Communism and that his nation could not abstain itself from participating in the anti-Communist crusade. It was hoped that the Axis forces could deal a massive blow against Communism, but that Italy would also gain control of some of the precious oil fields in the Caucasus. Italian support was hastily pledged shortly after the outbreak of hostilities between the Soviet Union and Germany despite the fact that the Italian armed forces by all standards were not prepared for a war of long duration. The navy, for instance, entered the war in June 1940 with a total of 113 submarines, seven battleships, and no aircraft carriers. The submarines would be the only units to be deployed near the port of Sevastopol and that would play a role in scuttling a few Soviet ships. The air force, on the other hand, had approximately 3,000 aircraft. 'The mainstay of the Italian fighter force throughout 1940 was the Fiat CR.42 biplane. Despite quite exceptional manoeuvrability, it had less armament than its British counterpart, the Gloster Gladiator'.[21] By 1941, the air force was able to introduce the Macchi MC.200, which was faster than the CR.42 and would see service in Russia as well. The Italians also had a powerful torpedo bomber, the Savoia-Marchetti S.79, which according to a British aeronautical expert was 'an extremely efficient machine and perhaps the most successful torpedo bomber of the war'.[22]

The torpedo bomber, however, was mostly deployed against British shipping in the Mediterranean and saw no significant action against the Soviet Union. The air force epitomised Italy's campaign against the Soviet Union. In 1941, Italian planes were still being manufactured at a slow pace by semi-artisan aircraft manufacturing companies, while the Soviet Air Force had a much larger fleet and its domestic industry was at the cutting edge of industrial production. While the Soviet Air Force had more than 20,000 planes, the Italian had only a few thousands and its industrial base was unable to catch up. The army was based on the infantry division, which was comprised of two infantry regiments and one artillery regiment totalling 8,000 to 10,000 soldiers. Although the army had forty-four divisions of infantry soldiers, the latter were armed with many antiquated weapons such as the rifle from the First World War and the machine gun. Most importantly, the Italian infantry lacked a powerful anti-tank gun that could be deployed in forward positions to knock out enemy armour. The main tanks were the Fiat L-3 light and the M11/39 medium tank with a fixed 37-mm gun. Both were very light units that offered little firepower against bigger Soviet or British tanks. The artillery was probably one of best trained branches of the army although many artillery units were obsolete and from the First World War. Some of the largest artillery units were the 210-mm and the 149-mm guns and howitzers, which represented the most effective firepower available to the Italian Army. In some cases, the artillery firepower was bolstered by the availability of the German Flak 88-mm guns or 90-mm units. In both North Africa and in Russia, the Italians would often use these weapons as truck-mounted units deployed primarily in halting enemy armoured attacks. The army had only three motorised/armoured divisions at the beginning of the war, and a large section of this force was dispatched to North Africa. In fact, the army's biggest shortcoming in the Eastern Front was the lack of trucks to transport troops to and from the frontline and most importantly supplies and ammunition. Initially in the summer of 1941, Italy dispatched the *Corpo di Spedizione Italiano* in Russia (Italian Expeditionary Force in Russia or CSIR), which consisted of 62,000 soldiers subdivided into three divisions: the Pasubio and Torino, which had two infantry regiments and one artillery regiment each, and the 3rd Mobile Division Celere, which consisted of a *Bersaglieri* Regiment, two cavalry regiments, an artillery regiment, and a light tank unit with sixty tanks. On one hand, the mechanised elements of the Celere Division were very weak when compared to the Soviets or the Germans. The tanks, for example, which only weighed 3 tons, were primarily sixty L3/33 units, very light tanks that were totally inadequate when facing larger, more powerful Soviet tanks and anti-tank guns. On the other hand, its mechanised forces and its greater degree of motorisation *versus* standard Italian infantry divisions made the Celere more mobile than the other two infantry divisions. The latter were in essence standard infantry divisions with very low levels of motorisation.

As Burgwyn asserts: 'Although the Italian expeditionary force was put together hastily, many were veteran and elite troops who arrived with Italy's best equipment'.[23] The troops comprised above-average trained units, while the Celere's degree of motorisation was the highest possible within the Italian Army of 1941. Despite the fact that the country was unprepared for a major war, its High Command had gathered all available resources for the campaign. The biggest commitment, for instance, was made by the artillery branch, which would dispatch to Russia some of the most advanced and largest artillery batteries at its disposal. The artillery compartment was comprised initially by 200 guns ranging between 20-mm and 105-mm, and ninety-two 47/32-mm anti-tank guns.

The Italian units' major issue from the onset was logistics and mainly had to do with how to effectively resupply the troops in Ukraine from far away bases in Romania. According to the pre-established agreements between the two countries, the German Army was to provide key logistical support, but as the war wore on, logistics and supply would become a much bigger problem for Germany as well. This would have repercussions on all Axis forces deployed in the Eastern Front given the lack of substantial quantities of supplies for frontline troops especially during the winter of 1941–42.

The *Regia Aeronautica* (Italian Air Force) pledged the following forces: fifty-one C.200 Macchi fighter planes and forty Fiat CR.42 fighter biplanes.[24] The Macchi planes were more advanced from a technological standpoint *versus* similar Soviet planes, but they were without de-icing equipment and were not expected to take off in sub-zero temperatures.

The CSIR also had approximately 5,500 vehicles. These troops and equipment were soon followed by the 63rd Assault Tagliamento Legion, a Blackshirt volunteer unit that symbolised Italy's commitment to the anti-Communism fight. The unit was comprised primarily by assault battalions and by soldiers that had greater combat experience than soldiers in the standard infantry divisions. In addition, it had two machine-gun companies and one heavy weapons artillery battalion. Together these forces fought during the initial advance into Russian territory and during the second, more defensive minded phase of the campaign. In March 1942, Mussolini doubled down by deciding to dispatch more units to Russia including the II Army Corps (Sforzesca, Ravenna, and Cosseria infantry divisions), and the elite *alpini* units (Vicenza, Tridentina, Julia, and Cuneense divisions). The latter were comprised by experienced and well-trained mountain troops, which were suited to fighting in the mountainous sector of the Caucasus, while the former were less specialised and had few motorised elements. This larger unit was merged into the CSIR and renamed *Armata Italiana* in Russia (Italian Army in Russia, or ARMIR) and renamed Italian 8th Army. By mid-1942, the Blackshirt contingent was also considerably augmented with respect to the beginning of the campaign. By then, it was comprised by four M Battalions (Tagliamento, Montebello, Leonessa, and Valle Scrivia) subdivided into two major M Battalions groups. The *Raggruppamento* CCNN M 3 *Gennaio* comprised the Tagliamento and the Montebello, while the *Raggruppamento* CCNN M 23 *Marzo* Group included the Valle Scrivia and the Leonessa. Thus, by mid-1942, eleven battalions, or half of the total force of the M Battalions at the disposal of the MVSN and the Italian Army, were deployed on the Eastern Front thus demonstrating how critical this campaign was for the MVSN and the Blackshirt movement. Each group had its own artillery battalion armed primarily with anti-tank guns, mortars, machine guns, and machine pistols.

The total strength of the ARMIR by the summer of 1942 was 227,000 soldiers fighting alongside some of the best and most potent artillery units available to the Italian Army. By then, Italy had committed a total of 960 pieces of artillery of various calibre: fifteen units of 210/22-mm (the only large-calibre guns available to the Italian Army); three batteries (thirty-six pieces) of 149/40-mm guns, twenty-four Krupp guns 149/28-mm, fifty-two guns of 75/46-mm; thirty-six guns of 75/32-mm; seventy-two guns of 75/18-mm calibre, 380 outdated 47/32-mm guns; 220 guns of 20-mm; seventy-six guns of 105/32-mm calibre; and, finally, 119 100/17-mm guns, which had been seized by the Italians from the Austrians during the First World War. An additional 16,700 vehicles were also dispatched to Russia along with 1,130 artillery tractors.[25]

The Italian forces, although autonomous from the Germans, acted in close co-ordination with the other Axis forces and they were placed under the command of General Giovanni Messe, the commander of the CSIR, who had risen through the ranks mainly by leading the IX *Reparto d'assalto*, a famous *arditi* unit during the First World War. In the spring of 1942, the command of the ARMIR was assigned to General Italo Gariboldi, an older, more conservative officer with few of the qualities of boldness and foresight that characterised his predecessor. Gariboldi's tenure as leader of the ARMIR would not be a positive one, especially when the Russians began their major offensive in the winter of 1942–43 and the Italian command failed to take effective countermeasures to avoid the rout.

Despite the fact that Italy's main theatre of operations was North Africa and despite the fact that the Italian High Command had warned the political authorities against dispatching additional troops to the Russian cauldron, by mid-1942, a large build up of troops was thus sanctioned and authorised.

This large army that was dispatched in 1942 was ultimately detrimental to Italy's true interests in the war since the move negatively impacted the needs of the North African front, which were sacrificed in favour of those on the Eastern Front. In 1942, the Germans had been halted and were in trouble because they faced a numerically superior Soviet Army both in terms of weapons and soldiers. Thus, their allies had to make a greater contribution to the Eastern Front campaign. As a result, modern artillery, tractors pulling heavy guns, vehicles of all kinds, and vast amounts of ammunition were assigned to the ARMIR.

In vain, General Messe (CSIR commander) had warned against further increasing Italy's commitment to the Eastern Front. He had urged to bolster the existing CSIR units with additional trucks and tanks rather than sending more foot soldiers from Italy. But neither Mussolini nor Ugo Cavallero, the chief of General Staff, heeded his message. The decision sealed the fate of the Italian–German Panzer Army commanded by General Erwin Rommel, whose strength was undermined by the vast build up by the British 8th Army in the summer of 1942. By the summer of 1942, for example, Rommel's Army was in dire need of more and heavier artillery units to properly confront the build-up in American tanks (Grant and Sherman) that the British were receiving in large numbers in order to prepare for their much anticipated offensive. But the bulk of the heavier Italian guns, including the fifteen 210/22-mm guns and howitzers, were hastily dispatched to Russia at the expense of the North African campaign. The decision in favour of the build up in the east ultimately also sealed the fate of the ARMIR, which was destroyed by the vast Soviet offensive of the winter of 1942–43. Even the dispatch to Russia of a larger artillery and infantry force resulting in the creation of the ARMIR could do little to match the much greater deployment of forces by the Red Army.

Within the confines of this large build up of troops, the Blackshirt units comprised a very small presence, not even coming close to representing 10 per cent of the strength of the ARMIR. Despite their relatively light presence, and despite the fact that many officers of the Royal Army disliked the militia, the Blackshirt legions and M Battalions would distinguish themselves during the campaign, especially when the Soviet attack of the winter of 1942–43 crippled the Italian defences, causing a widespread rout and a hasty retreat toward the west. The Blackshirt units, for instance, would maintain their composure and cohesion despite the huge losses and continue to fight while many other Axis soldiers abandoned their weapons and fled west.

The next chapters will detail the origins and combat deployment of the Blackshirt units deployed in the Eastern Front. Chapter 2 will focus upon the birth of the Blackshirt units, their evolution from a military police of the state to a large combat unit and their status and organisation at the outset of the Second World War. The chapter will also detail the weapons, training, and battle tactics deployed by the Blackshirts. Chapter 3 will focus upon the first phase of the Eastern Front campaign, which saw the Tagliamento fighting alongside the Germans and the Italian troops of the CSIR. It will focus upon the first advance into Ukraine and then detail the events surrounding the Christmas Battle. Chapter 4 will consider the reorganisation of the Blackshirt units on the Eastern Front in mid-1942, as well as detail the first and second offensive of the Don River, which saw both M Battalions group heavily, engaged in repelling the enemy advance. Chapter 5 will analyse the formation of the M Division, the armoured unit that was constituted in the spring of 1943 from all the Blackshirt troops that had survived the Eastern Front campaign. The concluding chapter will provide an assessment of the Blackshirts in a comparative perspective.

Italian soldiers training for the anti-tank defence somewhere in Ukraine in 1942. (*Ufficio Storico*)

The T-34 tank and its crew knocked out by Italian artillery units. (*Ufficio Storico*)

A Blackshirt with a mule in the Balkans. Mules, sleds, and motor vehicles were the Blackshirt units' primary movers to carry equipment and ammunition. (*Archivio Centrale dello stato*)

Right: Parade at the training ground. M Battalions mid-1942 Trastevere. (*Archivio Centrale dello stato*)

Below: Galbiati inspects a rangefinder. (*Archivio Centrale dello stato*)

Order of Battle, CSIR, August 1941

Divisione Pasubio (General Giovanelli)
- 79th Infantry Regiment.
- 80th Infantry Regiment.
- 8th Artillery Regiment.
- Mortar units, sappers, and divisional headquarters and services.

Divisione Torino (General Lerici)
- 81st Infantry Regiment.
- 82nd Infantry Regiment.
- 52nd Artillery Regiment.

3a. Divisione Celere Principe Amedeo Duca D'Aosta (General Marazzani)
- Savoia Cavalry Regiment.
- Lancieri di Novara Regiment.
- 3rd *Bersaglieri* Regiment.
- Artillery Regiment.
- Light Tank unit.
- Sappers and anti-tank units.
- XXX Cavalry Group.
- 63rd Tagliamento Legion (*Console* Niccolo' Nicchiarelli).
- 63rd Udine Battalion (*Seniore* Ermacora Zuliani).
- 79th Reggio Emilia Battalion (*Seniore* Alberto Patroncini).
- 103rd Machine Gun Company (Centurion Marco Gentile).
- 183rd Machine Gun Company (Centurion A. Zanotti).
- 63rd Artillery and Heavy Weapons Battalion (*Tenente Colonnello* Vincenzo de Franco).

2

A History of the MVSN

Introduction

The 63a *Legione Tagliamento* was the first unit of the MVSN to be deployed against the Soviet Union when it was attached to the CSIR in the summer of 1941. The unit was then followed by the other Blackshirt units such as the *Gruppo di Battaglioni* CCNN M Montebello, *Gruppo di Battaglioni* CCNN M Leonessa, and the *Gruppo di Battaglioni* CCNN M Valle Scrivia, which arrived on the frontline in mid-1942. By that time, the basic structure of the Blackshirt units had already evolved from the light legion structure to the sturdier *Gruppo di Battaglioni* CCNN M (M Blackshirt Battalions Group), which was slightly different from the bare-bone organisation of the Blackshirt units of 1940–41. By then, the Blackshirts had been organised into two distinct *Gruppi di Battaglioni* CCNN M: the 3 Gennaio and the 23 Marzo. Each had four infantry assault battalions and two heavy weapons/artillery battalions, plus support services. Together the two groups they comprised a Blackshirt division with eight infantry battalions and four heavy weapons/artillery battalions and additional support services.

The role of these Blackshirt units was to be attached to the infantry divisions of the Royal Army to be used as a tactical reserve. The original intent was to use them strictly as assault battalions much like the *arditi* of the First World War. But as we will see in the next chapters, the Blackshirts never had a specific combat role, but were used by the Royal Army to carry out a multiplicity of defensive and offensive tasks. We will see, for example, that they fought effectively, especially when deployed in a defensive and counterattacking capacity. As a result, some of their major successes would come when they effectively fought off large-scale Soviet offenses.

In the summer of 1941, a few weeks prior to its departure for the Eastern Front, the Tagliamento's initial strength consisted of two infantry battalions, two machine-gun companies, one heavy weapons/artillery battalion, and various support services. Its structure reflected the rather light standard organisation of the Blackshirt legions in 1941, which roughly equated to the strength of a standard infantry regiment of the Italian army. The only exception *versus* other legions dispatched to North Africa and Greece in 1940–41 was that the Tagliamento Legion had been reinforced from the onset with a heavy weapons/ artillery battalion, which other legions at the time did not have.

Its structure was organised as follows:

-Legion Command Company
-LXIII *Battaglione* CCNN (LXIII Assault Infantry Battalion)
-LXXIX *Battaglione* CCNN (LXXIX Assault Infantry Battalion)
-103a *Compagnia mitragliatrici* CCNN (103rd Machine-Gun Company)
-183a *Compagnia mitragliatrici* CCNN (183rd Machine-Gun Company)
-LXIII *Battaglione Armi Accompagnamento* (LXIII Heavy Weapons Battalion)
-*Autieri* (Support Services Group)

At the start of the campaign the 63rd Legion had fifty-two officers, seventy-six NCOs, 1,230 soldiers, 284 artillery soldiers, 133 drivers and support services, and five Carabinieri. It also count could count upon approximately 150 trucks, forty-eight assault rifles, twelve machine guns, eighteen 45-mm mortars, six 81-mm mortars, and eight 47/32-mm anti-tank guns.

In contrast to the early Blackshirt Legions deployed in North Africa in 1940, the Tagliamento was dispatched into combat on the Eastern Front with the addition of a heavy weapons artillery attachment from the Royal Army armed with the 81-mm mortars and the 47/32-mm guns listed above. One of the reasons the Blackshirt units in North Africa had performed poorly was because they lacked artillery and firepower, especially when fighting against armoured units. The MVSN did not want to see a repeat of the North Africa campaign in Russia and therefore had strengthened the Blackshirts with an artillery battalion armed primarily with six 81-mm mortars and eight 47/32-mm anti-tank guns. In addition to artillery, the Tagliamento was further strengthened by two machine-gun companies, whose ranks also came from the Royal Army.

Each infantry battalion was structured upon three infantry assault companies and one machine-gun company. Each company was based upon four platoons. The latter was the basic combat arm of the legion and its strength was designed around the carrying capacity of the standard Italian military truck, the Fiat 666nm. Each truck was capable of carrying a *squadra* (squad) or a half platoon. A *squadra* was comprised by twelve soldiers: one NCO, two machine gunners, two machine-gun ammunition carriers, and seven riflemen. The unit's basic assault tactics involved the NCO and the riflemen advancing against the enemy position, covered by the machine-gun fire of one (sometimes two) Breda model 30 units. While the machine guns pinned the enemy down, the attackers hurled hand grenades into the enemy trenches and then engaged him in hand-to-hand combat with their rifles and bayonets. The basic tactic of the Blackshirts resembled those of the *arditi* assault units of the First World War, which used machine guns as flanking fire and then engaged the enemy in close-combat fighting with hand grenades, bayonets, and daggers. What characterised their operations was the speed in which their assaults were conducted, which usually began on the heels of a brief but most destructive artillery barrage that kept the enemy from being able to react during the early stages of the assault. If everything worked according to plan, the *arditi* were at the enemy trenches as soon as the artillery barrage was complete. Not having suffered many losses by the enemy machine-gun fire, the *arditi* could then penetrate the trenches and begin to mop up the enemy positions. The Blackshirts used the same tactics and their actions relied upon the close collaboration between artillery and assault units since the timing of the assault had to coincide with the tapering off or the moving forward of the barrage. The latter typically consisted of both field guns, small mountain type units and mortars, or enough shells per minute to tie down the enemy and keep him in the dugouts. The speed of the assault units was essential since arriving at the trenches quickly was critical to the success of these type of offensive operations. In certain small-scale raids, the barrage was not used in order to achieve complete surprise. In the latter stages of the assault, the Blackshirts used primarily rifles, daggers, and hand grenades. Beginning in mid-1942, these assault units could also use a limited number of 9-mm Beretta model 38 light machine guns.

Although not part of the Italian Army, the Blackshirt units (Legions or later the M Battalions), which organically belonged to the party militia (MVSN), took part to all Italian campaigns of the Second World War (between 1940–43) and fought alongside standard infantry and under the command of the Royal Army. In 1940–41, the legions fought in all theatres of operation—in some cases they fought effectively, while in others less so. Then, in 1942–43, the Blackshirt units fought primarily on the Eastern Front, France, Tunisia, and in Yugoslavia. Since these units were not very large and lacked basic services and functions such as a full medical staff, an engineer and sapper company and teams of motor vehicles drivers, they had to rely on other units of the Royal Army for some of these services. The Blackshirts' basic organisation was typically comprised of a slimmed down version of the standard infantry regiment with two infantry battalions and one light artillery battalion. Because of their light organisational structure, the Blackshirt legions were subsequently assembled under bigger, more durable organisations as the war wore on.

The following sections will discuss the origins of the Blackshirt units as well as their training and weapons. They will seek to answer such questions as what spurred the creation of the MVSN and the legions? What type of men did the legions recruit? How many Blackshirt units were there at the start of the war in

1940? What is the history of the Blackshirt units deployed on the Eastern Front? What weapons did they have and how effective were they? How well were the Blackshirts trained? What distinguished their units from the Royal Army?

Origins

The origins of the Blackshirt legions date back to the period immediately after the First World War when Italy was mired in political violence and economic insecurity as a result of the so-called 'Mutilated Victory'. The Italians had won the war by defeating the historical enemy, the Austro-Hungarian Empire, but the country experienced a terrible time in transitioning out of the war and the war mentality. As Crociani and Battistelli assert:

> The origins of the *Camicie Nere* date back to the months after the end of the World War One, when Italy was riven by social and political struggle. The *squadre d'azione* [action squads, their members being called *squadristi*] came into being in reaction both to the mutilated victory which deprived Italy of what she considered her rightful gains, and to the rise of the socialist-communist party.[1]

The country had come out of the war with its economy in tatters and with a large majority of public opinion that maintained that the Allies had not kept their promise made before the war and hence had blocked Italy's territorial expansion on its eastern border. A large majority within the Italian nationalist movement maintained that the country had a rightful claim to the city of Fiume and to the greater Dalmazia region with its large Italian-speaking population. But the Allies had unjustifiably awarded this region to Yugoslavia. In addition, to the international dispute regarding Dalmazia, in 1919, a resurgent Socialist Party had also began to mobilise workers and farmers against the state and the military and its radicalism called into question Italian nationalism and all the efforts that had been made during the First World War. The militant left had particularly channelled its anger against decorated and non-decorated ex-servicemen that had been singled out for violence and verbal abuse in Italy's major urban centres. As a reaction to the left, which had occupied factories and assaulted ex-servicemen, the Fascist Party of Benito Mussolini assembled the *arditi* and other ex-servicemen, the Futurists, and many others in a broad anti-Socialist, nationalist political alliance. In 1919, the movement gave rise to the *squadre d'azione* (action squads), which aimed to confront the socialists and the communists in the streets by political violence. The *squadre* were particularly strong in regions such as Emilia Romagna, where the workers and labour movements had many adherents. In these regions, the *squadre* acted with extreme violence against the unions of farm labourers and factory workers and clashes between the two sides were daily occurrences especially during the two years of the so-called *Biennio Rosso* (1919–20). When the political regime of Fascism became established in 1922, the MVSN, a volunteer party militia, was formed shortly thereafter to help stabilise it. It was comprised mainly by the members of the *squadre d'azione*, the early adherents to the movement. Its official creation was on 12 January 1923, when the Grand Council of Fascism created by Royal Decree No. 311/1923 the *Milizia Volontaria per la Sicurezza Nazionale*. Initially, the MSVN functioned as a police force to maintain public order. It also served Mussolini's regime as a way to channel violent ex-combatants into a structured organisation that tempered their extremism.

The main body of the MVSN was the legion that had a local basis as all the cadres came from the same town or region of Italy. The legion's headquarters were typically located in the regional capital and each battalion was assembled from the same major town or province within that region. Legions typically held an administrative office in their region, but did not have their own training grounds or barracks.

It is estimated that by 1926, there were approximately 130 legions distributed fairly evenly throughout Italy. Statistical examination of the Blackshirts in 1931, however, shows that most of them came either from the most developed areas of Italy or those closely tied to the state apparatus. Approximately 41 per cent of the Blackshirts came from northern Italy, 31 per cent from central Italy, and the remaining 28 per cent came from the islands and from the southern regions. The majority of the Blackshirts were state employees, farmers, artisans, and ex-military men, while approximately only 9 per cent were students and professionals. The majority at the time was comprised by young males between the ages of twenty and thirty.

Enlistment in the MVSN was open to all card-carrying party members between the ages of seventeen and fifty years of age. The two requirements that each volunteer had to meet were physical fitness and not to be serving concurrently with the armed forces.

The members of the MVSN were easily identifiable by their clothing, which consisted initially of a black shirt, light grey pants, and a black fez hat, and the colour of their shirt gave them their nickname the *Camicie Nere* (in short CCNN, or Blackshirts).

From the onset, the MVSN was created as an alternative to the armed forces and the national police as it served the purposes of the regime. Once the regime consolidated its hold on political power, however, the MVSN membership beginning in 1924 was required to swear a pledge of loyalty to the king. The latter was the nominal head of the armed forces so that this pledge was seen as a way to normalise and institutionalise the MVSN and the Blackshirt movement. The MVSN in fact experienced a similar institutionalisation process that characterised the Falange in Spain, which after some time was downgraded by Franco from the official party of the regime to an organisation that channelled support for the authoritarian regime. Thus the legionary or the Blackshirt had to swear a dual pledge of loyalty to the regime and to the king. As we will see, this decision will have profound influences on the history and future development of the MVSN. The importance of the dual pledge of loyalty would become very relevant when, in mid-1943, the Blackshirts were faced by a very stark choice: choose between loyalty to the regime or to the king. As a result of this stark choice, the unity of the MVSN would be undermined by deep differences of opinion. On the one hand, as will be seen later, the leadership would initially switch their loyalty from the regime to the king, while the bulk of the rank and file would retain loyalty to the regime.

In the early days of the MVSN, one of the most controversial issues regarding the future and the make-up of the organisation was whether to entrust the militia's leadership such as the head of the militia itself or of the individual legions (*Luogotenente Generale della Milizia*, which equated to a general of an infantry division in the Royal Army, and the *Console*, which equated to a colonel) to a cadre of military professionals or to ex-*squadristi*. In a speech held in the Senate on 8 June 1923, the *Duce* opted for a compromise solution where the ex-*squadristi* were to be given command of the rank and file by being awarded the lower to middle-level positions such as *Centurione* (captain), *Capomanipolo* (lieutenant), and *Caposquadra* (sergeant). In turn, senior military officers were to take the top positions within the MVSN.

The decision thus established that the most senior positions within the militia were to be assigned to professional military officers. These were typically officers that were either retired or that did not have a permanent commission in the armed forces. This choice at the time was strongly criticised because it was seen as a way to weaken the militia. Quirino Armellini, for instance, an ex-Royal Army General and a leader of the MVSN, a few years later argued that too many top officers of the MVSN were not effective since for the most part they had been forced to retire from the military being older, conservative thinkers and lacking a true military, professional culture. In fact, as the officers retired from the army, they joined the MVSN and thus collected a pension and a salary. But often times, the ones that did retire and join the MVSN were those older generals that no longer had a clear role in the military and were in fact forced into early retirement. Another issue that plagued the militia was its promotion system. It based career advancement not primarily on seniority or merit, but often on how well the MVSN officer could relate to his troops through his charisma, oratorical skills, and personal history in the *squadrismo* movement. Character and charisma were thus more important in many instances than technical, military skills and know-how to gain a top job within the legions. This debilitated the militia and made it an organisation that was highly dependent upon the government and the party authorities for promotions and career advancement. In fact, charismatic authority and ascendancy on the masses of the militia were not infrequently more relevant than the technical and professional abilities of the leader. As we will see later in the chapters dedicated to the Second World War, one of the major issues that plagued the militia was the lack of effective and capable mid-level officers and NCOs. The problem thus persisted well into the 1930s and the 1940s, although by 1941, steps were taken to improve the quality of the officers within the MVSN and the M Battalions specifically with an increased emphasis on officer training. Another well-known ex-*squadrista*, Enzo Galbiati, also criticised the compromise solution of 1923 stressing that it did not do away with the dualism between the militia and the army. The solution in his view favoured the army at the expense of the militia since the former had a budget that funded its schools and its army bases, while the latter relied on more unstable sources of funding that were subject to political agreements at the highest level. In Galbiati's view, the militia was secondary to the armed forces in terms of budgets and the quality of its leadership. Both elements pointed to a weaker militia *versus* the Royal Army. In addition, the militia without its own training bases was seen as more and more reliant upon the Royal Army for weapons, equipment, and uniforms given its semi-permanent nature.

The MVSN organisation was based on the legions that were spread out throughout Italy. The Blackshirt legion resembled the structure of the *arditi* units, while the nomenclature and the official titles of officers and soldiers drew from the ancient roman legions. The leader of the standard legion, the *console* (consul), was typically an ex-officer of the army or a well-known *squadrista* leader from the early days of 1918–21. Other officers called *primo* or *secondo seniore* (first officer or second officer) or *centurione* (centurion) were also primarily drawn from the ranks of ex-army officer corps, and the majority of them had also been *squadristi* after the First World War. The soldiers, called *camicia nera* (Blackshirt) or *legionario* (legionary), the NCOs, and the sergeants came primarily from the MVSN and typically belonged to the lower classes.

The legion's individual and crew served weapons were virtually the same as those of the standard infantry units, while the uniform was singular and unique. It consisted of a black fez hat, a black shirt, and tie, black boots, and grey trousers. The distinctive badge of the Blackshirts was a black flame pin attached to the collar of the grey jacket, a symbol of the *arditi* of the First World War.

First Combat Engagements

In 1923, as Italy entered a decade where it waged continuous wars, the MSVN began to slowly evolve and its units assumed a more complex role from just providing public order. The legions were now expected to fight alongside the Italian Royal Army during military campaigns as well as provide railway, border and port and airfield security. Thus, between 1924 and 1934, the MSVN was expanded much beyond its original role. In 1927, a MVSN for the territorial air defence was created. This unit was furnished with artillery batteries that could be deployed in Italy's major cities to protect infrastructure and army bases from enemy aerial attacks. Three years later, the MVSN was further expanded with the creation of coastal battery units to safeguard harbours and important marine observation positions.

In 1939, these two units were further institutionalised. The former was renamed MACA (*Milizia Artigleria Contraerea*, or anti-aircraft artillery militia) with a total force of 80,000 militia soldiers, 4,286 Saint Etienne machine guns, 116 model 1935 Breda machine guns, ninety Skoda 77/28-mm, ninety-four Skoda 5/27-mm from the First World War, 232 Vickers 76/45-mm guns, and finally 480 Ansaldo 76/40-mm guns.

The latter was renamed MILIMART (*Milizia Artigleria Marittima*, or maritime artillery militia) with 33,000 soldiers and 300 mostly older batteries and some machine guns from the First World War.[2]

Additional smaller units were also created for forest, rail and border defence and security.

The MVSN had its own autonomous medical, religious, and administrative services, in addition to a specific social security fund, although it did not have its own military bases. The medical staff were organised by legion. Each of these units had a medical officer with his own staff who was supported by three junior doctors and staff, which served the battalions. The latter, for instance, was a much slimmed down version of the medical staff made available to the standard Royal Army battalion and this deficiency would become very evident during the Second World War when many Blackshirt units experienced extreme hardships due to the lack of adequate medical services. As far as the military bases are concerned, the MVSN had only two bases under its direct control: Trastevere (downtown Rome) and Civitavecchia (outskirts of Rome). These two hubs served as the elite training grounds of the Blackshirts, while the bulk of the legions did not have their own bases and utilised those of the Royal Army. Before the war, for instance, the legions trained sporadically and for short periods of time. The organisation also had its own music band.

A few months after its constitution, the MVSN was called to conduct its first military operation and this experience would have a profound influence on the organisation. In September 1923, three legions were mobilised and deployed in Libya. The legions not only fought in some of the most important engagements of the campaign, but also helped to colonise Libya by carrying out police and security tasks after the conflict. As a result of their preponderant role, the Royal Decree No. 1166 of 1 May 1924 instituted two permanent legions to be stationed in Libya: the 1. Oea in Tripoli and the 2. Berenice in Benghazi. These units mostly supplemented the local police in maintaining public order and trained at least once annually to prepare for a potential conflict against other European armies stationed in Africa. This first experience was a determining factor in the expansion of the militia into a full-fledged combat role.

The first major test for the MVSN came with the Ethiopian War of 1935. During the campaign the militia deployed seven infantry divisions (23. Marzo,

28. Ottobre, 21. Aprile, 3. Gennaio, 1. Febbraio, Tevere, and Cirene), as well as two battalions of forestry services troops and additional smaller groups for a total of 5,611 officers and 162,390 Blackshirts.[3] At the time, each infantry division was comprised by three legions, a machine-gun battalion, a 65/17-mm guns artillery group, two reserve battalions, and several services units.

During the operations in East Africa, the Blackshirts fought fairly well even though they were deployed against an enemy that did not have advanced weapons such as heavy artillery, motorised units, and poison gas. Despite the enemy's lack of preparedness for the war, the Blackshirts did suffer one major defeat. 'Only in the Uaerieu Pass Battle did they suffer a bitter setback, losing on one single occasion 19 officers and 245 militia'.[4]

Their overall military performance, however, was satisfactory and many MVSN units gained valuable combat experience.

The true test of combat for the MVSN came with the Spanish Civil War when the Italian government responded to the call for help of Franco's insurgents by dispatching both Royal Army and militia units. Within a few months of the start of hostilities, three Blackshirt divisions were hastily dispatched to Spain (*Dio lo vuole*, 2a. *Fiamme Nere*, and 3a. *Penne Nere*), with a force comprised by 20,000 *legionaries* primarily armed with rifles, small artillery and light guns. These units fought alongside the standard Italian infantry and the Spanish military against the Republican Army and suffered large casualties. In fact, while fighting against a well-equipped army, the Blackshirts combat effectiveness was definitively less robust than in Ethiopia. In the battle of Guadalajara, for instance, the Blackshirt units were overrun by an enemy battalion and severely beaten. Although the Italian contribution was key to Franco's final victory, the haphazard, uneven, battlefield performance of the militia induced the Italian government to halt the further expansion of the Blackshirts, and it also explains why at the outbreak of the Second World War the troops of the legions were ill-equipped, fought with antiquated guns, and their battalions were endowed with very limited services.[5]

In Spain, the Italians also deployed some of their armoured units, which at the time were expected to provide support to the infantry rather than fight in an autonomous fashion. The performance of the armour, for a host of different reasons, was poor, and as a result, the military authorities failed to recognise their future role and potential. By 1939, for instance, the development of the armoured units was de-emphasised and this is one of the reasons why although many of the German Wehrmacht and Waffen SS units were in essence panzer/grenadier units, the Italian Blackshirt units were primarily infantry units with no armoured component and more akin to line infantry divisions.

In April 1939, six legions participated to the invasion of Albania. The militia together with the standard army took the country with a brief campaign that mostly highlighted the weakness of the Albanians.

The Second World War

On 10 June 1940, the day Italy entered the Second World War, all militia units were integrated into the armed forces, while the legion commanders were still in charge of administrative, training, and recruitment functions and reported directly to the head of the MVSN.

In Italy and Libya, there were 112,000 Blackshirt soldiers subdivided into 194 assault battalions, mountain troop units, and reserve forces. In the Empire, there were another 26,000 Blackshirts under the command of the Duke of Aosta. The marine coastal guard had an additional 33,000 *legionaries*. The anti-aircraft units had 80,000 soldiers while some Blackshirts also belonged to the special units such as the railways, ports, forestry, and postal units. In total, the militia had approximately 313,000 *legionaries* that could be mobilised for the war.

The infantry assault or mountain battalions were comprised by men aged between twenty-one and thirty-six years of age, who, after having served in the army, navy, or air force, voluntarily joined the MVSN militia for a ten-year period.

The *Milizia Contraerea* and the *Milizia Costiera* were instead constituted mainly by older veterans of the First World War, by individuals that were either blind or deaf by birth, or by ex-soldiers that had sustained a serious injury during the war.

Thus, on that fatal day of 10 June 1940, the militia was very rich in terms of number of soldiers, but fairly poor when it came to equipment and training. As MVSN historian Carlo Rastrelli asserts: 'The limits of the organization were well known. It was always subordinated to the needs of the Army and it lacked experienced officers and NCOs.'[6]

In 1940, the militia, even though it was an integral component of a regime that emphasised war making, was not a particularly healthy military machine, lacking heavy weapons such as anti-tank guns and tanks, and most critically lacking training in modern warfare. Most importantly, its overall state of readiness for war was not unique or an exception since the Royal Army was also deemed unprepared for war and its ranks also lacked training. The regime was primarily responsible for talking tough and for advocating a belligerent and expansionist foreign policy. But such aggressive foreign policy was based on vastly overestimating the country's military resources. In fact, in 1940, Italy not only lagged behind all European powers in terms of steel, coal, and other major production goods, but its army was much weaker in terms of equipment and weapons than the great powers such as Great Britain, Germany, and France. In fact, according to pre-war estimates, Italy could not be ready for war until at least mid-1943. Cognizant of the nation's weakness, the participation to the war was a gamble on the part of its leadership who maintained that Germany was about to sweep Europe and that Italy, by entering the war, would gain a seat at the post-war bargaining table.

The legions, not having their own bases, were not combat ready as the troops lacked training. Since the legions relied upon the Royal Army for weapons, few of its units were fully armed. Moreover, at the beginning of the war, there was a real dearth of experienced NCOs and the problem would even get worse as the war progressed due to high casualty rates and older officers being retired from service. The legions also shared with the rest of the army the overall lack of viable advanced fighting equipment especially with regards to tanks and anti-tank guns.

Initially, each legion was to comprise an assault battalion at the disposal of the infantry divisions.

> According to existing plans each Army Division had a CCNN [CC.NN stood for *Camicie Nere* or Blackshirts] battalion. In reality, only half of the existing divisions received one. On paper the CCNN battalion was supposed to emulate the *arditi* [highly trained assault troops of the First World War], but in reality they were light infantry not particularly well trained, but [it was supposed] enthusiastic and aggressive, destined to operate in offensive support of frontline units.[7]

As will be shown later, the war would be a true test of strength for the Blackshirts, which especially during the first year of the conflict would suffer tremendous losses. Italy's first campaign of the war was the brief engagement in the Western Alps against the fortified French positions held by specialised mountain troops, the so-called Maginot line of the Alps constructed on the border with Italy. Even though, in June 1940, France was on the verge of collapse on the Western Front against the rapidly moving German armoured units, in the Alps, the Italian troops were stalemated by French mountain artillery. In search of a quick victory, Mussolini ordered the Italian Army to be deployed from Switzerland (Mount Blanc) to the sea (Liguria Riviera) with two armies: the 4th to the north and the 1st to the south. These two units faced across the mountain chains the French *Armée des Alpes*, which were units of experienced mountain soldiers assigned to defend the alpine front consisting of a series of bunkers and pillboxes located on mountain tops and on key mountain passes.

> Although most of the *petit ouvrages* of the Little Maginot Line in the Alps consisted of little more than a few infantry weapons positions, they were well sited. A few *gros ouvrages* included reinforced forward firing artillery casemates, since turrets were impractical in the mountainous terrain.[8]

The fortified positions were well-equipped and armed. Each blockhouse of the alpine line, for instance, consisted mainly of two 149-mm field guns, two anti-tank guns, several machine guns, and automatic rifles.

Given that the French controlled the high ground, this campaign would result in an extremely tough engagement for the Italian Army, which had to advance along rough hills and mountain peaks, through territory that had almost non-existent transportation channels (such as roads) and under poor conditions given the very harsh weather. In fact, it was a fight that the Royal Army and the Blackshirts would engage not only against determined French opposition, but also against the mountains and their bitter climate. The only way to proceed forward was for the mountain troops 'to force the mountain passes between the coast and the Swiss border' and to do this under the watchful eye of the enemy.[9]

From the onset, the Italians deployed 300,000 troops while the French deployed 200,000 soldiers, positioned in their high mountain fortifications. The 4th Army was deployed near the glaciers with seventy-eight battalions, eleven of which were Blackshirt units, while the 1st Army, deployed from the Gran Granero to the sea, consisted of 110 battalions, of which seventeen were Blackshirt battalions. The following Blackshirt battalions would experience the bulk of the fighting during the brief yet costly campaign: I, II, IV, V, XI, XII, XV, XVII, XX, XXIII, XXIV, XXVIII, XXX, XXXIII, XXXIV, XXXVI, XXXVIII, XL, LXXIX, LXXX, and LXXXVI. The vicissitudes of I, II, and IX Battalions, for example, are representative of the type of combat operations these specialised Blackshirt mountain troops were engaged in during the French campaign. Their experience during the campaign will be detailed in the following paragraphs.

Days prior to the start of the campaign, both I and II Battalion where assembled at Ghigo di Pralì, near the border.

For these troops the campaign started in the worst possible way, since they were stationed for days in the mountains and without the proper equipment or clothing. In fact, on the first day of hostilities, the two battalions suffered their first losses due to frostbite, caused primarily by very violent rain/snow mix precipitations, the intense cold especially during the night, and the lack of proper mountain clothing. On 16 June, the units received their marching orders of operations and began a very tortuous hike through the mountains in order to reach the enemy positions. After four days of continuous uphill hiking the troops finally inched closer to the enemy. On the 21st, at 5 a.m., both battalions finally crossed the border. I Battalion was charged with taking Mount Epiol, which was conquered after the peak position was surrounded and invested with hand grenades, while II Battalion also experienced heavy fighting. In rapid succession, the Blackshirts then advanced upon the Preveyre Valley, which was seized at 8:30 p.m. and drove on to Chapelle S. Barthelemy where they were invested by violent machine-gun fire that caused several casualties. After another harsh fight engaged for the capture of Bois Noir's garrison, which was taken at 11:30 a.m., I Battalion was forced to halt its advance because it was again targeted by the fire of well-concealed and emplaced machine guns and artillery. After a long pause caused by the fact that the troops could not progress, having instead to shield themselves behind boulders and rocks to avoid the enemy fire, the advance was then able to resume when darkness descended. Thus, by the end of the day, I Battalion reached Rio de Combe where it stationed under a heavy snowstorm. Meanwhile, II Battalion had also invaded the Preveyre Valley, reaching Reyscasse La Roux-Costone, which was occupied after the loss of a dozen wounded due to heavy enemy fire. This last assault, conducted under the constant threat of enemy machine-gun and rifle fire, saw the Blackshirts overcome walls of rock in order to finally arrive within striking distance of the enemy positions. By the end of the campaign, both battalions had reached their destinations and contributed to the disarming of several French units.

Another Blackshirt battalion that fought alongside the *alpini* and that had to complete a very complex alpine manoeuvre was XI Battalion. The latter, reinforced by the Susa *Alpini* Battalion, had been given the task of advancing to Monte Clapier and Monte Rocciamelone with a flanking manoeuvre through glaciers and mountain passes in order to pave the way for the attack by the Brennero and Cagliari Divisions.

The mountain troop column began to march on 21 June, and after twelve hours of tough uphill walking through several mountain peaks, it was able to descend into the Ribon Valley. On the 22nd, the Blackshirts and the *alpini* continued to advance along the Ribon Valley and first reached Bressan in the morning and the Arc Valley in the afternoon where they skirmished with several enemy alpine patrol units. On the 23rd, the two battalions reached Lanslevillard, then Lanslebourg, and later pushed up to Thermignon, while dispatching some patrols up to the Doron Valley. The latter were able to reach the valley after negotiating a high mountain peak with ropes and pickaxes. When the order to cease hostilities arrived, the column had already reached Chalet La Fontanelle.

The report by the Commander of the Cagliari Division underlines how the two battalions' demonstrated good mountain climbing skills that allowed them to reach the enemy in such a short time:

> The action of the Arc Valley was conducted with decision and speed. Twenty-three hours after it had began; the advanced patrols had already reached Bramans. The French later stated to us that it was almost impossible for the two battalions, (Susa and XI CC.NN) to have penetrated the Ribon Valley from the Chapeau Rocciamelone hill in such a short time.[10]

The column commander's reported the amazement of the French officers for the bold mountain manoeuvre conducted by IX Battalion:

> A French officer that surrendered at Thermignon on 27 June stated that he would never have expected that a single column could descend into the Ribon Valley by trekking through the Rocciamelone glacier. He further stated that no fixed defences had been set up in the Ribon Valley since it was almost

> impossible to descend from the Rocciamelone and then force the peaks and mountain passes of the Arc Valley. Another French officer, commander of the troops deployed at Col de La Vanoise, was deeply amazed that our column had reached the Doron Valley in such a short time.[11]

Along with the *alpini*, which were deployed in large numbers, the twenty-eight Blackshirt battalions deployed in the Western Alps all suffered some casualties. The campaign however, was too brief to provide a real assessment of the battle performance of these troops, which despite their background as able mountain troops, were mobilised without training and subsequently deployed in a hasty manner and without much planning. The French surrender brought all hostilities to an abrupt end. The campaign resulted in the capture of the glaciers on the Italian–French border and of Menton. The official German history of the French campaign described the two weeks of fighting by the Italians as a debacle. In reality, it was not a debacle but a stalemate. According to a specialist historian of the Maginot Line: 'Most Italian units fought bravely but in most cases faced insurmountable challenges and when they did storm a few French positions, they did not have demolition equipment like the German hollow charges to neutralize them'.[12] As a result, the Italians suffered 631 dead, 2,631 wounded, 616 missing, and 2,151 were the victims of frostbite. In contrast, the French had thirty-two dead, forty-two wounded, and 150 missing. Specific losses for the Blackshirt battalions are not known.

The next deployment for the Blackshirt legions was in the muddy, wet mountains of Greece where fifty-six battalions suffered very high losses. This would be a much more meaningful test of fire for these units, which found themselves fighting against an army that had similar weaponry but had greater logistical support. Since the campaign was badly planned in terms of timing and poor logistical support was provided to the troops, the losses, almost from the start were staggering, and the MVSN was no exception. The initial offensive took place during the fall and winter of 1940–41 and the torrential rains, the mud, and the snow much hampered the advance to the point that the weather not the enemy became the number one opponent of the invading Italians. In addition, key ports in Albania were too small and did not have the capacity to unload and then transfer large quantities of supplies to the frontline troops. The slow supply chain further undermined the effort of the frontline troops in fighting a better stocked and fed Greek Army. The MSVN losses suffered during the offensive were so high that twenty-seven out of fifty-six Blackshirt battalions had to be dissolved by the spring of 1941. Initially, CIX, CXLI, and CLXVI legions, for instance, participated to the first offensive of the campaign in late October 1940. All three suffered heavy losses while advancing against Greek machine-gun and artillery fire. Twenty legions were then hurriedly dispatched to the frontline when the Greeks undertook their bold counteroffensive and the Blackshirts again suffered heavy casualties. Here they were mostly deployed in static defensive positions even though it was not their primary combat role. Their deployment was likely a stopgap solution of the Italian commanders facing an aggressive enemy bent on pushing the Italians back all the way to Albania. Despite their usefulness in plugging defensive holes, not all Blackshirt units fought effectively.

According to military historians Battistelli and Crociani during the Greek campaign, the Blackshirts' 'battlefield performances varied from poor to good, often with units being deployed at the front for a few weeks only'.[13]

Their performances were impacted by the hurried conditions of their deployment, the lack of proper winter clothing and equipment, and the overall logistical nightmares of a campaign that had been badly planned and timed.

Despite the non-stellar performance of some of the Italian units deployed in Greece, some Blackshirt legions such as the Leonessa fought valiantly and their efforts were for the first time recognised by the Italian High Command, which praised their combat activities in an official army bulletin. After a brief Italian offensive over enemy territory, which lasted from 28 October to 10 November 1941, the Greeks launched a major counteroffensive that by then had given them the upper hand in terms of momentum and initiative and that was facilitated by the proximity of their reserve units' depots and the ease of communications. The Leonessa Legion, in particular, was one of the Blackshirt units that distinguished itself while fighting in dire conditions and against an enemy that could more readily deploy more troops and equipment. Despite being hurriedly thrown into combat to shield the retreat of the Italian units that were faced with the major Greek counteroffensive of February 1941, the Blackshirt battalions made a key contribution toward halting the enemy advance. The Crete Greek Division, which was twelve battalions strong and reputedly the strongest division of the Greek Army, attacked the Italian battalions of the Leonessa (XIV and XV Battalions) with brute force, which was engaged in continuous combat for several weeks. In fact, the latter took the biggest brunt of the enemy attack and the following paragraphs recount its battle experiences during the counteroffensive.

On 2 February at 6 p.m., a day characterised by gusty winds, snow mixed with torrential downpours, and very muddy almost unmanageable roads, the Leonessa was transferred on foot to Scialesit to bolster the defences of the Pinerolo Infantry Division that had already been heavily tested by the Greeks. The approach march conducted on foot was conducted under torrential rains and with very cold winds. The mountain road that the Blackshirts travelled on was muddy and slippery and the soldiers could hardly stand up and walk. In the darkness, the unit even lost its way and, until the next morning, was trapped for many hours by huge mud slides. Without having had any sleep or food, the next day the troops reached their destination and were hurriedly deployed on the line on Hill 800. After conducting repeated counterattacks, the troops of the Leonessa resisted and maintained their positions facing wave after wave of enemy troops. On 5 February, the weather continued to offer no let up with more torrential rains, mud slides, and hailstorms. Under these pitiful conditions, the Greeks continued to attack Hill 800, which was defended by two companies of the Leonessa. The attacks during the day were unsuccessful due to the flanking machine-gun fire of the Blackshirts units. As a result, the Greeks attempted several thrusts during the night, which ultimately were also repelled.

The next day, the situation was unchanged, but the Greeks attacked again in large numbers. Once again they were repelled by the defenders. On 7 February, the fighting continued again unabated. This time the troops of the Leonessa were deployed in a counterattack that failed to recapture Hill 802, which had been lost to the Greeks on 1 February. The action being poorly planned exposed the attacking columns to the deadly fire of the enemy guns and there were heavy casualties.

On the 8th, the Leonessa was ordered to counterattack again the enemy positions in order to take Hill 802, but the attacks once again were checked by the staunch Greek opposition.

During the night, enemy patrols executing repeated assaults managed to get close to the positions held by the Blackshirts but they were ultimately forced to withdraw by heavy machine-gun fire leaving behind in the slopes of the mountain several dead soldiers. The next morning on 9 February at 6:30 a.m., the Greeks with a large force came forward again with a frontal attack against Hill 800 supported by a heavy artillery barrage. After nearly two hours of fierce fighting and a last-ditch counterattack by the Blackshirts with hand grenades, the opponent was finally pushed off the high ground, leaving 100 dead, a machine gun, various weapons, and four prisoners.

Finally, on the 10th, the Leonessa positions were reinforced by additional Blackshirt troops including the 3rd Company of XV Battalion and a platoon of the 15th Machine-Gun Company, which had until then been kept in reserve. On 11 February, again with great stubbornness, the Greek infantry, preceded by a violent artillery preparation, came forward again to assault Hill 800. The fierce attacks lasted for over two hours and the troops of the Leonessa put up a strong resistance, supported by the machine guns, mortars, and the heavier guns in the rear. As a result of thundering fire, the enemy suffered great losses and finally stopped the attack, leaving on the ground several dead soldiers, various automatic weapons, and five prisoners. After a few hours of calm, the enemy attacked again at 8:30 p.m. This time it attempted to envelop the Italian troops from the left flank with a column fast descending from Hill 802. But once again the prompt reaction of the Blackshirt battalions restored the situation by concentrating heavy fire upon the Greeks. Several dead and wounded soldiers were left on the battlefield. On the morning of 13 February, following a pinpoint mortar barrage, the Greeks advanced in great numbers once again only to be mowed down by the dogged resistance of the Blackshirts. Once again they were forced to leave on the battlefield many dead and wounded, numerous weapons, and five prisoners, including an officer. At 11:30 p.m. on the same day, while the Cagliari Division infantry was in the process of relieving the Blackshirts, the Greeks attacked with successive waves of infantry troops hoping to catch the Italians off guard. But the prompt reaction of the Blackshirts supported by heavy machine-gun fire once again broke up the surprise enemy attack. By that date, the Leonessa had suffered the following losses: forty-five dead, 150 wounded, and 144 soldiers missing or hospitalised. Of the 1,023 men still able for combat, 120 had to be taken to hospital after a few days because they were suffering from rheumatic fever or frostbite. The bulletin issued by *Comando Supremo* remarked: 'On the Greek front, the enemy suffered significant losses. In the last battles the XIV Battalion CCNN of the Leonessa Legion particularly distinguished itself'.[14]

Thus, for more than ten days, these troops, faced by an overwhelming enemy force, resisted the onslaught often recurring to close quarter's combat and frequent counterattacks to re-establish Italian defensive lines. One of the Blackshirt NCOs involved in the fighting recalls:

> A large enemy unit attempted to outflank us and assailed our positions while uttering wild screams. But with a bold counter with hand grenades and bayonets we were able to seize from the Greeks a small height from which we began to fire our machine guns effectively targeting the packed enemy columns advancing on the right flank of our defensive line. Our second platoon could now retreat in an orderly manner as all resistance on the line was pointless at that point since we were fighting against a much greater enemy force that held a 10 to 1 advantage against us. As we retreated we were targeted by several machine guns positioned in well concealed heights and on Hill 802. A large enemy unit led by a senior officer attempted to cut us off as we pulled back. I placed myself at the head of a few Blackshirts to head off and check the enemy attack. I then grabbed a rifle from one of the wounded Blackshirts and began to fire very rapidly against the approaching enemy troops. Our unit then launched several hand grenades against the enemy troops which were forced to retreat.[15]

According to the testimony above, the Blackshirts often had to engage the enemy with hand grenades and flamethrowers in order to repel them from key positions. In other cases, the fighting took the form of rapid raids and counters against enemy positions such as the troops advancing with bayonets while receiving the support of flanking machine-gun fire. Their resistance ultimately would prevent the envelopment of the entire Italian line and was responsible for halting the Greek advance. After the counteroffensive had been checked, the Blackshirt legions were deployed on the frontline, mostly carrying out defensive and reconnaissance duties until the final Greek collapse.

Positive results during the Greek campaign were also obtained by the *Ragguppamento Galbiati* (a unit which took the name of its commander Enzo Galbiati), which was comprised by VIII, XVI, and XXIX Blackshirt Battalions.

The unit was created on 24 December 1940 in Valona (Albania) and it was comprised by experienced mountain troops from northern Lombardy. Its initial goal was to organise a number of legions into a more durable combat structure that could be used as a tactical reserve. Its first major operation was during the Battle of Maritzait when on 13 February 1941 it was called upon to prop up the infantry to defend against the major counterattack of the Greek Crete Division. Together with the support of II Mortar Battalion of the Sforzesca, the *Raggruppamento* fought from 13–23 February in order to halt the enemy advance. Facing only three lightly armed Blackshirt battalions, the Greek commanders were certain of a breakthrough in the sector held by Galbiati's troops. But the fierce response of the Blackshirts fought the Greeks into a standstill and forced them to ultimately abstain from attacking any further due to the high casualties. The *Raggruppamento* later in the campaign distinguished itself once again in the Battle of Drino Valley on 17 April 1941 when the Blackshirt assault detachments together with the standard infantry broke through the enemy lines and penetrated deep into Greek territory.

This breakthrough, together with the concurrent advance from the north by the German armoured units, forced the hand of the Greek Army, which later surrendered to the Axis.

The Greek campaign and the consequent stalemate that was forced upon the Italian Royal Army, although it was a true trial of fire, exposed some of the major weaknesses of the Italian Army. The Blackshirts also demonstrated that they were armed with very light equipment unsuited for the defensive tasks and that their units, due to their lack of firepower, were a far cry from the *arditi* units of the First World War.

Despite the heavy toll suffered by the Blackshirts, the Greek campaign was instrumental, however, in beefing up and ultimately strengthening their organisation with the consolidation of many of their more experienced and battle-hardened units into larger, better-equipped, and more durable structures. The *Raggruppamento Galbiati* was the first unit to consolidate three Blackshirt battalions under a single command. But once the campaign was over, they received further training in Rome and eventually became one of the first units (*Gruppo di Battaglioni*) of the M Battalions.

Once Greece was conquered, several Blackshirt battalions were deployed in policing and counterinsurgency operations along with some of the infantry divisions of the 2nd Army Corps and the Carabinieri in Yugoslavia, Albania, and Greece. The Yugoslavian campaign witnessed the formation of two other M Battalions groups such as the *Ragguppamento Biscaccianti* (80th and 109th Legion and XCIII Battalion) and the *Raggruppamento Diamanti* (28th, 108th, 115th, 136th, and 152nd Legions).

The campaign, which began on 6 April 1941, saw the Luftwaffe carry out a devastating three-day air strike on the Yugoslav capital, which was soon followed by a swift advance of the German Panzer Divisions that overcame any resistance. Within a short time, the Yugoslav Army disintegrated, and the state, undermined by deep internal political and ethnic conflicts, dissolved.

During this campaign, the Italian troops of the 2nd Army of General Vittorio Ambrosio attacked the Yugoslavs from their bases in Friuli Venezia Giulia and seized the Dalmatian coast and the city of Fiume. Concurrently, the 9th Army of General Alessandro Pirzio Biroli attacked from bases in Albania. The *Ragguppamenti Diamanti* and *Biscaccianti* fought under the command of the 9th Army, while eight legions attacked Yugoslavia from the north (5th, 17th, 73rd, 75th, 88th, 89th, 98th, and 137th Legions).

After the Yugoslavian Army was dissolved, the 108th and 49th Legions were deployed in Herzegovina; the 73rd and the 89th in Dalmatia; the 55th, 75th and 137th were active in both Croatia and Slovenia; the 98th, 15th, and 105th were utilised to patrol sections of northern Slovenia; and the 82nd and 72nd Legions were deployed in Montenegro. These units were augmented by other legions and autonomous battalions that were dispatched periodically and rotated into service to help put down major revolts. Several legions were also garrisoned in barracks near Gorizia to patrol the Italian–Slovenian border.

All units deployed in the Balkans were involved in very tough fighting and, unlike on the Russian Front, the Italian troops in several instances committed grave deeds against both enemy combatants and civilians to put down rebellions and local insurgencies. As Italy occupied a section of Yugoslavia in 1941, the Yugoslav partisans in fact fled to the mountain regions and waged a guerrilla campaign against the Axis forces occupying their country. As a result, the Italian General-in-Charge Mario Roatta issued on 1 March 1942 a circular (3C) that outlined the policy of systematic reprisals against Partisan units based in modern-day Slovenia, which attacked Axis units. The policy included executions, burning partisan held villages or homes and capturing partisans and sending them to prisoner camps. A total of 25,000 civilians in Slovenia were taken to the camps, and by 1943, several thousands died in the camps. Both sides, including Tito's Communist partisans, committed atrocities between 1941 and 1943. This included random shootings, executions by firing squad, killing of civilians, and mass arrests.[16]

The Italians, as the occupying force and therefore as one of the main culprits of the guerrilla war and its illegal methods, attempted to rule by creating local, pro-nationalist groups to fight against the Communists. In some cases, the local nationalist militias fought alongside the Italians, while in some cases the latter fought autonomously. Most recently, the role of the Blackshirts in the fight against the partisans has been the topic of a heated debate among military historians and Balkan history specialists. The debate originally began when a special parliamentary commission was set up in the post war to investigate Italian war crimes. Subsequently, as military archives released most of the information historians began delving into the history of the Axis occupation of the Balkans. After reviewing the available information, some have argued that the Blackshirts behaved much worse toward civilians than the troops of the standard army, while others have argued that they did not behave any differently than the troops of the Royal Army. Historian Andrea Rossi argues that 'as early as 1941 the MVSN distinguished itself for its repressive zeal, its merciless treatment of civilians and because it never withdrew from what was unanimously considered the worse of the dirty work of occupation armies, executions and firing squads'.[17]

In contrast, historian Osti Guerrazzi argues: 'An analysis of the Diario Storico of the 98th Blackshirt assault battalion, which was part of the Isonzo Division, does not show any difference between the behaviour of the Blackshirts and that of the Army's soldiers'.[18]

Both units, argues Osti Guerrazzi, committed atrocities to the same degree. This type of behaviour mirrored that of the partisans that killed soldiers randomly in ambush attacks and then fled the scene, often exposing and leaving civilians helpless and open to Axis reprisals. In 1943, when Italy exited the war, Tito's partisans would in turn commit even worse atrocities against Italian soldiers but especially non-combatants targeting easy civilian targets (the elderly, women, and children) in what has become known as the Foibe of Dalmazia. Italian-speaking civilians (especially women and children but also teachers, policemen, and local administrators) and soldiers alike were dumped alive in mass graves in the caves in the mountain areas near the border and perished by a slow and terrible death.[19]

For many years, the Italian Communist Party kept a lid on these tragic events for much of the post-war period. Then, in the 1990s, with the fall of the Soviet Union, these events came much more to light revealing the brutality and unlawfulness of Tito's troops and its Communist regime. Another fact that came to life was Palmiro Togliatti's, Italian Communist Party leader, disinterest for the fate of Italian prisoners of war held by the Soviets after 1945. In fact, the vast majority would die of hunger and disease, while Togliatti, fully aware of the situation, never addressed their predicament with the Soviet leadership.

Heavy losses were also sustained by the Blackshirts in North Africa. In this theatre of operations, three divisions were deployed (23 Marzo, 28 Ottobre, and 3 Gennaio) between 1940 and 1941 and spearheaded the original advance ordered by General Rodolfo Graziani. While these troops originally advanced against the British to Sidi el Barrani, they were later overrun during the first British counteroffensive (Operation Compass) that led to the loss of most of the Italian possessions in Cyrenaica. Most of these units fought valiantly but lacked the tactical acumen and the weapons of the British Army. All three divisions, for instance, experienced great difficulties in confronting British armoured units due to the lack of heavy anti-tank weapons. The 3 Gennaio, for instance, was virtually destroyed at Sidi Barrani in December 1940 and was later disbanded.

Meanwhile, the 28 Ottobre and the 23 Marzo divisions were also badly beaten and pulled back to Sollum and Bardia respectively. Both were defeated again and later disbanded in January 1941.

Battistelli and Crociani argue that the performance of the Blackshirts in North Africa during Operation Compass was fairly bad.[20] This was not necessarily the result of the Blackshirt units themselves but because they were deployed in static defences by commanders that did not provide viable tactics to halt the British armoured units. The troops had not been trained properly and had little experience in fighting against armoured units. In addition, given the lack of training, they had few soldiers within their ranks that could properly operate the crew served weapons. Their performance, however, was not inferior to that of the Italian standard army units deployed in North Africa. This view differs from that of military historian Paddy Griffiths who has argued that the militia in 1940–41 held back the standard army due to its lack of training, weak armament, and lack of motorisation.[21]

By late 1941 (4 December), however, the fortunes of the Blackshirts improved. A unit comprised of volunteer university students accounted itself well when assigned the defence of a critical Axis position and faced by a large armoured brigade of Commonwealth troops. British historian Michael Carver wrote that the action of the Giovani Fascisti was a contributing factor in halting Operation Crusader, the first British counterattack against the Axis forces commanded by General Erwin Rommel:

> Although Norrie had an overwhelming superiority in every arm in the area of Bir el Gubi, the failure to concentrate them and coordinate the action of all arms in detail had allowed one Italian battalion group to frustrate the action of the whole corps and inflict heavy casualties on one brigade.[22]

The Italian positions were defended mainly by two battalions of Blackshirts of the Giovani Fascisti, two MILIMART 102-mm guns, an L tank company deploying tanks dug in deep gun pits as artillery support, and a battery of 20-mm guns.

To better understand the dynamics of the battle, it is worth quoting at length the Official History of the 11th Indian Armoured Brigade:

> At 1245 hours the artillery laid a smoke screen on the southern approaches to el Gobi; behind it two companies of the 1/6 Rajputana Rifles moved to the attack. Four I tanks accompanied the assault, but owning to wireless failures fought independently and were not on call by the infantry. After initial progress the Rajputana Rifles were held up. A company of Camerons joined the fray on the left flank. At 1430 hours Lieutenant Colonel Butler (Rajputana Rifles) reported that he had reached the outskirts of a comprehensive defence position organized in depth. His tanks and carriers (Bren) had penetrated the

> outpost line but were unable to deal with the enemy in their deep and narrow slit trenches. A number of tanks had been knocked out by Molotov cocktails. A similar report came from the Camerons, who added that enemy machine gun squads had occupied one of the disabled I tanks and were enfilading them. At 1600 hours the Rajputana Rifles commander again reported the situation as stalemate. A few minutes Lieutenant Colonel Butler was killed by a mortar.[23]

The operation resulted in over 400 infantry casualties and several knocked-out tanks suffered by the British and Commonwealth forces. It was also one of the first operations where relatively lightly armed Italian infantry forces had been able to halt a powerful armoured assault. Historian John Gooch has argued that the action of the Giovani Fascisti is a valid example that illustrates why 'Italy's military component was so different in the first and second stages in the campaign in North Africa'.[24]

According to Gooch, 'the change in performance stemmed mainly from increased battle field experience, coordinated and centralized artillery action that stifled more effectively enemy armoured attacks and more mobility and greater assimilation of German tactics by Italian armoured and motorized units'.[25] As far as the Blackshirts are concerned, the upswing in performance can be attributed to improved training and a more coordinated effort between assault infantry and anti-tank artillery units. By that time, following the German lead, the Italians had understood the full ramifications of using primarily the anti-tank guns and not tanks to knock-out enemy armoured units. In addition, the Giovani Fascisti were decisively better equipped than the three Blackshirt Divisions under General Graziani. They comprised a force of sixty-nine officers and 1,500 NCOs and volunteers armed with daggers, hand grenades, and rifles. As far as the crew served weapons, the unit had twenty-seven automatic guns, nine machine guns, four 81-mm mortars, four 47/32-mm anti-tank guns, and fifteen Solothurn rifles.

In 1942, the MVSN coastal defence units deployed in Tobruk also distinguished themselves when they participated to the defence of the port and its infrastructure during the daring British Commando raid of 13–14 September 1942. The British destroyer *Sikh*, for instance, was sunk by the coastal batteries of the MVSN while it was taking on commando troops during the last stage of the raid.

Meanwhile in East Africa, there were thirty Blackshirt battalions (the 11th Legion, comprised of two battalions, and I, II, III, IV, V, XI, XII, XIII, XIV, XLIV, CXVI, CXXXI, CXXXVI, CXLI, CXLVI, CLI, CLXIV, CLXVI, CLXX, CCXL, DII, DIV, DV, DVI, DLXXXV, DCXXXI, DCCXXXI, and DCCXLV Battalions) stationed there at the outbreak of the war. These units fought all major engagements of the campaign from the initial conquest of British Somalia to the defence of the Empire to the final British counteroffensive. Although, this was a secondary front for the Italians, which failed to properly supply the Duca d'Aosta with troops and equipment, the Blackshirts were deployed *en masse* in the Battle of Cheren, where they fought well despite the final negative outcome of the campaign. After being defeated, some Blackshirts together with other elements of the Italian Army engaged the British in a guerrilla campaign that lasted for almost a year and caused the British troops some headaches forcing them to tie down a larger forces than initially planned. The campaign was disastrous for the Blackshirt, which were either destroyed or captured by the British during the final counteroffensive.

The Blackshirts were then involved with Operation Barbarossa as the 63rd *Tagliamento* Legion was dispatched to Russia in support of the CSIR. This would be their major campaign of the war not only in terms of their massive deployment, but also because it was where most of the militia casualties were sustained. The combination of fighting against the Communists and on behalf of an ideology that abhorred the Soviet Union made the campaign the most critical deployment for the militia of the entire war. From the onset, the fighting against the Red Army was very tough and as the campaign evolved more and more Blackshirt units were sucked into the conflict. From the onset, the Blackshirts fought well and even received praise from not only the Italian commander but also from German generals and headquarter staff. Their ranks would be depleted by the constant fighting and by the rough Russian winter weather.

From the Legions to the Elite M Battalions

As the war continued, placing huge demands on the scarce resources of the Italian Army, on 1 October 1941, the High Command together with the MVSN opted for a reorganisation of some of the legions. The change stemmed from many factors but the main one being the consolidation of the Blackshirts under heavier, better-equipped, and better-trained assault units. The *Battaglioni d'assalto* M (M for Mussolini assault battalions) specifically were created to form elite assault units within the Blackshirt legions during the Second World War. The majority of these battalions were formed out of those legions that had fought particularly well in Albania, Greece, or Soviet Union in 1940–41. The first M Battalions were those from the *Raggruppamento Galbiati* (VIII, XVI, and XXIX Battalions), which were veterans of the Battle of Maritzait in Greece, followed by those of the Leonessa (XIV, XV Battalions), which had also made a key contribution during the Greek campaign and had been cited for their actions in the war bulletins of February 1941. The bulk were trained and raised in the Trastevere and Civitavecchia military bases and then later dispatched to the frontline. While a minority of these units, such as the Tagliamento, were designated as elite assault battalions in the field during their deployment in Russia. The Tagliamento, for example, considered one of the best units of the MVSN, was reputed as not needing any extra training in order to receive this important designation.

These special battalions were the brainchild of the head of the MSVN *Luogotenente Generale della Milizia* Enzo Galbiati in order to assemble under select, few divisions the cream of the crop of the Blackshirt legions comprised of the type of soldier that 'responded more effectively to the modern battlefield'.[26]

The latter had been nominated by Mussolini as the head of the MVSN upon his return from Greece on 25 May 1941. Galbiati succeeded Achille Starace, the pompous and ineffective leader that was dismissed abruptly by Mussolini because he had done little to prepare the MVSN for war, and quickly distinguished himself from his predecessor. In contrast to Starace, Enzo Galbiati worked strenuously to make the MVSN and the Blackshirt units more autonomous from the Royal Army by placing a strong focus on improved training, the introduction of new weapons and new equipment, and the introduction of more rigorous selection processes. Galbiati's original intention was to constitute Blackshirt elite units by adopting the German Panzer Grenadier model, these being mixed units of highly specialised infantry (engineers, assault platoons, and specialised crew served weapons platoons) and of tank and armoured vehicles units. Unfortunately, however, the Italian Army in 1941 did not possess enough tanks and motorised units and therefore the M Battalions remained for the most part non-motorised or lightly motorised infantry units, although endowed with a greater degree of specialisation than the standard infantry. When Galbiati proposed the formation of the M Battalions, he also launched several new ideas that were mainly based on his observations of German special infantry units. The first idea was a proposal to improve the relationship between the Royal Army and the Blackshirts through more extensive collaboration in the planning and execution of military operations. Galbiati envisioned that units that were to be deployed in battle would conduct prior joint training exercises to increase collaboration and prior joint detailed reconnaissance of enemy positions. Up to that point, Royal Army and Blackshirt units had rarely trained together.

Second, in Galbiati's view, the Blackshirts should have been made more autonomous from an organisational standpoint from the Royal Army. Not only should they be supplied with more effective armaments, but also they should have their own training bases and shooting ranges. This was seen as an essential step in improving the battlefield performance of these units. The elite battalions were to be trained at the Trastevere and Civitavecchia bases with an increased focus on the intensity and duration of the training.

Third, Galbiati aimed to improve the efficiency of the units through quantitative and qualitative reforms. The Blackshirts were to be endowed with more and better weapons and the selection process was to be more rigorous. For example, no soldier that was shorter than 1.7 metres was to be accepted in the M Battalions. Soldiers must have had prior combat experience and have familiarity with crew served and individual weapons before being accepted into the Blackshirts.

Fourth, to improve Blackshirt training, each unit was required to go through a more exhaustive training regime much like the training of the *arditi* units. Training with self-propelled guns, heavy artillery such the Flak 88-mm gun, and with portable German flamethrowers was to be initiated as soon as possible.

The dearth of equipment and weapons was one of the main factors that slowed down the constitution and the rapid development of the M Battalions. In Ugo Cavallero's diary, there are two entries that refer to the M Battalions and to the early debates regarding their constitution. They both point to the fact that lack of equipment hampered their development. On 19 June 1941, the topic of the M Battalions was preliminarily discussed between Cavallero and Galbiati. The latter proposed the formation of twenty highly trained MVSN units styled along the Panzer Grenadier model armed with tanks and self-propelled guns. Cavallero, on the other hand, argued that there were no tanks available for these units and not enough trucks to make these units fully motorised. Therefore, his view was to constitute units of highly trained, experienced volunteers that could be deployed as tactical reserves of the Army Corps or for militia and territorial garrison duty.[27]

On 12 September 1941, there is another mention in Cavallero's diary of a meeting with MSVN head Galbiati were the topic of the M Battalions was more fully discussed:

> I met with his Excellency Galbiati. The M Battalions (three in Rome and two in Fregene) have been rigorously selected, trained and are comprised of battle hardened soldiers. Currently they lack crew served weapons such as flamethrowers, anti-tank guns and artillery pieces. Galbiati demands these weapons for his troops. But I reply that the Army does not have the weapons. Mussolini had asked that 16 M Battalions be constituted by the end of the year. But I believe that we can only constitute 6 units at this time...I envision these troops to be deployed in anti-partisan garrison duty and I do not see the need for arming them with anti-tank weapons. Galbiati disagrees he envisions them to be deployed in battle to fight alongside the standard infantry. I therefore urge him to train these troops as assault battalions. He concurs with me and argues that we should be able to constitute 100 battalions in three years.[28]

Thus although the early development of the M Battalions were characterised mostly by the scarcity of viable equipment and weapons, their later consolidation was marked by a greater focus on training and by slight improvements in their weaponry. The M Battalions were structured similarly to the legions, but had slightly larger cohorts. Each M Battalion Group typically was comprised by about 1,650 soldiers on two assault battalions and one accompanying artillery weapons unit, while the legions typically had on average 1,500 soldiers. The former had a larger command company, which was not only better equipped with Beretta machine guns but also had more trucks at its disposal. The M

Battalions were generally comprised of better-trained troops, although for the most part their crew served weapons were no better or more effective than those available to the legions in 1940. The standard Blackshirt Legion had 126 officers and NCOs, 1,230 soldiers, one automobile, five trucks, forty-eight assault rifles, twelve machine guns, and eighteen mortars. In 1940 or 1941, for example, no provision had been made to arm the legions with an anti-tank gun unit.

Whereas the standard M Battalion Group had 162 officers and NCOs, 1,350 soldiers, 134 drivers, four cars, 124 trucks, thirty-six motorcycles, forty-eight assault rifles, twenty-four automatic rifles, twenty-four heavy machine guns, eighteen 45-mm mortars, six 81-mm mortars, and eight 47/32-mm anti-tank guns.[29] Some M Battalions Groups such as the Leonessa had even slightly larger cohorts with a total of 1,792 all ranks.[30]

By comparing the strength of the legions to the M Battalions, it is evident that the latter had a greater degree of motorisation, more weapons, some automatic machine guns, and also had an engineer/sapper and a reconnaissance component that the former clearly lacked. The M Battalion Groups were a step in the right direction of modern mechanised warfare, with the formation of more specialised units, although their greatest weakness remained the absence of a viable anti-tank weapon. While the German Panzer Grenadier divisions received more powerful artillery, *panzerfaust* and later on even more deadly guns, the Italian Blackshirts, like the infantry, had to settle for the 47/32-mm units, the mostly ineffective Pazzaglia bombs and the Solothurn anti-tank rifle.

The M Battalion Groups were to be assigned as a tactical reserve of the Army Corps or the High Command. Their main function was to act as a tactical reserve to be allocated to carry out particularly demanding actions such as to open up the way for the standard infantry during offensive actions, conduct raids beyond enemy lines, and reconnaissance work. Thus the bulk of these elite units was mainly deployed in the campaign against the Soviet Union, in the anti-partisan fight in Yugoslavia and for the planned invasion of the British-held island of Malta. In essence, apart from North Africa, they were deployed in Italy's main theatres of operation.

In 1942, not only the Blackshirt assault units but also the MVSN as a whole was expanded further in order to brace the militia for a prolonged war of attrition. First, the existing coastal and aerial defence units were expanded although their equipment remained largely the same as a result of shortages and the overall slow production output by Italian industry during the Second World War. Second, a new specialty was created within the M Battalions, which specialised in seaborne landings, the *Gruppo Battaglioni* M *da Sbarco* (M Battalions Group for Seaborne Landing). The unit, comprised of four battalions (XLII *Battaglione da Sbarco* M Vicenza, XLIII *Battaglione da Sbarco* M Belluno, L *Battaglione da Sbarco* M Treviso, LX *Battaglione da Sbarco* M Pola) was supposed to take part in Operation C3, the invasion of Malta in mid-1942. In addition to the infantry companies, the unit was comprised of a command company, two companies of 47/32-mm guns, one mortar company (81-mm units), and one company of engineers. The Blackshirts M *Gruppo Battaglioni da sbarco* were relatively even better equipped than the standard M Battalion Groups and had a strength of 353 officers and NCOs, 2,978 soldiers, 108 assault rifles, forty-two machine guns, thirty-six 45-mm mortars, and eight 47/32-mm guns. The soldiers began training in late 1941 in Tuscany and Liguria where fire brigade ladders were used to allow the troops to scale rocky cliffs in a Malta-like hilly and rugged environment. Their purpose during the operation would have been to link up with the paratroopers, which would have gone into Malta first. The Blackshirts units would land through barges and small boats and once effectuated the seaborne landing they were required to take out British coastal batteries and machine-gun posts. For many months, with this sole purpose in mind, training continued to the point that this unit was probably the better equipped and most prepared of the entire MVSN. It had the largest number of Beretta automatic light machine guns ever allocated to a Blackshirt unit and it trained longer and with more resources than any other unit. As Battistelli and Crociani assert: '… to a limited extent some special individual equipment was also made available, in the form of certain number of Beretta M38A machine guns, and the special Samurai load carrying vests used to carry extra magazines and hand grenades'.[31]

But eventually as the operation against Malta was cancelled, the soldiers, even though excellently trained, were deployed in other fronts. Some of these units later took part to the occupation of Corsica after the Allied landings in North Africa and were later moved to France to provide garrison duty of important military bases near Toulon. It is interesting to note that throughout the conflict, they never carried out an important operation even though the resources that had been made available to them had been very considerable.

By mid-1942, there were a total of twenty-two M Battalions (if you exclude LXIII Heavy Weapons Battalion of the Tagliamento, which at that point was comprised primarily by Royal Army), while the legions slowly declined in numbers due to losses in the field of battle and the inability of the MVSN to replace their debilitated ranks with new recruits. Of the twenty-two M Battalions, half were dispatched to Russia, six to the Balkans, four to France, and one to Tunisia.

If the M Battalions were expanded, the number of the standard legions declined as the war wore on. In September 1941, a total of 197 legions/battalions had been deployed on the major fronts. But shortly thereafter, eighty-one of them had experienced high casualties and had been disbanded.[32]

The problem was that there was little manpower available and the MVSN was forced to call up reserve soldiers and older veterans to fill the void. 'The lack of manpower and dispersion of forces meant it was not possible to make good the losses and attrition incurred, especially for the *legioni* attached to the divisions employed in garrison and anti-partisan duties'.[33]

The lack of NCOs and officers particularly affected the legions and many were disbanded because of the lack of leadership cadres.

On July 1942, the number of Blackshirts Battalions had declined to 105, while in January 1943, the number had gone up slightly to 110 but by this time most were organised into either M Battalion Groups or larger groupings. However, most of the legions by then were under strength and in some cases battalions had less than 60 per cent of their initial ranks.

By the end of 1942, the MVSN had the following M Battalions:

-V *Battaglione d'Assalto* M (from the V *Legione* Valle Scrivia based in Tortona)
-VI *Battaglione d'Assalto* M (from *Legione* Sforzesca based in Vigevano)
-VIII *Battaglione d'Assalto* M (from *Legione* Cacciatori delle Alpi in Varese)
-X *Battaglione d'Assalto* M (from *Legione* Montebello from Voghera)
-XII *Battaglione Armi Accompagnamento* (from *Legione* Monte Bianco from Aosta)
-XIV *Battaglione d'Assalto* M (from *Legione* Garibaldina from Bergamo)
-XV *Battaglione d'Assalto* M (from *Legione* Leonessa, Brescia)
-XVI *Battaglione d'Assalto* M (from *Legione* Alpina, Como)
-XXIX *Battaglione d'Assalto* M (from *Legione* Antonio, Chinotto di Arona)
-XXX *Battaglione d'Assalto* M (from *Legione* Roberto Forni, Novara)
-XXXIV *Battaglione d'Assalto* M (from *Legione* Premuda, Savona)
-XXXVIII *Battaglione Armi Accompagnamento* (from *Legione* Vittorio Alfieri, from Asti)
-XLI *Battaglione Armi Accompagnamento* (from *Legione* Cesare Battisti from Trento)
-XLII *Battaglione da Sbarco* M (from *Legione* Berica, Vicenza)
-XLIII *Battaglione da Sbarco* M (from *Legione* Piave, Belluno)
-L *Battaglione da Sbarco* M (from *Legione* Trevigiana, Treviso)
-LX *Battaglione da Sbarco* M (from *Legione* Istria, Pola)
-LXIII *Battaglione d'Assalto* M (from *Legione* Tagliamento, Udine)
-LXIII *Battaglione Armi Accompagnamento* (Royal Army unit into M Battalion Group)
-LXXI *Battaglione d'Assalto* M (from *Legione* Manfreda, Faenza)
-LXXIX *Battaglione d'Assalto* M (*Legione* Tagliamento, Reggio Emilia)
-LXXXI *Battaglione d'Assalto* M (from *Legione* Alberico da Barbiano, Ravenna)
-LXXXV *Battaglione d'Assalto* M (from *Legione* Apuana, Massa)

As previously mentioned, the bulk of the Blackshirts M Battalions were deployed in Russia (Tagliamento, Montebello, Leonessa, and Valle Scrivia) and organised into two major groups: *Raggruppamento* CCNN M 3 Gennaio and *Raggruppamento* CCNN M 23 Marzo (Blackshirts 3 January and 23 March Groups).

The former was comprised by the *Gruppo Battaglioni* CCNN M Tagliamento and *Gruppo Battaglioni* CCNN M Montebello legions, while the latter by the *Gruppo Battaglioni* CCNN M Leonessa and *Gruppo Battaglioni* CCNN M Valle Scrivia.

The Tagliamento consisted of LXIII Assault Battalion; LXXIX Assault Battalion; and LXIII Artillery Battalion.

The Montebello consisted of VI Assault Battalion; XXX Assault Battalion; and XII Artillery Battalion.

The Leonessa consisted of XIV Assault Battalion; XV Assault Battalion; and XXXVIII Artillery Battalion.

Finally, the Valle Scrivia consisted of V Assault Battalion; XXXIV Assault Battalion; and XLI Artillery Battalion.

Historian Carlo Rastrelli reports that the total losses during the campaign against the Soviet Union were staggering: 90 per cent of battalion commanders, 70 per cent of officers, and 55 per cent of *legionaries* fell during the harsh fighting. By February 1943, total losses on the Eastern Front were as follows: 172 officers and 3,480 Blackshirts with the Tagliamento and Leonessa taking the brunt.[34]

Most of the losses were sustained during the last phase of the campaign in the winter 1942–43 when the Axis faced the massive Red Army counteroffensive on the Don River. The Blackshirts were heavily involved and were often used to counterattack the Red Army or to defend key advanced outposts or machine-gun positions. During the pullback from the Don line and while other Axis units retreated in a disorganised fashion, the Blackshirts maintained their composure and fought to the end.

Meanwhile, the XM Battalion was dispatched to Tunisia in February 1943 and was initially assigned to the 136th Armoured Division Giovani Fascisti. It fought fairly well on the defensive line of Mareth and later at Enfidaville until the surrender of the Axis in Africa. Even though they fought mostly a defensive battle that was typically not suited for these special assault troops, the Blackshirts contributed to halting several attacks and delayed the advance of the Allied troops for several weeks.

There was a further expansion of the MVSN in 1943 with the creation of the 1a *Divisione Corazzata Camicie Nere* M (1st M Blackshirts Armoured Division). This unit, which will be dealt with in Chapter 5, was constituted in May 1943 from the remnants of the M Battalions that had fought in Russia and newly trained volunteers. Thus it was comprised by the most experienced soldiers within the M Battalions with ranks who had fought in Greece and the Soviet Union. The unit, equipped with very advanced armoured vehicles and guns supplied by the Germans, was still being trained at the time of the fall of Fascism (25 July 1943). The M Division was also the brainchild of Enzo Galbiati, which saw in this armoured division the last step in the specialisation process of the MVSN that had begun with the creation of the M Battalions. The

German leadership, however, was essential to its creation by furnishing to the Italians key weapons and equipment.

The development of the *Divisione* M represented an important turning point in the history of the MVSN. Since late 1941, the MVSN had privileged, better-equipped and trained units, at the expense of a large, non-motorised, poorly trained, and equipped standing army. This development mirrored the broader evolution of the Italian Royal Army, which by 1942 had favoured the constitution of elite units such as the Folgore, the Ariete Armoured Division, and the Monte Cervino *Alpini* Battalion. Most likely the effort was too late in coming given the turning of the tide in the war in 1943, but it was nevertheless an important advancement for the MVSN.

After the turning points of the Battle of El Alamein and the fall of Tunisia, the Axis war effort reached its lowest point in the summer of 1943. Italy was now threatened directly by the Allied invasion, which began with the attack on Lampedusa Island. The operation, meant to gain a foothold on southern Europe for the invasion of Italy, was initially effectively countered by, among others, the artillery troops of the 9th Legion. American intelligence officers had conducted detailed reconnaissance of the MILIMART units and had determined that the majority were comprised by small calibre and outdated gun units. But these same units a few days later faced a major enemy onslaught against Pantelleria Island were they fought waves of bombers and Allied naval raids. Then, in July, MILMART fought alongside other militia units (17th, 95th, 171st, and 173rd Legions) and standard army battalions to counter the Allied landing in Sicily. Despite an initial reaction by the Royal Army, the Germans, and the Blackshirts, the Axis troops quickly collapsed faced by the overwhelming fire of the American military, especially air power. Many units, including the Blackshirts, simply melted away. As historian Elena Aga Rossi asserts: 'The operation of scant Axis air forces was reduced by the Anglo-Americans' systematic destruction of the island's air bases. The clear disproportion between the forces was the main reason for the Italian army's disintegration'.[35]

Enrico Francisci, who had fought in Russia as head of the *Raggruppamento* CCNN M 23 Marzo and then held the position of *Luogotenente generale della milizia* for Sicily, however, died while fighting against the Allies and was posthumously awarded a Gold Medal of Military Valour.[36]

On 10 July 1943, during the Allied landing in Sicily, General Francisci was charged with coordinating the Axis counterattack against the Allies near Licata. After having surveyed the field of battle, at dawn on 11 July, Francisci led a swift armoured manoeuvre by the 177th *Bersaglieri* and the 161st self-propelled group against the 7th Army of General George Patton. While the latter was forced to retreat to the beachhead, Francisci was killed by a grenade while leading his troops forward. Accordingly, on that day, the Allies realised that 'not all Italian forces had lost the will to fight'.[37]

The MVSN and the Armistice of 1943

On 8 September 1943, General Badoglio's newly established government announced the switch in alliances by signing a peace treaty with the Allies. This drastic foreign policy change pushed the MVSN units that were located in Rome or north of Rome to join the Germans and to continue to fight against the Allies. The XVI M Battalion headquartered at Ponte Galeria, near Rome, the next day marched on the capital and it was stopped from clashing against units of the Royal Army by the prompt intervention of a senior officer of the MVSN, which dissuaded its *Console* Gustavo Marabini, from continuing its action. The M Division together with the German officers that were in charge of training contacted the head of the 3rd *Panzergrenadieren* Division, which was also in Rome, in order to also march on the capital.

In central-northern Italy, the various militia support units (rail, forest, harbour, border, and road security units) together with the *coorti territoriali*, the so-called territorial cohorts, charged with managing the M legions ammunition and weapons garrisons refused to abandon their weapons and reactivated the ammunition depots giving the MVSN units access to weapons and supplies. According to Andrea Rossi: '… it was really the political soldiers of the MVSN and not the leaders that were the first elements of the old regime that created the conditions for the formation of reorganized armed forces allied to the Germans in 1943'.[38]

Thus while the top leaders of the old regime such as Farinacci, Pavolini, and even Mussolini's son had fled to Berlin, the rank and file of the MVSN, despite being less leaderless, took the political and military initiative.

In Friuli-Venezia Giulia all the legions passed to the Germans to continue the fight against Tito's partisans. The Udine (63rd), Gorizia (62nd), Trieste (58th), Pola (60th), and Fiume (61st) legions transferred in mass to the German side.

A large number of those in the *Divisione* M, for example, left the unit, which was disbanded and reorganised by Badoglio and joined the Germans. The remnants of the Tagliamento, Leonessa, and the Montebello also joined the German Army. The Blackshirts units located in France and Yugoslavia also, for the most part, opted to continue the fight against the Allies. In Toulon, for instance, a battalion of Blackshirts comprising 580 soldiers, was given a stark choice from its commander. Either continue the fight or, for those that did not wish to continue fighting for the Axis, return to Italy. Over 350 soldiers opted to remain in France and were later attached to a German Grenadier unit, while the remaining soldiers returned to Italy and to civilian life. Thus in Toulon the bulk of XLII and L M Battalions joined the Germans under a new unit that was named *Compagnia* Zardo, taking the name of its commander. In Ljubljana, the bulk of the *Raggruppamento* CCNN M 21 Aprile (VIII, XVI, LXXI, LXXXI, and LXXXV) also joined the Germans. In the same city the 75th Legion also sided with the Germans and was later dispatched to Ferrara to carry out anti-partisan activity.

In the town of Split, the 89th Siena Legion decidedly sided with the Germans, who later trained and armed the unit with German weapons. In 1944, the unit was then transferred to Italy where it carried out anti-partisan raids in Piedmont and Lombardy. In Zara, the 107th Legion also sided with the Germans. It was later also transferred to Italy to fight against Tito's partisans. In Montenegro, the following units: the San Marco Legion (33rd, 40th, and 49th Battalions), LXXII, LXXXII, LXXXVI, LXXXXIV, CXLVI, and CLXII Battalions joined the Germans and where deployed in Croatia until the end of the war and engaged in anti-partisan activity against Tito's troops. In Albania, two Blackshirt units—the XXIX M Battalion of the Raggruppamento CCNN M 21 Aprile and the 92nd Legion—joined the Germans the day after the armistice was signed. The latter was dispatched to Russia in late 1943 and later fought against the Russians in Hungary in 1944. In Greece, all thirteen Blackshirt units stationed there in September 1943 joined the Germans. Some were transferred to Germany for training and later deployed in Italy. In Greece, the 19th Legion was the first Blackshirt unit to side with the Germans. The XXXVI Blackshirt Battalion took a week before siding with Germany and was later dispatched to Germany for training as well. XXIII and XXVIII also joined the Germans a few weeks later. Little is known about the other ten Blackshirt units present in Albania in 1943, but presumably they too joined the Germans and then went to Germany for training. CXLI Battalion was garrisoned in Crete, while the 24th Legion was headquartered in the Dodecanese islands, they too refused to disband and joined Germany.

The only units located north of Rome on the day of the armistice that refused to ally themselves to the Germans were XLIII and LX M Battalions, which together with the Royal Army units stationed in Corsica fought for the Badoglio government. These units took on none other than the 16th Brigade Reichsführer of the Waffen SS. The fact that the latter received a bloody nose and suffered casualties in spirited clashes against the two M Battalions in the outskirts of Bastia demonstrates how fairly well trained were the elite units of the MVSN.

Historian Andrea Rossi's estimates drawn from analysing Wehrmacht documents reveal that approximately 90,000 Italians, belonging to all units of the armed forces, sided with the Germans in September 1943. Of these 13,000 at the time of the armistice were in Italy, 45,000 in France, roughly 32,000 were in the Balkans. It is estimated that the 13,000 soldiers in Italy were all from the MVSN while in France there were only approximately 500 militia members in Toulon and the bulk were Royal Army troops. In the Balkans and Greece, over 32,000 sided with the Germans, and 20,000 of them belonged to the militia. Thus Rossi concludes by stating 'that approximately 33,000 Blackshirts after the armistice rebelled against the Badoglio government and joined their old ally'.[39]

Historians Marco Avagliano and Marco Palmentieri in their *L'Italia di Salo'* argue that according to their estimates, approximately 40,000 Blackshirts joined the old German ally when Badoglio's government signed the Treaty of Cassibile. In addition, they also argue an additional 25,000 belonging to the special militia units (port and railway security, forestry, border security, and postal units) also joined the Salo' Republic. Lastly, in 1943, the militia raised an additional 11,000 volunteers from the classes of 1922–26.[40]

Considering the reduced force of the MVSN and the Blackshirts in mid-1943, it can be argued that a sizeable minority of the militia opted to continue fighting on the side of the Axis alliance, while the vast majority of the remaining members of the MVSN, especially those in the south, most likely disbanded and returned to civilian life.

In due course, the Blackshirt units in northern Italy or Europe were disbanded and the militia soldiers joined the army of the Republic of Salo' of Marshal Rodolfo Graziani. The Blackshirts were in fact merged with newly formed *Guardia Nazionale Repubblicana* (Republican National Guard), which acted as a police and anti-partisan force between 1943 and 1945.

In the south, with the exception of Sardinia, the Blackshirt units joined the Royal Army and fought alongside the Allies. In Sardinia, the Blackshirt troops rebelled against some of the officers and joined the Germans. Most of these soldiers eventually made it to the north of Italy and were deployed within the *Guardia Nazionale Repubblicana*. Meanwhile, the Blackshirt units that opted to fight for the Badoglio government were disbanded in November 1943.

As historian Andrea Rossi asserts:

> The picture that emerges from the study of the reaction of the Blackshirts of the MVSN after 8 September is one of a great mass rebellion by these units. It was probably the biggest act of insubordination against the government in the history of the post-unitary Italian army. These units took their weapons and equipment and placed themselves under the command of the former German ally.[41]

Meanwhile, historian Stefano Fabei argues that the decision of the Grand Council to depose Mussolini created a fissure within the militia. On one hand, the top hierarchy of the MVSN, including its leader Galbiati and many senior officers, sought an accommodation with the new government and the monarchy, while on the other the bulk of the rank and file of the militia ultimately continued the fight against the Allies and the new government. In his view, the lack of a reaction by the M Division, can be explained largely by the fact the 'militia was betrayed by the leadership of the MVSN'.[42]

On 6 December 1943, Badoglio's government enacted a decree that dissolved the MVSN and its Blackshirts armed units. It abruptly ended the MVSN's twenty-year history.

An Assessment of Combat Efficiency

The Blackshirt units had a troubled history throughout their twenty-year existence. They were first used by the *Duce* to help consolidate the regime. Then their role changed from providing internal security to fighting Fascism's expansionist and colonial wars. In 1940, they faced the biggest test of their existence when deployed in Italy's major theatres of operation in the Second World War against well-equipped armies such as the British and the Soviet Red Army.

Historians have different opinions with regards to the combat effectiveness of the MVSN during the war.

Gian Luigi Gatti, a historian of the MVSN, has argued that the Blackshirts were not an effective fighting force since they lacked military professionalism given their political closeness with the regime. Moreover, the pack of viable junior officers and NCOs also limited the MVSN's combat effectiveness since its units lacked the cohesiveness and discipline of Royal Army infantry units. Moreover, those that held leadership positions lacked the necessary military prerequisites to lead a modern armed force.[43]

Similarly, Greek historian Phoebus Athanassiou has argued: 'However, the incorporation of Blackshirt units was not completed until well after the Greek campaign had diminished enthusiasm for the Fascist cause, the efficiency of these units was lower than that of the regulars and their overall role in the war effort was patchy'.[44]

In contrast, Greene and Massignani assert:

> According to most scholars, the performance of the CC. NN. units during the Second World War was generally always inferior to the equivalent German units, with the only exception being the CC. NN. units sent to Russia. In partial mitigation of this judgment, it should be remembered that equipment and training of the CC. NN. units, along with their cadres, was on average inferior to the German units.[45]

Similarly, Battistelli and Crociani have argued that the Blackshirt units:

> When tested on the field of battle, Blackshirt units performed with mixed results. Their overall performance during the 1935–36 war was good, much less so during the Spanish Civil War and in the early stages of World War Two, when only some *legioni* and battalions proved themselves competent in battle. Later on, Blackshirt units gave good accounts of themselves on the Eastern Front, and in the Balkans where, in a sense, they felt at home fighting against Tito's partisans. The main shortcomings among the Blackshirts units were their lack of service elements and their armament, which they shared with the army.[46]

The above assessments of the Blackshirts during the Second World War appear to be correct as far as they perceive a difference in performance between the first year of the war and the period of 1942–43.

Brian Sullivan's work, titled *The Italian Armed Forces, 1918–40*, can help us to better understand this seesaw trajectory of the Italian units and specifically of the Blackshirts during the Second World War.[47] In his view, the Italian effort during the war can be subdivided into three stages. The first stage between 1940 and 1941 was one where the troops, poorly trained, equipped, and led, performed fairly poorly especially in Greece and in North Africa. In Greece, as discussed previously, the Italian Army as a whole did not succeed principally because of the lack of planning and the timing chosen to initiate the campaign. In addition, the Greek Army proved a capable opponent bent upon defending its land from a foreign opponent. North Africa represented another debacle as the Italian troops were overrun by the fast-paced British armoured counteroffensive. The third year (1942) of the war, however, was the watershed moment for the Italian Army during the war as better-trained troops alongside elite units such as the Folgore and Ariete Divisions fought effectively in North Africa coming close in the summer of 1942 together with General Erwin Rommel's *Panzerarmee*, in dealing a fatal blow to the British 8th Army. In the Soviet Union, 1942 saw the Axis troops conduct a successful offensive in the summer in the Ukraine thus building upon the earlier victories achieved 1941. Here the performance of all troops was much improved thanks to a host of factors. The third phase was one of general collapse in both the defence of the Tunisian bridgehead, during the Red Army assault on the Don River and later during the invasion of Sicily. Despite fighting effectively, especially in Tunisia and in the Soviet Union, the troops were overrun by overwhelming enemy forces. The historical trajectory of the MVSN and the Blackshirt units experienced a similar path to that of the Royal Army. The first units deployed in France, Greece, and North Africa generally did not perform well due primarily to lack of training, the poor weapons at their disposal, and their overall lack of preparedness for war. But most specifically, it was their deployment in static defences that were ill suited for defending against the rapid advance of the British armour units that led to their lacklustre performance in North Africa. In Greece, after the first offensive had been checked by the Greeks, the Italian troops reorganised and fought a mostly defensive battle with the Blackshirts playing a key role in halting the Greek counteroffensive. Then towards the end of the campaign the Blackshirts achieved some success rolling over Greek units during the final advance toward Athens. Similarly, there was a marked difference between the Blackshirts performance during the first offensive in 1940 and the defensive battles fought in 1941.

The Blackshirt units deployed in Russia on the other hand, fought valiantly to the bitter end. Moreover, while most of the ARMIR had melted away during the retreat from the Don River, the troops of the M Battalions along with the *alpini* retained their fighting spirit despite the calamitous collapse.

In his work *Desert Tactics*, the British historian Paddy Griffith has made a similar argument regarding the performance of the Blackshirts in North Africa. 'Their infantry,' argues Griffith referring to Operation Compass, 'and especially their supposedly elite Blackshirt fascist militia, were badly trained and equipped. They could not make anything like the best use of the defensive works provided for them and were easily cut off'.[48]

But almost a year later, during Operation Crusader, a noticeable change had occurred. Again it is well worth quoting Griffith:

> Even Mussolini's political troops were fighting well by this time, as the Giovani Fascisti mechanized reconnaissance group demonstrated on 4 December, again at Bir el Gubi, when it beat off several attacks by the 11th Indian Brigade. The Italians were again in a static defensive role, but on this occasion they did stick to their guns, and achieved effective all-arms co-ordination between infantry field artillery, AT guns and light tanks.[49]

What explains the change in performance with respect to the first year of the war? The first factor is training. In fact, the first units of Blackshirts deployed in 1940 had received almost no training and had most likely just conducted one or two live fire exercises prior to the war. In addition, no combined arms training had been conducted prior to the war to establish greater cooperation between the various arms of the modern battlefield such as the tanks, anti-tank, and artillery units, fighter planes, and bombers with the infantry. The M Battalions of 1941 were not only comprised by experienced soldiers that had already fought in France, Greece, or North Africa, but these same units trained more extensively before being transferred to the Soviet Union. Just to give an example, these troops conducted much more intensive live fire training, and in addition, their units conducted rehearsed drills that simulated typical battlefield conditions. The second factor was the lack of experience of real combat against tanks and heavy guns. In North Africa, for example the troops that fought under Graziani were green including the Blackshirts. As a result, their defensive positions were easily overrun by the speed of the British tanks and armoured vehicles. But by December 1941, the Giovani Fascisti Regiment had already faced several enemy armoured attacks and had also learned simply by observing the more experienced German units in combat. These experiences gave them greater ability in the anti-tank defence, including building deeper anti-tank ditches, locating and camouflaging anti-tank and machine guns in more dynamic defensive positions, and having at their disposal additional anti-tank weapons such as Pazzaglia bombs. Greater experience had also been gained at that point on how to disaggregate the enemy armoured units from their infantry by using machine guns and heavy artillery. The third factor was a greater assimilation of the use of crew served weapons during defensive battles. By then, for example, the Italians in North Africa were using truck mounted Flak 88-mm guns or Italian anti-aircraft guns to repel armoured attacks. These units were not only highly mobile, but packed a much heavier punch than the obsolete guns used at the start of the war. The fourth factor was the constitution of elite units within the Royal Army and the MVSN. With regards to the Blackshirts there was a consolidation of the best legionary units into the M Battalions, which were not only heavier with more extensive services such as reconnaissance, sapper, and flamethrower sections, but also with some improved weapons. Generally, however, the light crew served weapons remained the same as those used at the beginning of the war and the lack of an effective anti-tank gun, for instance, was keenly felt. This continued to be a major weakness of the Blackshirt units and the Italian Army as a whole. Thus, overall, and despite inadequate equipment especially in the crew served segment, a marked increase in effectiveness can be gleaned from an examination of their battlefield performance just prior to and after 1942.

To compare these units with the German Waffen SS or other similar volunteer units is probably unfair since the former had modern weapons such as automatic light guns, tanks, anti-tank guns, and *panzerfaust* that the M Battalions could only dream of. Moreover, it is probably also not completely correct to compare the Blackshirts with similarly situated units such as the Spanish Blue Division since the former did have a similar pool of soldiers (it was a volunteer unit drawn from the Falange militia), but it had been armed and extensively trained by the Germans prior to entering into service near Leningrad. Thus its equipment was much more similar to that of the standard German infantry division and decidedly superior to anything available to the Blackshirts. Each battalion, for instance, of the Blue Division was composed of three companies of infantrymen armed with bolt-action K98 7.92-mm Mauser rifles, which were more effective than the First World War Italian rifles. Moreover, the machine-gun company of the battalions of the Blue Division had six MG34 machine guns and six 81-mm mortars. The standard Blue Division regiment included an anti-tank company with twelve PAK37 37-mm anti-tank guns, a combat engineer battalion, and a company of ski troops. Further artillery and heavy weapons support was provided by Reserve Battalion 250, composed of three companies of infantrymen armed mainly with submachine guns. An anti-tank gun section with three PAK40 75-mm anti-tank guns from the German 2d SS Brigade was also attached to the Blue Division. In addition, the Blue Division had its own artillery gun company comprised with two 75-mm guns, thirty-two 105mm howitzers, and twelve 150mm howitzers. The Tagliamento and other M Battalions in contrast could only field light anti-tank guns, which were comparable to the PAK36 37-mm gun, but had nothing that compared to the PAK40 75-mm or the heavier howitzers and guns.

When looking at the history of the MVSN in comparative perspective to the Falange and other similarly situated organisations, one must not forget the tortured existence of the militia in post-First World War Italy. The MVSN was an organisation that from the onset was characterised by weak institutionalisation. All major political decisions that were taken between 1923 and 1940 were the result of attempts to not purposely weaken the militia, but aimed at making it on one hand dependent on the party for patronage and on other to subordinate it to the Royal Army. Unlike the army, the decisions taken in 1924 stripped the militia of a continuous source of funding. Then political patronage played a part during the 1920s and 1930s in deciding who should hold the leadership positions within the MVSN and the legions. Lastly, the generous and costly, yet non-stellar performance played by the militia during the Spanish Civil War induced the government to halt a further expansion of the legions and their military capabilities. As a result of all these decisions, the militia retained a weak organisational structure to the point that the legions did not have their own training grounds and could only be activated for short periods of time prior to the Second World War. During the war, the leadership of the MVSN under Galbiati began in 1941 to attempt to bridge the gap by placing an increased focus on the training of elite Blackshirt battalions and later the armoured division. But most likely this attempt came too late into the war and only thirty or so battalions could be properly trained by mid-1943. Although the achievement was considerable, it was not nearly enough to close the initial gap and in the greater scheme of Italy's war effort, it was not nearly enough to tip the scale in any way.

History of the Blackshirt Units Deployed in the Eastern Front prior to 1941–42

The 63rd Legion was one of the original Blackshirt Legions constituted in Udine by the MSVN in February 1923. Its first commander, *Console* Luigi Russo, was a decorated war veteran of the First World War. He had originally fought in the Carso as a captain of a *Bersaglieri* unit and in 1917 as the major of one of the first *reparti d'assalto* (assault battalions) of the *arditi*. Many of the original members of LXIII were also war veterans. During the 1930s, the unit was mobilised periodically at least three times a year for two weeks' training sessions at the time. These sessions comprised mainly of sharpshooting and long marches. It was then involved in Africa during the campaign that led to the creation of the empire and then during the Spanish Civil War fighting alongside General Franco and his supporters. When the Second World War broke out, LXIII was mobilised along with LXXIX Battalion based in Reggio Emilia, the 183rd Blackshirt Machine-Gun Company based in Piacenza, and another machine-gun company from the Cuneo area. These four units comprised the core of the Tagliamento Legion. As Battistelli and Crociani assert, the initial basic training was fairly limited due to budget limitations and the absence of true inter-arms collaboration:

> A good deal of the training comprised basic drill and long marches, with few live firing exercises characterized by the limited amount of rounds available (particularly for the automatic weapons). Summer field exercises involving several units would be held, though with little reference to inter-arms and inter-service cooperation.[50]

When the Blackshirt units were mobilised their field exercises were very limited due to scarcity of weapons and ammunition that continued to plague the Italian Army even as the Second World War inched closer. Again, according to Battistelli and Crociani:

> To that end, each Blackshirt could fire up to a maximum of 12 rounds per handgun, 60 rounds for rifles, and 40 rounds for automatic rifles, while 100 rounds were available for machine guns. The rank and file were allowed to throw two hand grenades, and 60 mortar grenades were available for training. The reality was that many Blackshirts were thrust into battle in 1940 in the Western Alps or in Greece without having fired a single shot.[51]

In February 1941, the legion was attached to the Pistoia Infantry Division, which was based in Crotone. At the time, the legion's officers were for the most part ex-armed forces officers typically between the ages of thirty-five to forty-five, while the legion commander was initially an ex-*squadrista* but subsequently a senior army officer assumed command of the unit during the Eastern European campaign. The soldiers were typically volunteers aged between twenty-six and thirty-six, while a small minority was even older being veterans from the First World War. The majority of the soldiers had already seen combat action prior to 1941. As with all the legions and the M Battalions, the elite Blackshirt assault units, the Tagliamento was comprised of assault troops. Accordingly:

> The men were used to hard labour in the rural fields or in manufacturing plants, they were all close to the age of thirty. They were mature soldiers not prone to excessive enthusiasm or to bouts of low morale when things did not go well in the battlefield. The officers belonged to the same towns from where the infantry recruits were selected from. Both knew each other simply because they lived in the same towns or the same regions of Italy (Friuli Venezia Giulia and Emilia Romagna). This commonality facilitated the work of the officers and enabled them to command the troops without the recourse to strict discipline.[52]

Ermacora Zuliani's military career is typical and representative of the officers of the Blackshirts of the Tagliamento or of any other M Battalion unit. Born in 1897, Zuliani joined the Italian Royal Army in 1916 to fight in the First World War against the Austrians. On 15 June 1917, Zuliani fought on Mount San

Gabriele and earned the badge of the *arditi* for his deeds during this major Italian offensive. After the war, Zuliani enrolled in the MVSN. During the Ethiopian War, he was promoted to *centurione*. On his return to Italy, he continued to lead a group of Blackshirts of the Gorizia area, which was responsible for protecting the eastern border.

In 1937, Zuliani volunteered to take part in the Spanish Civil War and fought during the famous Battle of Guadalajara, then saw combat at Gondramendi, Guernica, Bilbao, and Santander. Upon his return to Italy in 1939, Zuliani became the commander of LXIII Assault Battalion based in Udine. In 1940, at the age of forty-three, he volunteered once again and in 1941 led LXIII Battalion of the 63rd Tagliamento Legion during the Russian campaign. He returned to Italy in the spring of 1942 after fighting in the Christmas Battle. In 1943, he assumed command of the 63rd Tagliamento Legion, which was assigned to the M Division.

On the other hand, Roberto Maluberti is representative of the typical MVSN/Blackshirt soldier. He was born in 1912. In 1935, he was enrolled in the Royal Army within the 65th Infantry Regiment. In 1939, Maluberti was recalled to the army within the 90th Infantry Regiment. A few months later, he was dismissed by the Royal Army. In 1940, he volunteered in the MVSN and was enrolled in the V Legion's command platoon. Maluberti then participated to the campaign against Yugoslavia in 1941 and later in the campaign against the Soviet Union in June 1942 as part of the Valle Scrivia M Battalions Group. In 1943, he was dismissed from the Blackshirts due to an injury sustained to his left eye.

The reasons for enlisting in the Blackshirt volunteer units varied. Some were attracted to the strong anti-Communist stance of the M Battalions, while others sought to join to gain access to enhanced social services such as pensions, medical benefits, etc. Others joined because they wanted to climb the ladder of the civil service, while still others entered the M Battalions because they were too old to enlist in the army but desired to fight anyway. The pay rate and the conditions of service were not as good compared to the standard army and therefore a soldier in his prime typically did not volunteer to be a Blackshirt unless he really believed in the cause or saw enlistment as a way to better himself at the war's end.

The unit's commander, General Niccolo' Nicchiarelli, who had already a long and distinguished career in the Italian Army prior to 1941, wrote a report for the head of the MSVN in November 1941 in which he detailed the morale status of his troops.[53] By then, the initial enthusiasm of his troops for the war had already been tempered by the extremely tough conditions found on the Eastern Front. Moreover, the type of deployment of the Blackshirts, which entailed always plugging holes in the defensive line, counterattacks, and raids, also weighed heavily on the morale of the men. General Nicchiarelli wrote that his troops were doing well physically, although they were waiting with great anticipation for their winter clothing. As far as their morale, Nicchiarelli wrote 'that it was still high', even though several men were depressed by the negative conditions of service in the Eastern Front.[54]

He argued that his *legionaries* could be subdivided into two broad groups. On the one hand, there were those who were fighting the war without great enthusiasm and mainly had volunteered to get ahead within the party hierarchy and clime the economic ladder once the war was over. On the other hand, there were those that believed in the motivations behind Italy's entry into the war and some of them had even set the example for the unit has a whole by fighting with great vigour and tenacity. But even the morale of this group was not has high as when the campaign had begun since many of these soldiers felt that the Tagliamento was not being deployed properly by the CSIR. Some felt that the standard army infantry divisions received better treatment and services while on the frontline. Others felt that the unit was deployed by the CSIR in the most dangerous stop gap assignments that required strenuous tasks such as attacking enemy positions or defending under siege positions often at night and/or in deplorable weather conditions. While others argued that contrary to the initial expectations, the campaign would be long and strenuous. Overall, however, the morale of the *legionaries* was always higher than of those soldiers deployed in the standard infantry units. Indeed, it can be argued that it remained always high even though the *legionaries* frequently bore the brunt of major enemy attacks and infrequently broke under the strain of combat even when attacked by much larger forces or by tanks.

According to historian Maria Teresa Giusti, the soldiers of the CSIR could be classified in terms of their ideological motivation into three ideal types. First, a majority of soldiers that was not ideological but carried out their duties by fighting with determination even though they ultimately longed to return home. Another group of soldiers mainly from the Blackshirts units and from the officers corps that was vehemently anti-communist, Catholic, and right-wing traditional, while another group was comprised primarily of careerist who served because they ultimately aspired to climb the economic ladder after the war.[55] Her research correlates nicely to General Nicchiarelli's observations regarding the three sets of soldiers that fought for the Tagliamento and demonstrates that between the two polar opposites, there was a large chunk of the armed forces that were not particularly ideological but nonetheless carried out their duties.

During several months of 1941, the Tagliamento was stationed at Crotone were trained extensively. The training program at the barracks followed a set of established procedures and was conducted by ex-army officers. First, individual training was emphasised, such as sharpshooting, handling of individual and crew served weapons, and physical exercises. The second part of the training focused upon group drills, training by single patrols, and crew served weapons training, while special officers' teams conducted very specialised training, such as field reconnaissance, intelligence gathering, and setting up proper defensive positions. Third, large-scale exercises and manoeuvres were conducted at the company or battalion level with live fire practice and with the use of other weapons, such as hand grenades and machine guns. The training was not too different from what was administered to the standard infantry since resources were scarce and few provisions were made for large-scale combined-arms drills. However, what distinguished the Blackshirts of the Tagliamento from other standard units was the fact that the majority of the former had already fought in combat and were therefore generally more experienced than the standard soldier.

In March, the unit began to train more intensively in the barracks where the soldiers continued to perfect their shooting skills at the range and rehearsed how to attack enemy positions with hand grenades. Outside of the barracks, the soldiers completed long marches with full pack and weapons as well as special drills such as attacking an uphill position. The soldiers were particularly put off by the marching assignments with full pack, but these drills would ultimately turn out to be beneficial since they reflected the prevailing fighting conditions on the Eastern Front.

On 10 March, each battalion was required to constitute and train a special unit dedicated to patrols aimed at finding and destroying units of enemy paratroopers. It is likely that the intent was to develop tactics to fight off the Russian Commando tactics that were so prevalent during the First World War and were especially deployed against the Austro-Hungarians. Each team was also administered drills to fight off potential enemy British commando landings by learning special intelligence and patrol skills.

By April 1941, the Tagliamento could count upon a force of fifty-two officers, seventy-six NCOs, 1,230 soldiers, 284 artillery soldiers, 133 drivers and support services, and five Carabinieri.

Sometime in July 1941, the Tagliamento was transferred to military barracks in Mantova where it made last minute preparations before being dispatched to Russia.

Although the Tagliamento had trained fairly well during its extended stay in Crotone and the temporary stay in Mantova, its preparations had been limited due primarily to the scarcity of resources that hampered the Italian Army in general.

The M Battalions, which were constituted later in 1941, would receive more extensive training, mainly because they had greater amounts of ammunition, had their own training bases, and more time to prepare for combat operations. At the time, certain Blackshirt officer groups, such as the special reconnaissance patrol or headquarter staff intelligence officers, underwent much more rigorous preparation. Although this training was only reserved for junior officers and NCOs, it nonetheless allowed for the formation of special units that could deploy specially trained sharpshooters as well as fast moving motorised intelligence teams to ambush or simply to collect intelligence on the enemy.

Experience by the standard soldier was thus gained primarily during combat. For example, Italy was one of the few countries almost continually at war during the decade that preceded the Second World War. Since the Blackshirt units were comprised primarily by older soldiers, this meant that many had already gained viable combat experience prior to the outbreak of the war. What they did not receive, however, was either training or combat experience fighting alongside armoured vehicles and this remained a major limitation that was clearly evidenced during the Eastern European campaign. The lack of motorised units also undermined the tactics of the assault battalions in two ways. During offensive operations, the lower ratio of motorisation to men undermined the units' mobility and ability to maintain the pace of its major ally. It also undermined their ability to breakthrough particularly strong enemy defences. During defensive operations the M Battalions were often used to prop up weak positions or to counterattack. If only the units had more vehicles at their disposal, they could have conducted both tasks at a much quicker and strategically important pace.

The training received by the M Battalions, however, represented a vast improvement *versus* the scant training administered toward the legions in 1940. But the major leap forward in the training of the M Battalions was only achieved in 1943 when the units were consolidated into the M Division, which not only received advanced training with modern German tanks and self-propelled guns, but also trained alongside experienced German units that shared their know how. Unfortunately, this development came too little too late to have a meaningful impact upon the course of the war.

Raggruppamento CC NN M 3 Gennaio

In mid-1942, the Tagliamento was merged into the *Raggruppamento* CCNN M 3 Gennaio M Battalions Group along with the Montebello. The latter was constituted by the two assault battalions: VI Vigevano and the XXX Novara Assault Battalions, which initially fought in Greece/Albania in support of the Sforzesca Division as the 30th Legion, and by XII Aosta Artillery Battalion. The Sforzesca and the 30th Legion were originally headquartered in Novara and Vigevano, respectively, where they conducted a few pre-war field exercises. Both were deployed for the attack against Greece and began their approach to the front by parading in the streets of Novara. The parade, which involved the troops marching from the barracks to the train station, was cheered by a massive civilian crowd. In Greece, both units fought primarily in a defensive capacity to halt the Greek counterattack in early 1941 and were often engaged in hand-to-hand combat in defence of the main thoroughfare that led to Valona. In January 1941, they arrived on the frontlines and were deployed on the hills between Maritzait and Scindeli and for the entire month of February fought against the Greek Army mainly with rifles, machine guns, and mortars. The Greeks continually attacked the Italian lines, while the latter dug in their lines and utilised the crew served weapons and the rifles to break up enemy attacks. On certain days, the Italians were also required to counterattack and retake possession of positions that had been lost to the Greeks during the first few days of the counteroffensive. On 28 February, the 30th Legion was barricaded on Scindeli, when the offensive impetus of the Greek Army was finally halted after countless casualties were sustained on both sides. On 9 March 1941, the Sforzesca and the Legion attacked the Greek lines and captured the frontline positions of Chiaf and Merzgoranit. On 15 April 1941, the Sforzesca and the Blackshirts again advanced through Greece by taking Kilsura, a key thoroughfare. In contrast, XII Battalion initially fought in the Western Alps in support of the Monte Bianco Legion. It subsequently fought with the *Raggrupamento* Galbiati in Greece/Albania by providing key artillery support mainly to break Greek counterattacks. All three units were designated as M Battalions following the end of the Greek campaign in the fall of 1941. In the early spring of 1942, the unit was transferred to the MVSN training ground of Trastevere in the heart of Rome, where it began to train intensively. In the summer of 1942, they were transferred to the 3 Gennaio Group.

Raggruppamento CCNN M 23 Marzo

The *Raggruppamento* CCNN M 23 Marzo was comprised of two main M Battalions units: the *Gruppo Battaglioni* CCNN M Valle Scrivia and the *Gruppo Battaglioni* CCNN M Leonessa. Each unit also (like the 3 Gennaio) consisted of two assault battalions and one of the heavy weapons. Each assault/infantry battalion had a command platoon, a reconnaissance platoon, three infantry assault companies, and a machine-gun company. The heavy weapons battalion also had a command platoon, a mortar company, and anti-tank gun company. The *Gruppo Battaglioni* Valle Scrivia was formed on 11 February 1942 in Ovada (near Alessandria) with soldiers from the V Assault Legion Valle Scrivia. It was constituted by V and XXXIV Assault Battalions and XLI Heavy Weapons Battalion, which came from XXXXI Cesare Battisti Legion based in Trento. The Valle Scrivia was comprised primarily by mountain troops that had fought during the Western Alps campaign against France. XXXIV Assault Battalion was deployed together with other Blackshirt units (including XXXXI) and attached to the Modena Infantry Division. At 10 a.m. on 22 June 1940, the division began to attack the French troops located on Mount Meras, where it was fiercely opposed by intensive machine-gun fire. Despite the blocking fire, XXXIV managed to conquer the important position of Colle Raget and subsequently hold it despite numerous enemy attempts to counterattack and retake the mountaintop.

At the conclusion of the campaign against France, the two battalions were deployed for the attack against Yugoslavia. In 1941, XXXIV Assault Battalion, led by *Seniore* Antonio Monticelli, was attached to the 5th Legion based in Piedmont.

At the beginning of April, the legion (constituted by XXXIV Assault Battalion, V Assault Battalion, and the 10th Machine-Gun Company) was dispatched by rail to the Tolmino mountain pass on the border with Yugoslavia.

On 6 April, when the hostilities against Yugoslavia began, the legion was deployed and its objective was to guard the pass to prevent potential enemy infiltrations. On 15 April, the *legionaries* of the 5th Legion then crossed the border and were stationed at Kasalice until the beginning of May.

Similarly, XLI Trento Artillery Battalion came originally from the Cesare Battisti Legion which was founded in 1923. The legion would then participate to the campaign against Ethiopia and then to the Spanish Civil War. During 1940, it saw service with the Pistoia Division carrying out patrol, sentry, and coastal defence duty in Italy.

During the first week of May 1942, the Valle Scrivia M Battalions Group was moved to Racconigi, where it was joined by the two machine-gun companies: 359th and 234th. In this location, it began the training, which lasted until mid-June. On 20 June, the unit left Cuneo's train station destined for the Eastern Front. On 1 July, it arrived at Merefa, near Charkow (Ukraine), from where it began a long march to reach the frontline on the Don River.

The Leonessa Legion and later the M Battalions Group rose from the ashes of the 114th CCNN Legion Garibaldina, which was originally constituted in 1935 to take part in the Ethiopian War. The unit, under the command of *Seniore* Giovanni Ricciotti, was comprised of XIV Battalion based in Bergamo and XV Battalion garrisoned in Brescia. The majority of the ranks were ex-*alpini* troops.

Prior to the start of the war, the unit trained near Formia where together with two other legions it formed the 2nd Division CCNN 28 Ottobre. It then took part to the war in East Africa by participating to all of the most relevant battle engagements.

When Italy entered the Second World War by launching an attack across the Alps against France, only XV Battalion was mobilised and it saw action during the campaign against the French Chasseurs Alpins. When Italy initiated the campaign against Greece, both battalions were mobilised, forming the 15th Legion CCNN M *d'Assalto* Leonessa.

The role of the Leonessa during the Greek campaign was to be deployed in a stopgap fashion to prop the standard infantry. The unit received several recognitions for its worth and key contribution to the campaign. One of the most important awards was given to *Legionnaire* Giuseppe Pesenti Gritti, which merited a gold medal for military valour for his efforts to lead the Blackshirts after all the officers had fallen during the February battles against the Greek Crete Division. During February 1941, every Greek attack was thwarted with heavy losses and with key contributions from both the Leonessa and the *Raggruppamento* Galbiati. Subsequently, in April 1941, the Leonessa participated to the final offensive against Greece.

Later on, two units of the Leonessa, XV and XXXVIII Brescia and Asti Battalions, performed garrison duty in Ljubljana.

The *Gruppo di Battaglioni* CCNN M Leonessa was constituted on 1 April 1942 in Rome from the ashes of the 15th Leonessa Assault Legion. It was constituted initially by XIV Battalion and XV Battalion and inherited the name of the units that had fought valiantly during the Greek campaign.

After their repatriation from Albania, the battalions had spent a few months at their respective mobilisation centres and were then transferred to Rome where they began proper training in March 1942. At that time, they were joined by the 138th Machine-Gun Company, which was attached to XIV Battalion and the 15th Machine-Gun Company that was attached to XV Battalion. On 22 April, XXXVIII Heavy Weapons Battalion (originally from the 38th Alfieri Legion based in Asti) was also attached to the Leonessa. The unit spent forty days in Rome where it trained in preparation for the Eastern Front. On 5 June, it reached Saluzzo where it joined other Italian units destined for the Eastern Front. The *Raggruppamento* CCNN M. 23 Marzo was to be assigned to the Italian II Army Corps as its tactical reserve, while the *Raggruppamento* CCNN M CC.NN. 3 Gennaio was assigned to XXXV Army Corps.

The MVSN and the Italian Royal Army

The MVSN was an anomaly in the history of modern Italy since the organisation did not belong to the state but to the party militia. The MVSN therefore had a difficult and sometimes adversarial relationship with the organs of the state such as the Royal Italian Army. Just to give an example one of its first roles in the 1920s, the MVSN was to provide public security, which rivalled the traditional official role given to the national police and the Carabinieri. First, the MVSN had its own infantry battalions via the Blackshirt legions and later the M Battalions and these units competed for scarce resources against the standard army. Second, both organisations had contrasting loyalties with the army being loyal first and foremost to the king and the house of Savoy, while the latter was loyal to fascism. These differences manifested themselves at particularly difficult times and during major crisis. For example, in the summer of 1943, when the monarchy and the high command of the army were preparing to shift sides and sign a treaty with the Allies, the Blackshirts M Battalions accused the standard infantry of cowardice for not putting their all in the war effort and especially at a time when the Allies had landed in Sicily. The Blackshirts were not above criticism, however. In North Africa in 1940–41, for example, many Blackshirt units came under strong criticism from the army for their lack of professionalism and for their poor showing at Bardia. The army observers noted how badly trained the units that comprised the Blackshirt battalions were and how their overall lack of preparedness had been one of the reasons that Bardia fell to the British.

Third, like in Nazi Germany many in the Italian Army had little sympathy for the extremist views of some of the Blackshirts and they did not share their enthusiasm for the war. Some Blackshirts were thus more politicised than the army espousing a fervent anti-Communism.

Fourth, as will be seen in the chapters dedicated to the campaign in the Eastern Front, the frontline generals of the army often deployed the Blackshirts in the most difficult tasks in some cases in order to preserve the royal armed forces. Therefore, the Blackshirts were deployed to plug holes in the defensive line, to counterattack at the head of all Italian troops, or to carry dangerous reconnaissance operations or raids where high casualties were expected. In other cases, they were misused by the frontline generals who placed them in the line to fight with the standard infantry even though the M Battalions were fairly lightly armed and were meant to be used in offensive operations. The Blackshirts were under the command of the Royal Army, but the latter did its outmost to preserve the integrity of the armed forces sometimes at the expense of the Blackshirt units.

The differences between the two entities would clearly re-emerge and intensify with great force in the summer and fall of 1943 when the army, or large sections of it, sided with the Allies while the Blackshirts opted to continue fighting with the Germans.

Blackshirt Uniform and Weapons

The standard Blackshirt soldier wore a dark grey helmet (model M 1933) with a black stencilled militia badge. A grey coat with white fasces on a standard black collar badge. A black shirt, black sweater, green/grey mountain troop like pants, and white socks with ankle high black mountain boots. The boots were designed for rock climbing but had little padding to protect from the cold weather of the Russian winter. As one Bersagliere soldier Bruno Doni commenting on the Italian Army asserted:

> I want to let you know how soldiers died. It appears to be banal but the principal cause was frostbite to the feet. After a day or two of marching in those cold temperatures, with our shoes, which were not suitable for such extreme weather, our feet would freeze and we were no longer able to walk. We remained therefore blocked on the road and many of us would die after ten minutes in the open by freezing to death.[56]

Armaments were generally light considering the fact that these units were to be deployed primarily in raids and assaults rather than in defensive tasks. The main weapons included a dagger, rifle, and hand grenades. Initially, no provisions were made to furnish the troops with winter camouflage equipment such as white overcoats or helmet covers or special items to brave the Russian winter.

The Tagliamento—and basically all Italian troops in Second World War—lacked an effective anti-tank gun, and this handicap had to do with the pre-war dispositions of the Italian High Command. At the time, the Italian general staff was convinced that Italy would end up fighting a war in the Alps against France or Yugoslavia, where it was envisioned that infantry was unlikely to encounter heavy tanks. For this reason, it was believed that the Breda model 35 47/32-mm gun, which functioned much like a small mountain cannon, was a viable weapon to fight the type of war envisioned.

In addition, once the Second World War began, High Command showed a high degree of inertia—ignoring the great relevance of armoured tank units in Germany's successful campaign against France in 1940.

The 47/32-mm anti-tank gun had originally been developed for the type of mountain warfare that Italy experienced in 1915–18. It could be broken down in different components for mule or light vehicle transport, but it could not be towed. In the Russian steppe, the Italian Army lacked transports and, in most cases, the gun had to be towed by hand. The gun performed satisfactorily during the first year of the war against light armoured vehicles. As the enemy introduced bigger and more powerful tanks, the 47/32-mm gun became obsolete because it could not penetrate heavy armour. The lack of firepower of the anti-tank guns would force the 47/32-mm artillery platoons to deploy the weapon within a quarter-mile range of enemy armour, or else it had little or no effect upon it. At a distance of three-quarters of a mile, its grenade could pierce light tanks or light and medium scout and reconnaissance vehicles. The gun was not effective against heavier tanks, especially against the Soviet T-34 tanks, and its only chance of success against these larger units was by aiming at the tracks, the turret, or the back of the tank. As a result of this type of close-combat deployment, many anti-tanks units were captured or destroyed during the campaign primarily for being positioned too close to the enemy's line.

The lack of firepower was determined by its inability to damage the more robust enemy tanks that were introduced in late 1941 and 1942. After 1941, there were only two somewhat productive ways to use the gun:

1. It was effective if the servers aimed at the tracks to immobilise the tanks
2. It was deployed in well-fortified defensive sectors—allowing the servers to aim for the more vulnerable sections of the tank, while the latter manoeuvred to negotiate an obstacle (typically a trench or a ditch).

Overall, it was a poor weapon, but even in 1943, when it had become virtually obsolete, it was the only anti-tank gun supplied to Italian infantry units. Lack of technological innovation and a small manufacturing base did not allow for the design and the mass manufacture of a more powerful anti-tank gun unit. This presented a unique conundrum for the Italian infantry. As Rottman asserts: 'By the end of 1940 the tank had undeniably proved to be a dominant weapon on European and North African battlefields. Most of the period's anti-tank weapons were woefully inadequate, and by 1942, mostly obsolete'.[57]

Rottman goes on to argue how the German Army began to develop effective anti-tank weapons to deal with the growing threat of enemy tank attacks against static infantry defences. The Italians on the other hand, even in 1943, failed to develop an effective anti-tank weapon and their infantry would continue to experience enormous difficulties when faced by massive enemy armoured attacks. The Tagliamento units were no different to the standard infantry when it came to the anti-tank defence since they had the same weapons.

The rifle used by the Blackshirt legion soldiers was the standard 6.5-mm Carcano model 1891, which was also used by standard infantry units. The rifle came with a foldable bayonet and it could fire eight bullets per minute. Although a reliable weapon, it was no match for the automatic guns used by the Soviets, which fired up to 100 bullets per minute.[58] Hand grenades included the Breda M35, OTO 35, and the SRCM 35, which were less powerful than Allied or German grenades and were generally very light. Italian grenades typically produced plenty of smoke, but had a low explosive charge. In the harsh temperatures of the Russian winter, the Italian hand grenades would lose much of their effectiveness since the fuse frequently jammed when snow and ice prevailed.[59]

The automatic rifle was the Breda Model 30 6.5-mm. It worked through a fixed cartridge clip of twenty rounds and a rate of fire of 400 rounds per minute. This weapon also did not fare well during the Russian winter and many units were abandoned voluntarily by the soldiers as a result of their ineffectiveness.[60] The Breda Model 37 machine gun was the standard automatic of the Tagliamento. It was operated typically by a three-man unit. One soldier would fire the gun, the second soldier would be responsible for inserting the ammunition clips (twenty-eight rounds per clip), while the third soldier—armed with a rifle—would act as a sentry and cover both flanks of the firing point.

The Swiss-made Solothurn 20-mm anti-tank rifle was also used by the Italian soldiers as an anti-tank weapon during the Second World War. It was called *Fucile Anticarro* S and it was employed either as a standalone infantry weapon, or mounted on vehicles. Each clip had ten rounds and they were used primarily against light vehicles and tanks. It was effective at a range of 400 feet or less—and especially if positioned upon the flank of an enemy tank.

The 45-mm Breda mortar was a much more effective weapon. It was capable of firing both a 3.4- and a 6.8-kg high-explosive grenade, with a firing range of three-quarters of a mile. The fragmentation of both types of grenades was effective particularly against assaulting enemy infantry units, but also, in a more limited extent, against armoured vehicles. This mortar proved to be very effective during the eastern campaign, when it was used to repulse both infantry and armoured units at a relatively close combat range.

Perhaps the most effective weapon of the Tagliamento was the Beretta Model 38 MP 9-mm submachine gun, which represented a vast improvement over the gun used by the infantry, the 6.5-mm Breda Model 30. While the former was relatively light (it weighed half as much as the American Thompson gun, which was used by both the British and the Americans), it was only carried by few officers. This 9-mm weapon fired ammunition at a rate of 600 rounds per minute—typically using thirty- or forty-round magazines—and could reach a distance of 230 feet.

The flamethrower used was the Model 35, capable of throwing a flame 22 yards and making untenable a zone 39 yards long by 17 yards wide. It could produce ten intermittent jets of flame, representing twenty seconds of continuous fire.

Blackshirts had no tanks and had only approximately 150 trucks, which were used primarily to transport food provisions and heavy weapons. For a unit that was considered an assault division, its low ratio of motorisation was particularly harmful since the infantry battalions had to travel on foot. In many cases during the Eastern European campaign, the anti-tank guns and the mortars had to be hand towed through the Ukrainian plains, which in the winter were completely covered in snow and ice and in the fall and spring were muddy and wet. The troops were not able to function effectively in the muddy conditions of the Russian steppe and generally functioned at a slower pace than the Germans.

In conclusion, the basic issue was that the Blackshirt Division like other Italian infantry divisions deployed in Russia/Ukraine was only motorised in part and generally there were not enough trucks to transport the troops who as a result were forced to move on foot. This caused severe problems both during offensive and defensive operations as the lack of transportation slowed down the Italian troops which in most cases could not keep pace with the more mobile German troops. Another major issue was that most weapons did not perform well during the Russian winter. In some cases, the weapons, including the anti-tank artillery, froze and could only be operated after oil lubrication or by storing it overnight near a fireplace.

As far as the weapons were concerned, there were two other specific problems. Italian rifles were no match for the Soviet automatic guns and their anti-tank guns could not damage a T-34 tank. Both weaknesses presented unique problems. On one hand, the Italian troop's rate of fire was comparatively low. Secondly, lacking heavy weapons, they would have a hard time repulsing enemy attacks every time the Soviet Army attacked with large masses of tanks in conjunction with the infantry. The T34/76 model Soviet tank was armed with a 76.2-mm anti-tank gun and a 45-mm frontal armour that could not be penetrated by anything the Italian infantry could deploy against. Both the crews of the anti-tank guns and the Solothurn rifles must have felt a sense of dread every time they faced large numbers of T34 units. The only way that such large tank formations could be immobilised or damaged was by deploying the divisional artillery with its larger field guns.

Given their ill-suited weapons, the Tagliamento and the *alpini* units deployed in Russia found themselves in the same predicament. In the words of a commander of the *alpini*, the war in the Caucasus plains was different than waging war in the mountains. Moreover, the weapons available such as the small mountain cannons, anti-tank weapons, and small mortars 'could not effectively match against the enemy's much larger field guns'. During the defensive stage of the battle, these weapons 'would have forced the *alpini* to fight in very adverse conditions due to the lack of armoured units and anti-tank guns'.[61]

The only troops of the Italian contingent that were on par in terms of weapons and equipment *versus* the German or Russian special forces were the *alpini* of the Monte Cervino Battalion, a highly trained and well-armed unit that had been trained to execute raids against enemy raiding parties. The soldiers had 'a white camouflage windbreaker with a leather lining, mountain hat, gloves, thick white socks, mountain pants, snowshoes, and a Beretta automatic gun which was distributed to officers and NCOs while binoculars were only given to proven military leaders'.[62]

But this unit was an exception within the *alpini* and the Italian infantry being an elite battalion. It was dispatched to Russia only in mid-1942 and it was fairly small, being comprised by less than 1,000 soldiers. All other units deployed by the Italian Army did not even come close to the level of training, the equipment and weapons made available to a unit such as the Monte Cervino.

Blackshirts Tactics

Since the M Battalions were not as heavily equipped as their Russian shock troop counterparts or the German storm battalions and seldom attacked with tanks, they were therefore assigned more specific and limited tasks. As Battistelli and Crociani assert: '... they could only be used in fast, opportune raids before a main attack and, following a breakthrough, in widening any breaches made in the enemy defences. In defence, they could only be used in counterattacks against targets of opportunity, and for manning the line'.[63]

The assault tactics of the M Battalions were similar to those of other infantry units of the Italian Army and relied heavily upon the weapons and training of the *arditi* of the First World War. Their offensive actions, whether small-scale raids, counterattacks, or large attacks, were typically preceded by a period of intelligence gathering on the enemy defences. The information collected through aerial photographs, patrols into no man's land, and the careful observation of enemy movements and positions, was used to fully plan out the attacks. The attacks typically did not rely on brute force alone or on mass waves of infantry attacks, but on careful preparation and on leveraging the element of surprise. They were then based on a preliminary barrage that would primarily aim to wear down the enemy's defences. In the interest of secrecy, there should be just a short artillery barrage before the M Battalions attacked. The artillery would intervene with no prior registration in order to achieve complete surprise as the crews of each gun should be certain of their targets based on prior knowledge of the enemy positions, and ready to factor in the meteorological conditions.

The infantry attack had to be coordinated with the artillery preparation in the sense that it needed to be timed in conjunction with the different phases of the barrage. The troops were to surge forward on the heels of the barrage, which was meant to take the enemy by surprise and immobilise him in the trenches. The artillery would then switch to a rolling barrage moving the fire forward toward the rear defences as the infantry advanced. Finally, the air force would also be expected to support the attack by targeting from above the enemy's defences with both machine guns and bombs.

The infantry would then run toward the enemy's positions in small, scattered groups and under the cover of the Breda 37 machine guns and mortars, which were used to pin down the enemy and impede his reaction. The former were considered the most effective weapons of the assault infantry, which were to be brought forward as far as possible. Heavier machine guns were also utilised during the attack to support the advancing waves of assault troops as well as to fend off enemy counterattacks. To facilitate the infantry's advance special light artillery groups armed with mortars and light artillery carried by sleds would also follow in the wake of the assault troops. Their role was to knockout particularly stubborn pockets of enemy resistance or to fend off tanks. In the final phase of the attack, the assailers would start to throw hand grenades into the enemy trenches followed by hand-to-hand combat. During the assault phase, in some cases, large numbers of flamethrowers, ten or more, were also deployed. The Italians on the Russian front in fact made extensive use of flamethrowers as supporting weapons for infantry action and also to mop-up enemy defences. It was an imperative that the infantry forces should move in as quickly as possible thus not giving the enemy time to recover from the effects of the barrage or from hand grenades flying into its positions.

These assault tactics resembled those adopted by the *arditi* and the onus was placed upon unleashing maximum force against the enemy with a combined arms approach. What was lacking for the Italians, however, was the use of tanks during the assault. Throughout the Eastern European campaign, the use of tanks in Italian offensive operations was much more limited than, for example, in North Africa. This had to do with the fact that the lightweight Italian tanks were no match for the Russian T-34 but also because the CSIR had a negligible number of tanks.

Tanks were in short supply because of specific reasons that had characterised the course of Italian tactical thinking between the wars. 'The need to overcome the stalemate situation characteristic of the First World War battlefields was acknowledged in the early 1930s by General Francesco Saverio Grazioli, who had emphasized the need to use machines on the battlefield while demanding quality before quantity'.[64]

But the experiences of the Spanish Civil War, where several tanks were lost to enemy forces induced many generals to think that armour was not critical for winning future wars. General Emilio Canevari drew from the Spanish Civil War the following conclusions:

> Tanks could not spearhead an assault, given their need to be constantly protected by the infantry. Once again small arms firepower was regarded as critical; tanks were regarded as better suited as a weapon support for the infantry, more of a self-propelled gun than a real tank, while the need for a massive artillery fire support was once more emphasized.[65]

Many military planners also realised the limited viability of Italy's light tanks during the Spanish campaign and they argued the need for more durable, larger, medium, or heavy tanks. Approximately eighty medium tanks were delivered to the army in 1939, but that number was not nearly enough to sustain a major campaign in 1940

The supreme commander of the army, Pietro Badoglio, shared some of the negative views on tanks given his experience in Africa, and as a result, Italy had few tanks compared to the greater powers at the start of the war and little had been done to train the infantry to fight alongside armour. Moreover, even the German victories of 1940 in France, in which the armoured units had played a central role, failed to spur a debate within the Italian High Command, which continued to maintain a conservative tactical outlook.

First, the Italian Army at the outbreak of the war had only one large armoured division that was deployed in Italy's main theatre of operations (North Africa) while two armoured divisions in training were held back in the mainland to be deployed as a tactical reserve. Therefore, there were only few light weight tank units that were readily available for the Eastern Front, a force that was obsolete even before the start of the campaign. The Italian military interest in tanks deepend in 1938–39 where a shift to mechanised warfare occurred.

Second, tactically there were few provisions for Italian infantry and armoured vehicles collaborations to begin with. As John Sweet asserts:

> The 1938 manoeuvres and the operational plans show both the development of armoured warfare and the weaknesses. On both the European and the colonial fronts, the army planned the use of tanks and armoured units as a main feature of operations. In Italy the armoured corps formed the spearheaded of the attack.

> In Libya the infantry would have close tank support. One the other hand most units had not trained with tanks.[66]

In contrast, tanks and specialised infantry capable of fighting alongside the armour were critical to both German and Soviet tactics. Both deployed specially trained shock troops as they were considered essential to achieve a breakthrough in battle. But in both armies, the shock troops fought alongside armoured units. Tanks carried or hauled the heavily armed storm detachments and engineers to deal with the anti-tank defence and to probe the weakest points of the enemy's defence. Large tank formations were central to the attack plans of both the Soviet and the German Army, and by 1943, the decisive battles between the two antagonists (such as Kursk) were fought with massive deployments of armour. Despite their relevance and centrality throughout the campaign, the Italian assault units such as the M Battalions were forced to fight without their aid placing them at a severe disadvantage. By 1942, for example, the Soviet Army had adopted most of the successful tank tactics developed in 1940–41 by the Germans. Accordingly, as Fugate asserts, the Soviet Army had made major strides and its infantry was accustomed to fighting alongside the tanks.

> NPP tanks were to carry out their operations never allowing gaps of more than two hundred to four hundred meters to develop between them and the following infantry. Instead of allowing NPP tanks to be flung into battle without proper support, where they had in practice incurred heavy losses, the directives required that artillery be used to counter German tanks. Tank to tank battles were to be avoided unless the terrain conditions and number of relationships were highly favourable. The role of the infantry was to scout for, mark, and if possible, destroy enemy antitank mines and obstacles. After the initial phase of an assault, the infantry would then carry out the crucial mop up operations that had often been neglected.... Artillery and support aviation were to coordinate their operations with the armour and infantry as closely as possible.[67]

The Italian troops such as the Tagliamento could only aspire of carrying out such far reaching, deep penetrations through combined arms operations.

The M Battalions defensive tactics were hampered by the lack of effective anti-tank weapons as the troops had to rely upon equipment that for the most part could not match on par the large Soviet T-34 tanks. As a result of this deficiency, their training placed a great emphasis on the use of incendiary devices, bundles of grenades, or Molotov cocktails to disable enemy tanks. Despite the training, these weapons could only do so much against the large Soviet units and their utilisation caused high casualties, and as a result, they were used sporadically and mostly in desperate circumstances. The standard tactics relied upon building two parallel defensive lines in a zigzag fashion. The line itself was interspersed by anti-tank and machine-gun units, which were typically camouflaged and the weapons were positioned in gun pits. When faced by a large-scale enemy attack involving large numbers of tanks, the soldiers would typically lay low and let the tanks overstep their positions to be dealt by the artillery screen while they would come out of their positions when facing enemy infantry. The latter was repelled with the use of mortars, machine guns, and flamethrowers. Despite their inferior equipment, the M Battalions often demonstrated a greater capacity of resistance to enemy attacks given the fact that their ranks were comprised by more experienced soldiers. Although comprised of more mature soldiers, the Tagliamento would still experience numerous difficulties while fighting against the T-34 Soviet tanks and the heavily armed shock troops that usually accompanied them in battle. In numerous instances, its defences were overrun by powerful enemy combined arms attacks where the tanks played a lead role in smashing through the fortified strongpoints.

The defensive tactical procedure adopted by the Tagliamento can be summarised by a directive issued by the Italian High Command. The document, which was meant to provide guidelines for anti-tank defence to standard infantry units, stated:

> The infantry battalion's defences shall be deployed upon three strongholds, two at the front, one at the rear of the main position.
>
> Each stronghold shall be surrounded by a number of small dugouts. These positions should be deep enough to protect small groups of soldiers from an enemy aerial attack or from machine gun fire. In addition, if these dugouts are well concealed, the enemy tank crew while advancing will not be able to spot its in-occupants. During an enemy attack it is imperative to separate the tanks from the mass of the infantry units. The defenders shall allow the tanks to proceed past their position, while the machine guns and the anti-tank guns, situated in the main strongholds, shall focus their fixed line of fire upon the infantry. Once the tanks have passed over the advanced firing points, the infantry shall leap out of their dugouts and concentrate fire against enemy infantry units that are advancing behind the tanks. The enemy armour shall then be dealt with by the artillery units situated to the rear of the main stronghold.[68]

In general, the defensive tactics were successful during the early stages of the campaign but once the Soviet Army became more adept at making wide-sweeping attacks put forth by large numbers of tank battalions accompanied by specially trained shock troops, even the well-trained soldiers of the Tagliamento were unable to stop them. Like the standard Italian infantry, the Blackshirts were unable to stop the tanks, even with the aid of the divisional artillery. Once the tanks had made the initial breakthrough, its soldiers were forced to retreat and to abandon or destroy their heavier weapons.

Above: A *legionnaire en route* to the train station to reach the frontline being cheered on by the crowds. (*Archivio Centrale dello stato*)

Left: Blackshirts of the Tagliamento during one of the training sessions before the war. (*Legione Tagliamento*)

Above: General Messe reviews the Tagliamento Blackshirt Legion. (*Archivio Centrale dello stato*)

Right: Soldiers of the Tagliamento during a pre-war training session. (*Legione Tagliamento*)

Tagliamento Legion being reviewed by a senior MVSN officer in Mantova prior to the unit's departure for the Eastern Front. (*Legione Tagliamento*)

The officers of the Tagliamento Legion with the unit's chaplain monsignor Guglielmo Biasutti. The latter participated to the Eastern Front campaign. He celebrated Christmas Eve mass of 1941, a day before the start of the so-called Christmas Battle. (*Legione Tagliamento*)

Soldiers of the Tagliamento Legion training with full pack in southern Italy in the summer of 1941. (*Legione Tagliamento*)

Mussolini reviews a Blackshirt battalion, who are saluting with raised daggers. (*Archivio Centrale dello stato*)

Blackshirts returning home after the conclusion of the campaign against France in the western Alps. (*Archivio Centrale dello stato*)

Blackshirt unit advancing towards the front under rain along the Albania–Greece border. The poor weather conditions limited the Blackshirts combat effectiveness. (*Archivio Centrale dello stato*)

Blackshirts in the Balkans manning a roadblock in Montenegro. Several Blackshirt units carried out garrison and anti-partisan duties at the conclusion of the Balkan campaign. (*Archivio Centrale dello stato*)

The Tagliamento Legion *en route* toward Ukraine in the summer of 1941. (*Archivio Centrale dello stato*)

An example of typical defensive bunker sited by the French Army along the Italian–French border to defend against an Italian attack. (*Archivio Centrale dello stato*)

General Messe, commander of the CSIR, inspects a German anti-tank gun (Pak-38, 50-mm gun). (*Ufficio Storico*)

Italian artillery piece 65/17-mm used throughout the Eastern Front campaign. Although outdated, the gun was more useful than the 47/32-mm unit to contrast Soviet armoured units. (*Ufficio Storico*)

Blackshirts surrounded by Greek children. (*Archivio Centrale dello stato*)

Blackshirts on their way to Greece in the fall of 1941. (*Archivio Centrale dello stato*)

Soldiers of the Tagliamento on their way to the Eastern Front.

Above left and right: A Blackshirt on sentry duty in the Balkans. (*Archivio Centrale dello stato*)

Battaglioni M da Sbarco. (*Archivio Centrale dello stato*)

A group of Blackshirts in Greece. (*Archivio Centrale dello stato*)

A group of Blackshirts in Greece. (*Archivio Centrale dello stato*)

Above: A casemate overlooking the bay during the invasion of Sicily in 1943. (*Archivio dello Stato*)

Right: Italian artillery unit during the battle for Sicily. (*Archivio Centrale dello stato*)

Captured French position on the Alpine Maginot Line held by *alpini* troops. (*Archivio Centrale dello stato*)

Giovane Fascista soldier training/launching a Pazzaglia bomb somewhere in North Africa in 1941. (*Archivio Centrale dello stato*)

3

From the Initial Advance into Ukraine to the Christmas Battle

Fighting Conditions on the Eastern Front

The conditions of service on the Eastern Front for Italian soldiers were influenced by three main factors: the weather, the logistical nightmare of supplying troops entrenched in frontline positions far away from their supply bases, and the overall sufficient but not abundant availability of services.

The troops arrived in the Soviet Union during the summer of 1941 when the weather was still mild. At the time, they had no idea what was in store for them. Then reality kicked in when in October torrential downpours ground to halt the movement of almost every means of transportation, including vehicles, bicycles, and even sleds. The soldiers were then forced not only to march on foot but also to pull and hand tow their weapons and ammunition through the muddy and wet roads of Ukraine. The commander of the Tagliamento, for instance, wrote that the fall advance against the Ukrainian heartland took a heavy physical toll on his Blackshirts forced to pursue the enemy through muddy roads and torrential rains. The unit began the campaign with approximately 150 trucks, which were used primarily to transport the heavy weapons, the ammunition and the food provisions and medical service. But in October, it became very difficult to move the equipment and the weapons with motor vehicles given that most roads in Ukraine were not paved and were then waterlogged. Thus, the guns and the ammunition in certain phases of the advance had to be hand towed while the troops were continually digging trenches and gun pits given the fast pace of the operation. The weather greatly slowed down the pace of the advance and even the better-equipped German Army experienced difficulties during the manoeuvre. However, the real surprise came when the dreaded Russian winter arrived and even the *alpini* troops or the Blackshirts from the mountain troops were not used to the extremely cold weather even, though they came from the northern and mountainous area of Italy. The sudden dip in the temperature created all kinds of problems, especially frostbite and other ailments that affected the physical and mental life of the soldier fighting in the trenches. Frostbite became the number two killer of the Italian troops during the winter of 1941. If frostbite did not kill a soldier, it caused innumerable other problems such as, in some cases, the forced amputation of limbs and the inability of the soldiers to use their hands for simple everyday tasks. It was even more difficult to operate the trucks during the winter months and the troops that by then were deployed on the Don line, far away from their supply bases, experienced shortages of food and ammunition on certain days. Thus, the Eastern Front campaign replicated on a larger scale the problems experienced during the attack against Greece of 28 October 1940. That campaign had highlighted the complete unpreparedness from a logistical and organisational standpoint of the Italian Army. Just to give an example, of the 63,000 wounded soldiers in Greece 12,300 were related to cases of frostbite due to the lack of winter clothing and equipment.[1]

On the Eastern Front, for example, many soldiers died as a result of lack of proper equipment. The soldier's boots, for instance, were not sturdy enough for the Russian winter, and when the soldiers marched on foot, they would often experience frostbite or colds and fever as the sole of the boot, which was designed for rock climbing, retained excessive amounts of ice and mud. Another problem experienced by the soldiers was the lack of heavy coats when the first burst of cold weather kicked in. The soldiers of the Tagliamento, for instance, only received their overcoats in late November 1941. The winter weather would also make life for the frontline troops even more difficult in other ways. Sentry duty was extremely dangerous as the Red Army would send out raiding platoons every night and it was not uncommon for these special units to lunge at the sentinels or the troops laying in their bunkers and then kill them or take them prisoners. Tunnelling through the snow was another tactic widely used by the Red Army to reach the Axis lines and kill opponents by stealth. A third tactic used was for special agents or partisans to destroy road signs in the hope of leading enemy troops into ambushes. Another major worry evidenced by the commander of XIV Battalion of the Leonessa was the use of special agents or infiltrators, especially women, 'that carry poison with them to the rear to contaminate Axis field kitchens'.[2]

Finally, another tactic that was widely used was for raiding parties to fake surrender and then pick up their weapons and fire at close range at sentries or small platoons on trench line duty.

The second problem faced particularly by the Italian troops was related to supply. The CSIR initially relied upon the German support services for keeping the frontline troops supplied with food and water and well-stocked with ammunition. The problem from the start was that the few Italian trucks that were used to supply the troops were often out of fuel and when they had fuel they did not perform well in the below zero temperatures during the Russian winter. In the fall, when the trucks were still operating the stock of fuel was the primary problem. As the troops moved deeper into Ukraine, more fuel was necessary to supply the troops. Since the stocks of fuel were not unlimited many convoys had to be cancelled due to shortages. In December 1941, the fleet for the most part ground to a halt since the trucks could not function properly in those bitter freezing conditions. What little supplies could be brought forward were carried by teams with pack mules or with sleds. As a result, the troops had to rely on the German ally more and more for their supplies. Initially there were no problems, but once the Axis troops drove deeper and deeper into Ukraine and the winter set in, the German supply chain also encountered tremendous difficulties. Hence the frontline troops, both German and Italian, at times suffered privations and shortages. There was always a problem with the quality and quantity of the food that arrived at the front. Meals, in many instances, came to the frontline frozen—wine and water were also frozen. In addition, the frontline troops were forced to scrounge for enemy equipment such as the Russian shoes, which were more suited than German or Italian boots for the rough winter weather. Some units such as the Blackshirts were not furnished with the camouflaged white overcoats due to shortages. Then in January only a few special Blackshirt assault units received this very vital equipment. Another item that was in short supply was the white helmet cover that was especially useful for sentries and for assault platoons. While some Italian units had camouflaged helmet covers, some did not.

The Blackshirts of the Tagliamento, for instance, experienced shortages of all kinds including ammunition for the machine guns and the rifles especially during the Christmas Battle when some of their units had been surrounded and cut off from the bulk of the CSIR. This lack of equipment was compounded by lack of effective weapons. The infantry rifles dated from a model first produced in 1891, the artillery units did not have a real antitank weapon and the machine guns, unless kept warm, froze due to the cold weather. In addition to the lousy conditions of service the Blackshirts were also disadvantaged from a purely economic perspective since soldiers that were on active duty received a lower wage than standard soldiers in the Royal Army. Many of their perks, if they can be labelled as such, were only obtainable when the soldier had retired from active duty. At that time, the soldier received a lump sum payment for his services and could possibly obtain career advancement or a job within the state bureaucracy. He could access state benefits such as enhanced social services, paid vacations, medical and health insurance, life insurance, and a pension. These were all perks that could not be obtained while in service, and as a result of the low pay, many Blackshirts, like other Italian soldiers, were forced to barter and steal from the local population.

Another major issue impacting the Italian troops and the Blackshirts in particular that fought against the Soviet Union was the lack of services, especially medical and signal/engineer services. The Tagliamento at the start of the campaign had only one doctor for each infantry battalion. The soldiers that were only lightly wounded were typically treated on the spot and then sent back to their battalion headquarters, whereas the badly wounded were taken back to field hospitals. The trip was always a challenge in itself. The Blackshirts had some medical trucks at their disposal, but when the temperatures dipped and the trucks could not function or were already full, the soldiers had to be brought back by sleds or pack mules and the journey could be extremely long and debilitating. Since the fighting against the Red Army was continuous, the wounded were many more than the unit's scant medical services could handle. This is another factor that impacted upon the soldier's morale together with the harsh fighting conditions, the weather, and the fact that the troops fought in a very distant place from the homeland. The lack of adequate medical help continued to plague the Blackshirts units particularly and until the end of the campaign.[3]

Another service that was in short supply among the Blackshirts was a combat engineer and sapper unit. Initially, the Blackshirts only had a few soldiers that had experience in this realm and very little equipment. This limitation presented important problems when the troops were required to breakthrough enemy defences with barbed wire or bunkers that could only be ruptured by detonating explosive devices. With the arrival of the M Battalions this problem was only partly mitigated.

Troop Morale

The Italian Army of 1941 was comprised primarily by factory workers, farmers, low-level state employees, and artisans that had been conscripted into the armed forces. Although the upper-middle classes also participated in the war, they only comprised a small share of the troops at the front given several exemptions to military service. The biggest one was enrolment into a four-year university degree, which was widely used by the sons of the middle and upper classes to avoid fighting in the war. The majority of the soldiers at the front had limited knowledge of the Soviet Union and of its ideology, although the propaganda machine in Italy had focused upon the red peril and the dangers posed by a Communist regime. Accordingly, the officers and the Blackshirts were considered the two groups within the armed forces that were the most ardent anti-Communist. The Blackshirts because of their ideological beliefs and their adherence to the government's propaganda, while the officers because of their higher level of education, their rather conservative and religious values. The bulk of the soldiers, although not fervent anti-Communist did carry out their duties while at the front but generally did not share the German soldiers hatred for the local population and its political regime.

Unlike other wars where life on the static frontline was for the most part dull and uneventful, on the Eastern Front even the static phases of the campaign were characterised by frequent fighting and high casualties. Trench raids, rapid patrol actions and ambushes by partisans and paratroopers were common even during the winter. As a result, the troops found themselves always on a state of alert even when they were not taking part to an offensive campaign. To counteract Soviet raiding, Axis generals instructed their soldiers to always improve their defensive positions as well as create special elite platoons to capture partisans and check enemy raids. Unfortunately, most soldiers disliked digging or hammering to upgrade or maintain the trenches. This type of work also had a negative impact upon the morale of Axis soldiers especially if the work had to be completed during the winter months. It was also difficult to enrol in one of the special anti-raiding platoons since many Italian units lacked adequate weapons.

One of the most important ways in which the morale of the Axis troops was raised during the excruciating Eastern European campaign was through the award of decorations. Such policy served a dual purpose: to improve morale and to instil a sense of comradeship between allies fighting against a common enemy.

As a unit of the Italian Army, the Blackshirts could be awarded Italian decorations for military valour, but they could also receive decorations from the Wehrmacht. The most important decoration that could be awarded to the volunteers was the Italian Gold Medal of Military Valour followed by the Silver Medal and finally the Bronze Medal. On the other hand, the most relevant German medals were the first and second class Iron Cross.

Throughout 1941–43, the soldiers of the Blackshirt units deployed in the Soviet Union received the following decorations: one collective gold medal; one collective silver medal; seven gold medals; fifty-two German Iron Cross Second Class; and countless silver, bronze, and Italian iron crosses.

The number of awards for the Blackshirt units (that all together equate roughly to a division), for instance, compares well to the awards made to a similar unit such as the Spanish Blue Division. The latter received eight Spanish crosses; forty-two individual merit metals; and 138 Iron Cross Second Class.[4]

Another factor that contributed to the boosting of the morale of the frontline soldiers was the delivery of special packages of food and wine. The Blackshirts, for instance, received a special package during the Christmas week of 1941, which did wonders to make the soldiers feel less homesick during such an important time. The Blackshirts also took great pride in maintaining their uniforms crisp and as clean as possible. In contrast to the soldiers in the Royal Army, for instance, the Blackshirts always appeared more distinctively dressed, well-shaven, and neater and more organised.

In general, the Blackshirts units had higher morale than the standard infantry units to begin with. They were more receptive to the state's anti-Communist propaganda, and many soldiers were experienced veterans of other campaigns, hence less prone to bouts of low morale. While others were new recruits from those born in 1923 or 1924, many of which had only known the fascist regime. The M Battalions in particular were comprised of many 'believers' that were loyal to the regime and opposed to any political evolution away from the *Duce* and the old state apparatus. For many, the war against the Soviet Union was perceived as something more than an ordinary war but as a clash of regimes and cultures. It was seen as an opportunity for many individuals to make their mark by enrolling in the MVSN units and also as a way to advance socially after the conclusion of the war. Giovanni Dell'Aglio, who became a *centurione* in the Montebello, enrolled as a volunteer without letting his family know that he was about to join the ARMIR. While his friend, an ex-major in the army, was driven to tears because he had not been accepted into the ARMIR.[5]

Fidia Gambetti, another Blackshirt, enrolled as an ordinary soldier and gave up his right to be enrolled in the officer corps in order to leave for the frontline sooner. In his war memoirs, Gambetti described the campaign on the Eastern Front as a collision between two ways of life and a titanic struggle for the soul of Europe.[6]

Another Blackshirt, Danilo Ferretti, first volunteered for the campaign against Yugoslavia and then as a *capomanipolo* of the MVSN in Russia. The house-to-house guerrilla campaign against the partisans had disgusted him to such an extent that he had decided to volunteer to fight against the Soviet Army.[7]

The volunteers, however, were not all from the militia. Some also came from the *Bersaglieri*, the *alpini* or the infantry units. Carlo Hendel, for instance, who was exempt from military service since he was a university graduate, volunteered, demanding to be sent to the Eastern Front as an infantryman.

According to the war diaries of the Tagliamento, the soldiers during the first offensive in 1941 could be subdivided into three broad groups: the believers, the opportunists, and the moderates. Each group was fairly homogeneous, but the harsh winter conditions and the heavy fighting, would later test the morale of even the most hardened anti-Communist. Ultimately, troop morale, even among the Blackshirts, was impacted by the fact that soldiers realised how uneven a fight they had been forced to wage.

> Mussolini had no sense for the realities of his own country and the situation of his soldiers. They fought hard under difficult conditions with wretched equipment, impossible supply lines reaching all the way back to Italy, and no goal even remotely visible as they quickly lost their initial enthusiasm. The eagerness with which Mussolini squandered the lives of his soldiers only contributed to the weakening of the Fascist regime at home.[8]

Relationships between Allies

How were the relationships between the German and the Italian soldiers and especially between the Germans and the Blackshirts? It is widely known that the relationship between the two armies was fraught with difficulties mainly because of their uneven capacity.

At the official level, the Germans always expressed positive opinions regarding the fighting abilities of their allies. However, the Germans clearly held different views when one looks at confidential army reports of several officers that worked closely with the Italians or with the other Axis partners. In these documents, the Germans often expressed very critical and negative opinions regarding a whole host of the factors that impacted the performance of the Italian Army. For example, some of the major critiques were centred on the leadership qualities, or the lack thereof, of the officers and the non-commissioned officers. In many cases officers were singled out for having very little combat experience or for being too old and conservative when it came to strategy and tactics. For example, while many Blackshirt *consoli* or *primo seniori* were praised for their commitment, other Royal Army officers were accused of not co-operating well with the Germans. During the Second Battle of the Don River, for instance, German General von Tippelskirch, the official liaison attached to the Italian 8th Army praised the work of *Consoli* Italo Vianini and Graziano Sardu as they kept order and discipline among the troops (even Royal Army units) retreating on foot during the dead of winter. But the same officer criticised the leadership and the officers of some of the infantry divisions for not having enough experience in fighting against armoured units and for their lack of leadership during the retreat.

Other critiques included the lack of military discipline of many Italian soldiers, while some of the most prevalent critiques regarded the way in which the troops were deployed in concentrated and static defences. In the German view, this defensive posture not only was ineffective but it also led to running the risk of being overrun by superior enemy forces. Despite the differences in opinion regarding the fortress or stronghold defence (or what the Italians called *caposaldo*), the Italians continued until the end of the campaign to adopt this static and fortified garrison like defence. The reasons for this were twofold: the frontline sector assigned to the Italians was considered as being too long and extended for the number of troops available and most divisions lacked trucks and armoured units and hence could not but organise a static defence. During offensive operations, the major critique was the lack of speed and mobility of Italian soldiers due to their lack of motorisation. When the Italians would have to march to the front on foot, the Germans looked at them with contempt. Generally, both the defensive and offensive tactics of the Italian Army were criticised by the Germans and the Blackshirts tactics were no exception to this critique since they were the same as those of the Royal Army. On several occasions, German officers, however, praised the Blackshirt units for their fighting abilities such as when they shored up the defensive garrisons during the First Battle of the Don River in August 1942 or when they conducted forceful counterattacks during the Second Battle of the Don River to restore Axis frontline positions.

Another relevant difference between Germans and Italians was the difference in the quality of the officers and the NCOs where the latter did not compare well with the former. Many post-campaign reports, for example, highlight the fact that many officers were not experienced and hence not capable of making sound decisions under emergency situations or within a short time frame. In contrast, the NCOs and the junior officers were the backbone of German Army, which prided itself in decentralising the decision-making process as far down the chain of command as possible by giving autonomy of action to junior officers and NCOs.

Another major difference between the two was the relationship between the soldiers of the two armies and the local population. When reading many of the numerous books written by veterans of the campaign one of the most glaring differences between the Germans and the Italians was the treatment of civilians. While many Germans generally treated civilians with disdain and extreme brutality, the Italians generally had more positive relationship with them. In much of the post-war Italian literature of the campaign, many historians and intellectuals stressed that the Italians were not like the Germans and were much more respectful toward civilians and Russian prisoners of war. Mario Rigoni Stern, for instance, recalls in his works that the relationship between civilians and Italian troops was for the most part based on mutual respect. Similarly, most recently, Hope Hamilton has also discussed how the *alpini* troops generally maintained positive relationships with the local population often treating it with dignity and respect.[9] Although this benign interpretation of the Italian invasion of Ukraine and Russia certainly helps to distinguish between the behaviour of the German and Italian soldiers toward civilians, the reality and the historical facts are more nuance. German historian Thomas Schlemmer, for instance, has argued that the Italians were not victims of the Eastern Front campaign, but perpetrators belonging to an invading army. Maria Teresa Giusti has also argued in her works that the Italians did commit some atrocities against civilians and prisoners, although she underlines how their behaviour was generally much more restrained than that of the German Army. Therefore, did Italian units commit grave atrocities against civilians in violation of international law? How did they treat prisoners and partisans? Most importantly, did the Blackshirts also take part in negative and criminal behaviour against the local population and its armed forces?

There are three elements that must be reviewed when discussing these topics. First, we must evaluate the relationship between the occupying force and the civilians. Second, the relationship between opposing armies and especially the treatment reserved to prisoners. Third, we need to evaluate how the Axis forces—and the Italians specifically—treated or dealt with the Russian partisans.

There are several examples and testimonies furnished by Italian soldiers attesting to the positive relationships that existed between civilians and the Italian military. When the Red Army attacked the Italians during the Christmas Battle in 1941, for example, a lot of the Italian positions were located near small towns where the civilian population did help the troops on a daily basis. Often this took the form of sheltering the troops from the weather in their homes. On the other hand, the Italians often gave some of their rations to children and women of the civilian population that lived near Axis bases, while the Germans usually threw away the food that they did not need.

The work of Mario Rigoni Stern, a sergeant-major in the *alpini* of the Vestone, recalls of positive relations between Italian soldiers and civilians. Often the Italians were helped and fed by Russian civilians during the retreat, while German soldiers were treated with much less respect by civilians.

In one instance of the retreat after the Don front had been broken Mario Rigoni Stern recalls that he stopped for food in a Russian home:

> There are Russian soldiers there. Prisoners? No. They're armed. With red starts on their caps. My rifle is in my hand. I look at them, turned to stone. They're eating round a table, taking the food with a wooden spoon from a common bowl. And they look at me with their spoons held in mid-air. *Mnie khocetsia iestj*! I say. There are also some women. One takes a plate, fills it with milk and meal and offers it to me with a spoon from the common bowl. I take a step forward, sling a rifle over my shoulder and eat. Time doesn't exist any more. The Russian soldiers look at me. The women look at me. The children look at me. No one breathes a word. The only sound is of the spoon from my plate and each of my mouthfuls. *Spaziba* I say when I've finished. And the woman takes my empty bowl from my hands. *Pas austa*, she replies simply. The Russian soldiers watch me go out, without moving.[10]

An infantryman with regards to the relationship between the Italian soldiers and the local population stated that:

> Our relationship with the local population was good. Every time that we distributed food to the soldiers many within the local population would approach our camp. For the most part they were kids and women speaking a mixture of Italian and Russian and they would ask us for food. Typically, we ate first and then walked back to the kitchen to get extra food such as pasta, rice, minestrone and bread that we would hand over to the locals. The Germans on the other hand threw away the food that they did not need in order not to give it to the population, while we left it for the civilians.[11]

Italians, were favourably disposed toward the Ukrainian rural population, which shared many similar traits and common beliefs. The Ukrainian, for instance, were, for the most part, anti-Soviet, they retained their Catholic religious traditions despite Stalin's police, and were generally conservative and socially deferential. All traits that the Italians shared and admired.

Another soldier from the *alpini* stated: 'I used to give to the civilians tobacco, soap, bread and many images of the Madonna. Efforts were taken to feed the population of civilians that lived close to our camps'.[12]

Generally, the Italian troops, including the Blackshirts, admired the effectiveness and the organisation of the German Army, but disliked its brutality in the treatment of civilians. However, the Italians were part of an army of occupation and in this capacity sometimes their troops did commit crimes against civilians. These included taking their food and clothing and in some cases hurting or killing civilians.

After the war, the Soviet government set up a commission to pursue Axis soldiers that had committed war crimes between 1941 and 1944. The vast bulk of the more than 40,000 Axis soldiers that were the target of the investigation were either German or Austrian, while only thirty-six were Italians. This included a few generals and some officers of the *alpini*, infantry, *Bersaglieri*, and the *Carabinieri*. No Blackshirts were included within this group of thirty-six soldiers. German historian Schlemmer reports of a Blackshirt officer, which supposedly torched a Russian village including several homes, but there is no concrete evidence to back up the assertion.

The major accusations against the Italians made by the Soviet inquiry were the killing of civilians in retaliation to partisan attacks, the inhumane treatment of certain civilians whose houses were ramshackled and often burned to the ground, and violence against women. One of the major crimes was supposedly the killing of a dozen Soviet prisoners that had attempted to escape. The commission identified a *Bersaglieri* unit as the perpetrators of the killings. Apparently, the *Bersaglieri* retaliated against the Soviets as they attempted to flee after killing a few Italian guards. Another crime identified by the commission was supposedly carried out by General Roberto Lerici of the Torino Division, who was guilty of ordering the destruction of large industrial complexes in Ukraine. Captain of the Torino Division Luigi Grappelli was guilty of having ordered the killing of 615 civilians and the deportation of 2,683 others and that under his command several hospitals, industrial complexes, and homes had been burned to the ground. General Paolo Tarnassi, who was responsible for maintaining law and order in the rear, was guilty of having ordered the execution of several civilians in the town of Kantemirovka, while Colonel Mariano Pinzi of the *Carabinieri* was guilty of ordering the deportation to Germany of several civilians. Major Romolo Romagnoli was accused of having ordered the destruction of a home and the torture of its owner and her daughter. Colonel Attilio Banda, who was in charge of anti-partisan activity, had supposedly ordered the destruction of a village, while Colonel Raffaele Marconi had ordered the execution of thirty-one civilians. Some of these accusations were probably the result of Soviet propaganda, but it appears from the evidence uncovered by the Soviet commission that indeed even the Italians had committed atrocities against civilians and that in some cases the troops had retaliated against captured Soviet prisoners. It must be stressed that these crimes were not investigated or confirmed by an Italian commission after the post war. But even assuming that some of them did not take place and were indeed the fantasy of Soviet propaganda, it can be argued that even one of these crimes would be enough to blemish those Italian troops that fought as part of the CSIR and the ARMIR.[13]

However, it appears that the Soviet Union never made any accusations of war crimes or crimes against humanity to which the Blackshirts could be held responsible. It is possible, I would argue, that some Blackshirts might also have committed atrocities although not on a scale as great as that of the German Army or the units of the Waffen SS. If indeed, the Blackshirts did commit atrocities against the population, it must be argued that they were probably isolated, sporadic incidents. When the *Raggruppamento* CCNN M 23 Marzo arrived in the Soviet Union in July 1942, for instance, the army had issued firm guidelines and instructions on how the Blackshirts should interact with the officers of the Royal Army. It is clear from these documents that the relationship between Blackshirts and the military were still fairly tense. This was because the former were less respectful and deferential toward military commanders than standard infantry soldiers. An inspection by the commander of the II Army Corps of the camp set up by the Leonessa revealed that 'the *legionaries* did not use the proper protocols when interacting with the commander. In addition, too much commingling between Blackshirt officers and troops was observed'.[14]

But most importantly guidelines were also issued by the Royal Army on how to deal with the local population. One of the problems the commanders of the militia had to deal with was that some Blackshirts were bartering or stealing from the local population. Given the fact that resources at the front were always an issue, many Blackshirts made deals with the local population for the exchange of goods and in some cases stole from the local population. One report issued by the commander of XIV Battalion of the Leonessa stated: 'I continue to receive complaints from the local authorities and from the population regarding damages made by the *legionaries* to harvest fields and vegetable gardens. In some cases the roots of plants have even been pulled out of the ground and these actions are to be considered as pure acts of vandalism'.[15]

Another problem identified was the bartering of the legionary uniform for food or other objects prompting again the commander of XIV Battalion to issue another guideline: 'Any commercial-type action or exchange between Italian soldiers and soldiers from other nations or with the local population is strictly prohibited'.[16]

Both types of actions were against army regulations and were punishable with sentences up to three years in military penitentiary.[17]

With regard to Soviet civilians historian Maria Teresa Giusti has argued:

> We can conclude that there were instances when Italian troops committed atrocities and took advantage of the local population during the occupation. But it is also true that the Soviets also forced some of the captured soldiers to submit to unfair legal proceedings that were based on forced confessions and untrue information. Many were committed for crimes they didn't commit or simply for what the Soviets considered to be anti-Russian and anti-Soviet propaganda that these soldiers in their view espoused during the campaign.[18]

As far as the treatment of prisoners is concerned, we know that generally Russian soldiers tended when possible to surrender to the Italians rather than to the Germans in expectation of a more benign treatment. After the creation of the ARMIR, agreements between Germany and Italy stressed that those Soviet soldiers captured by the Italians were to remain in Italian run and controlled prison camps. The living standards in these camps were generally of a higher quality than of those run by the Germans. For the most part, the prisoners were treated according to the rules of war, they were sheltered and were fed on a regular basis. Generally, Italian-run prisoner camps were much more in line with the traditional treatment administered to captured enemy soldiers, while in both the German and Soviet camps, a much more brutal treatment was meted out to enemy soldiers and very few Italians that were imprisoned returned home after the war. On some occasions, there were reprisals by the Italians against Soviet prisoners but these appear to be for the most part isolated incidents. In one incident a unit of *Bersaglieri* killed several Soviet prisoners, but in retaliation to their attempt to flee and only after they had killed or wounded several *Bersaglieri*. Both the German and the Soviet Army treated prisoners with great contempt. In many cases, the Russians would shoot captured prisoners of war or subject them to inhuman treatment in reaction to the way the Wehrmacht treated their own comrades. In many cases, during offensive operations, Red Army troops received orders to not bother to take prisoners into custody but to shoot them on the spot.

A majority of those that were captured never returned home and died of malnutrition or ailments provoked by bad living conditions in the camps. The Blackshirt units were always deployed in the frontline and therefore did not use some of their platoons to guard or escort prisoners. It therefore can be categorically excluded that they shot or killed prisoners in the camps. There is also no evidence to determine whether they killed any prisoners near or in the frontline positions, although this cannot be clearly ruled out.

Axis troops also utilised specially trained troops to hunt down partisans during the period of the occupation. Partisan activity became very strong in the fall of 1942, in anticipation of the Soviet operation on the Don River. This forced the Italians to form specially trained platoons that were charged with conducting reconnaissance and surveillance to prevent Partisan attacks. As far as the archival evidence is concerned, the *Carabinieri* were specifically deployed for this task, while some *alpini* platoons were also formed to patrol the area near the Don River. It also appears from the archive information that the Blackshirts of either the *Raggruppamento* CCNN M 3 Gennaio or *Raggruppamento* CCNN M 23 Marzo groups did not participate to the anti-partisan actions because they were always deployed in the frontline and rarely carried out garrison duty in the rear. During the retreat, the partisans attacked several columns of Italian soldiers and also committed acts of sabotage to destroy bridges and make the retreat more difficult. But once again, the Blackshirts were never deployed in rear areas garrison duties.

Partisan activity was light throughout 1941 in the sector of the frontline held by the Italians. An Italian intelligence document from September 1941 states that the partisan movement was not very active but that troops were urged to be vigilant. Their tasks were to identify Soviet spies in their midst and track down prisoners that had escaped from the camps and were now feeding information to the Soviet Army. Some women and children, the document warned, also pretended to be friendly toward the Axis troops but were secretly collecting information for the Soviet Army. Finally, the document warned Italian soldiers to be vigilant against Soviet paratroopers that could be dropped behind the frontline to spy against the Axis forces. From the data that is available in 1941, the Italians had detained 2,652 civilians, of which 249, based upon prior agreement with the German Army, had been handed over to the German special police, while twenty-seven partisans had been captured and executed by the Italians.[19]

In 1942, Soviet partisan activity intensified considerably. As a result, the Italians were forced to create special units dedicated to hunting them down. Special *cacciatori* (hunting units) were comprised after undergoing considerable training. These units were typically comprised by one officer, a sergeant-major, an NCO, and twenty soldiers. All underwent special training, had to have above average physical endurance skills, and be proficient in non-conventional fighting skills. Unfortunately, due to the destruction of most intelligence documents during the retreat from the Don River, little is known about the activities of these units.

What we do know is that on 20 January 1943, for instance, Soviet partisans attacked and killed a group of 250 *alpini*, while the heaviest fighting between Italian troops and partisans took place in the town of Pavlograd when a motorised column of *Bersaglieri* was forced to put down an insurrection by the local population.

In conclusion, none of the Blackshirts officers and NCOs appear in the report authored by the Soviet Union commission headed by Vyacheslav Molotov to identify Axis soldiers guilty of crimes against Soviet civilians. Moreover, no evidence was found during this research of any wrongdoing against Soviet prisoners. This does not confirm nor deny that the Blackshirts committed atrocities, but it is at least an indication that they for the most part stayed away from large-scale shootings and executions of civilians and soldiers, which both the Germans and the Russians carried out extensively during the campaign.

As Miller asserts: '… the CCNN bore some resemblance to the German Waffen SS, wearing not only blackshirts, but also an entirely black uniform, but the Italian organisation was never as ruthless and brutal as its German counterpart, nor did its military ambitions ever extend beyond the divisional level'.[20]

The Start of the Campaign

The CSIR was initially deployed within the Army Group South commanded by General von Rundstedt along the Dniester River in Ukraine and sandwiched between the 17th German Army and the 4th Romanian Army. The goal of this group was to spearhead an armoured advance (led by tank corps commander General Paul Ludwig von Kleist) into Ukraine against the main cities of Kiev and Stalino (Donetsk) and then continue in a south-eastern direction toward the coasts of the Black Sea and the Sea of Azov. The CSIR, for the most part, was tasked with flanking von Kleist's armoured forces while the advance unfolded. In this capacity, it carried out numerous roles, including covering the left flank of the Axis deployment, freeing up the German armour for the spearhead advance, cutting off Soviet troops retreating from the German advance, and general reconnaissance and mop operations.

Arrival and First Operations

The first Italian units began to arrive at the front four weeks into the Barbarossa campaign, and by the time the Blackshirts arrived, the CSIR already deployed three infantry divisions. The unit and its performance in combat were considered by the MVSN as two factors of primary importance that would help preserve the reputation of the Blackshirts after their non-stellar performance during the Greek campaign. The opening of a new campaign on the Eastern Front was also seen as an opportunity to showcase the worth of the militia to both the regime and the Italian High Command.

To this effect: 'Its constitution, on the other hand, reflected not only the intent to dispatch an effective unit of the Militia to fight the Soviet Army, but also to demonstrate that the unit was able to collaborate well with the Royal Army'.[21]

The Tagliamento was chosen to represent the militia on the Eastern Front since it was reputed to be one of the most experienced and battle hardened units of the MVSN. A unit that was comprised of many soldiers that had already fought during the Spanish Civil War and that were considered to be some of the best Blackshirt assault soldiers. Although the role of the Tagliamento was to be a subordinate unit of the CSIR, it was still believed that the unit would have plenty of opportunities to showcase its worth and even conduct autonomous operations. The Tagliamento Legion began its journey toward the Eastern Front in order to reach the positions held by the CSIR from Mantova train station between 9 and 10 August 1941. At the train station, commander Nicchiarelli remembered that 'the local party authorities and the population assembled to bid us farewell and to wish us the best of luck. Many people assembled for the farewell since the Tagliamento had trained extensively near Mantova prior to the departure and during its stay it had captured the goodwill and sympathy of the local population'.[22]

Five trains left the station and within a few hours reached Bolzano where the local women's fascist party federation came out in large numbers to cheer the *legionaries*. After five days, the convoy arrived at Trusesti having travelled through Austria, Hungary, and Romania. On 23 August, the march toward the front was resumed as the troops were transported by trucks to their first assembly point. On the 26th, the legion was assembled at Pervomajsk where it was reviewed by the CSIR commander Messe. Two days later, the Tagliamento along with a motorcycle *Bersaglieri* unit, an infantry battalion and an artillery regiment of the Torino Division and an anti-tank battalion paraded in front of Mussolini and Hitler and the High Commands of both armies. The Italian ambassador to Berlin, Dino Alfieri, recalled:

> Given the disastrous conditions on the ground, the parade was conducted in a fairly disorganised way. The drivers despite the mud did their best to keep their vehicles on a straight line and to avoid swerving off the road. The infantry units were well organised, the soldiers were clean and shaven and held up their weapons well. When they passed by Mussolini they turned their heads toward him.[23]

During the next two weeks, the legion continued to advance toward the front on foot and on 8 September 1941 reached its final destination where it took up defensive positions along a 15-mile stretch of frontline on the right bank of the Dnieper River. On 9 September, the legion replaced the Novara Lancieri Regiment on the line and it was placed under the command of the Celere Division. In this capacity, the Blackshirt unit had its baptism of fire. The Soviet infantry was aligned on the opposite side of the river and the troops exchanged artillery fire daily and on occasion the Soviets attempted to raid the Italian positions especially during the night.

The next day, while positioned on the right bank of the river, the unit experienced its first combat operations of the Eastern European campaign. In fact, until 25 September, the legion would fend off three enemy raids and would also be on the receiving end of several artillery barrages, which caused its first casualties. In total during September, the Tagliamento lost twelve soldiers and suffered eighteen wounded. The first casualties were the Blackshirts Ugo Scarpin and Igino Casali. *Soldato* De Apollonia recalled in his diary:

> On 10 September at 1330 two medium calibre grenade shells fell very close by my position and took in one fell swoop the life of two men from the mortar unit of the 1st Company—Scarpin and Casali. Apart from this incident the frontline remained fairly calm. After the two deaths the commander of the Legion visited our trenches.[24]

The unit's war diary reported that between 9 and 25 September, the legion experienced: '... numerous attempts by the enemy to shell our positions and inflict casualties with multiple artillery rounds. Numerous small scale raids were also attempted on our side of the river. Also numerous Ukrainians deserted the Soviet lines and turned themselves in'.[25]

At the end of September the bulk of the CSIR was still deployed along the Dnieper River, but it was on the verge of moving forward in support of the Axis push toward the industrial heartland of Ukraine. At the time, the goal was to prepare the next phase of the offensive, which entailed cutting off the retreat of the Soviet infantry that had been trapped by the rapid advance of the German armoured units. On 28 September 1941, the CSIR carried out this autonomous large-scale operation that involved all of its units in support of the Wiking and Westland Panzer Divisions that aimed to advance in Ukraine and take the industrial hub of Stalino. The CSIR was charged with creating a bridgehead on the Russian-held side of the Dnieper River through the rupture of the Soviet Army defences. This manoeuvre would have allowed the trapping of large numbers of Russian forces, while the German forces were to converge and make a final advance on Stalino.

After having crossed the Dnieper River the Pasubio troops established a bridgehead on the Russian held side. Then the Pasubio on one side and the Torino and the Tagliamento on the other conducted a pincer movement aimed at surrounding and capturing the Soviet forces deployed in defence of Petrikovka, who had been left cut off and isolated as a result of the rapid German advance. The manoeuvre, which began on 28 September, was opposed every inch of the way by determined Russian counterattacks, but ultimately by 30 September five Soviet infantry divisions (over 10,000 enemy soldiers) were captured. The Tagliamento's own contribution first entailed storming Dnepropetrovsk and then to lay siege to Petrikovka. At 7:30 a.m. on 28 September, after the Italian artillery blasted the enemy defences, the forces of the Torino and Tagliamento began to advance upon the positions held by the 261st Infantry Division. The 82nd Regiment advanced on the left flank, while the 81st and the Blackshirts moved ahead on the right. The officers of the Tagliamento led the *legionaries* forward in hand to hand combat with bayonets and hand grenades while several machine guns pinned the enemy down with flanking fire. In the trenches, hand-to-hand combat ensued and several enemy soldiers were killed or wounded, while some retreated back to the safety of the ravines. Two hours later, the Russians after having regrouped counterattacked on the heels of a mortar barrage. The cries of Hurrah broke the morning silence but the effective fire of the Blackshirts mowed down several waves of Soviet attackers and as a result the latter were not able to slow down the pace of the advance. The Soviet units fought valiantly, but ultimately the Italians penetrated into their defences and captured large quantities of men and material. A Tagliamento soldier recorded in his diary that the Soviet troops kept on attacking even though they had been cornered:

> During the night between 28 and 29 September there were several clashes between opposing patrol units. The Bolshevik dead are so many that they cannot be counted. Cadavers are scattered all over, the smell is unbearable.[26]

The next day, the same forces continued to advance against the remaining forces of the 261st and the 273rd Infantry Divisions in defence of Petrikovka. Once again, the troops were involved in a pincer movement with the 82nd Regiment advancing against Kurilovka and the Blackshirts and the 81st Regiment advancing directly against the main hub of Soviet resistance. General Messe had issued the following instructions: 'The 81st Infantry Regiment followed by the Legion shall advance at 0500 against Petrikowka. The Legion will begin its advance at 0600 and take the same route. It will then halt at Novosiloka'.[27]

The Blackshirts fought all day in tough clashes against numerous enemy strong points by pinning down Russian forces under the fire of the machine guns and then overcoming their resistance during the last stage of the assault with the aid of rifles and hand grenades. The advance was slow and extremely laborious given the fierce resistance of Soviet rearguards and due to the fact that the manoeuvre took place in a soggy and waterlogged area. In the morning, they clashed against several Russian patrol units. From these encounters, the Italians suffered one casualty, while the opponents suffered several more. In the afternoon, the same Tagliamento units were assigned the task of mopping up various scattered enemy units that were attempting to avoid capture. A unit of Soviet fusiliers entrenched in a pillbox and a machine-gun strongpoint put up determined opposition and refused to surrender even though their position had been completely surrounded. The unit was first subjected to a mortar barrage, which had come on the heels of a failed infantry attack that claimed two lives. The barrage was followed by another unsuccessful attempt by the infantry to reduce the determined enemy opposition. Finally, a third attack was put forth this time with a team of flamethrowers that opened up the way. As the flames invaded the trenches and entered through the embrasures of the pillbox, the few Russian soldiers that managed to survive the attack were forced to come out of their dugouts and surrender. At 6 p.m., the legion had achieved all objectives by capturing 646 prisoners, 220 rifles, five machine guns, and 1,000 horses and mules. In turn, it had suffered three dead and fourteen wounded. For the CSIR, the operation revealed itself to be a great success considering that collectively the Italian troops were able to capture over 10,000 enemy soldiers. According to the CSIR commander, the operation 'was the first complex manoeuvre carried out entirely by Italian troops with our own means of transportation. It therefore constituted a true and explicit affirmation of our strength and capability'.[28]

The next objective of the German and Italian troops was the capture of Stalino, one of Ukraine's most industrialised urban centres with large steel mills and several coal-fired plants. The advance was conducted at a fairly rapid pace in order to surprise the Russian forces despite the cold weather and the roads that were beginning to be fully immersed in mud and water. The troops of the Tagliamento moved primarily on foot and particular difficulty was experienced in hand towing the anti-tank guns through muddy roads since the trucks could not be used. The difficulty in advancing was compounded by the fact that the Soviet Army by this time had already begun to adopt the strategy of leaving nothing behind while retreating by destroying bridges, knocking out key infrastructure, burning fuel depots, and food storage centres. This made the Axis advance even more troublesome and in some cases casualties were sustained by the actions of Russian rearguard troops that attempted in several instances to slow down their pursuers with machine-gun fire. In some cases, the Russians had even managed to lay traps and ambushes by placing scattered mine and explosive traps under small bridges or on roadsides, which caused further casualties. A Blackshirt, for instance, was severely injured when he stepped into a mine that had been left behind by the Russians on a small bridge while another was killed by a sniper that fired his weapon from a concealed position in a forest and then fled to avoid capture.

Between Stalino and the Axis forces stood the town of Pavlograd that was defended by the 15th Soviet Fusiliers Division and had been heavily fortified by the latter with multiple rounds of barbed wire, pillboxes, and other fortifications. The town was to be captured by the German 198th Infantry Division, by motorised Italian units from the Celere Division and the Tagliamento. As part of the preliminary reconnaissance of the Pavlograd defences a platoon of the LXXIX Battalion was sent ahead of the main assault to locate the enemy's main machine-gun nests. Armed with two light machine guns, several rifles, and hand grenades, the platoon identified an advanced concealed enemy position. While the latter was subjected to heavy machine-gun fire to pin it down, the rest of the members of the platoon slowly moved behind it and then suddenly attacked it with hand grenades. This type of operation is an example of the storm tactics perfected during the First World War and representing the basic tactics of the Blackshirts, which used speed, deception, and special assault weapons to surprise and overwhelm enemy positions.

The unit's war diary regarding this operation reported:

> The *legionaries* Bruno Benatti, Dismo Caffarri and Sante Soliani of the LXXIX Battalion distinguished themselves for their decisiveness. Once they spotted the enemy platoon in the distance they immediately fired their weapons forcing it to flee. Captain Caloiro communicates that driver Dino Renzo Marin from Rovigo died instantly when his truck carrying ammunition blew up after receiving a direct hit from an enemy shell.[29]

On 6 October, the Germans opened up a powerful barrage against the Russian defences, but when its infantry attacked, it was repulsed by the intervention of special sniping teams. Sensing that his non-motorised forces could not break through the stubborn defences, General von Kleist launched into the battle the tanks and armoured units of the Celere along with the Tagliamento. The latter attacked on 10 October the heavily fortified village of Mavrino where the unit's mortar groups played a key role in breaking down the enemy defences and allowing the infantry to roll them up with hand grenades. Shortly thereafter, Pavlograd was captured by the Italians, and the key bridgehead on the Russian side was established by the Tagliamento Blackshirts. An engineer/sapper platoon threw a temporary bridge to allow the troops to invade the enemy positions. Machine gunners positioned on both flanks began firing their weapons while two assault platoons ran across the bridge hurling hand grenades against the enemy positions. Due to heavy fire, the Russian defenders were forced to pull back and abandon their crew served weapons, while the infantry units that continued to fight were quickly surrounded and captured. This breakthrough enabled the bulk of the infantry to advance on a temporary bridge and reach the Russian positions. By then, the unit had suffered three dead and thirty-six wounded, while it had captured an additional 373 Russians.

On 13 October, the Axis forces finally narrowed in on Stalino by eliminating small groups of Russian troops acting in the rearguard. The Celere and XLIX *Gebirgskorps* then attacked Stalino proper. The Italians took the railway station in the outskirts of town, while the Germans were the first to enter into the town centre. By the 16th, Stalino had fallen and the Axis forces had captured a prominent Soviet industrial hub and the area surrounding it, which was rich in natural resources. Vast amounts of weaponry were captured and Soviet losses were severe.

Having succeeded in trapping large quantities of enemy troops and weapons in Stalino, the new goal of the Axis forces was to continue the advance as fast as possible in order to reach the main objectives prior to the start of winter. The CSIR was thus asked to continue to cover the flank of the armoured spearheads of the German Army by advancing behind them and mopping up enemy troops that had not been able to escape the Axis pincer movement. The next objective assigned to the CSIR was the seizure of the heavily fortified town of Nikitowka and some of the smaller villages nearby which were defended by three Soviet infantry divisions. The Soviet Army positions in this sector bulged into the Italian defences, and if the bulge was not eliminated, it was likely that the troops would be subjected to a major enemy counterattack. The 80th Regiment of the Pasubio was thus tasked with this objective, which also would have served the purpose of better aligning the Italian troops with the 17th German Army Corps that was advancing north. Despite fierce Russian opposition, the Italian infantry regiment was ultimately able to break through the defences and occupy the town. The next day, however, the Soviet 74th Fusiliers Division counterattacked and surrounded the Italian infantry cutting them off from the rest of the CSIR. The Italian infantry resisted for six days but suffered heavily due to casualties and a shortage of ammunition. Numerous attempts were made by other units of the Pasubio to lift the enemy siege and come to the aid of the 80th Regiment, but none succeeded.

On 12 November, at dawn, the Italian air force, which was by then based at Stalino, bombed the Soviet positions. Soon after the bombing, the 1st Company/ LXXIX Tagliamento Battalion, followed by troops from the 81st Infantry of the Pasubio, were tasked with breaking up the enemy siege.

The Axis artillery began the preparatory fire, but this caused the enemy to react with its own guns. At their starting points, the attackers suffered some losses from the Russians' counter preparatory bombardment, but the infantry was not prevented from moving forward at the designated time. The Blackshirts attacked on the left flank, first storming some preliminary advanced defences and then parts of the unit pushed on to the town centre which they took around 2 p.m. after a particularly fierce struggle. They captured 500 men and several field guns. On the right flank, the standard infantry slowly fought its way into the town with hand grenades and flame throwers, and at 2:30 p.m., it had liberated the remaining forces of the 80th. The defenders of Nikitowka where then pulled back to the Italian lines and the town was later evacuated by the Blackshirts after they had finished covering the retreat of the infantry. The attack had cost the Italians 150 dead, thirty-six missing, and 550 wounded, but it had allowed them to halt the dangerous enemy counterattack that aimed to create a dangerous fissure between the former and the Germans in the north.

This first operational cycle of the CSIR revealed that the troops of the Tagliamento were well-trained and generally more mobile than standard Italian infantry units. On one hand, the pre-war assault drills of the *arditi* of the First World War had evidently helped to shape these units into capable storm detachments well-versed in the use of hand grenades, flamethrowers, and machine guns. In addition, the troops, which were also well-trained in fighting in small teams, were often used by the CSIR to complete patrols beyond enemy lines and mop up enemy groups or to conduct the reconnaissance of enemy positions. On the other, the Tagliamento's 150 trucks had consistently helped the troops during the fast paced advance and had given the unit an advantage over others. Although the number of vehicles was not nearly enough to transport the foot soldiers of the legion, it allowed for at least the transportation of the heavy weapons, the ammunitions, and the soldiers own packs and rifles. This enabled the soldiers, who still travelled on foot like the rest of the Italian infantry, to move at a much quicker pace. In certain cases, the trucks could also be used to transport one company or a few platoons to a troubled spot with considerable haste. This was an asset that the standard infantry did not have and that greatly benefited the Blackshirt legions. The German Army, for instance, thought that the Tagliamento was a storm trooper unit, given the literal German translation of the term *Battaglione d'assalto*, and that it could thus be deployed in highly mobile operations. During this early phase of the campaign, both the German and Italian divisional commanders demanded its deployment in several instances as they deemed the Blackshirts to be highly reliable soldiers. The capture of Pavlograd, for instance, was made thanks to a key contribution by the Blackshirts, which on that day were fighting under German divisional command and had been deployed after the first German infantry thrust had been forcibly pushed back.

Despite the rapid Axis advance, the Soviet Army attempted in several ways to slow down the progress into Ukraine of the Axis forces. First, isolated Soviet troops that had been cut off by the fast-paced advance in most cases did not surrender. Their resistance in many cases forced the Axis forces to destroy the scattered isolated groups in long and extenuating clashes, which caused high casualties on both sides. While deployed on opposite banks of the Dnieper River, the Soviet Army's activities were very intense. This included frequent artillery barrages, railway guns firing at point-blank range into Axis defence, constant raiding and sniping from Russian Commando platoons. Moreover, the Soviet Army frequently disrupted enemy positions with dedicated teams of snipers or raiders to inflict casualties, capture prisoners, and weaken their morale.

As a result of this intense enemy activity, the Italians were forced to deploy many small platoons to constantly patrol vast areas often located on the banks of the rivers. The Tagliamento troops due to their training were particularly skilful in conducting these very dangerous tasks, which often required fighting at night.

On 16 September 1941, for instance, a platoon of the Tagliamento was deployed in a typical night action to intercept an enemy raid. It was approximately 1:30 a.m. when two small boats carrying six enemy soldiers and two men not in uniform were spotted by the sentries of LXXIX Battalion. Given the fact that there were men not in uniform involved, it was initially believed that they had either lost their way or that they were deserters.

As soon as the eight men landed on the Italian-held side of the river, they first pretended to surrender but soon after began hurling hand grenades and firing a machine gun. The sentries did not have time to react as three soldiers of the Tagliamento were injured by the sudden burst of enemy fire. When the Italians responded to the enemy fire, the Russians fled and managed to escape capture by running into a forest.

After the firefight, a small team was assigned to canvas the area where the Russians had landed. A wounded Russian soldier was found lying on the ground and stated that the raiders, who belonged to the 273rd Infantry Division, knew the area well and that their goal initially was to pretend to surrender and then ambush enemy soldiers. Two weeks later, Red Army commandos struck the rear of the Tagliamento in a surprise raid. They managed to destroy a supply depot and to wound three enemy soldiers. While the Russians were retreating, a unit of the Tagliamento attempted to intercept them, but the former rushed back to their lines and during the chase two Tagliamento officers were severely injured.

These types of operations involving the reconnaissance of enemy positions or the interception of enemy raiding parties were frequently assigned to the Blackshirts, which often sustained losses due to the dangers inherent in night time or early dawn raiding.

In mid-November, the CSIR was defending frontline positions that were 50 miles long, along the so-called Z Line (Chacepetovka, Ivanovka, and Petropavlovka). Its forces were spread out rather thin and could barely cover such a wide section of the front. Attempts were made to straighten out the defensive line and improve the overall line of resistance. This was considered an important task in light of the fact the CSIR defended the vital sector that hinged the Italian to the German positions. If the enemy could get past it, not only was the CSIR in grave danger, but the whole southern Ukrainian Axis front would be put at great risk of being outflanked.

General von Kleist had urged the CSIR to continue to advance on the left flank of the German deployment, but General Messe, cognisant of the difficulties of advancing in such precarious weather conditions, urged caution. His decision not to continue to advance but rather improve defensive positions would turn out to be the correct one, since in late December, the Italian troops were heavily attacked by the enemy. If the enemy had attacked against non-prepared defensive positions, it is likely that it would have penetrated deeply into the Axis line and possibly have encircled the German armoured units.

On 13 November, LXIII Legion was assembled on the defensive line near the town of Gorlowka. The next day, it was assigned under the command of the Pasubio Division in order to take responsibility for holding a section of the defensive line, where on the night of the 17th, three enemy attacks concentrated in the section held by LXIII Assault Battalion.

On the 18th, the 1st company of LXXIX Battalion received the order to conduct a reconnaissance in depth of the enemy's defences. The order that it has been given was to act very aggressively in a bid to fully probe the opponent's positions.

But after having advanced approximately half a mile, the unit became the target of a fierce barrage. Over fifty shells fell within a few minutes on the location where the Blackshirts were concentrated. The commander of the platoon requested the intervention of its own artillery, which was denied because the artillery had been ordered to preserve has much ammunition as possible. The Blackshirts were therefore stuck under a torrent of enemy fire for several hours and then at night time ultimately managed to return to their lines. On 19 November, one assault company of LXXIX Battalion carried out a successful raid against enemy positions together with other units of the Pasubio Division. The soldiers left their trenches during the early morning and without the support of a preliminary barrage so that the enemy would not be forewarned. A storm troop platoon of the Blackshirts continued to advance and soon took an enemy fortification, which had been garrisoned by one Soviet infantry company. The following assault units, however, were not able to follow the leading detachment because the enemy unleashed a heavy round of shells. Caught in no man's land, the troops suffered casualties and were forced to lay low for most of the day. Finally, as night descended, the survivors of the raid were able to retreat to the Italian lines. The raid had inflicted fifteen enemy casualties and had led to the capture of two machine guns.

On 27 November, LXIII Legion moved to the Shelesnoje area, to defend the left flank of the CSIR. On 3 December, LXIII Assault Battalion reinforced by mortar and machine-gun units was moved to prop up the sector of the Celere Division reinforcing its left flank. On the 6th, the remaining units of the legion reached the same position. On the day of the 1st Company of LXIII Assault Battalion carried out a successful offensive exploration on Ploski, capturing three enemy soldiers.

On 7 December, the legion's commander and his officers were headquartered at Krestowka, while LXIII Assault Battalion was garrisoned at Malo Orlowka, LXXIX Assault Battalion in Michajlowka together with the heavy weapons battalion and a horse-drawn battery unit. The commander of the legion was assigned the command of the left sector of the Celere Division responsible for both Royal Army and Blackshirts units. On the 9th, two enemy raids were promptly repelled. The first took place in the sector defended by LXIII and the second in the area defended by LXXIX. On the 13th, the Michajlowka garrison (LXXIX Assault Battalion) repelled three enemy raids inflicting several casualties against the Russians. Then, on the 19th, the Russians attempted again to raid the Italian lines. This time they came at night under the cover of darkness and were also advantaged by a dense fog. But despite initially overrunning an advanced position, they ran into several concealed machine-gun nests that broke up the infantry attack.

Until Christmas Eve, the unit was then engaged in additional patrols as well as in fighting off a multiplicity of Red Army small-scale raids. During this stationary phase of the campaign, the unit suffered few losses: two dead, sixteen wounded, four missing, and seven afflicted by frostbite.

The winter of 1941–42 would not only reveal how ill-equipped the Axis forces were in braving the harsh Russian winter, but it also revealed a renewed found determination by the Soviet Army to resist and in some cases counterattack forcefully. In the southern sector, for instance, von Kleist took Rostov, the gateway to the Caucasus, on 22 November, but a particularly fierce Soviet counteroffensive recaptured it on 28 November. During the early stages of the campaign, the Soviet Army saw its infantry repeatedly being overrun by the fast-moving German armoured units time and time again and its tank groups were destroyed by being deployed in uncoordinated and piecemeal actions. By the winter of 1941–42, however, the Soviet Army's anti-tank defence was not only better organised but also much better positioned in defence of its major urban centres. At the same time, the Soviets had successfully managed to save most of their equipment from the steel and munitions plants in the Ukraine industrial heartland and had started to produce record numbers of T-34 tanks and other weapons in the east. Their armoured units were also beginning to be deployed more effectively. Less than a year later, they would be already used to effectuate deep drives into the enemy's lines. German General Erich von Manstein commented by that point that 'it was just as if we had showed them what to do'.[30]

Faced by the resurgence of the Soviet Army, the CSIR would bear the brunt of one the major Soviet counterattacks during the winter of 1941–42. The counterattack was not only unexpected because of the cold weather, but also because the Italian troops were overstretched having to cover a large area of the frontline.

The Christmas Battle

During mid-December 1941, the intelligence services of the CSIR communicated to High Command that the Russians were most likely gearing up for a major offensive against the Italian troops during the week of Christmas. On several reconnaissance missions, Italian pilots had spotted large-scale movements of Soviet troops that were incrementally being amassed directly in front of the sectors held by the Celere and the Tagliamento. In addition, several motorised columns carrying artillery and ammunition were also spotted moving toward the CSIR sector of the frontline. The Russians were indeed planning a large-scale attack against the Italians, which were believed to be especially vulnerable during the most special religious holiday in the Catholic calendar. It was hoped that their 'sentries and intelligence officers would be distracted by the festivities' and that their overall attentiveness to defensive tasks would be less rigorous than usual.[21] The suggestion to attack the Italians on Christmas day had originally come from the Italian Communist party leaders, especially Palmiro Togliatti. The latter had fled from Italy before the war to join the Communist International and in 1941 was paid by the Soviet party apparatus to direct Communist and defeatist propaganda aimed at the Italian troops of the CSIR.[32] The idea to strike at what was believed to be an extremely opportune time had then been taken up by the army, which had planned to execute it during the early hours of 25 December.

Another motivation behind the Russian attack was the dire conditions of the German Army after their failed attempts to conquer the Soviet Union's largest urban centres. General Messe had specifically warned his troops, stating: 'Our ally is currently facing a momentary crisis, we must be on full alert and everyone should put forth their best effort to stifle any enemy attempt to take advantage of the situation'.[33]

The final plan, which was trashed out by the high command of the 136th Infantry Division, envisioned an attack that was to concentrate upon the meeting point between the Celere Division and XLIX German Army Corps and with the ultimate objective being the recapture of Stalino. The Russians had determined that the weakest point in the Axis defences was located on the left flank of the Celere Division. This sector was selected for two reasons: because being a meeting point between two armies it was less populated by the troops and second because it was the shortest route in order to recapture Stalino and outflank the armoured units of General von Kleist. The plan was to achieve a breakthrough to sever the two units with the deployment of the 136th Division, the 68th, and 35th Cavalry Divisions supported by two artillery regiments.

The Russians also envisioned the deployment of two tank units to punch through the defences. In choosing the sector held by the Tagliamento and *Bersaglieri* units, the Russian High Command followed its favourite infantry assault tactic of attacking at a meeting point or juncture of two major enemy units. As we will detail, only the hard-fought, often hand-to-hand and counterattacking defensive action of the Blackshirts and the *Bersaglieri* troops against overwhelming odds would prevent a major Soviet success.

The Italians, however, knowing that the enemy attack was imminent, thanks in part to information provided by the intelligence services and later confirmed by Soviet soldiers (most likely Ukrainian nationals) that had given themselves up to the troops of the Pasubio, had taken proactive countermeasures. General Messe on 24 December had placed the bulk of the Celere and the Tagliamento in the frontline positions targeted by the Soviet Army and had kept the Pasubio and the Torino in the rear to be used to counterattack the enemy thrust. The frontline positions had also been bolstered by additional teams of anti-tank guns and machine guns to specifically fend off the tanks.

On 24 December, the Tagliamento was deployed to the left flank of the Celere Division and sandwiched between the former and the Torino Division. The troops on that day gathered for the Christmas Eve mass and then for dinner. The frontline was eerily silent and the temperature had dipped to -20 Celsius.

The command of the legion was headquartered at Krestovka, while the bulk of LXIII Battalion was at Maloorlovka along with a 81-mm mortar company and two 47/32-mm anti-tank platoons. The 2nd Company of LXXIX was positioned at Novaja Orlovka with an 81-mm mortar platoon and an anti-tank platoon, while the 2nd Company of LXIII was at Sevcenko along with a Breda 37 machine-gun platoon. Finally, the bulk of LXXIX Battalion was stationed at Michajlovka with a 47/32-mm anti-gun company.

The Italian artillery support to the back of the Legion was comprised by one battery of 75/25-mm and one of 105/32-mm guns, while LXIII Heavy Weapons Battalion was interspersed in small groups at the platoon level among all the frontline positions. An additional reserve unit was comprised of two mobile horse-towed batteries of 20-mm guns.

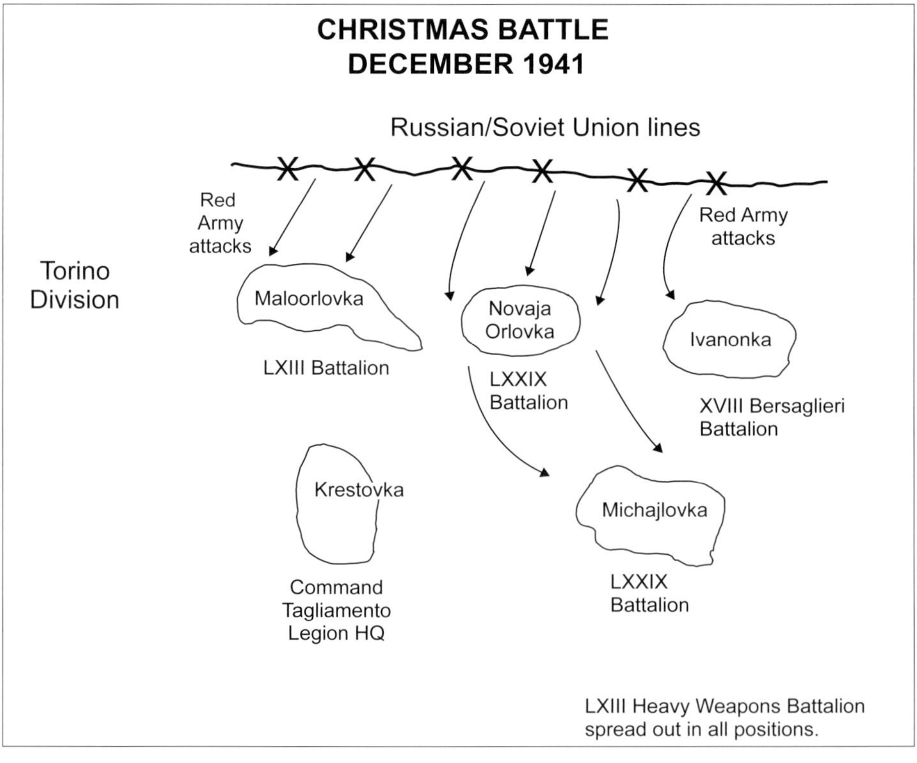

On Christmas Day, as expected, at 6:30 a.m., the Soviet artillery blasted all of the Italian positions including those of the Tagliamento and the barrage was soon followed at 6:40 a.m. by a series of multiple concurrent infantry attacks spearheaded by tanks. The brunt of the attack was taken by the Celere and the Tagliamento as the Soviet infantry concentrated their main thrust on the boundary between the CSIR and the XLIX *Gebirgskorp*.

At 6:45 a.m., while the Italian artillery began responding to the enemy barrage, a small unit of Blackshirts left the trenches at Novaja Orlovka to patrol no man's land and reach Ploskj. But a few minutes later, the soldiers spotted a large group of heavily camouflaged Soviet infantrymen that were dashing toward the Italian position at a very fast pace. Without wasting any time, the Blackshirts immediately ran back to their defensive positions and sounded the alarm. The Novaja Orlovka strongpoint was shortly thereafter attacked by two battalions of the 296th Soviet Infantry Division and by armoured cars. At 7:30 a.m., *Centurion* Mengoli, the unit's second in command, radioed that the position was practically 'surrounded being attacked frontally and from the flanks. We need urgent reinforcements.'[34] A few minutes later, all communications between the strongpoint and the Blackshirts' command headquarters had been interrupted as the former was completely cut off by the enemy encirclement.

At first the Russians used their mid-range weapons to further degrade the defences. Particularly strong enemy mortar fire poured down on the Blackshirt strongholds causing several casualties. Then the armoured cars came bearing down on them by firing their machine guns at point-blank range. Although the attack was halted mainly by the anti-tank guns, it had caused additional casualties reducing even further the strength of the Blackshirt garrison. In the third instance, the Soviet infantry charged against the Novaja Orlovka position with the aid of hand grenades and flanking machine-gun fire. Initially, the attack was repulsed with blistering machine-gun fire moving down the ranks of the attackers as they dashed forward. But after several hours of intense fighting, the position was overrun despite fierce resistance and the Russian infantry captured several Blackshirts. According to the war diary of the Celere: 'Despite heroic resistance the strongpoint was destroyed. Its commander, the *Centurion* Gentile, was killed while all the officers were either killed or captured. Only 50 soldiers managed to escape the encirclement by breaking the enemy siege with hand grenades and reaching Michajlovka'.[35]

Shortly thereafter, the *centurion* who was the second in command had also died leading his officers and men in a violent last stand with hand grenades and daggers. During the most dramatic phase of the battle, he had urged his men forward but was quickly cut down by enemy machine-gun fire. Leaderless, the soldiers attempted one last stand in their positions, but by that time, the Soviet infantry had already submerged the trenches, the walkways and fortified strongpoints and had begun to capture some of the crew served weapons.

The positions of the Tagliamento had subsequently been completely surrounded and the few survivors were captured. The following is the testimony of machine gunner Toso:

> We fired our weapons the entire morning, then we went inside our barracks.
>
> … We were cleaning our weapons when all of a sudden we were alarmed by one single shot and then later by an exchange of gunfire followed by screams and by more weapon fire.
>
> I turned around and saw Cavicchio di Varazze falling to the ground. His hands were covering his face and he was asking what had happened to him. As soon as he took his hands away from his face I saw a lot of blood. His face had been badly injured and an explosive bullet had blown away his left eye. He had pulled himself to the side in order to allow us to fire the weapon. The machine gun was being fired by Tibaldi Natale from Cortemilia, who was born on Christmas Day and who fell on that Christmas Day in 1941.
>
> Our group had four machine guns one of them was manned by Frencia from Saluzzo. He would fire the gun than seek cover behind it while observing if the enemy had gotten behind his position. Then he would resume firing. During one of the breaks, he placed his weapon to the ground and was shot in the stomach and died instantly.
>
> Soon after there were only two of us left from 2nd Company Captain Mengoli and I. Mengoli had been shot in the neck but luckily he had not been shot with an explosive bullet. He was not well and he was having difficulty standing. Others came to his aid. They had him lay down but he was still urging us to fight shouting 'Come on boys, *viva l'Italia*!' After a while he was able to resume the fight but soon after we were both captured.[36]

By night time, the command centre of the Tagliamento had not only received no further communications from the strongpoint of Novaja Orlovka, but it could ascertain after detailed reconnaissance that the position had been completely overrun and that its defenders had been killed and/or taken prisoner.

During the day, the Soviets had also overrun the nearby position of Ivanovka held by *Bersaglieri* units of XVIII Battalion, which were forced to pull back to Michajlovka. At the same time, another battalion of the Soviet 296th Division had attacked the Maloorlovka strongpoint, but the Blackshirts from the onset reacted with extreme force causing several casualties among the attackers. While LXIII Battalion was busy repelling the enemy attack at Maloorlovka, the Soviets troops of the 136th Division dashed against the Michajlovka strongpoint in a determined attempt to surround and cut it off from the bulk of the Italian troops. The Blackshirts of LXXIX, however, managed to hold firmly on to their positions aided by machine guns, artillery, hand grenades, and daggers. A powerful barrage into no man's land caught the bulk of the Soviet attackers in exposed positions causing several casualties. As a result, the bulk of the Soviet infantry was forced retreated into the woods to avoid the deadly machine and mortar fire. A little while later, the soldiers regrouped and spearheaded new attacks together with tanks and armoured cars. The former in particular, fired several shells from close range into the Italian strongpoints, eliminating several advanced centres of resistance and knocking out one of the anti-tank guns. But as the Soviet tanks got even closer—a range of 200 metres of the Italian positions—they were met by heavy concentrated fire from the anti-tank rifles and guns. One of the leading tanks was shot at five times. On the fifth attempt, the tank was hit on the left track and it could no longer manoeuvre. As the crew emerged from the tank and attempted to flee, it was targeted by the Blackshirts machine-gun fire. Seeing the leading tank immobilised by enemy fire, the other tank crews quickly made an about turn and retreated back to their lines. But there was no let up by the Red Army. After twenty minutes, another strong battalion of infantrymen sallied against the defenders by hurling hundreds of hand grenades. Luckily, the strongpoint had enough guns and mortars still in operation to keep, albeit temporarily, the enemy at bay.

Blackshirts and *Bersaglieri*, firing from well-concealed positions inside houses or immediately in front of them, began to mow down with rifles and automatic guns the attackers that were coming forward in great numbers.

The Krestovka strongpoint, which at the time was held by 100 soldiers, was also attacked by a much larger enemy force that had penetrated from Novaja Orlovka. The Blackshirt artillery, which had been placed on high alert, opened fire immediately. It repulsed several enemy attempts to encircle it, but eventually it ran out of ammunition and the artillery pieces had to be withdrawn. The position was soon after evacuated due to overwhelming enemy pressure and the troops were subsequently ordered to reach the Maloorlovka strongpoint, which was still holding out. Despite several attempts by the Russians to cut off the retreating Italian troops, the latter managed to reach their destination. Thanks to the deployment of a battery of horse-drawn 20-mm guns, which fired numerous shells at point-blank range against wave after wave of enemy troops, the Blackshirts were able to keep the enemy at bay and without losing too many men finally managed to reach their comrades at Maloorlovka.

This strongpoint faced additional enemy assaults undertaken by great deployments of enemy infantry. However, all attempts were repelled by the tenacity of the Blackshirts and the few from the Torino Division that had come to their aid. After the battle had ended, several prisoners revealed that the Russian units had lost up to 50 per cent of their ranks without having been able to gain control of the position or to inflict grave casualties upon the Blackshirts.

In the afternoon the Michajlovka strongpoint was threatened again, this time by a much greater force comprised of several infantry battalions, two mortar battalions, and several tanks. The enemy repeatedly attempted to break through the defences, but the troops of the Tagliamento aided by XVIII *Bersaglieri* Battalion/3rd Regiment held firm and repelled all attacks.

At first, it appeared that the Russians were going to overtake the position since they came in wave after wave, courageously disregarding the enemy fire. In fact, as the Soviets kept coming, it appeared that the predicament of the Italian defenders was hopeless as one officer recalled: 'The fallen increase by the minute in the most exposed and advanced positions. Our main positions are obliterated by the shelling of the enemy mortars. All communications are interrupted'.[37]

Soon after, the infantry was aided by the armoured units. The tanks came storming into the defensive positions by continuously firing their deadly shells while in rapid movement toward their objectives. They smashed through some of the advanced positions and destroyed several machine-gun posts. Fortunately for the legion's soldiers, the Soviet Army tactics were still not fully developed. The tanks advanced, but their initial success was not fully exploited as the infantry failed to follow in their wake. As a result, the tanks were isolated and they became targets for the artillery guns. In addition, they were also targeted by Blackshirts armed with Molotov cocktails and hand grenades. In the confrontation that ensued, two tanks were destroyed and one was strongly debilitated. Once the tanks had been dealt with, the infantry battalions belatedly charged the defensive positions but were met with strong machine-gun and rifle fire. The guerrilla-like fighting for control of the town continued throughout the night between 25 and 26 December. The unit's war diary reports:

> The Russians came down from a hill on the left flank of the town and managed to occupy several houses ... the battle raged for the control of each street and house and both troops exchanged fire at a very short range. In certain instances the fighting took the form of hand to hand combat with bayonets and hand grenades.[38]

Eventually, the legion's troops were able to muster enough firepower to keep the Russians at bay and the position was finally preserved from an enemy occupation.

Meanwhile, the Russians of the 733rd Infantry Regiment along with units of the 361st and two battalions of Cossacks cavalry charged against the village of Ivanonka held by the 18th *Bersaglieri* Battalion/3rd Regiment and a unit of horse-drawn light artillery. Due to massive enemy pressure in the afternoon, Ivanonka had to be evacuated and ceded to the enemy and the *Bersaglieri* were forced to pull back to the main garrison of Michajlovka.

In another section of the Celere Division, other Russian forces had overrun Orlovka Ivanonka and were in the process of enveloping the rear strongpoint of Stozkovskoe when the prompt intervention of the reserve battalion of the 20th *Bersaglieri* later reinforced by the 318th Regiment of the German 213th Division hurried to the scene to parry the blow.

In a nearby section of the frontline, the Russians had even managed to surround Katyk, the main headquarters of the Celere. Here a unit of Cossacks cavalry had penetrated deep into the Axis deployment and had managed to sally against the vital divisional hub. But the prompt response of the anti-tank artillery ultimately dispersed these troops by firing at a very close range.

Other Russian units in the meantime had rushed against the villages of Petropavlovka and Rassypnaja managing to capture the former with a bold stroke. As a result, all *Bersaglieri* units of the 25th Battalion were forced to pull back to Rassypnaja.

At the end of the fighting, the command of the Tagliamento was able to piece together various pieces of information on the Russian attack to determine the scale of the enemy operation. Information was gathered from the intelligence services, from the depositions of the prisoners and from documents found in the pockets of dead Red Army officers to determine that the legion had been attacked by several infantry and fusiliers battalions, artillery and cavalry units, and armoured units. The Nowaja Orlowka strongpoint, for instance, had been attacked by two infantry battalions, a mortar battalion of the 733rd Regiment, motorised and armoured units supported by two artillery regiments, and one mortar regiment. Meanwhile, Malo Orlowka had been assaulted by two enemy battalions supported by one anti-tank company, a mortar and an artillery regiment. The Michajlowka garrison had been attacked by three infantry battalions and by armoured units and supported by one artillery regiment, an anti-tank company, and a mortar battalion.

Finally, the Krestowka strongpoint was attacked by one infantry battalion supported by armoured and motorised units and artillery support units. In essence, the Red Army had attacked with a two in some cases four to one advantage in infantry and a four to one advantage in mortar/artillery battalions. In addition, several armoured and cavalry units had also been deployed, thus giving the Red Army an even greater advantage. A Russian officer that had been captured during the battle, Lieutenant Mikael Semionovic Iljic, stated during the post battle interrogation: 'I can't understand why our attack failed. We outnumbered you by a large margin and fought decisively'.[39]

Despite the advantage in men and arms, the attack did not succeed being thwarted by the prompt response of the defenders concentrated fire. In his analysis of the engagement on Christmas Day, the general of the Celere Division praised the decisions made on that day under difficult conditions by the commander of the Blackshirts, which had promptly defended the main Italian garrison.

> 'I must underline,' wrote general Marazzani of the Celere Division, 'that the commander of the Tagliamento instead of retreating to Mikailowka, were the headquarters of the divisional high command was located, instead

> preferred to head with his troops where the enemy was coming through in large numbers in order to parry the blow. Thus he headed in the direction of Malo Orlovka which was being valiantly held and tenaciously defended by the LXIII Battalion. Despite countless enemy attempts to overcome its defences, the latter held on to the village and managed to eliminate 50 to 60 percent of the attacking force.'[40]

Thus, after a day of very heavy fighting, the Russians had occupied Ivanonka and Novaja Orlovka but had suffered many casualties. In addition to the two positions defended by the Tagliamento and *Bersaglieri*, the Soviet infantry was also able to seize the strongpoints of Petropavlovka in the sector defended by the Celere.

Undeterred by the huge losses sustained on the first day of battle, the Soviet commander was determined to attack again on 26 December. These plans, however, were initially thwarted by a swift counterattack launched by XLIX *Gebirgskorp* and by Italian infantry detachments. These units supported by ten tanks promptly retook possession of Ivanonka and Novaja Orlovka and pushed even beyond by occupying Hill 331.7, a strategic position that overlooked a large sector of the frontline. While the Axis forces were retaking possession of the two positions, the 962nd Soviet Infantry Division attacked the troops of LXIII Tagliamento Battalion under a heavy barrage of mortar fire. Their position had been blanketed by a winter storm and the rapidly advancing and highly camouflaged Russian units were able to advance almost undetected toward the stronghold of Maloorlovka. At the same time, the Soviet loudspeakers blurted out in Italian: 'We respect the Italian soldiers and their will to resist at all costs, but don't you know that you are surrounded? Your resistance is in vain! Kill your officers and join us'. Shortly after, at 8 a.m., they surprised the forward defences and managed to overrun several firing points. Despite the initial confusion, the Blackshirts were able to quickly regroup and inflict very heavy casualties upon the enemy force, which was promptly repelled back to its start line. During the morning of 26 December, the Michajlovka position was once again targeted by two Soviet battalions (2nd/733rd and 3rd/966th Infantry Division) supported by a large-scale artillery and mortar deployment. In the early stages of the battle, the Russians had overrun some of the advanced positions tearing up a gap in the Italian defences. Then the troops advanced still further past some abandoned machine-gun positions. But they eventually ran into numerous concealed outposts, out of which the Blackshirts fired with automatic rifles from all sides. To overtake them, the Soviet infantry took much time and used up their hand grenades. This blunted the pace of the attack and allowed the Axis forces to gear up for a counterattack. The counter, spearheaded by LXXIX Tagliamento Battalion, by XVIII *Bersaglieri* Battalion, and by ten German tanks of the 10th Panzer Regiment, drove the two Soviet battalions from the field.

An eye witness recalls:

> At 10:30 on 26 December all of a sudden and unexpectedly several German tanks came down from a hill and rolled into town to make contact and engage the Soviet infantry which was in the process of enveloping the Axis defences. The tanks began to fire in rapid succession against the columns of attacking enemy soldiers silencing both machine guns and their small field artillery pieces. The barrage caused several losses and the unexpected arrival of the tanks was greeted by the Blackshirts, the *Bersaglieri* and the artillery men with loud shouts such as Victory and Hurra.
>
> Energized by the support provided by the armoured units, the soldiers went on the counter attack with their bayonets and with great impetus forced the Soviet infantry out of the homes and dugouts. As the Soviet infantry retreated, many soldiers hopped on the tanks and with one hand holding on to the hulk and with the other hurling hand grenades against the enemy which by now was in full flight.
>
> Lastly, the tanks pushed forward by chasing the retreating soldiers. Some of them had barricaded behind some fortifications which were quickly overrun forcing the Russians to scatter.[41]

During the night, however, a strong counterattack by the Soviet 964th Infantry Division retook possession with a bold stroke of Ivanonka and Novaja Orlovka. Thus, by the end of the second day of battle, the overall situation was unchanged.

On 27 December, the snowstorm that had blanketed the plains ceased and the clear sky allowed the air force to also intervene in the fight. Several Soviet bombers accompanied by I-16b fighter planes took off from nearby air fields to carry out saturation bombing attacks against the Italian positions, but promptly, the 22nd *Stormo*, made up of several Macchi C.200s, took flight to intercept the bombers and the faster Italian planes had a field day by knocking out of action fourteen enemy planes. With the air force having gained control of the skies, the infantry was in a position to resume its counterattack. This time, it was to be undertaken by LXIII Tagliamento Battalion and a battalion from the 81st Regiment. These units stormed ahead and reoccupied the position of Novaja Orlovka following a withering mortar barrage. This barrage caused much destruction and the Russian commander was forced to concede terrain by instructing his men to evacuate the position. When the Blackshirts arrived on the scene, the trenches were full of wounded or dead enemy soldiers and the few that had survived the barrage were still under shock and were quickly taken prisoner. Meanwhile, Ivanonka was also retaken by the Blackshirts together with detachments from the German 318th Infantry Regiment. The infantry troops were initially stalled in the face of heavy machine-gun fire and hand grenades. But a second wave of assault detachments came behind the first. Within a few minutes, the Soviet defences were overrun and the units occupying the advanced positions were killed. After the troops had mopped up the trenches capturing some Soviet soldiers, they patrolled the trenches to see if there were any Axis soldiers that had been taken prisoner that needed medical treatment or any other assistance. What they were presented with was a truly horrendous scene. After they had taken the position, the Russians had taken over the hospital where the Axis wounded soldiers were being sheltered and had killed all of them. Among the first casualties of the butchery was a *Bersaglieri* officer, Angelo Vidoletti, who had been wounded twice in the legs and had attempted to shield the other wounded soldiers from the murderous attack. Despite his protestations to the Soviet officers and Communist Party representatives, Vidoletti was killed with a bullet to his neck. He was later awarded with a gold medal for military valour with the following motivation:

> Twice he had refused to be repatriated in order to remain at the command of his platoon. The same unit that he had laboriously shaped into a fierce fighting machine and had recently completed a very strenuous operational cycle. On a day of particularly harsh combat, Vidoletti continued to lead his men with great impetus despite the violent fire of the enemy's automatic weapons and mortars. Wounded first in the throat he persisted in the defensive effort. He was then hit in the chest by a gunshot, but refused medical treatment and continued to fight on the frontline inciting the few survivors to resist at all costs. He was finally captured by the enemy when the position was overrun. A Soviet political commissioner then interrogated him, even threatening him with a revolver pointed at his chest. While being escorted to the rear, he was shot from behind by the vicious enemy. A great example of the heroism and strong virtues of the Italian soldiers. Iwanowskij (Russian Front), December 25, 1941.[42]

On the same day, the 318th German *Infanterie* Regiment was able to recapture Hill 318.7, which had been ceded to the Russians the day before.

But a night-time assault by the Russians managed to seize it once again, forcing the German units to fall back to the so-called Z line.

After the recapture of the two towns lost during the Russian attack, the CSIR command ordered a further counterattack to improve the positions of the frontline troops in the sector held by the Tagliamento. According to the commander of the Celere Division, the objective was to form three attacking columns, which would assault the enemy positions simultaneously and retake the town of Woroscilowa.[43]

On 28 December, the legion was deployed as follows: the commander's platoon and headquarters were at Malo Orlowka, LXIII was stationed at Nowaja Orlowka, and LXXIX was stationed at Mikailowska. On that day, the commander of the legion assumed command of the tactical reserves of the Celere Division, mainly the Blackshirts and XVIII *Bersaglieri* Battalion to begin a number of counterattacks and localised jabs to push back the Soviet infantry.

After having recovered some of the terrain lost, the objective was to continue the counter thrusts to occupy more of the advanced positions to consolidate the defensive line. Accordingly, on the same day, LXIII Tagliamento Battalion reinforced by two 81-mm mortars platoons, one anti-tank platoon, and one machine-gun company from the Torino Division attacked the enemy positions on Hill 331.7 and the town of Woroscilowa with the objective of taking from the Soviets a key post located beyond the starting positions of the Christmas Battle.

The fighting began with the field artillery shelling the Soviet positions while the infantry advanced in small groups toward the objective. Initially, the artillery fire was strong enough to push the Blackshirts forward and to enable them to charge against Hill 331.7, which was conquered with the aid of hand grenades and bayonets. But once this first objective had been reached, the Soviets began to respond to the enemy fire with even greater firepower, which ultimately silenced the Italian guns. After having neutralised the enemy's artillery, the Soviet field guns and the mortar units concentrated all their firepower into no man's land, targeting the Blackshirt units as they were slowly negotiating their way past icy and snowy terrain and thick vegetation. The murderous fire forced the attackers to the ground and into any crevice or ditch they could find to avoid getting blown to bits. Greatly bogged down by the enemy's machine-gun and mortar fire, the Blackshirts asked for artillery support, but the latter was not readily available mainly because all communications had broken down and the Soviet artillery had overpowered any Axis response. As the fighting continued, unexpectedly several German tanks burst on the scene and commenced firing at the Soviet defenders. As the tanks began to smash their way through the enemy's forward defences, the Blackshirt infantry made a determined effort to reach the Soviet positions by advancing behind them. In a very bitter engagement, the Blackshirts drove the enemy from their position despite a determined stance. Forty enemy soldiers were captured along with two machine guns. The following is the testimony of Tagliamento *legionary* De Vittor:

> The enemy began firing at us with both mortars and artillery from the onset of the operation. As a result of the enemy fire we suffered our first casualties. Our attack was also bogged down by the knee deep snow that hampered our movement.
>
> We advanced past the town that on the 25th had been staunchly defended by the *Bersaglieri* and that now laid in ruins. There were dead bodies scattered all over as the Russians had killed all the wounded soldiers that we had been forced to leave behind at the field hospital. We then continued to advance and

> we conquered hill 331.7. We then later approached Woroscilowa at 1400 which was still defended by the Russians. The enemy's machine guns never ceased to operate. We got down to the ground on the snow. It was very cold and we were forced to lay motionless to avoid the enemy fire. Then all of a sudden three German tanks come to our aid. They drove onto the enemy positions and we followed them. We moved against the enemy positions and we conquered them.[44]

There were further counterattacks put forward by the Axis troops on that day. The 2nd *Fallschirmjäger* Regiment, those valiant troops that had been parachuted into Crete and were now deployed on the Eastern Front, were tasked with charging against the Russian positions of Nikitino, but the action failed due to stubborn Russian opposition.

The 81st Regiment of the Torino was also unsuccessful in the capture of Kurgan Ploskij despite an initial positive start.

On the night of 28 December, the Soviet infantry surrounded Woroscilowa after the enemy positions had been thoroughly barraged by over 100 guns. The heavy snowstorm that began at 6 p.m. allowed the troops to infiltrate some of the houses and to completely surround and overrun two machine-gun strongpoints. But the prompt response from the remaining units of the Tagliamento was enough to see off the attackers. The unit's war diary reports: '... by counterattacking the enemy with much force we were able to maintain our positions'.[45] On the morning of 29 December, the survivors at Woroscilowa alerted that 'we have little ammunition left. We ask for immediate artillery support.'[46]

On the 29th, the situation was still hanging in the balance as the Blackshirts of LXXIX were still hanging on to their positions but were totally isolated from their comrades and their ammunition stocks were almost depleted. The commander of the Celere reported:

> Yesterday afternoon an attempt was made to reach Woroscilowa but the two platoons that were tasked with making contact with the men of the LXXIX were heavily targeted by enemy rifle fire and by night time were forced to retreat back without having achieved their goal.[47]

On the 29th, an additional attempt to relive LXXIX was made. To aid the troops, two trucks full of ammunition and food began the slow approach march from the base of the legion to reach Woroscilowa. But soon after the small convoy had travelled less than a half-mile, the trucks could no longer proceed given the ice on the roads and the continuing snowstorm. It was then decided to transport the supplies with a small convoy with sleds, which promptly reached its destination after a long march and much tribulation. Once Woroscilowa had been resupplied, the troops began to harden their positions by attempting to build several pillboxes, trenches, and other defences, but the constant artillery enemy fire gave them no let up and prevented most of the work from being carried out.

At dawn on 30 December, the enemy attacked the Woroscilowa forces, but was promptly repelled. But while the bulk of his troops were focused on the town, a smaller Red Army unit succeeded in overwhelming two German infantry platoons who had been deployed in defence of Hill 331.7. With this bold manoeuvre, the Red Army had completely isolated the *legionaries* defending Woroscilowa. As a result, all communication with the rest of their deployment had been cut off and their position was completely surrounded by the enemy. Two of its platoons attempted to open up a path to reach the rear of the Italian positions, but were soon beaten back by the violent fire concentrations of the Russian automatic guns.

On 31 December, the Red Army renewed its attacks against the advanced outpost of Woroscilowa, but it was unable to make gains. The next day, a platoon of the Tagliamento broke through the enemy's cast-iron curtain, and with a surprise attack was able to reach Hill 331.7 and finally manage to link up with the vice-commander of the Celere and some of his units. During the same morning, some German armoured units with *Bersaglieri* soldiers following closely behind broke through the Russian defences and regained possession of Hill 331.7, which by then had already been occupied by the Blackshirts. The defensive battle, the so-called Christmas Battle, thus came to a conclusion with a victorious outcome for the Axis forces.

While the enemy refrained from attacking due to the extremely cold temperatures, during the month of January, the Tagliamento was still busy improving its positions, but the cold weather prevented much of the work from being completed. The terrain was completely frozen and the troops were unable to build deep into the ground.

Unexpectedly, on 18 January, two Soviet infantry battalions attacked the Tagliamento positions of Woroscilowa supported by strong mortar fire. Initially, the enemy fire reaped many casualties mainly because of its accuracy and secondly because the defensive positions were not deep enough due to the frozen temperatures. But the strong response comprised by machine-gun and mortar fire allowed the Blackshirts to fight off the enemy attack. The defensive battle was won primarily by holding the strategic possession of Hill 331.7, which allowed the Blackshirts to effectuate a pinpoint mortar fire that caused widespread casualties in the Red Army ranks and deterred further attacks. Moreover, the defenders were helped by the appalling weather conditions as several enemy soldiers froze to death while bogged down to the ground for long periods of time due to the combined mortar and machine-gun fire. Even the well-equipped Russian soldiers with their special valenki shoes and their white overcoats could not survive for long while the temperature had fallen to -43 Celsius. The Tagliamento soldiers' reminiscences of this battle, for instance, state that it was impossible to handle the rifles without gloves or to stay outside for more than five minutes at a time. The sentries on duty could only carry out their rounds for no more than ten minutes and a constant rotation had to be set up to ensure the safety of the troops.

By the last week of January 1942, the troops of the 2nd *Fallschirmjäger* Regiment had arrived in the sector held by the Tagliamento as reserve units. Their commander observed that the Italian troops on the frontline were war weary given the daily Soviet barrages and the continuous raiding by their infantry. Every day and night, assault detachments comprised of 100 or 200 soldiers attempted to infiltrate the Italian lines by stealth and deception. Every time these units had been fought off, the Soviet artillery would typically cover the return of their infantry to the trenches by firing both mortars and small howitzers, which typically caused casualties:

> When the Soviet infantry was far enough away from the village, the Soviet artillery began to fire. The barrage became heavier and heavier. Heavy rounds exploded among the Italian positions, inflicting casualties. The Italians in Woroscilowa had twenty-six killed on this bloody Sunday. The Blackshirts were depressed because it was clear they were facing an enemy several times more powerful.[48]

The last offensive action of note was conducted on 25 January when a company of the Tagliamento's LXXIX Battalion charged enemy positions and fought effectively by occupying several trenches near Woroscilowa, which were cleared of all enemy presence.

On 25 January, the German paratroopers' war diary reported: 'The Italians have done it. They have retaken Woroscilowa. Over there their reserves are moving up'.[49]

> During this counterattack the Tagliamento advanced furthest to Woroscilowa, which was a Russian supply depot taken and held against repeated enemy counterattacks. It is said that when the survivors of the Legion marched back past Ivanovka, a German major (Patoka of the 2nd *Fallschirmjäger*) ordered his detachment to present arms, commenting to *Console* Nicchiarelli that a new term should be invented to describe the *legionaries* of Woroscilowa: Panzer Soldaten.[50]

While the losses of the Tagliamento between 25 December and 31 January included ninety-one dead, 235 wounded, 359 affected by frostbite, and ninety-six missing (approximately 60 per cent of its original strength), the unit received the recognition it deserved from both the commander of the CSIR and of the German command. The CSIR awarded the following medals of military valour: fourteen silver medals, ten bronze medals, while the Germans awarded ten Iron Crosses.

Historian Maria Teresa Giusti has argued that the Christmas Battle was a success for the CSIR and that despite the obsolete Italian anti-tank weapons the troops managed to hold off a major tank attack. 'Even though the Christmas Battle did not produce important results or the conquest of new positions, it can be argued that it had been a success for the Italian troops. The latter's artillery forces even if heavily outnumbered by the Soviets were able to thwart the Soviet attack'.[51]

It is important to stress that although Soviet tactics had much improved with respect to the start of the campaign, the enemy still did not possess the tools and knowhow to effectuate deep penetrations behind enemy lines by tanks accompanied by special shock troop detachments. In contrast, German historian Thomas Schlemmer has argued that the Christmas Battle revealed the inherent weakness of the CSIR (i.e. the lack of heavy anti-tank weapons and tank units) that forced it to fight in a non-autonomous role *vis-à-vis* the German Army.[52]

Although the first signs of this weakness were manifested in December 1941, argues Schlemmer, the evident lack of firepower of the Italian infantry ultimately led to collapse on the Don River positions when a year later the Soviet Army attacked in larger numbers. The CSIR suffered high casualties (1,347 dead, missing, or injured), but it can nonetheless be argued that the Christmas Battle had been undoubtedly an Italian success. Not only had the troops retaken all of the positions seized by the Russians during the first day, but very heavy casualties were inflicted against the Soviet infantry and cavalry. Some enemy tanks had also been destroyed, even though the Russians had refrained from deploying more than thirty tanks, including ten T-34: 'The Russians suffered 2,500 casualties, 1,300 were taken prisoner, twenty-four 76-mm guns, nine anti-tank guns, twenty-two machine guns, many rifles, trucks and other material had also been seized'.[53]

The battle demonstrated that the Italian infantry with the support of the artillery regiments was able to fight on par with the Soviet forces that employed the armoured units according to pre-combined arms tactics where the armour was deployed incrementally, not in large numbers all at once and mainly as a support to the infantry. The tanks were targeted by the divisional artillery regiment, and particular success was achieved by using the anti-aircraft artillery pieces in the anti-tank mode. The infantry had also performed well. The Tagliamento in particular was singled out by Messe for its determined efforts against overwhelming opposition: 'Although we had suffered casualties after the first day of heavy fighting the enemy thrusts had been decisively repulsed and we had also taken the initiative to re-establish our positions'.[54]

The Soviet Army was able to overrun some of its positions only after numerous hours of heavy fighting and by the deployment of a much larger enemy force. It succeeded only in two out of five sectors after a fierce resistance and after all the officers had been killed or wounded. The fight increased in its intensity by the hour and the Soviet infantry finally penetrated the Tagliamento strongpoints, which were surrounded and then destroyed after excruciating hand-to-hand combat.

The Blackshirts had fought an effective defensive battle in the midst of a snowstorm and facing both armoured and infantry attacks. Mortar and machine-gun fire had provided the core defensive fire to break up enemy attacks or to enable swift counterattacks to regain territory and positions. The troops were well-versed in the construction of well-concealed and camouflaged machine-gun strongpoints and all too often they would lie in wait and suddenly open up tremendous fire once the enemy had bypassed or approached their positions. Their biggest weakness, however, remained the anti-tank guns, which were not effective against the large T-34 tanks. Even well-trained troops could not stop enemy armoured attacks with little or no firepower. The heavy divisional artillery often had to pick up the task of stopping the tanks and supporting the Blackshirts with its greater firepower.

Regarding the Christmas Battle, General Marazzani of the Celere wrote:

> The enemy was first contained and then pushed back beyond the starting point of the battle. New positions were captured and the new defensive line appears much more solid and offers a jumping off platform for new offensives. We have also successfully defended the main road leading to Stalino.
>
> The enemy was also unable to capture the meeting point between the CSIR and the LXIX German Army Corps. The Division has bore the brunt of the enemy attack on 25 December undertaken by two infantry divisions, and two cavalry divisions. During the fight the enemy had a 1 to 4 and in some cases a 1 to 7 advantage in infantry. Our casualties were high (1,300 men) but the enemy's casualties were massive. Over 2,000 Russian cadavers were buried by our troops. We captured 1,300 prisoners and with all the wounded involved it is estimated the enemy lost between 6,000 and 7,000 men. The battle was hard fought and it lasted for seven days against an enemy that continued to attack even when it suffered casualties after casualties.[55]

During the following winter months, the Tagliamento Legion was not engaged in combat but kept in the rear to reorganise and replenish its much-depleted ranks within the compound of the command headquarters of the Celere. Most of the officers had died or had been wounded during the winter battle. As a result, the wounded were rotated out of service and new officers and NCOs arrived from Italy. The ranks were also reinforced with new recruits arriving from Italy or from other fronts were the Blackshirts were deployed. During the spring of 1942, a large build-up of Blackshirt units was planned for the Eastern Front, and a few months later, almost half of all the M Battalions (eleven out of twenty-three) were dispatched to Russia. These units were to take part in the massive new offensive that was being planned by the German High Command. In mid-April, the Croatian Legion arrived at the front and took defensive position on the frontline previously held by the Tagliamento. The latter continued to be held in the rear to rest and complete its reorganisation. As part of this reorganisation, the Tagliamento Legion became the *Gruppo di Battaglioni* CCNN M Tagliamento (Tagliamento Blackshirts M Battalion Group). The *Gruppo di Battaglioni* M Montebello was to be dispatched from Italy to constitute *Raggruppamento* CCNN M 3 Gennaio. During the reorganisation, *Console* Nicchiarelli was replaced by *Console* Domenico Mittica.

General Messe, commander of the CSIR, at an award ceremony of the Tagliamento Legion in 1941. (*Legione Tagliamento*)

Left: The standard of the Tagliamento Legion during a ceremony on the Eastern Front. (*Legione Tagliamento*)

Below: The photo depicts the commander of the Tagliamento with the commander of the Croatian Legion in the spring of 1942 somewhere on the Eastern Front. (*Legione Tagliamento*)

The commander of the Tagliamento instructs the commander of the Croatian Legion on the frontline positions held by the Soviet army. (*Legione Tagliamento*)

Two *camicie nere* at an award ceremony summer of 1942 on the Eastern Front. (*Legione Tagliamento*)

Tagliamento unit at award ceremony summer of 1942 on the Eastern Front. (*Legione Tagliamento*)

Italian Blackshirts at the end of the Greece campaign spring of 1941. (*Archivio Centrale dello stato*).

Award ceremony summer of 1942 on the Eastern Front. (*Legione Tagliamento*)

Above left: Two Blackshirts eating their food ration on top of a Soviet statue (a decapitated statue of Stalin). Blackshirts and Royal army officers were known to be the most pronounced anti-Communists of the Italian army. (*Archivio Centrale dello stato*)

Above right: A profile photo of an officer of the Tagliamento: *Capo Manipolo* Angelo Cristofoli. (*Legione Tagliamento*)

Blackshirts saluting by raising their daggers in the typical roman salute. Enlistment in the Blackshirts was open to those who were members of the party that were also physically fit and between the ages of seventeen and fifty. (*Legione Tagliamento*)

Officers of the Tagliamento talking to General Messe commander of the CSIR. (*Legione Tagliamento*)

This photo shows a group of Blackshirts charging forward in the attack on the Eastern Front; the one to the left is providing flanking fire with a Breda Model 30 machine gun. (*Archivio Centrale dello stato*)

A military parade depicting the Croatian Legion and the Tagliamento Legion standard in the background. (*Legione Tagliamento*)

This photo shows a group of Blackshirts firing the machine gun during the Christmas Battle in the winter of 1941–42. (*Legione Tagliamento*)

Blackshirts saluting by raising their daggers in the roman salute while the Italian flag is being raised. The Blackshirts had to swear loyalty to both the regime and to the king. (*Legione Tagliamento*)

This photo shows a group of Blackshirts firing the machine gun during the Christmas Battle in the winter of 1941–42. (*Legione Tagliamento*)

This photo shows a group of Blackshirts firing the machine gun during the Christmas Battle in the winter of 1941–42. (*Legione Tagliamento*)

Summer of 1941: Blackshirts marching in front of Hitler and Mussolini. (*Legione Tagliamento*)

General Nicchiarelli in the forefront. Commander of the Tagliamento. Note civilian women and children in the background. (*Legione Tagliamento*)

This photo shows a group of Blackshirts charging forward in the attack on the Eastern Front in the area of the Dnieper basin in the summer of 1942. The photo captures the standard assault tactics of the Blackshirts. On the left, a machine gun is providing flanking fire to pin the enemy down, while the bulk of the assault troops advance against the enemy position. (*Archivio Centrale dello stato*)

General Messe reviews the Blackshirts who salute with their daggers in September 1942.

A horse-drawn Italian artillery battery. Horses, sleds, and motor vehicles were the three means of transportation of heavy equipment to the frontline. (*Ufficio Storico*)

Italian Blackshirt sitting beside an artillery unit on the Eastern Front. (*Tagliamento Legion*)

Above: Tagliamento unit outside the barracks in Cosenza being reviewed by an officer of the Royal Army. (*Tagliamento Legion*)

Right: The standard of the Tagliamento Legion. (*Tagliamento Legion*)

4

First and Second Battle of the Don River

Introduction

By the spring of 1942, the Axis offensive had stalled, running into a strong and very determined Russian defence that had successfully repulsed a number of attempts by the German armed forces in late 1941 to seize Moscow and Leningrad. As a result of the Germans inability to take Leningrad and Moscow before the winter, Hitler and the German High Command in the spring of 1942 changed course and began to plan an alternative operation. The goal this time was not to renew the siege of Moscow but to launch a large offensive to seize the grain and oil fields in the Caucasus. It was hoped that the operation would cripple the Soviet Army's ability to fight by occupying its main source of grain and fuel supply. The final plan took shape in late spring of 1942 under the codename of Operation Blau, and it was to take place from the two jumping off positions of Volcansk and Kursk. The goal was first to take the Voronezh hub by annihilating the bulk of the Russian infantry there deployed along the Don River. Secondly, the offensive was to continue by advancing along the Volga River to Stalingrad and finally with the seizure of the grain fields at Kuban and the oil fields of Groznyj and Baku.

During the winter and spring of 1942, the *Duce* exerted significant pressure upon the German leader in order to increase the size of the Italian contingent in Russia. Presumably, the Italian leader was still convinced, despite the stalled offensive, that the Axis forces would ultimately win the campaign. He believed that the Soviet Army would be difficult to overcome given its great size and its thousands of weapons, but that the Axis, after a prolonged struggle, would ultimately prevail. In the spring, a letter was written to Hitler urging him to take additional Italian troops destined for the Eastern Front. The letter was followed by a series of meetings between the Italian military *attaché* in Berlin General

Efisio Marras and the German High Command to determine where in the Soviet Union the additional Italian troops were most needed. Then, on 29 April, the two leaders met at Salzburg in order to examine developments related to all theatres of operation of the Axis forces. At the meeting, it was decided that the Axis would launch two major offensives in the summer of 1942, one in North Africa and the other in southern Ukraine/Russia.

Following this meeting, the German High Command headed by Wilhelm von Keitel began to plan the phased arrival and deployment of the additional Italian troops and of the other Axis forces such as the Romanians and the Hungarians, which had also been asked by the Germans to increase their respective contingents. The German High Command determined that these additional troops would best be suited to support the thrust toward the Caucasus oil fields and that they would fight primarily in southern Russia. Part of the renewed offensive was to take place in the mountains of the Caucasus where the advance of the German alpine troops had been stalemated by strong Soviet opposition. It was hoped that the Italian *alpini* troops, which constituted the bulk of the new divisions of the Italian 8th Army, would succeed in helping the German *Gebirgsjäger* in taking the mountainous terrain.

Despite the planned build-up by the Axis on the Eastern Front, there was considerable opposition on the part of the Italian military. On 2 June, General Messe held a confidential meeting with Mussolini in which he attempted to dissuade the *Duce* against increasing the Italian Army presence in Eastern Europe. His argument was based on the fact that the Italian presence on the Eastern Front, even if enlarged, was always going to be of small significance given the much vaster troop deployments by the Soviet Union and Germany. The lack of motorised forces and of heavy weapons, argued Messe, could put at risk the troops and especially expose them to the potential threat of an enemy encirclement by the fast-paced Soviet armoured units. Messe asserts in his memoirs that he told Mussolini: 'It's a grave error to send an entire army to the Russian front. Had I been consulted I would have advised against this, as I did the dispatch of the 2nd Army Corps last year'.[1] But the *Duce* countered that there was a rationale behind the troop build-up and mainly that a larger Italian presence would ensure greater territorial and economic concessions by the Soviet Union and greater influence at the bargaining table at the end of the war. The *Duce* stressed that Italy needed to gain access to some of the Soviet oil fields production to prosper after the war. Therefore, a large build-up of troops, despite the objections within the military, was ultimately authorised, which resulted in the constitution of the Italian 8th Army, the so-called ARMIR.

This time, as opposed to the summer of 1941, however, the dispatch of more Italian troops was more warmly welcomed by the German High Command since their offensive had been halted and the Soviet Army detained a considerable numerical advantage of both men and weapons. The Germans particularly welcomed the arrival of the elite mountain units of the *alpini*, of more artillery batteries, and of additional Blackshirt legions. The former were to take part in the planned offensive in the mountainous region of the Caucasus while the latter were particularly welcomed by Germans for their high fighting spirit and their ability to rally and prop up the infantry during defensive operations. The latter were expanded considerably in anticipation of the push toward the Southern Russian oil fields. The Tagliamento was renamed *Gruppo di Battaglioni* CCNN M Tagliamento (Tagliamento Blackshirt M Battalions) comprised by LXIII and LXXIX Infantry Assault Battalions, which were fully replenished, and LXIII Heavy Weapons Battalion. Although the unit had been reinforced, the Tagliamento's new recruits, its commander observed, were not of the same quality and combat expertise as the veteran campaigners. In his view, they tended to be shorter and of less robust physical condition and generally less experienced. In addition, a new Blackshirt unit was also to be dispatched to the Eastern Front, *Gruppo di Battaglioni* CCNN M Montebello (Montebello Blackshirt M Battalion Group). Similarly to the Tagliamento, this unit was comprised of two infantry assault battalions (VI and XXX) and one artillery battalion (XII). With regards to the Blackshirts of the Montebello, Battistelli and Crociani argue that their training, even though marred by a number of limitations, was somewhat of an improvement with respect to the standard Blackshirt training of 1940.[2]

Not only did they conduct live fire exercises, but they had also managed to train a number of specialists' platoons and support service units that the earlier Blackshirt units clearly lacked.

The Montebello was comprised for the most part of experienced soldiers ranging between the ages of twenty-five to thirty-two that had already fought in Albania and Greece. Although they were experienced, their training as M Battalions was rushed due to the rapidly unfolding events in Russia. It began in the spring of 1942 at the MVSN base in Trastevere and lasted only a few weeks. According to *Legionario* Pietro Calamai of VI Battalion:

> Our training consisted of shooting practice at the range and throwing a few hand grenades SRCM on the banks of the Tevere River. At the base they also showed us the new Berretta automatic rifle that was offered for sale to the officers for the egregious sum of 4,000 Lire. Most likely the people that ran the Ministry of War were not aware of the fact that the Russians by then were armed with the *parabellum* machine pistol able to fire 70 rounds per minute! While handling the Berretta most soldiers were impressed by its range and rate of fire, although when we finally arrived at the front the weapon did not function as effectively. We were then taught how to sing a few patriotic songs and were then rushed to the frontline.[3]

The training was then resumed on the Eastern Front where the unit trained more extensively and conducted several live fire exercises, inclusive of the use of heavier anti-tank weapons.

Meanwhile, in July, it had been decided that the Montebello was to be merged into the *Raggruppamento* CCNN M 3 Gennaio (3rd January M Blackshirt Group). The commander of the unit (Lieutenant General Filippo Diamanti) and his staff arrived in the area of operations in mid-August 1942 and initially had under his command the Tagliamento and the Croatian Legion. Subsequently, the latter was assigned to the Pasubio Division. For a short time, the CCNN M 3 Gennaio was comprised only by the Tagliamento, which was held as a reserve to the Sforzesca Division. Then, in August, when the Tagliamento suffered huge losses due to the Axis renewing the offensive, the Montebello Blackshirts were hurried to the front to provide support. The delay in forming the 3 Gennaio group was due a host of factors but most importantly to the long approach march to the front by the Montebello. The latter spent several days on the trains in order to reach Ukraine. Then the troops were taken closer to the frontline by trucks. Finally, on the night between 10 and 11 September, the Montebello reached the headquarters of the *Raggruppamento* CCNN M 3 Gennaio near the frontline.

The Montebello arrived at the front in full force with two infantry assault battalions and one artillery battalion. Its force was comprised by 162 officers and NCOs, 1,350 soldiers, 134 drivers, while its main crew served weapons included six 81-mm mortars and eight 47/32 anti-tank guns.

Initially, the Montebello was held in the rear to complete its training. *Legionary* Piero Calamai of the VI Battalion recalls:

> At Millerovo it was necessary for our unit to complete the training that we had begun in Rome. Mainly to rehearse how to go on the attack in combined arms operations as this was our *raison d'être* to begin with. In Germany it took four months to train an assault division. We on the other hand, were asked to complete training in less than two weeks. We completed two live fire exercises per day and we were even required to collect the shell casings after training due to the scarcity of the equipment. At the completion of our training the whole unit was able to move on the battlefield with both great ease and agility. Two assault battalions and one of artillery with mortars and guns. The assault platoons advanced close to the ground in small groups while backed up by the fire of the machine guns and the mortars. When the platoons were within 100 meters of the enemy position each soldier fired their rifle six times while leapfrogging toward the enemy. When we reached the enemy trenches each soldier hurled against them up to five hand grenades in order to suppress the enemy resistance. These were the dreaded last 100 meters where we had to fight our way through with our weapons and without the support of the

> machine guns.... By the end of the training we had reached a high degree of readiness and our unit was at least as effective as the training received by the best assault units in Europe.[4]

This much larger unit (*Raggruppamento*) comprised of the Tagliamento and the Montebello was to supersede the legion structure, which was considered to be too small and inadequate to meet the demands of the Eastern Front. Each group was led by a *console*, which had under his direct command eleven officers and a command platoon. The assault battalions were led by a commander (*seniore* or *primo seniore*) who relied upon a staff comprised of three officers, a reconnaissance platoon, and a command platoon. Each assault battalion had three infantry companies and one machine-gun company with six guns. The Heavy Weapons Battalion was organised slightly differently with one commander, two officers, a command platoon, a mortar, and an anti-tank gun company. As Crociani and Battistelli assert:

> If the *gruppo battaglioni* was a development of the former *legione* organization, the *Raggruppamento Camice Nere* formed with twin *gruppo battaglioni* in Russia were to be the largest Blackshirt units deployed on the battlefield since 1940. These brigade sized units ranked as the elite of the Blackshirts, being allotted both motor vehicles and adequate weaponry, including anti-tank guns.[5]

Despite these improvements, the M Battalions continued to be plagued by the lack of heavy anti-tank weapons that could effectively pierce and disable T-34 tanks. Moreover, their degree of motorisation, although improved compared to 1941, was still fairly low compared to similarly deployed German or Soviet units. Each group had approximately 300 trucks—a fleet of vehicles that was not much higher than the combined number of trucks available to the two legions in 1941.

The new Blackshirt organisation was to assemble under these larger units comprised almost exclusively with experienced soldiers. In addition, their support services and the artillery battalions were to be expanded. For example, the reconnaissance platoon of the M Battalions Group was, by mid-1942, fully motorised and used primarily for scouting and intelligence-gathering missions. While the artillery battalions did not receive new weapons, their artillery shells were much improved with the introduction of the new high-explosive shells (EP) that were considered to be more effective when defending against an enemy tank attack. The officers and NCOs of the Montebello arrived at the front armed with the Beretta 9-mm machine guns, which represented a vast improvement with regards to the weapons of the Blackshirt legions. By that time, the Tagliamento was also under the command of a new *console* (Domenico Mittica) as General

Nicchiarelli was called back to Italy to take on a more onerous assignment, while the Montebello was commanded by *Console* Italo Vianini.

In the summer of 1942, the ARMIR Order of Battle was as follows:

-II Army Corps: Ravenna, Cosseria, and Sforzesca Divisions and CCNN M 23 Marzo.
-XXXV Army Corps: Pasubio, Torino, Celere Divisions, and CCNN M 3 Gennaio.
-*Alpini* Army Corps: Julia, Tridentina, Cuneense, and Vicenza Divisions.

The Blackshirts order of battle in mid- to late 1942 was as follows:

63. *Gruppo di Battaglioni* CCNN M Tagliamento *Console* Domenico Mittica

Unit	Commander	Original Base
LXIII Battalion	*Primo Seniore* E. Zuliani	Udine
LXXIX Battalion	*Primo Seniore* Patroncini	Reggio E.
103a machine gun Company	*Centurione* M. Gentile	Cuneo
183a machine gun Company	*Centurione* A. Zanotti	Piacenza
LXIII Battalion	*Colonello* V. De Franco	Reggio E.

Gruppo di Battaglioni CCNN M Montebello *Console* Italo Vianini

Unit	Commander	Original Base
VI Battalion	*Seniore* O. Goldoni	Vigevano
XXX Battalion	*Seniore* G. Pollini	Novara
XII Battalion	*Seniore* S. Superti	Aosta

In August, the II Army Corps was further strengthened with the arrival of a tactical reserve group comprised of six Blackshirt battalions (from the Valle Scrivia and Leonessa), which took the name of *Raggruppamento* CCNN M 23 Marzo (23 March Blackshirt Battalion Group).

Gruppo di Battaglioni CCNN M Leonessa *Console* Graziano Sardu

Unit	Commander	Original Base
XIV Battalion	*Seniore* Bianchi	Bergamo
XV Battalion	*Seniore* Albonetti	Brescia
XXXVIII Battalion	*Seniore* Vannini	Asti

Gruppo di Battaglioni CCNN M Valle Scrivia *Console* Mario Bertoni

Unit	Commander	Original Base
V Battalion	*Primo Seniore* Masper	Tortona
XXXIV Battalion	*Seniore* Gloria	Savona
XLI Battalion	n/a	Trento

Similarly to the CCNN M 3 Gennaio, the CCNN M 23 Marzo was the second (*Raggruppamento*) dispatched to Russia and constituted by its two M Assault Battalion Groups (Valle Scrivia and Leonessa). Each standard M Battalions Group was typically comprised of 162 officers and NCOs, 1,350 soldiers, 134 drivers, four cars, 124 trucks, thirty-six motorcycles, forty-eight assault rifles, twenty-four automatic rifles, twenty-four heavy machine guns, eighteen 45-mm mortars, six 81-mm mortars, and eight 47/32-mm anti-tank guns (while the Leonessa battalions were slightly larger with approximately 150 more soldiers).[6] The Heavy Weapons Battalion had eight 47/32-mm guns and six 81-mm mortars.

Thus, by mid-1942, the two standard M Battalions Groups formed a Blackshirt Division that could count upon 6,500–7,000 soldiers of all ranks, 144 motorcycles, sixteen cars, and 496 trucks. In late August 1942, in order to strengthen this tactical reserve, the High Command of the 8th Army assigned to the Blackshirts the following additional artillery units: the Valle Scrivia received the III *Gruppo* Cannoni from the 201st Artillery Regiment, which was armed with six 75/28-mm guns, while the Leonessa received an additional battery of 47/32-mm guns from the 3rd Granatieri Regiment. The *Raggruppamento* CCNN M 3 Gennaio, however, was not reinforced with additional artillery detachments.

Although the ARMIR was numerically superior to the old CSIR, its overall lack of equipment such as heavy tanks and motorised units made it look like an enlarged CSIR. Its weapons offered little or no improvement *vis-à-vis* 1941. Indeed, the ARMIR had a larger battery of heavy artillery guns, but it still trailed the Red Army's and the German Army's capabilities in the field of motorisation, tanks, and super heavy weaponry. As far as the heavy weaponry was concerned, its most glaring weakness was the lack of effective anti-tank guns capable of producing the same effects against T-34s as the German Flak 88-mm gun. Second, most infantry units of the ARMIR were not motorised and predominately moved on foot. The *alpini*, for instance, relied on pack mules to transport the heavy equipment. Therefore, the Italian units, although more numerous than in 1941, were still forced to advance on foot and remained therefore less mobile than their German ally.

The dearth of motorisation by this enlarged Italian Army is very evident when reading the diary of Roberto Maluberti, a *legionnaire capo squadra* (or NCO) of the V Assault Battalion of the Valle Scrivia, who recounted the long approach march that his unit had to complete in order to reach the front. It is a testament of the very long and strenuous journey that the Italian troops had to complete in order to reach the frontline on the Don River.

Upon leaving Italy, Maluberti writes: 'The first part of the journey consists of the train ride from Italy to Charkov in Ukraine: It's the seventh day of travel but we are getting closer to our final destination. We are in Russian territory near

Minsk [27 June 1942]'. A few days later, he writes: 'I am still travelling [29 June]'. The next day, he writes: 'Finally we arrived at the train station. Now we will start with the most interesting part of the journey: the march on foot. [30 June]'. Then, on 1 July, he writes: 'We are still waiting to march from Charkov to Stalino'.

On 3 July, he reports that the unit was getting closer to the frontline: 'We are headquartered temporarily in a forest. We are close to the frontline as we can hear the roar of the artillery'. Two days later, the troops of the Valle Scrivia were still marching toward the front: 'The day ends very early since at 1500 it gets dark already. On the other hand, the sun rises very early at around 0300. We are waiting for the order to resume our march to the frontline. [5 July]'.

The never-ending journey continued throughout the month of July and into August: 'We marched forward yesterday for another 40 kilometres. [26 July]. We are still marching [1 August]. I was not able to respond to your letter sooner since this morning at dawn we were again marching. It's our daily routine, but my body is handling well the approach to the frontline. [2 August]'.[7]

The unit would finally arrive on the frontline on the river banks of the Don River in mid-August, where the Valle Scrivia became a tactical reserve at the disposal of the Cosseria, Ravenna, and the German 294th Infantry Divisions.

Renewed Offensive

In July 1942, the 17th German Army Corp began preparations for a renewed offensive against the Soviet defences on the opposite bank of the Donetsk River. As part of the general plan of operations, the Tagliamento along with the Croatian legion was to act as the offensive spearheaded of the Celere Division, which was to follow in the wake of the faster moving German troops. Its objective was the capture of Nikitino.

On 9 July, the unit had reached the jumping-off platform for the offensive. Its LXXIX Battalion took position on the peak of Hill 331.7 near Woroscilowa village, while LXIII Battalion took up several positions near the railroad station of the same village. On 10 July, the positions held by the Tagliamento were heavily targeted by the Soviet artillery, which kept the troops under severe pressure for more than ten hours, causing several casualties. The next day, several Blackshirt platoons went over the top to conduct detailed reconnaissance of the enemy positions as well as test their defensive preparedness. A few skirmishes took place between opposite raiding parties when the platoons approached the enemy positions, but these encounters did not result in any casualties.

On 12 July, LXIII Battalion received the order to attack and seize the Soviet Army-held town of Nikitino. The goal was to pinch the enemy's positions from two separate directions with the Italians converging on Hill 331.7 while the Croatian legion was to attack Hill 253.4.

The attackers were to move forward after a thirty-minute destructive barrage and while the enemy troops were still seeking shelter. Accordingly, in the early morning, a powerful destruction fire was unleashed by five heavy, fifteen medium, and thirty-two light guns along a front that reached 5 miles behind Nikitino.

After the fire was moved forward, two engineer and sapper platoons were sent ahead of the main attack to make gaps in the wire and to disable sections of the minefield so that the infantry could advance along a secure path. After several large charges were detonated, which breached sections of the wire, the troops came forward in small groups. But even though a passage had been made for them in the minefield, the Soviet Army opened up a blistering fire that immobilised the Blackshirts in no man's land, resulting in a few casualties and several wounded. In addition to the heavy machine-gun fire, the Soviets began lobbing several mortar shells into the minefield, which caused further casualties and prevented the assault teams from moving forward.

While the enemy barrage was still targeting the main assault columns in the middle, a number of platoons moved away from the fire, heading toward the flank to reach a heavily wooded area that was out of the field of fire of the enemy guns. From these concealed positions, the wooded terrain near the outskirts of the city, the assault units moved forward. When they had advanced and were within small arms range of the enemy positions, they opened up tremendous fire. Initially, the Russians could not locate where the fire was coming from and began to fire their weapons in all directions with little or no co-ordination, resulting in a heavy consumption of available ammunition. While some of the Blackshirts were still stuck in no man's land, others continued to press forward from the flanking position and shortly thereafter overran several enemy trenches. But the gains were only temporary as, within less than twenty minutes, a strong Soviet counterattack pushed back the *legionaries* into no man's land. Again the Italian batteries and trench mortars were called into action to hammer the enemy positions for half an hour while the infantry units on the flank inched forward before rushing to the attack. Once the artillery relented, at several enemy strong points, there was combat with hand grenades or bayonets, in which the Blackshirts gained the upper hand. But a strong enemy counterattack once again nullified any progress made by the Italian troops pushing them back. The fighting had swung back and forth all day, and as darkness descended on the Russian steppe, the advancing columns had difficulty co-ordinating their actions. Thus, by late evening, it appeared that the chance to take the town had evaporated due to the enemy counterthrusts. But when all seemed lost, a platoon led by *Capomanipolo* Menegozzo persevered in the offensive action. At 8 p.m., it then advanced through an area with tall vegetation, proceeded to the back of an enemy machine-gun strongpoint, and infiltrated the Russian defences by hurling hand grenades. It proceeded to capture the main mortar and machine-gun positions, and it was soon followed by the rapid advance of the bulk of the *legionaries*, which began to mop up the enemy defences.

By nightfall, the Tagliamento had broken the enemy defence and had entered Nikitino, where it subsequently headquartered for three days to reorganise and rest. The next morning, at 3 a.m., the Blackshirts pushed forward and occupied the town of Molotowa, while an advanced platoon was able to reach Kruglij.

Thus, on the morning of 13 July, the Russian Army had been pushed back. The breakthrough was completely successful, and tore a gap 2 miles wide in the enemy front. The occupation of Nikitino had yielded 200 prisoners, including ten officers along with ten guns.

On 15 July, the Blackshirts together with the Croatian legion, who were still under the Celere Division, were transferred to Wladimirovka in order to take responsibility for the positions that up to that point had been held by units of the 198th German Infantry Division.

On the night of 16–17 July, the troops took over the sector of the frontline that had been assigned to them while the German units after the handover were assigned to new tasks. On the line, the two *legionary* forces were buttressed by one artillery battery of 75/39-mm guns and the 3rd *Gruppo a Cavallo*, a horse-drawn artillery unit with 20-mm weapons.

On 17 July, LXXIX Battalion was requested by the commander of the Celere Division to carry out a reconnaissance mission of the Soviet positions of Sterovka. The positions were believed to be heavily defended by several infantry units, a minefield, anti-tank ditches, and barbed wire. The objective assigned to the Blackshirts was to identify the location of the gun nests and test the enemy's defences. At 11 a.m., two platoons led by *Capomanipolo* Mario Zago began their approach toward the enemy positions without the aid of the customary artillery preparation in order not to draw the enemy's attention. But even without the preliminary barrage, after they had walked half a mile, the Blackshirts were spotted by the enemy and subjected to heavy machine-gun and mortar fire. While the first platoon took up flanking positions and began to pin down the enemy with machine-gun fire, the second platoon advanced against the objective taking the brunt of the enemy fire.

Slowly the advancing platoon reached the outskirts of the town, which was defended by Soviet troops barricaded inside houses and farms. While the Blackshirts inched closer to these positions, they were targeted by more machine-gun fire. One of these guns severely injured *Legionary* Marco Paolucci, who, despite the open wounds and openly disregarding the enemy fire, attempted to rescue the officer *Capomanipolo* Mario Zago, who also had been wounded by enemy fire. As the brave *legionary* continued to make his way toward his injured comrade, Paolucci was shot and injured for a second time. Although injured one more time, the soldier had the strength to continue fighting and to eventually rescue his officer.

While helping the officer to retreat, Paolucci was shot to death by more rounds of machine-gun fire and was later awarded a Gold Medal of Military Valour for his generous deeds.[8]

After having tested the enemy's mettle, the Blackshirts concluded their patrol action and made their way back to the Italian position. As the platoons were slowly retreating, the Russians counterattacked the positions held by LXXIX Battalion and engaged the Blackshirts in a prolonged exchange of fire. In the evening, even more extensive exchanges of fire ensued, but the Russians were unable to take any positions. By nightfall, the fighting finally ceased and the Russians returned to their trenches. Altogether, the reconnaissance action had been successful, having identified the location of the major Soviet strongpoints held by the 1st and 3rd Battalions/674th Infantry and several heavy weapons groups, far too many Blackshirts had fallen, including one officer and seventeen *legionaries*, while seventy-two had been wounded.

On 18 July, LXXIX Battalion occupied Sterovka with a bold thrust that yielded the capture of 200 enemy soldiers from the 674th Infantry Regiment, nine mortars, an anti-tank gun PTRD 1941, and two heavy machine guns. The operation began when a strong barrage invested the enemy positions forcing many soldiers to flee the frontline strongholds. The artillery fire in essence opened up the way into the enemy defences and allowed the Blackshirts to take them without facing very strong opposition. Once upon the enemy trenches, the soldiers were able to capture several enemy infantrymen that had not been able to flee the artillery fire, as well as several weapons. The trenches and the homes where the Russians had assembled had been obliterated by the artillery, the bodies of more than 100 enemy soldiers were scattered in the trenches, and over twenty crew served weapons of different type and size had been abandoned in position by the Russians.

Pushed back by the great strides made by the German armoured units, the Russian frontline on the Don collapsed and the Tagliamento sought to further exploit the situation by pursuing and rounding up scattered groups of Russian soldiers. Together with the Croatian legion on the night of 18 July, they pushed forward and reached the town of Krasnaja Poljana, which had been evacuated by the Russians a few hours before their arrival. Thus, by the end of the month, the German armoured units reached the Don River. This movement had trapped many Soviet infantry battalions between Donetsk and the Don which were captured in large numbers. The offensive had been a huge success especially because the Axis commanders had initially expected much stronger opposition from the Soviet Army. Record numbers of prisoners and equipment of all kind had also been seized.

During the last three days of fighting, the Tagliamento had lost several soldiers and its strength on 18 July was reported to be as follows:

-Command Platoon: nine officers and 102 soldiers.
-LXIII Battalion: eighteen officers and 535 Blackshirts.

-LXXIX Battalion: sixteen officers and 501 Blackshirts.
-LXIII Artillery Battalion: fourteen officers and 236 soldiers.
-Motorised unit: three officers and 129 soldiers.[9]

On 27 July, Messe recognised the efforts made by the Blackshirts during the seizure of Nikitino and awarded twelve medals of military valour, highlighting the hard work carried by the Tagliamento.

The unit had proved itself worthy of being one of the foremost assault detachments of the Italian ARMIR. In his speech, Messe outlined how the Blackshirts had been instrumental in pursuing the enemy with rapid patrols and in breaking down pockets of resistance with its assault and crew served weapons. In addition, he asserted that the newly formed CCNN M 3 Gennaio and the CCNN M 23 Marzo, the two M Battalion groupings, were now expected to play a key role in the advance toward the Caucasus.

First Battle of the Don River

At the beginning of August 1942, the ARMIR was deployed along the right bank of the Don River sandwiched between the 6th German Army to the south and the 2nd Hungarian Army to the north. The northern sector of the ARMIR was held by the Cosseria, Ravenna, and the 294th German Infantry Division. The middle was held by the Torino and the German 62nd Infantry Division, while the southern sector was held by the Pasubio and Sforzesca Divisions. *Raggruppamento* CCNN M 23 Marzo was assigned to the II Army Corps. The Valle Scrivia was assigned in support of the 294th German Infantry Division and the Ravenna Infantry Division near the frontline positions of Novaya Kalitva and the Bogutschar Valley, while the Leonessa was held as a tactical reserve at the disposal of the commander of the II Army Corps and stationed at his headquarters at Kantemirovka. *Raggruppamento* CCNN M 3 Gennaio on the other hand was deployed as a tactical reserve of the Pasubio Division.

The troops of the ARMIR were responsible for holding approximately 270 km of the Axis defensive line and they faced the 63rd Soviet Army, which was positioned directly across the Don River. The latter was a fairly formidable force comprised by five infantry divisions, several tank battalions and over 10,000 artillery pieces. Both sides of the river were well-fortified, while the Russian held side was also comprised of a heavily wooded area that enabled them to camouflage anti-tank and artillery guns. In contrast, the side held by the ARMIR was more barren and hence more exposed to the Russian guns. Most of the strongpoints consisted of gun emplacements dug into the rock or ground and observation posts or sniper positions concealed behind rocks, trenches, or the sparse vegetation. In addition, some of the troops were concentrated on the advanced trench positions along the river, rather than in the more easily defensible hills further back from the river. At the time of the handover of the positions by the Germans, there had been disagreements between the Italian and German command. The Germans had arrived on the Don first and had occupied positions close to the edge of the river, while the Italians initially insisted that the further behind positions on the hills were more advantageous for a defence in depth. The Germans argued that the units were to be deployed close to the river as possible in order to strike more quickly at the enemy. Since the Germans had already begun to consolidate the defensive line on the river, the Italians ultimately continued this work once they assumed command of the sector. But they also built strongholds on the hills located nearby in an attempt to control the high ground and construct more durable anti-tank defences.

In late July, the Russians launched various counterattacks under the codename Operation Volga in order to disrupt Germany's Operation Blau. The goal was to probe the defences of the ARMIR and to exploit its weakest sectors in order to achieve a breakthrough.

The first Soviet operation was launched on 29 July and the fighting lasted five days. Its goal was to expand the bridgehead on the right bank of the river in the southern sector held by the ARMIR. The Celere Division clashed against the Soviet Army at Serafimovic on the banks of the river. The Italian anti-tank guns manned by the *Bersaglieri* had the better of the duel, knocking out thirty-one Russian tanks, half of which were T-34s. The Germans were also able to deal a severe blow to the enemy by destroying nine enemy tanks with their own anti-tank guns and some *panzerfaust*. This battle, however, was just the preliminary stage of the major operation that aimed with a greater deployment of forces to achieve a breakthrough in the sector held by the Sforzesca Division. The latter belonged to XXXV Army Corps, which also comprised the Pasubio Division, the Savoia and Novara Cavalry units, and *Raggruppamento* CCNN M 3 Gennaio, which was its tactical reserve. These units occupied a 40-mile-wide defensive line on the Don. The Sforzesca Division constituted the right wing of the 8th Army deployment and held the delicate meeting point between the latter and the German troops of the XVII German Infantry Division, which occupied the left flank of the 6th Army of General von Paulus. A few days before the battle, the *Raggruppamento* CCNN M 3 Gennaio was deployed on the right flank of the Sforzesca as follows: *Comando Raggruppamento* and the Command Platoon of the Tagliamento were stationed at Bolschoj. The bulk of LXXIX Battalion was there as well, along with LXIII Artillery Battalion. One assault company of LXXIX was stationed at Kotowskij, while LXIII Battalion was stationed at Blinoff.

The Italians were deployed along two parallel lines, the first was on the bank of the river and it was very thinly held, while the second comprised the resistance zone. The latter due to the scarce infantry resources was centred upon isolated strongpoints (each of which was held by a platoon with either machine guns or mortars) and sentry positions. The defensive strategy was based on each strongpoint garrison holding on to their position even if completely surrounded by the enemy. The strongpoint was to continue to resist at all costs while inflicting heavy casualties against the enemy, which eventually would be brushed aside from the tank units of the German Army. As Maria Teresa Giusti correctly points out: 'On one hand the Germans disliked this system of defence because it was subject to enemy infiltrations. On the other, the Italians counter argued that given the scarce manpower and the great extended frontline the troops could only offer resistance in well defended and concentrated strong points'.[10]

Moreover, the lack of an acceptable degree of motorisation by the Italians also hampered the viability of a more rapid response reaction force and hence favoured a more static defence approach. This defensive deployment openly flouted Hitler's directive, which indicated that all troops were to be positioned on the edge of the river.[11]

As we will see, the first Don offensive would reveal some of the tactical and strategic fissures between the Axis partners. Even though the Italian sector strongpoint-centred defence relied upon the armoured formations of the German Army as a tactical reserve to face off major attacks, the latter, having their troops and materiel tied up in and around Stalingrad, were not able to provide great support. It would thus be up to the reserve units of the Italian Army Corps, such as the Blackshirts, the cavalry, and the elite *alpini* battalion of the Monte Cervino, to come to the aid of the infantry and break up the sieges surrounding the strongpoints. Very little tank support was to be expected, even though the commanders masked the situation by telling their troops that the German armoured units were only within a few hours away. In reality, the German tactical reserve had sixty-five operational tanks, which were held in reserve behind the 8th Army. Such a force was not nearly enough to stop a major tank attack by the Soviet Army. Thus, the defensive troops were to rely almost exclusively upon their anti-tank weapons and the heavier divisional artillery.

Sforzesca Front

At dawn on 20 August, the Russians of the 197th Fusiliers Division launched a very heavy mortar and artillery barrage against the positions of the Italian XXXV Army Corp. This was comprised by both destructive fire aimed at breaking down frontline defences and concentrations of fire upon artillery and machine-gun strongpoints to nullify their reaction. Shortly thereafter, the Soviet forces crossed the river with thousands of small boats and then proceeded to attack the Italian division, which twice repelled the enemy attack. The 53rd and 54th Infantry Regiments of the Sforzesca bared the brunt of the Soviet attack.

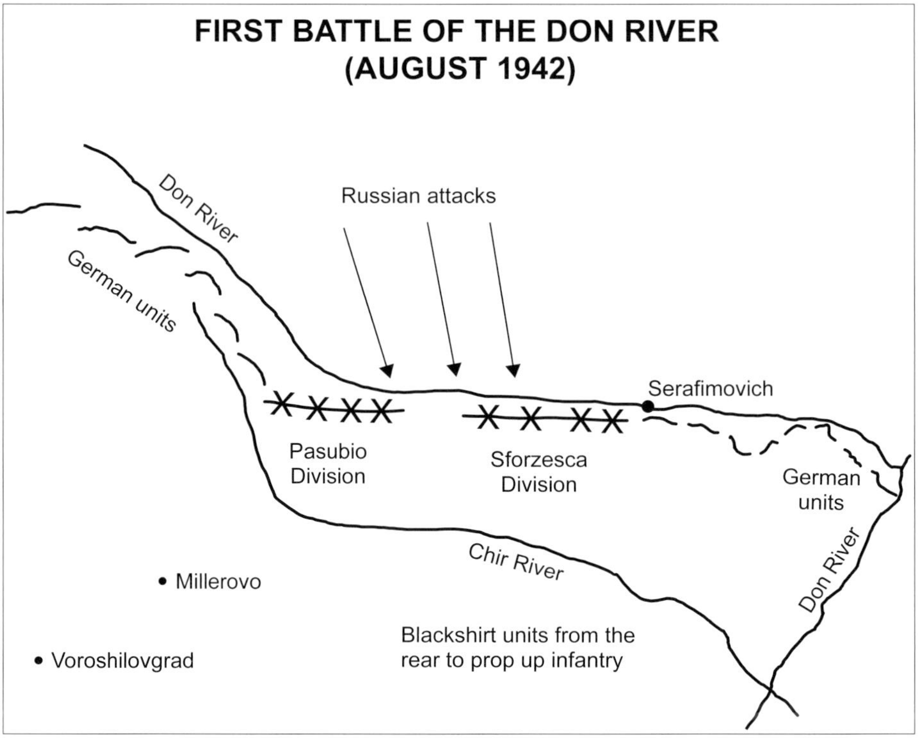

The troops of the latter, for example, were attacked head on and from the flank as a German unit of XVII Army Corps, due to the lack of communication between the German and Italian commands, had vacated prematurely their defensive positions. This enabled the Red Army to achieve a clear surprise against troops that were not expecting an attack to come from their right flank. Despite the tactical surprise, the defenders were able to repel two successive enemy attempts to overtake their positions by responding with heavy machine-gun fire. But the third attack, carried out by two shock troop battalions, proved fatal as the Russians tore a huge gap through which the special assault units penetrated in large numbers and then advanced on both flanks and specifically against the towns of Krutowskij and Simowskij in order to envelop and encircle the Axis deployment.

By midday, the troops of the 54th Infantry had been totally enveloped and the Russians had breached its defences and had even taken the high ground, the hills that were situated to the rear of their defensive positions.

> The Soviet mass attack involved seven infantry divisions against our Sforzesca Division. They came across the river in small boats and it looked as if there were thousands of them. We had asked for support by the *Regia Aereonautica* but the planes failed to come to our defence. At a certain point we deployed

> every man including cooks and drivers which were armed with rifles. We fought for as long as we could. For example, Sergeant Major Caputti, who came from Cuneo, although severely wounded, ordered his troops to retreat while he continued to fire his machine gun until he was killed. At the start of the battle we were 800, only 78 survived.[12]

After five hours of intense fighting near the town of Simowskij and sensing that the 54th in particular was in need of reinforcements especially because the numerous gaps torn in the defensive position made it untenable, General Messe dispatched several units including the Blackshirts to shore up the frontline.

LXIII Battalion was one of the first units deployed as it was immediately positioned on the right flank of the 54th Infantry together with additional infantry units of the Sforzesca, a cavalry squad of the Savoia and a horse-drawn artillery battery. These units quickly moved into the gap and reconstituted a new frontline. They set up machine-gun positions as well as infantry strongpoints each of which was occupied by at least one platoon of riflemen. The light artillery was positioned in the middle of the deployment and in a fairly advanced position to break up enemy attacks. Once more, the Red Army attacked, but its units this time ran forward in dense waves and collapsed under the effective defensive fire of the artillery and the machine guns. Especially with the key aid provided by the artillery batteries, the infantry troops were thus able to check the Soviet attack and prevent the encirclement of the 54th. Once this preliminary goal, to stave off the enemy infantry, had been achieved, General Messe called up additional troops including the Tagliamento's LXXIX Battalion, which was deployed on the opposite flank.

On the 21st, the Soviet Army threw additional troops in the fight by deploying the 14th Guards and the 204th Rifle Division to attack the much-enfeebled defensive deployment of the Sforzesca. The main thrust was to focus on seizing Hill 232.2, one of the main high-ground positions still in the hands of the Italian infantry.

During the morning, large groups of Soviet infantry were spotted moving at a rapid pace toward Hill 232.2. As a result of this build up at approximately 12 p.m., LXXIX Battalion was ordered to reach the main defensive positions of Hill 232.2 and prevent the enemy from encircling the infantry and taking possession of this key position. The unit was thus hastily transported by trucks to the troubled spot, but when the soldiers arrived to their destination, the head of the column, as it turned the bend, was heavily targeted by Russian mortar fire.

At that point, the Russians had already occupied the hill positions, and while in control of the high ground began to further target the Blackshirts with special sniping teams. As a result, as the unit dismounted, a number of soldiers were wounded by enemy rifle fire.

Since the positions had already been occupied by the enemy, the *legionaries* were initially tasked with wresting the higher altitude positions from the Russians. However, the latter continued to advance and assaulted the Blackshirts with the combined strength of two battalions of Soviet infantry. The rush forward forced the Blackshirts into a defensive position to fend off the thrust. The Blackshirts instead of attacking were thus tasked with acting as a rearguard to cover the withdrawal of the 54th and its artillery batteries in an attempt to salvage as many troops and weapons as possible.

Time and time again, the courageous Soviet infantry charged against the line held by the Blackshirts, but the latter were able to repulse all attempts. During the first assault, hand-to-hand fighting developed only at a few sections of the frontline, while in most sections, the thundering mortars of the Blackshirts checked the Soviet thrust. The fighting continued unabated with a second and then a third infantry thrust, but both collapsed under strong defensive fire. At 5:30 p.m., the Red Army put forth the most potent attack of the day with the deployment of three battalions and the accompanying medium weapons companies. The brave Soviet infantry came forward in large numbers once again even though they were expected to run through a field of fire. They dashed forward screaming their battle cry 'Hurrah' while hurling hand grenades and firing their rifles.

Nevertheless, the Blackshirts first defended the position with machine guns and rifle fire and then finally forcefully counterattacked the enemy with hand grenades and flamethrowers. In this final attempt, the courageous enemy was able to penetrate the most advanced positions and kill several infantrymen, but was soon forced out of the trenches again due to counter-thrusts put forth by the Blackshirts. Finally, the Red Army troops came forward one more time, but the defenders once again refused to budge from their positions, while inflicting several casualties in fighting with hand grenades or simply by counterattacking with rifles and bayonets. *Seniore* Silvio Margini recalled that in certain instances the fight grew in intensity:

> The numerous shouts of Hurra that accompanied the waves of enemy infantry coming forward were even louder than the crackle of the machine guns. But the Blackshirts stood firm fighting in a uniform and cohesive fashion. Several waves of enemy troops were repelled by the red hot machine guns that kept firing in the non stop fighting which prevented the soldiers from cooling them down. In certain sections where the enemy pressure was greater the Blackshirts countered with the aid of hand grenades and flame-throwers and pushed the enemy further back.... Ultimately the line held and the enemy was kept at bay.[13]

Similarly, the Tagliamento's war diary reported: 'Pressed from all sides due to the numerous large enemy units threatening our positions, we were forced to deploy our infantry in rearguard actions and to forcefully counterattack with bayonets due to the scarcity of ammunition'.[14]

Historian James Burgwyn states: '... involved in fierce defensive fighting as ammunition ran out the Italians of the XXXV Army Corps faced the last Soviet assault with fixed bayonets'.[15]

Another Tagliamento officers recalls:

> As soon as our motorised column turned the bend, we were targeted by heavy enemy mortar fire. The first three trucks were fired upon repeatedly while the rest of the column remained out of the field of fire of the enemy. Our reaction however, was immediate; the two platoons at the head of the column began to fire back at the enemy but were quickly outgunned by the greater firepower of the Soviet infantry. The remaining forces of the battalion came on and assumed their defensive positions as the enemy came at us in waves head on and from the right flank. In some sections of the line, where the enemy pressure was greatest, some of our platoons were forced to counterattack with hand grenades. The enemy tried repeatedly to outflank us but the Blackshirts fire was prompt and effective. *Capomanipolo* Walter Zampagna lead his machine gunners forward while occupying a high altitude position that offered a great view of the field of battle. While Zampagna stood up to better aim at the enemy, he was shot to death along with two other gunners. The mortar platoons were also discharging their weapons throughout the encounter battle and their fire thinned the ranks of the enemy soldiers with a pinpoint barrage. After many hours of continued fighting we pulled back to a slightly more advantageous position where we realigned along few altitudes. It was on this improved line that we faced the third and final onslaught of the day. The Soviets kept coming but their infantry was cut down by our effective machine gun fire.[16]

By night time, the predicament of the Tagliamento had become very dire due to the fact that it had lost many officers (only four were still on the frontline), ammunition was scarce, and their advanced positions were too exposed to enemy fire. However, the unit had been ordered to defend at all costs the positions to cover the flank of the infantry and it was not allowed to retreat. Luckily, by nightfall, the Soviets had also sustained considerable losses and failed to renew their attack against the enemy positions. Thus, despite a powerful artillery preparation, an equally powerful barrage by the mortar units and very determined fighting by the Soviet infantry, the day ended with severe losses and no considerable territorial gains for the Russians. The dispatch of the Tagliamento to prop up the infantry positions had saved the Italian frontline positions from a dangerous envelopment on its right flank.

While the troops of the Tagliamento were holding off, albeit with some difficulty, the Red Army, the infantry of the Sforzesca was retreating to a more easily defensible position. When the enemy realised that the troops were pulling back, it rushed assault battalions into the gap by penetrating in-between LXIII and the 1st Battalion of the 45th Infantry. This bold manoeuvre isolated the Savoia Cavalry from the bulk of the Italian troops and the former was forced to charge at the enemy in order to escape the encirclement. During the retreat, a platoon of LXIII Battalion lost its way and wound up being surrounded by the Russians. It managed to resist the assaults and at dawn was able to slip away and reach the new positions.

During the night, the troops bought some valuable time to reorganise the units and to strengthen the new positions. Thus, although the front had held, the situation of the infantry troops was also not well. The 54th Infantry, for instance, had lost the vast majority of its initial force, and it was down to only two infantry platoons. The 53rd had also sustained considerable casualties along with Blackshirts and the Savoia.

During the day, the Soviets refrained from attacking and the Blackshirts could therefore dedicate themselves to improve the new defensive positions. At night, a few Soviet infantry patrols advanced close to the wire to probe the enemy positions. Some of the soldiers lobbed several hand grenades into the Italian trenches, but the prompt response of the Blackshirts forced them to retreat. While LXXIX Battalion was gearing up for more enemy attacks, LXIII had been given the more arduous task of reconstructing a defensive perimeter and to reorganise the demoralised soldiers of the Sforzesca Division. With these two tasks in mind, the unit proceeded to form a new line with the heavy weapons, such as the anti-tank guns in the middle and the rifle and machine-gun platoons on the flanks. Meanwhile, the soldiers of the Sforzesca were gathered and organised into *ad hoc* frontline platoons. These were rounded up after scattered groups of infantry soldiers had stormed back to the rear when the Soviet had attacked. Seeing the tanks roll up and smash through their fortifications some troops had simply abandoned their positions and weapons to pull back and stream like an unorganised horde to the rear. The Blackshirts sought out groups of soldiers as well as lone survivors of the enemy assault in order to rearm them and position them on the line. Another immediate problem was the scarcity of ammunition, which had been spent in large amounts during the first day of the Soviet offensive. To resupply the troops, the Blackshirt motorised unit took the initiative to bring to the frontline much needed supplies.

The task of reorganising the line of defence took the entire day. By the 23rd, the commander of the Celere assigned LXIII Battalion to hold a section of the defensive line along with several platoons of *Bersaglieri*. It was envisioned that these more effective troops would corset string the standard infantry in an effort to provide leadership and greater firepower.

At dawn on 23 August, the Soviet infantry put forth a much more forceful assault on the heels of a powerful artillery preparation, but once again the troops were pushed back and heavy casualties were sustained on both sides. The operations began when over 200 medium- and large-sized field guns poured murderous fire on the defensive line. The largest Soviet guns deployed, such as the 200-mm and 220-mm guns, reaped havoc on the line; in some cases, burying machine gunners and sentry men under rubbles of earth and concrete. The Soviet infantry then came forward, submerging the more advanced positions with their greater numbers. But once they had passed beyond the preliminary defences, they were met with strong defensive fire and forced to retreat. During the fighting, the commander of LXXIX Battalion Silvio Margini, in order to relate the dire conditions of his unit, sent the following communication to the headquarters of the Tagliamento: 'My troops are being pressed from all sides, but especially from the left flank. We have little ammunition left for the crew served weapons. Some weapons are not functioning. Nonetheless we continue to resist'.[17]

At 9:30 a.m., the commander of the Tagliamento responded by stating that the unit must resist at all costs on its positions and that additional supplies were on their way. In order to relieve the troops, at 10:15 a.m., the command platoon managed to deliver to the frontline two trucks full of ammunition. These much-needed supplies arrived just in time, since at 10:30 a.m., the Soviets attacked again. Once again, the attack was repelled with losses especially by the crew served weapons that concentrated their fire upon the densely packed enemy troops.

> The Tagliamento and the 54th Infantry Battalion resisted for several hours in this never ending battle. The Legionnaires, in particular, displayed their marksmanship and bravery by standing up and taking aim at the enemy in order to better target them and prevent the waste of ammunition. Openly disregarding the enemy fire they persisted in shooting at the enemy from a very exposed position.[18]

An eyewitness from the Aosta Battalion wrote the following testimony:

> The frontline troops continue to resist the onslaught of shells raining in. Their garrison has been decimated and many of them have been cut to pieces but the few that remain are still holding on to their position. I could hear the distinctive battle cry of the Russian troops as they were assaulting the frontline units even though it was very dark and there was lots of noise from the blasts and the explosions from the artillery and mortar fire. The Russians were massacring all of them and the few soldiers still on the line were paying a dear price fighting tooth and nail after the pullback of the standard infantry division. When from time to time the darkness of the night was broken by the flashes of the guns, we could see a few helmets in the distance that were attracting the tracer bullets of the enemy guns.[19]

Undeterred by the losses, the Soviet Army attacked once again, but even this time 'gunned down by the fire of the automatic guns and the mortars, the Soviet soldiers were forced to retreat back to their lines. Despite the enemy losses and our ability to withstand their continuous pressure, our troops are beginning to show fatigue since they have now been without food and rest for three days'.[20]

On the 25th, the troops of the Tagliamento and those of the 54th Infantry faced yet again another major enemy blow aimed at splitting these units from the bulk of the Italian troops. The fighting continued unabated for several hours until the Soviet infantry desisted from putting forth more attacks given that they could not achieve a breakthrough.

Given the thinning of the ranks among the Blackshirts and the infantry, the few stocks of ammunition left and the fact that the troops had been completely cut off from the bulk of the Italian troops, the decision was made to attempt a further pullback and break the encirclement. It was decided that the troops were to retreat 9 miles west from the edge of the river. The decision taken by General Messe was originally opposed by the Germans. 'But to avoid a rout, and after asking vainly for the intervention of the XVII German Corps, Messe on the 25th ordered a retreat of fifteen kilometres'.[21]

The objective was to retreat on a south-west direction and reach Gorbatowo. Accordingly, the troops began moving in three columns, LXXIX Battalion on the left flank, the battalion of the 54th with LXIII Heavy Weapons Battalion in the middle, and LXIII Battalion on the right. As the Italian troops began to disengage, the Soviet infantry began to chase the three columns with considerable haste. In order to safely reach the rear position of the Sforzesca, the troops forcefully counterattacked with hand grenades and opened up a path for the retreat. While the bulk of the troops accompanied the trucks carrying the artillery units and the wounded, three platoons acted in a rearguard action engaging the enemy in hand to hand combat. After several hours of marching west finally, the troops broke off the encirclement and reached the safety of the Italian lines. During the retreat, the Blackshirts took the bulk of the losses with four officers and fifty-nine dead. In turn, during the almost week-long battle, the Blackshirts had managed to capture: three large mortars (82-mm), six mortars (52-mm), four machine guns, eight anti-tank rifles, twenty-three automatic guns, 150 rifles, 445 Russian soldiers, and three officers.[22]

Meanwhile, in other sectors held by the Sforzesca, the line had held thanks to the support provided by both the cavalry and the Monte Cervino Battalion. To alleviate the pressure, the 700-strong Savoia Cavalry charged the Soviet infantry in a memorable action, the only cavalry charge of the Second World War, and with the loss of thirty-two cavalrymen, it inflicted staggering losses on the Red Army: 150 dead, 300 wounded, and 600 prisoners. This was enough to buy time and allow the infantry units to reorganise their defences.

Ravenna Front

On the morning of 20 August, the Soviet Army also attacked along the front held by the Ravenna Division near the Verkhnij Mamon bridgehead, especially focusing their attacks on Hill 220. As a result, one unit of the Valle Scrivia was transferred to the Bogutschar Valley at Twjerdochlebowka, while a second group was also transferred to the frontline near Kussmenkoff. The successive infantry attacks were all checked by machine-gun and mortar fire.

On 21 August, the front was relatively silent and the Russian troops limited themselves to small-scale raids limiting themselves to lob hand grenades into the Italian frontline positions. These actions did not excessively bother the troops of the Valle Scrivia and only caused a few casualties.

On 22 August, XXXIV Assault Battalion as a preventive measure took position on the reverse slope of Hill 217.6 where it fought off numerous enemy attempts to reach the main defensive positions of Hill 220. Meanwhile, the V Assault Battalion moved to Twjerdochlebowka.

The Leonessa was also called to the frontline to help repulse the Soviet offensive when it too took up defensive positions at Kussmenkoff. Here it exchanged rifle and mortar fire against the enemy suffering several casualties. On the 23rd, it suffered further casualties due to enemy barrages that left one Blackshirt dead and two wounded.

On 24 August, due to the continuing pressure exercised by the Russians against the lines of the Ravenna Division, the V Assault Battalion was moved to Gadjutschje where it fought off several enemy attempts to take the positions.

A *legionary* of the V Assault Battalion Roberto Maluberti recalls:

> In the last few days we were deployed on the defensive line in a sector of the frontline that appeared to be very calm. Yesterday while we were waiting for the trucks to take us back to the rear we were targeted by the enemy artillery. The barrage caused a lot of panic amongst the troops which quickly scattered to more secure positions. A few of us were not so lucky and were on the receiving end of the enemy shells. To be exact we suffered one dead and two wounded. Therefore yesterday was my baptism of fire on the Russian front. I was calm throughout and then we quickly reached a rear position.[23]

On the 25th, the Soviet offensive subsided, but the CCNN M 23 Marzo Group units were held on the frontline until 6 September to block any potential enemy infiltrations.

On 26 August, the front stabilised. Both the Ravenna and the Sforsesca had been badly mauled but they held their main positions. The Sforzesca units had been forced to evacuate the advanced positions on the Don River allowing the Soviet Army to constitute a wider bridgehead on the Axis side, while on the positions held by the Ravenna the Soviets had also been able to seize an important jumping off position. Thus, the first offensive on the Don came to a conclusion with the Axis forces able to hold on and preventing the enemy from encircling the troops of the German 6th Army.

General Kurt von Tippelskirch served as the German liaison officer with the Italian 8th Army between 27 August 1942 and 1 February 1943. In this capacity, the German liaison officer *attaché* wrote a detailed report on the performance of the Sforzesca Division and the Italian II Army Corps in general, which is very revealing of the German view of their main Axis ally. The officer stated that the standard infantry had been led by inexperienced officers, which in some cases broke under the extreme pressure exercised by the enemy. 'Already during the course of the first engagements especially the officers of the Sforzesca Division showed some weakness and a few episodes of panic'.

He went on to argue that the sector of the Don River assigned to the Sforzesca was a difficult area to defend, but all Soviet attacks ultimately failed. These Soviet attacks had been thrown back by the 'energetic action of the Blackshirt Brigade of the 23 Marzo and 3 Gennaio'.[24]

The Blackshirts had indeed helped to parry the Soviet blow and their losses during the battle were a testament of their combativeness as line infantry. The Tagliamento in particular had lost many men during the six days of heavy fighting between 20 and 26 August. It had lost a total of 458 soldiers, including two dead, thirteen wounded, and four missing among the officers, forty-four dead, 259 wounded, and 136 missing among the soldiers. The losses by the CC NN M 23 Marzo Group were eleven dead, twenty-three wounded, and two missing.

The retreat from the banks of the Don River by the units of the Sforzesca had initially created considerable consternation in Rome. Mussolini was particularly preoccupied by how events were unfolding on the Don. On 26 August, Cavallero told Mussolini that indeed the unit had committed a phased withdrawal from the Don River but the enemy's uncoordinated, piecemeal attacks had all been pushed back. Cavallero was confident that the enemy would be prevented from making a major breakthrough and in addition, he argued, the *alpini* corps would soon arrive in its entirety at the front to bolster the Italian infantry.[25]

The Germans too were worried about the rupture in the centre of the II Army Corps, which made more fragile the supply road to Stalingrad. They stressed the need for counterattacks against the Russians to retake the bulge.[26]

After the phased withdrawal, the CCNN M 3 Gennaio was tasked with holding 10 miles of the frontline, which was comprised primarily by machine-gun strongpoints and observation posts. The Blackshirts were not only required to occupy the strongpoints but also to send out patrols periodically to reconnaissance the non-occupied areas.

To appease the Germans, on 28 August, one such patrol led by a platoon of LXXIX Battalion was dispatched over the top to conduct a raid against an enemy strongpoint. With a bold stroke, the storm detachment attacked Hill 228, which had been captured by the Soviets during their offensive with hand grenades, and wrested its control from a Red Army unit.

The unit's war diary states: 'The Russians turned back the first attempt, then successfully fought off the second thrust. The third attempt, this time spearheaded by a flame-thrower team and by assault infantry launching hand grenades forced the situation and caused the Russians to retreat from their position'.[27]

Subsequently, the platoon faced the enemy's attempt to retake the position, but by firing the machine guns at close range, it was able to repel the Soviets. The next day, the platoon retreated back to the Italian lines by handling over Hill 228 to the 1st Battalion of the 54th Infantry. The action had improved the frontline positions of the Axis with the capture of an important post overlooking the plains. During the operation, Blackshirt Vittorio Ferri distinguished himself for lunging alone against an enemy platoon with hand grenades and forcing it to flee. For his actions, he was awarded a Silver Medal of Military Valour. A few months later, Ferri was captured by the Red Army and would later die in a Soviet prisoner camp in 1945 of disease and malnutrition.

On 30 August, the Soviets attacked Hill 228 in large numbers once again. Promptly, *Console* Mittica dispatched an entire company of LXIII Battalion to provide support to the infantry. The unit counterattacked the Red Army infantry and temporarily pushed it back by capturing several prisoners and several automatic weapons. But unabated, the Russians stormed forward again and completely surrounded the position. Despite the enemy pressure, the Blackshirts and the infantry soldiers managed to hold out for more than a day. Then, on 31 August, the *alpini* of the Tridentina and Vestone lifted the siege and forced the Russians to retreat.

On 2 September, the CCNN M 3 Gennaio was withdrawn from the frontline for some much-needed rest and transferred to the rear as a reserve unit of the Sforzesca.

By then, the frontline positions of the Sforzesca had been consolidated in the new line, which was further back from the bank of the river. The soldiers had built several machine gun emplacements on the hills with commanding views of the battlefield rendering their overall deployment much more advantageous with respect to the earlier advanced positions. These positions also were more easily defendable from an armoured attack.

After the conclusion of the First Battle of the Don River, the Soviet Army continued to exert pressure against the Italian frontline troops. On 11 September, the 127th Infantry Division (I and II Battalions of the 555th Infantry Regiment) covered by the thick morning fog attacked the Deresowka area (specifically Hill 158 on the western side of the Verkhnij Mamon bridgehead), which was defended by the Cosseria Division.

With a bold attack, the Soviet troops irrupted with great force into the Italian positions capturing a number of machine-gun strongpoints.

The next day, south-east of Verkhnij Mamon, the enemy with two battalions of the 412th Infantry Regiment attempted to cross the Don River. The main thrust was concentrated against the Kusmenkin islet, while a secondary attempt aimed at occupying the town of Svinjuka. The former was nullified by the concentrated fire of the Italian artillery, while the latter was successful as the Soviet forces erupted by surprise into the Italian positions from a heavily wooded area. They managed to capture several soldiers and two machine guns.

Since the Soviet Army had gained another important foothold in the Verkhnij Mamon area, on 12 September, the command of Ravenna Division opted to forcefully counterattack Svinjuka in order to clear it of any enemy presence. The entire force of the CCNN M 23 Marzo Group of the Valle Scrivia and Leonessa subdivided into two tactical groups, and some infantry units of the Ravenna were to take part in this dangerous operation that was led by the Blackshirt Lieutenant General Enrico Francisci. Both units had distinguished themselves in Greece, but it was now their turn to take part in an important operation on Russian soil.

On that day, the two groups were organised as follows:

Valle Scrivia: *Console* Mario Bertoni
-V Assault Battalion.
-XXXIV Assault Battalion.
-One mortar company, with six 81-mm units.
-XLI Heavy Weapons Artillery Battalion.

Leonessa: *Console* Graziano Sardu
-XIV Assault Battalion.
-XV Assault Battalion.
-One mortar company, with six 81-mm units.
-XXXVIII Heavy Weapons Artillery Battalion.

After a brief but very violent artillery barrage lasting from 6:15 a.m. to 6:30 a.m., which opened up the way for the infantry battalions, the assault began with the launch of hand grenades toward the enemy positions. Hundreds of smoke and explosive grenades landed on the Russian-held positions causing widespread havoc among the ranks of the Red Army units. Blinding the enemy machine-gun units and destroying parapets and dug in rifle positions, the bombs initially paralysed the enemy impeding his reaction. Once inside the trenches, the assaulting troops began to exchange fire with the enemy, and after a brief struggle where the Russians attempted to resist with the aid of their rifles and automatic weapons, they managed to take the position. The assault units then continued their advance, but after having bypassed a heavily wooded area, they were mercifully targeted by Russian mortars of all sizes and forced to momentarily halt their operation. The enemy blocking fire caused several casualties, but it ultimately did not deter the assault units from continuing their advance. Half an hour later, the two main tactical groups had converged on Svinjuka, attacking the enemy from both flanks. The latter, invested by hand grenade and machine-gun fire, fled to the other side of the river with boats and other small crafts, while some soldiers swam to avoid getting captured. By 8 a.m., the position had been retaken and it was later occupied by units of the Ravenna.

In a letter to his wife, soldier of the Valle Scrivia Roberto Maluberti wrote of the attack that was carried out by his unit on 12 September 1942, which saw the M Battalions Group seize important enemy positions:

> It's now a time of peace and quiet for our unit. Today we paraded and greeted party secretary Vidussoni who paid us a visit. As you well know up until recently Ovada Bruni's brother was part of my V Assault Battalion of the Valle Scrivia. He died while fighting during the same operation that I participated to. He was hit by mortar shrapnel and he died a few minutes later. He died as a hero and demonstrating a high spirit of sacrifice.[28]

Upon completion of this bold stroke, Commander of the Ravenna Edgardo Nebbia congratulated *Console* Francisci's Blackshirts by issuing the following report:

> The meticulously prepared and executed action by three CC.NN battalions achieved its objective. Your troops, with a bold counter, regained full possession of the right bank of the Don River clearing it of any enemy presence. Once again, the M Battalions combativeness won the day. I am proud to have under my command these battalions and I am grateful for your directions and command during the operation.[29]

Thus, the first major operation of the CCNN 23 Marzo M Battalion Group in Russian territory had achieved success by pushing back the dangerous enemy infiltration. These troops were some of the most experienced and well-trained M Battalions units, having fought well in Greece and were now fighting equally effectively against the Soviets. The Blackshirt losses, mainly from the Valle Scrivia, were as follows: fourteen dead and fifty-two wounded. The Leonessa had also sustained losses, but the exact number is unknown.[30]

Although the action in the Svinjuka area was successful, the commander of the II Army Corps General Zangheri lamented the loss of too many soldiers during the two days of heavy fighting on 11–12 September, which totalled thirty-nine officers and 639 soldiers. This prompted General Francisci to issue a post-battle report, the focus of which was a supplemental lesson on tactics. His focus was on the fact that although the Blackshirts had fought with tremendous impetus, at times the offensive action had been disjointed, leading to excessive casualties. Francisci argued:

> Each platoon cannot be constituted by elements from other platoons and this principle applies also to larger units. Excessive commingling amongst soldiers of different units must be avoided at all costs. When this happens during the course of the battle, officers must put an end to it as soon as possible.... The rifle, reconnaissance and mortar platoons all belong to the same unit, but have divergent roles to play during the deployment.[31]

On 28 September at Gorbatov, Commander of Army Group B Field Marshal Maxmilian von Weichs bestowed forty Iron Crosses to the defenders of Hill 232.2, two-thirds of which were awarded to the Blackshirts of the Tagliamento. While handing out the Iron Crosses, General Kurt von Tippelskirch stated:

> The fierce resistance of the Italian troops deployed in battle and operating wholly by themselves has not only frustrated the enemy's attempts to achieve a breakthrough of the defensive line, but has also nullified its secondary intent to attract additional Axis forces to the area at the expense of the Stalingrad garrison. I thank you on behalf of the German Army and all German comrades deployed at Stalingrad for your tenacity and fighting spirit.[32]

During the same ceremony, Italian General Italo Gariboldi, who had assumed overall command of the 8th Army, awarded the Tagliamento with a Gold Medal of Military Valour with the following motivation:

> They were assigned to a supporting position in a strategically important sector, responding to the first alert, they jumped in unison against the Bolshevik columns which were trying to make ground on the right bank of the River Don and, after savage fighting, stopped the advance. Subsequently, after being surrounded, they bravely resisted for several days, suffering heavy losses and deaths. While ammunition was running out, the survivors would break out of the enemy siege using hand grenades; they broke the enemy's line and they reunited with the other Italian combatants in the nearby positions with unaltered attacking spirit and untamed desire for revenge. Russian Front (Mius-Jwanowka River, River Don, 12 July–15 August 1942).[33]

For the leadership capabilities shown during the battle, Silvio Margini of the Tagliamento's LXXIX Battalion was bestowed a Silver Medal of Military Valour with the following motivation:

> During six days of fierce struggle this Blackshirt battalion commander showed great expertise and exceptional leadership. In the midst of the fighting, he was a great animator leading his men in overcoming a particularly difficult predicament. He later led them in overwhelming the attacking enemy even though in the prevailing forces and forming with his men an insurmountable defence.[34]

General Messe underlined how his troops had saved the Axis offensive and how the supply line to Stalingrad had been preserved:

> For twelve days these same troops, deployed on the Don in contact with the German 6th Army, have been fighting heroically and bloodily to bar the way against Bolshevik hordes which, to the tune of three divisions of twenty-seven battalions, have hurled themselves savagely on the sector held by only one of our divisions, of six battalions, seriously threatening the supply line of the 6th Army itself, extending to Stalingrad. But they have not broken through.[35]

According to General Messe, the LXXIX Battalion was the unit primarily responsible for saving the day on 20 August. Its resistance prevented a rout and the outflanking of the defensive line:

> The LXXIX Battalion was deployed during the afternoon on the extreme right flank of the Sforzesca Division frontline. It had been charged with constituting a new line of defence and strongpoint. From the onset and even before it had reached its position, the Battalion faced numerous enemy attempts aimed at preventing it from reaching the positions. Most enemy attempts came from Hill 232.2 and the enemy pressure came head on as well as from the flanks.
>
> Strongly tested by the enemy's relentless push, the soldiers of the Tagliamento firmly held on to their positions and prevented the Soviet infantry from outflanking from the right the Sforzesca Division. At night-time the Battalion was able to pull back.[36]

After the Soviets had put forth the first major assault against the Don positions between 20 and 26 August, the front stabilised. As historian Giusti asserts, the Soviet Army had achieved very little with its first major offensive of the Don River:

> When the first Don offensive ended the Soviets had managed to occupy some important bridgeheads on the right side of the river that represented jumping off platforms for their much anticipated winter offensive. But the Red Army had achieved little else and had sustained huge losses.[36]

The Axis defences had held and as a result the German High Command continued to focus on the drive to Stalingrad at the expense of the beefing up of the defensive positions flanking the 6th Army. However, while the German intelligence services maintained that with regards to the Don River the 'Soviet units were all under strength,' the Soviet High Command continued to build up its forces in the Don/Caucasus front.[37] In September 1942 in the Southern sector, there were 188 German infantry divisions and seventy-five Axis allies divisions (ten of which were Italian), which were deployed in an area between the Don River to the north and the Caucasus to the south. In contrast, the Soviet Army deployed 339 infantry divisions, 143 infantry brigades, twenty-nine cavalry divisions, 138 armoured brigades, two anti-tank brigades, and held sixty infantry divisions in reserve. The Italian High Command of the ARMIR like the Germans was also under the delusion that the Soviet Army did not have the resources in the southern sector to complete a major operation. In fact, on 6 September, General Gariboldi wrote: 'The enemy does not have forces deployed in the rear area zone, but since their numbers are small, they are good only for supporting offensives'.[38]

Thus the seeds of disaster of the winter offensive had thus already been sown by wrongful and inaccurate intelligence. The German command had argued that the retreat had been caused by the lack of effectiveness in defence of the Sforzesca Division. However, it was clear that the Sforzesca's positions had been denuded of any armoured or motorised anti-tank German reserve units, even though they had been attacked by a much greater force. In addition, without the support of mobile artillery its troops could hardly have opposed a more significant armoured attack. If such conditions persevered, all the Soviets had to do was to retry the attack with greater deployments of men and tanks to achieve a breakthrough. The stage was thus set for the winter offensive which along with the Battle of Stalingrad would represent the true turning point in the east.

Meanwhile, on 6 September 1942, the *Luogotenente Generale della Milizia* Galbiati paid a visit to the frontline troops. After having visited the veterans of the Tagliamento as well as the newly arrived Blackshirt units, the impressions gathered were that 'the morale of both the Blackshirts and the *Bersaglieri* was high'.[39]

But he also observed that the Italian troops were being deployed primarily in a secondary front and mainly to cover the flank of the German 6th Army and were responsible, for the most part, for the defensive. He also observed that the *alpini* were being deployed as line infantry and that these units could be better utilised in the mountainous regions. In conclusion, Galbiati urged *Comando Supremo* to make better use of these troops by utilising them in more offensive-minded operations.

Operation Little Saturn

On 12 September, the German 6th Army under the leadership of General Friedrich von Paulus had arrived near Stalingrad. Shortly thereafter, the Germans began to siege the city with heavy artillery, tanks, and Stuka bombers. In order to support the drive into Stalingrad, General Maximilian von Weichs, as commander of Army Group B, began to transfer some of his rear troops from the Don River area to Stalingrad in order to support the 6th Army push against the Soviet city. As a result, the rearguard of the Axis frontline flanking Stalingrad was further depleted, especially along the Don River.

The fight for Stalingrad drew progressively more and more German troops as the Soviet Army put up such fierce resistance that by November the battle had come to a complete standstill. 'In a bold and unexpected move on 19 November, the Soviet command, realising that the enemy over extended with fragile supply lines, seized the strategic initiative against the German and satellite forces of Army Group B by launching a major offensive, Operation Uranus, to relieve Stalingrad'.[40]

This offensive shred to pieces the Romanian forces deployed to the left of Stalingrad and trapped the German 6th Army in a vice. The Romanians lines had been destroyed by a Russian force comprised by 1,500 tanks mostly T-34 and KV-1, and by a massive artillery barrage that preceded the tank attack. As Mike Syron and Peter McCarty assert:

> The operation wasn't a particularly risky one nor did the Russians suffer particularly heavy casualties, as they would have done if they'd encountered Germans instead of Romanians. The most striking thing about the operation was the way the Russians had used armour to effect deep penetrations, as the Germans had done in the great encirclement battles of the previous year.[41]

The Romanians had not fled from the battlefield or fought poorly, they had just been outgunned and outmatched by vastly superior Soviet firepower. In the words of the authoritative *West Point History of World War II*, the Romanian Army just like the German, Hungarian, and Italian armies deployed on the Don River comprised an 'ill-equipped infantry army, useful for little more than positional defense'.[42]

These were troops that had little or none armoured support and few effective anti-tank guns to stop the medium- and large-sized Russian tanks. Their mobility was further hampered by the lack of armoured vehicles and tractor trailer mounted artillery that could be used to push back enemy armoured infiltrations.

Ultimately, their infantry fighting with light weapons had been steamrolled by the Soviet tanks. It is likely, however, according to the *West Point History of World*

War II that a force of 200 German tanks and self-propelled anti-tank units held in the reserve could have stopped the enemy attack and repelled the Soviet deep penetration. Thus this operation by the Russians should have been a wakeup call for the Axis forces, but as we will see with the Russian offensive against the Italians and the Hungarians little was done to bolster their positions.[43]

After having attacked in force the Romanian Army positions between 19 and 21 November 1942 and surrounded the German 6th Army at Stalingrad, the Soviet Army began to plan another large-scale attack against the Italians and the German forces deployed on the Don River. The intent was to repeat what had been done against the Romanians with the ultimate objective of further surrounding the German 6th Army at Stalingrad. This operation, if successful, could in fact further isolate the 6th Army, while allowing the Red Army to completely envelop the Axis forces on the Don. The plan, codenamed Operation Little Saturn, was inspired by the pre-war deep battle principles, and it was drafted by General Alexandr Vasilevsky, the mastermind behind all Soviet offences of the war, and his staff of the Soviet High Command. The plan was to implement a combined arms operation where for the second time the Soviet Army would co-ordinate the deployment of large numbers of tanks to fight alongside specialised infantry units. The overall aim was to effectuate a deep penetration of the Italian sector defences, which, like the Romanians, had little tank and motorised support. It was believed that once the penetration had been achieved, the armoured units could attack the rear defences and destroy the main field artillery batteries, trap large groups of both German and Italian infantry forces, and recapture Rostov. To achieve a breakthrough, the Soviet amassed a massive force consisting of the 1st Red Guard Army (ten infantry divisions and four motorised brigades with 533 tanks), the 3rd Red Guard Army (ten infantry divisions and four motorised brigades with 212 tanks), and the 1st Tank Army (with 254 tanks). Not counting the reserve units, with regards to the forces deployed by the Italian 8th Army, the Soviets enjoyed an overwhelming advantage in both men and weapons. The Soviets in fact could count upon 300,000 infantry soldiers while the Italians had approximately 150,000 deployed on the line. The Italians had only fifty tanks (with an additional sixty-five German tanks in reserve) and less than 150 anti-tank guns and approximately 600 artillery pieces, while the Russians had a sevent to one advantage in artillery and a ten to one advantage in armour. As Forczyk asserts: 'None of the Italian armoured fighting vehicles had a chance against the T-34, nor did the primary tank gun, the 47mm, offer an effective defence against Soviet armour'.[44]

The defensive positions along the Don River in mid-December 1942 were held as follows: the German 6th Army surrounded Stalingrad, while the Romanian Army was deployed to the left of the Germans; and the Italians and then the Hungarians held positions to the left of the Romanians—this last unit had been badly mauled by the enemy offensive of November and had lost most of its artillery pieces.

Organisation of ARMIR within Army Group B, 15 November 1942:

Army Group B—Colonel-General Maximilian von Weichs
Italian 8th Army—Army General Italo Gariboldi
-*Alpini* Corps (2nd Tridentina, 3rd Julia, 4th Cuneense *Alpini* Divisions).
-II Army Corps (Cosseria, Ravenna Infantry Divisions, 318th German Infantry Regiment, *Raggruppamento* CCNN M 23 Marzo).
-XXXV Army Corps (Pasubio Division, 298th German Infantry Regiment, *Raggruppamento* CCNN M 3 Gennaio).
-XXIX Army Corps (Torino, Celere, Sforzesca Divisions, 62nd German Infantry Division, 71st Reconnaissance Air Group, 22nd Fighter Air Group).

The central staff of the German 6th Army was clearly aware of the lack of anti-tank firepower within the strongholds held by the ARMIR, but few provisions were taken to strengthen them prior to the mass attack.

> It is also clear that at headquarters of Army Group B and the Sixth Army the danger of a Soviet breakthrough in the sector of the Romanian Third Army and the Italian Eight Army was recognised, and that the Chief of Staff of the Sixth Army even reckoned with the possibility of a temporary encirclement of his army during the winter. However, the countermeasures proposed by these commands did not go beyond tactical measures to strengthen the Romanian Third and Fourth armies.[45]

The only German support unit that was held in reserve to the 8th Army was the 27th Panzer Division, which comprised an armoured unit of sixty-five tanks, two *Panzergrenadier* battalions, and two artillery battalions. The German tanks included some light and some medium units. It is estimated that there were only ten Panzer IIIL/M and five panzer IVG units that were a real match to the Russian T-34.

Thus, the fate of Germany's Axis allies was practically sealed in the summer of 1942 when these armies were tasked with taking up advanced very wide defensive positions on the Don River, while having no armoured support and weak anti-tank weapons. At the time, there were two divergent opinions within the Axis.

> The reduced combat power of the German forces at Stalingrad, as well as the precarious operational and logistic situation of the Sixth Army and the Fourth Panzer Army, should have demanded a timely withdrawal of these armies as well as the Romanian Third and Fourth armies to a much shorter and strength-saving position. In the autumn of 1942 important senior officers were in agreement about this and such an assessment is also the majority opinion expressed in the literature.[46]

Unfortunately, this was only the opinion of the German frontline commander and also of the Italian Commander Messe, but this position was not shared by the German High Command (or by Hitler), which still maintained that the Axis forces could reach the Caucasus oil fields by the spring of 1943. In contrast, in Hitler's view, the oil fields could only be reached from the advanced Axis positions on the Don River and after Stalingrad had been captured.

Regarding General Messe, British historian Paddy Griffith has argued that he 'had enjoyed an excellent combat record on the Russian front and was arguably the one man who might have averted Axis defeat at Stalingrad if only he had been maintained in his command there'.[47]

Messe had maintained in the summer of 1942 that the Axis position in Stalingrad and at the Don was too exposed especially in light of the coming of the Russian winter and because of the massive reinforcements that the Russians were dispatching to prop up their position. He had advocated for a phased withdrawal by the Axis forces behind more solid positions much further behind the Don River.

Ideally, the Axis forces would have taken positions on the hills behind the river, which by commanding the high ground gave the defenders greater freedom of action in holding off large masses of enemy soldiers or tanks. Instead, the defeat of the Axis forces during Operation Little Saturn, which was caused in part by the German directive urging the ARMIR of holding defensive positions that were very advanced and very close to the banks of the river, together with the encirclement of the German 6th Army at Stalingrad, determined a major turning point in the war. In the words of historian Magenheimer: 'In view of the loss of four allies armies, of 21 German divisions at Stalingrad, and the extremely high material losses in the fighting during the retreat, it is fair to claim that the devastating defeat of the German southern flank in 1942–43 was the turn of the war in the East'.[48]

The ARMIR occupied 220 miles along the river, subdivided into two tactical groups. The southern wing, closest to the German forces, included five Italian divisions beginning with the Sforzesca on the left, followed by the Celere, Torino, Pasubio, Ravenna, and the Cosseria. The northern group included the Cuneense, Julia, Vicenza, and Tridentina Divisions. To the left of these forces was positioned the Hungarian Army. The 27th German Armoured Division, with a much-reduced force of approximately sixty-five tanks, since the bulk had been dispatched to bolster Stalingrad, was deployed behind the ARMIR to be used in counterattacks or to prop up the infantry where the enemy pressure was greatest. This unit was supported by fifty light Italian tanks of the Celere Division. The *Raggruppamento* CCNN 3 Gennaio was deployed as a reserve to the Pasubio Division. It was initially held in the rear and its main objective was to intervene to either bolster the standard infantry positions or once the enemy had opened any gaps in the defences of the Pasubio. In November, the Blackshirts were deployed as follows:

the command of the group was headquartered at Liptschanska, the Tagliamento was assembled at Getreide, while the Montebello was split up into three groups; XXX Battalion was at Poltawka, VI Battalion was at Djatschenskoje, while XII Artillery Battalion was in the rear of Poltawka.

The other major M Battalions Group, the *Raggruppamento* CCNN M 23 Marzo, was deployed as a tactical reserve of the Ravenna Division, which was defending the Axis frontline against the second major bridgehead held by the Soviet Army at Verkhnij Mamon.

Its units were deployed as follows; the Command Platoon of *Raggruppamento* CCNN M 23 Marzo was headquartered at Winogradowka, the command platoon of Valle Scrivia and of XLI Assault Battalion, along with V Assault Battalion, were headquartered at Gadjutschje.

XXXIV Assault Battalion of the Valle Scrivia was stationed at Dubowikoff, while the command platoon of the Leonessa and of XXXVIII Battalion were positioned at Podoroshnyj along with XIV Assault Battalion. Meanwhile, XV Assault Battalion of the Leonessa was stationed at Zapkowo.

While taking possession of their assigned positions, the Blackshirt units were split into four main tactical groups, each of which was required to prepare entrenched positions while also occupying a few Russian izbas used as kitchens, temporary field hospitals, and all the other support units.

At the same time, they had carried out other projects, such as the construction of machine-gun and artillery emplacements and also began construction of secondary lines of defence. At night, the troops were instructed to fire their weapons at least twice in order to keep up with their training as well as to prevent the machine guns and the rifles from jamming due to the excessively cold weather.

By November 1942, several large German infantry units, which originally were to serve as a reserve force to the ARMIR, were redeployed near Stalingrad after the Russians had attacked both the Romanians and the Germans there deployed. Thus there were very few reserves to shift in the effected sector in case of an enemy breakthrough and few tanks to be used in a potential counterattack. Despite this predicament, Italian generals continued to be optimistic on the likelihood of successfully fighting off a Soviet attack against the Don. General Giovanni Zangheri of the II Army Corps, for example, sent a circular to his units stating:

> Today we are in a much better situation than the one in which we achieved the brilliant successes of August and September … there is no reason to worry: resist to the end and you will surely be liberated. Do not take a step backward, for Italian and allied reserves are assembling behind the lines to guarantee victory.[49]

The frontline soldiers were to hold fast at all costs by direct order by Hitler issued on 14 October 1942. Given this order, no provisions were made for an eventual phased withdrawal or a retreat to a more manageable rear position.

The Pasubio occupied positions on the Don that were 30 miles in length in the area of Radtschenskoje–Liptschanka. Although thinly held, the positions were beefed up by a powerful artillery force comprised of twelve light-, twenty-one medium-, and six large-calibre guns. In late November, the Italian divisional commanders were of the opinion that an enemy attack was imminent especially because the Russians were slowly building up their forces on the opposite side of the river. After having surrounded the German 6th Army at Stalingrad, the Russians were believed to be ready to attempt to breech the Italian positions on the Don River.

In anticipation of a Soviet attack, frontline positions were hardened even further. A first defensive line was constructed very close to the river and it consisted mainly of a huge anti-tank minefield, although by the time of the Soviet attack in December, the minefield had not been fully completed. The second line of defence consisted of a deep anti-tank ditch excavated along the edge of the minefield. The third line consisted of ample barbed-wire works and behind it a series of bunkers, gun emplacements, observation posts, and machine-gun strongpoints. Each regiment held one battalion along advanced positions on the edge of the river while the two other remaining battalions were positioned along a parallel line situated 500 meters behind. The troops here were thus concentrated into the strongpoints that dotted the defensive line. These troops were to defend their positions and stay put whatever the consequences until the German armoured units could rally a force and come to their aid.

Given that some battalions were held in reserve and some comprised the defences manned by the artillery and rear defences, on the frontline 'the medium density on the Don was of approximately one soldier for every seven meters of frontline. This deployment was insufficient to provide a proper defence or to repulse large scale attacks'.[50]

The most worrisome aspect of the defensive deployment of the ARMIR was not the thinly held infantry strongpoints, but the lack of an effective number of anti-tank guns that could muster the necessary firepower to stop a major enemy armoured attack. Since the outset of the campaign, the Italians had indeed faced Russian armoured units, but the latter had been deployed primarily as a support to infantry. In most prior battlefield engagements, small to mid-sized tank units had attacked their positions with the infantry, but the total number of tanks in each prior battle did not exceed 100–150 units. This time, the Soviet High Command was to deploy their armoured units in a very different fashion. By the fall of 1942, the Soviets were tactically more advanced and were using new methods of co-ordinating tank and infantry action. The emphasis was now placed on bringing all available firepower to bear simultaneously against the weakest and most under strength positions of the enemy. The concentration of firepower was to serve a dual purpose: wear down the enemy with heavy artillery and then breakthrough his positions with the use of large tank formations supported by infantry. The former was to establish new tactics guided by new principles. Long-winded First World War-type barrages were considered ineffective and only served to warn the enemy of an impending attack. The barrage's main purpose was now meant to neutralise the enemy while the infantry moved forward with quick but extremely concentrated artillery fire. The barrage would also serve as a screen against likely enemy counterattacks. Once the infantry had arrived at the enemy positions, the artillery was to exercise a highly mobile control of artillery fire. During this phase, self-propelled and truck-mounted guns were to be used to knock out enemy anti-tank guns.

The infantry was to deploy specially trained shock troops consisting of heavily armed special brigades. These troops were heavily armed by increasing their basic allowance of mortars, machine guns, and anti-tank rifles. One of the great innovations, for example, was the concentration, or the massed use, of mortars and anti-tank rifles to eliminate the anti-tank defence. The tanks were to transport heavily armed shock troops and sappers that were expected to go into action ahead of the tanks to disable minefields and knock out enemy guns. The tanks were to follow in their wake and steam roll the enemy defensive line.

In order to parry the blow, the ARMIR High Command in November 1942 had issued guidelines for the anti-tank defence, which originally derived from German field manuals:

> Since the success of the anti-tank defence is anchored primarily upon the effectiveness and the willingness to fight of the frontline units, special care must be taken to train especially the servers of the gun units. In fact, the most important factor in order to halt a mass tank attack is the flanking fire of the anti-tank units. Another factor is the constitution of special engineer units that can engage enemy tanks at a close combat range using mines and hand grenades. On the other hand, standard infantry units should not panic but stay in their trenches and engage the enemy infantry after the tanks have bypassed them. Although the latter shall focus upon the Soviet infantry, they can also contribute to the anti-tank defence by knowing how to identify different types of enemy tanks and their vulnerabilities and use crew served weapons to fire at the turret and other embrasures of the tank.[51]

Between 12 and 14 December, the Soviets began to shell both day and night the Italian positions, especially its weakest points, the positions held by the overstretched and under strength troops of the old CSIR (Pasubio, Cosseria, and Ravenna infantry divisions). At 8 a.m. on 16 December, the Soviet artillery began a massive artillery preparation that lasted for approximately ninety minutes.

After the barrage, the Soviet infantry accompanied by a large deployment of tanks and, supported above by the air force, attacked in large numbers. The Soviets were aided by the winter conditions, -40 degrees, which allowed the tanks and the troops to pass the frozen Don River with little or no losses. Once passed the river, the Russian forces attempted to capture the high ground, the hills located behind near the bank of the river. By occupying these positions, the Soviets could then fire upon their enemy from above and from behind creating great confusion among the ranks of the Italian infantry.

Initially, the Italian positions held, and despite countless attacks, the Russians were repulsed with heavy casualties. But with time the Soviets began to amass even more troops and the *coup de grâce* was delivered on 17 December when the defensive positions of the Ravenna and Cosseria Division were overrun by tanks and infantry.

According to Russian records of the operation, the Italian infantry fought effectively against an overwhelming enemy force, which made great use of the armoured formations that broke through, surrounded and then levelled the machine-gun and anti-tank guns strongpoints. Once the initial breakthrough had been achieved, the Soviets deployed their armoured reserves and it is estimated that on 18 December approximately 1,000 tanks were concentrated upon the positions held by the Ravenna and Cosseria Divisions. The former, for example, was broken in two sectors and it was completely annihilated.

The Soviets after having encircled the positions held by the Cosseria, Ravenna, and Pasubio Divisions forced them to a hasty retreat to avoid capture. As Forczyk asserts: 'Yet while tough, the Italian defences were thin in depth and once the Soviet Armour achieved a breakthrough, there was nothing left to stop them'.[52]

During this phase of the battle, large losses were sustained as the infantry divisions were forced to abandon their heavy weapons due to the lack of trucks and tractor trailers. As a result, without the anti-tank guns to defend against Russian tank units or strong German armoured units in the reserve, the Italians suffered tremendously every time the tanks came barrelling their way through. Moreover, as the Russians advanced past the defensive positions, they penetrated deep in the rear of the Italian main command centres disrupting the latter's logistic and communication bases and forcing them to abandon some of the heavy calibre guns. The Ravenna Division, for example, by 17 December consisted in a mass of disorganised soldiers attempting to retreat. As its commander asserted: '… by 18 December I no longer had control of my troops'.[53]

Another commander, Major Dario Tolloi, of the 8th Army headquarters' staff, recalled:

> On December 16 the Soviet troops crashed into the Italian line. On December 17 the front fell to pieces, and on December 18 the ring closed south of Boguchar, securely tightened by forces operating from the west and east. Many

> of the staffs lost contact with their troops. Units attacked by tanks tried to save themselves by scattering ... artillery and vehicles were abandoned.[54]

But let us examine the role played by the Blackshirts during the Second Battle of the Don River.

Pasubio Front

The Blackshirt unit of 3 Gennaio was initially held in the rear as a reserve to be used to prop up the defensive positions of the Pasubio Division. The latter was positioned right in the middle of the enemy's main thrust that aimed at overrunning the under strength Italian units, the old units of the CSIR that had been deployed since the outset of the campaign in 1941. The Pasubio was lined up almost in parallel to the enemy positions that also held a bridgehead at Ologew, which bulged into their defences and represented an advanced platform for attacks.

Between 1 and 10 December, the Soviet forces attempted to widen their two major bridgeheads (Ogolew in front of the Pasubio and Verkhnij Mamon in front of the Ravenna) facing the Italian defences located on the opposite side of the Don River. These bridgeheads would then be used on the day of the major

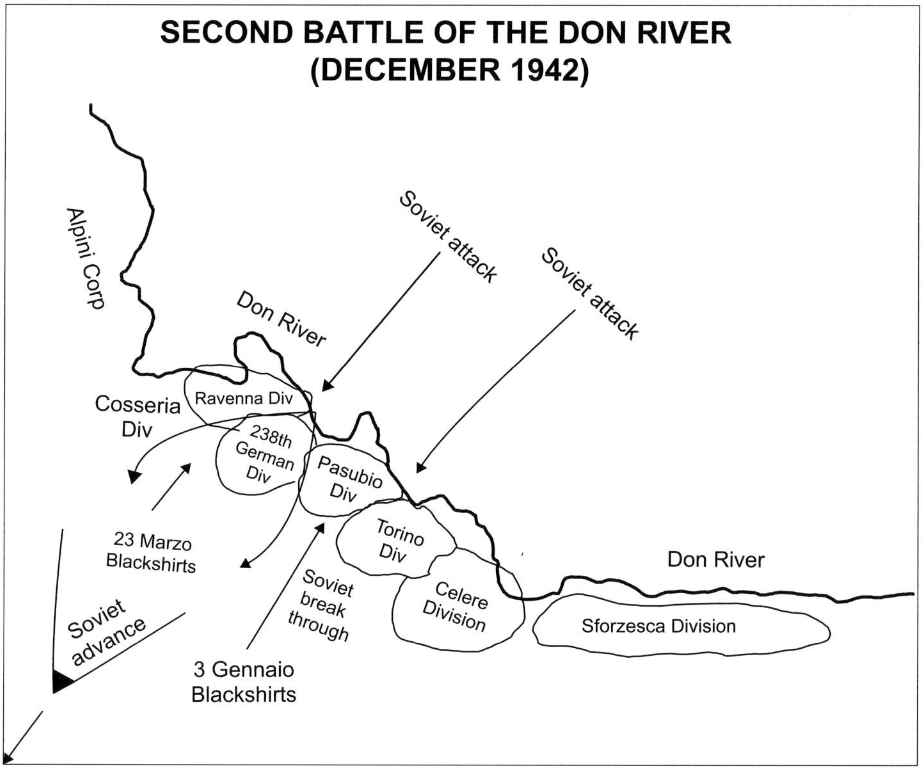

attacks to broaden the grip on the opposite side of the river and to facilitate the advance toward the heights on which some of the main Italian positions were situated. On the morning of 1 December, approximately 500 Russian infantrymen attacked in small groups and without the customary preliminary artillery preparation several positions held by troops of the Pasubio Division. But they were repulsed by the timely intervention of the defenders and elements of the Tagliamento, which counterattacked and inflicted casualties against the enemy.

Lieutenant Pedani of the Tagliamento recalled:

> The Russians had unleashed their great offensive. We figured it out during the early hours when our sentries sounded the alarm warning us that a unit of Siberian guards had managed to infiltrate our positions. We were able to capture an enemy officer and wasted no time to interrogate him. He was carrying a sand bag slung over the shoulder, and with his hair cropped. He warned us that the end was near. The events of the next few days later demonstrated that he was right.[55]

After the enemy had carried out three successive attempts to expand their foothold on the Italian side of the river, the assault units retreated back to their lines and the night was quiet.

During the next few days, the Soviets continued to dispatch aggressive patrols to degrade the adversary's defences in anticipation of the main assault. Most of these attempts were thwarted, however, by the infantry. Despite these early successes in wearing down the enemy attacks, the Italians also suffered casualties from both artillery and infantry fire.

On the 9th, faced by the constant pressure of the Red Army, interim *Console* Vianini, commander of the CCNN M 3 Gennaio (replacing Diamanti who had been injured previously), was instructed by the commander of the Pasubio Division to carry out a preventive strike. The aim of the action was to push back the Russians from the bridgehead and the banks of the river by destroying advanced enemy positions and capture or kill as many enemy soldiers as possible.

During the afternoon of the 9th, Vianini and several of his soldiers conducted the reconnaissance of the enemy positions in preparation for the raid that was to take place the next day. The appearance of the Blackshirts on the frontline was greeted by the soldiers of the Pasubio with considerable enthusiasm and relief. Historically, the standard infantry soldiers disliked the militia because the Blackshirts were volunteers while the former were conscripts. But on that day, *Legionary* Piero Calamai of the Montebello recalls that the soldiers of the Pasubio 'were happy to see us and their officers even went as far as padding us on the back.'[56]

The action was to be carried out by XXX Battalion of the Montebello, a machine-gun platoon, a flamethrower section, and a sappers group from the 79th Infantry of the Pasubio. The following day, the raiding party was deployed on its starting positions as follows: one infantry company was ready to go into action from strongpoint 3, while at strongpoint Z there were stationed the two other companies of XXX Battalion. Under the cover of darkness, at dawn, the troops sallied against the Russians with a surprise attack. Their action was conducted with great speed and the Soviets positions, invested by hundreds of hand grenades, were quickly evacuated by the infantry. While the sappers and flamethrower units blew up the trenches and torched the pillboxes, the assault companies continued to pursue the Russians on the opposite side of the river. By early morning, and despite some losses, XXX Battalion had achieved its objectives and was then withdrawn to the Italian lines having captured twenty prisoners and several weapons. In turn, XXX had suffered twenty-six dead, eighty-four wounded, and twenty affected by frostbite.[57]

The Pasubio Division war diary reports:

> The Blackshirts lunged forward with great impetuosity that the enemy was caught completely by surprise and suffered heavy losses. The sappers and the flame-thrower units destroyed several Russian positions and captured several prisoners by torching the entrances the entrances of their bunkers. The attackers also captured vast amounts of weapons and ammunition.[58]

The preventive strike, however, was not enough to dissuade the Soviet Army from launching its most massive attack of the campaign against the Italian infantry positions. The strike against the Pasubio and the Tagliamento in fact came a few days before the major push which began on 16 December, but it nonetheless saw a massive deployment of troops and materiel. At the battle of Ogolew, the forces of the Pasubio and Tagliamento, dug in hilly terrain, boulders, heavy vegetation, and balkas behind a barbed-wire line and protected by the heavy artillery, repulsed the Red Army infantry waves time and time again. The anti-tank guns together with the divisional artillery were the main bulwark of the defence knocking out several tanks and armoured cars, while the infantry companies fought off the enemy with their rifles and machine guns. When at times the enemy pressure was greatest they counterattacked repeatedly with the aid of the hand grenades.

The massive enemy attack against the Pasubio began on the morning of 11 December when several units of 38th Red Army Guards launched a major assault after two hours of mortar and artillery fire concentrated against the Italian positions near Ogolew, which were held by the 1st Battalion/79th Regiment and 2nd/Battalion 80th Regiment. But the prompt reaction of the Italian artillery and the timely intervention of several Italian and German airplanes, which bombed the starting points of the Soviet infantry, were able to repulse the attack at the onset with losses. At 9 a.m., the Russians, undeterred, attacked again with an even greater force. This time they were able to penetrate into the Ogolew defences and capture several Italian infantrymen. A soldier recalls:

> The first strongpoint to be subjected to heavy enemy pressure was the n. 2 which was on our left flank. We received an urgent message that the defenders of the position urgently needed mortar support to fight off the enemy about to encircle them. Quickly we got the weapons ready and began to fire. The Russians were advancing in large waves and one could see in the distance many soldiers in light yellow uniforms running toward post n. 2. Some were wearing white overcoats that most likely had been taken from our wounded or dead soldiers during prior engagements.
>
> The shells were falling at a very rapid rate on the ground. Each time a small cloud was formed followed by the shell creating a crevice in the snow and then a loud explosion. Once the shell hit the target what remained of the densely packed waves were only huge stains of blood on the snow and bits and pieces of human remains.
>
> The screams of the wounded and of those being hit by our fire were clearly audible from our positions.
>
> God was on our side that day as the Russians, which were still subjected to both machine and mortar fire, were first halted in their tracks and then forced to retreat to their start lines.
>
> Our comrades on the right flank had not been has lucky. Their positions had been overrun by the Soviet infantry attacking in great numbers and the 149mm artillery pieces there deployed could do little to stop them. The Soviets had occupied several positions and had captured Ogolew.[59]

Since some small pockets of resistance behind Ogolew were still fighting back, the commander of the Pasubio decided to deploy the Tagliamento for a quick counterattack to try to attempt to break up the Russian advance. At 10:30 a.m., the Blackshirts went into action led by *Primo Seniore* Mario Rosmini, and after a wild fight with hand grenades and bayonets, they were able to halt the enemy advance and rescue a small unit of the 1st Battalion/79th Regiment that was still fighting even though it had been completely surrounded. The next objective was to retake the town of Ogolew and push further back the Soviets. Accordingly, at 3:30 p.m., the Blackshirts supported by a pinpoint barrage by the Pasubio artillery attacked the town from three directions focusing the bulk of their infantry upon the left flank. Even though pushed back in certain sectors by the strong opposition of the Soviet infantry, the units of the Tagliamento were able to penetrate into the town. What followed was very violent hand-to-hand combat that ultimately led its recapture. Both sides suffered heavy casualties in the fighting. While the ranks of the Tagliamento were slowly thinning out, the Russians had lost many more and forty of their soldiers had been captured. But, most importantly, the loss of such a position earlier in the day had created a huge bulge into the frontline positions held by the Pasubio, which had finally been eliminated by the Blackshirts.

The Blackshirts war diary states:

> In a very violent counterattack the LXIII and the LXXIX battalions of the Tagliamento re-conquered with a bold stroke the town of Ogolew on the Don River.
>
> During the course of the operation Centurion Lupo and his 3rd Company particularly distinguished themselves and the former would later be rewarded with a Silver Medal of Military Valour.
>
> Unfortunately, a strong enemy counterattack executed during the night and on the heels of a heavy barrage allowed the enemy to gain the upper hand and once again take possession of Ogolew.[60]

The Tagliamento war diary reports that despite its loss in the night, the operation to recapture Ogolew was well-executed:

> The operation began at 1350 after a five minutes barrage. It was conducted very rapidly as a surprise raid into the enemy positions. The LXIII Battalion was on the left while the LXXIX was on the right and the supporting weapons were positioned on the so-called X strongpoint. The tactical manoeuvre was executed brilliantly and at 1530 the town was covered with heavy fire. At 1600 it had fallen into Italian hands. The pincer movement along with the speed of the attackers had allowed us to take the position with few casualties while the Russians lost many men, up to one hundred dead, forty prisoners and several automatic rifles.[61]

Undeterred by the losses, at 9 p.m., the Russians attempted once again to storm the town. The attack was once again preceded by a violent artillery barrage. The Russian artillery began to pound Ogolew very heavily to the point that the Blackshirts were forced inside the basements of the balkas to avoid getting killed by the murderous fire. Over 200 guns targeted Ogolew with continuous fire to the point that the Tagliamento, after half an hour of resistance, was forced to evacuate the town or risk the demise of the entire unit. Weakened by the loss of numerous soldiers and now about to face a massive enemy infantry attack, the forces of the Tagliamento were forced to effectuate a phased withdrawal under enemy fire. During the retreat, the Russian mortars continued their pinpoint action and succeeded in harassing the defenders, which suffered additional casualties.

Thus, by the end of the day, the Red Army had recaptured the much contested town. But the fighting for the control of Ogolew and the bridgehead on the western side of the Don River was far from over. Accordingly, on 12 December, the remaining forces of the Tagliamento supported by other Blackshirt units (VI Battalion of the Montebello) and reinforced by a company of combat engineers, a machine-gun, and a flamethrower company were ordered by the commander of the Pasubio to retake the burnt-out remains of Ogolew. After a brief pinpoint barrage, the storm assault units forced a path through the strong enemy defences, overwhelmed the Soviets despite fierce opposition, and captured many prisoners plus several weapons. After having penetrated the town, the same units drove two enemy battalions from the field and liberated the town. By the end of the day, the Tagliamento had lost considerable strength: fifty-nine dead, seventy-six injured, and twenty-four soldiers suffering from severe frostbite, but its success had been clear. The unit's war diary states:

> The barrage was extremely well executed and while the last few shells were about to land upon the Soviet positions the assault units quickly arrived onto the trenches and the remains of the homes where the enemy was shielded. The attack was conducted with speed and decision and the enemy positions were quickly overrun.[62]

Meanwhile, the Montebello was active on the opposite flank and pushed even further than the Tagliamento bypassing Ogolew altogether. Placed under the command of the 79th Infantry Regiment the unit was deployed for a quick counterattack against positions that the enemy had been able to seize at Ogolew and to relieve the pressure upon the troops of the Pasubio. After a quick barrage, the unit swung into action, and after two hours of heavy fighting, mostly with hand grenades and bayonets, it was able to kill more than 200 enemy soldiers in a close-combat confrontation. Some Blackshirt platoons pushed their way so far into the enemy's defences that they were able to cross the Don River and threaten the Russians on their own bank where they captured fifteen enemy soldiers. In turn, the Blackshirts of the Montebello had sustained the following losses: seventeen dead, seventy-eight injured, and twenty-four soldiers suffering from severe frostbite. Regarding the assault carried out by the Montebello units on 12 December, the 8th Army bulletin stated:

> At 0900 the Battalion moved to the attack and, after two hours of violent clashes with bayonets and grenades, it forced the enemy to flee as some *legionaries* reached the bank of Don River. Several prisoners and weapons have been captured from the enemy, who had left 200 dead on the ground.[63]

During the next few days, the forces of the Tagliamento were reorganised at Getreide, the rear hub of the Pasubio Division. But after only two days of quiet, the Russians resumed their attacks against the Pasubio once again, and the Blackshirts had to be quickly redeployed. This time, the Red Army attempted to overtake the strategic positions of Hill 201, which overlooked large swaths of the Don River. These positions at the time of the Russian attack (17 December) were defended by a force comprised by a battalion of the 520th German Infantry Regiment and the Tagliamento. After repulsing three consecutive enemy attacks, these forces went on the counterattack. Despite the Soviet artillery fire, they continued to pursue the enemy in a bold manoeuvre over forests and hills, and recovered some of the advanced positions near Hill 201. In mopping up the enemy positions, they also took a substantial number of prisoners, plus many machine guns and trench mortars.

Meanwhile, the day before, on the opposite flank of the bridgehead, the Montebello group was placed as a tactical reserve of the 80th Infantry of the Roma Division, which was faced with a massive enemy attack involving both armoured and infantry units. The barrage began in earnest at dawn, and it involved over 250 enemy guns. Its effects on the frontline troops were so fierce that many advanced positions had to be evacuated and the line infantry had to be reorganised on the resistance zone. Shortly after the barrage ended, Russian planes began dropping leaflets near the positions held by the Blackshirt, which read: 'Italian soldiers you are surrounded. To all soldiers and officers who surrender we guarantee life, good treatment and your return to your homeland when the war is over'. Then, at 8 a.m., the enemy attacked the Krassnogorowka–Abrossimowo–Monastyrschina front in force with a force comprised of three infantry battalions. By then, the Montebello, which had just arrived on the frontline, was able together with the infantry to check the enemy advance with rapid machine-gun fire. An hour later, the Soviets were back on the attack. Faced by a wide enemy envelopment, the commander of the Roma Division instructed the Montebello to take possession of the south-east flank of Hill 201. On the line the Montebello was flanked on the left by LXXIX Battalion of the Tagliamento and on the right by a small unit of the 80th Infantry. But the positions occupied on Hill 201.1 were completely devoid of any relevant field works or fortifications and the frozen soil prevented any emergency work from being completed. The absence of any real fortification led to casualties from the preceding Russian barrage, which with pinpoint accuracy targeted the Axis troops in their semi-exposed positions. Subsequently, the Soviets rushed these positions but were met by a hail of bullets and hand grenades to the point that they were prevented from advancing further. Thus, despite the lack of firm defences, the Red Army was stopped once again from advancing against Hill 201.1.

Undaunted by the large losses, the enemy resumed the attack in the afternoon of 17 December, but its attacking ardour was checked by the blocking fire of Italian artillery. Throughout the day, the Blackshirts and the infantry were faced by a continuous wave of enemy attacks, which were repelled by equally fierce counterattacks that wore down both contenders. To add to the misery, the very low temperatures on the night of 17–18 December proved fatal for several soldiers, who died of frostbite, some fell on the snow due to fatigue and were never able to get up again. Despite the bitter weather, the enemy continued to come forward in order to infiltrate the Italian lines. These continuous attacks forced the hand of the commander of the Roma, who, not having any reserves left to throw into the fight, in an act of desperation, resorted to dispatching to the frontline a battalion of railway workers of the Genova Division. It was clear that due to a lack of reserves the days of the Italian presence on the bank of the Don River were numbered. At dawn on 18 December, the enemy resumed the initiative by launching a blistering attack with two infantry battalions against Hill 201.1, but the Blackshirts together with the troops of the 520th German Infantry Regiment (298th Division), checked for one more time the enemy advance. To re-establish their lines, the German infantry and the Blackshirts counterattacked several times hurling hand grenades at the enemy. The enemy was also halted by the effective fire of the Italian artillery, which from the rear was able to knock out several enemy guns deployed in advanced and exposed positions in support of the infantry. During the night, several Italian patrols were sent out to reconnaissance the frontline. As soon as they exited the trenches, the Soviet Army attempted to interfere with this action and several clashes between opposing patrol units led to heavy casualties on both sides. At the end of the fighting, the Italian patrols made it back to their positions with some prisoners and a few enemy machine guns.

Ravenna Front

During the Russian offensive, the troops of the second M Battalions Group (*Raggruppamento* CCNN M 23 Marzo) were also deeply involved in the fighting on the second bridgehead on the Don River at Verkhnij Mamon as a tactical reserve in support of the Ravenna and Cosseria Infantry Divisions.

Before the major assault began, the Blackshirts were kept on high alert for several weeks in order to double the efforts to patrol the outer perimeter of their fortifications and trenches to prevent attacks by special enemy paratrooper units.

> With the arrival of winter and the freezing temperatures we must furnish our sentries with heavier clothing and rotate sentries in and out of service more often. We must not however, loosen our overall vigilance of the camps and especially when facing attacks by enemy paratrooper units.[64]

These were to be dealt specifically by *ad hoc* platoons whose dual role 'was to monitor enemy planes that could parachute enemy troops ... and open fire on the enemy especially before paratroopers have landed'.[65]

As the reconnaissance and patrol functions were beefed up considerably in anticipation of a major offensive, special teams were set up to carry out these functions. A reconnaissance platoon comprised of two NCOS and twenty-four *legionaries* was responsible to conduct patrols inside the camp, while a larger platoon of fifty-two *legionaries* was to patrol the outer perimeter of the camp. A special squad of ten *legionaries* was also set up to protect motorised teams bringing in supplies into the camp.

In order to tighten security at the camp, all commanders were ordered to shield crew served weapons from the harsh weather; rotate sentry duties among a larger pool of soldiers; keep a watchful eye on avoiding fires during the night; ensure sentries are dressed appropriately; shorten sentry and patrol duties; detain individuals stopped by sentries; and keep firing against enemy reconnaissance planes throughout the day.[66]

On 9 December, the Soviet artillery began to pound the Italian positions. The following is the testimony of Tullio Filippi, a Blackshirt from the Valle Scrivia XLI Heavy Weapons Battalion:

> The front line was all a succession of flashes, explosions, long snaking lines of tracer bullets, and terrifying thunders. It was an extraordinary scene, frightening, at times it seemed like day, the earth trembled, it seemed the end of everything. The bombing lasted about an hour; then came the calm of before, every noise ceased, the night descended, while the stars shone. And we all went to sleep; only the sentries kept watch.[67]

Based on advanced reconnaissance that indicated that the Soviets were about to attack, on 10 December, the commander of the Ravenna Division moved up the line some units of the Valle Scrivia, mainly XXXIV Assault Battalion, half a company of 81-mm mortars, and half a company of 47/32-mm guns of XLI Heavy Weapons Battalion, which were ordered to move from Dubowikoff and reach Gadjutschje. The frontline positions were held primarily by line infantry battalions of the Ravenna Division and were further supported by medium- to large-sized artillery batteries positioned further back in the rear. On the 11th, the frontline positions held by the Ravenna's 38th Infantry at Krassno Orechowo were heavily targeted by an enemy aerial bombing, which was later followed by an infantry attack put forth by the Soviet 195th Rifle Division. Although the enemy thrust was fierce with the deployment of special shock troops supported by advanced placed machine guns and mortar units that unleashed a torrent of fire on the trenches, the attack eventually bogged down. After an hour of fighting, it came under heavy machine-gun fire and the assault troops were initially forced to ground and they later retreated when darkness descended. At 3 p.m., V Assault Battalion was deployed near Krassno Orechowo to further bolster the 38th Infantry, which at the time was being subjected to small-scale enemy raids and attacks. After having reached the assigned positions, the Blackshirts occupied the forward trenches and set up the machine guns to provide flanking fire from both sides of their high-altitude position. As the Soviet troops attempted to approach them in order to throw hand grenades, they were dispersed by rapid machine-gun fire. Then, when darkness descended, V Battalion was tasked with counterattacking to secure two advanced posts that had been lost earlier in the day. Led by a special team of flamethrowers, which forced the bulk of the enemy troops to evacuate the positions, the Blackshirts erupted with force into the trenches engaging the enemy troops in close combat. As a result of this effort, the 2nd Company recaptured posts 9 and 9A, which were later held throughout the night despite several enemy attempts to dislodge the Italians from these forward positions.

Meanwhile, on the opposite side of the divisional deployment, on the Swinjucha plain, another offensive thrust was put forth by the 412th Riflemen Regiment/1st Soviet Division and by units of the 128th Regiment Riflemen/44th Siberian Division. After a powerful artillery barrage, the units attacked the eastern edge of the Verkhnij Mamon bridgehead with heavily armed platoons armed with automatic guns, small mortars, light, and heavy machine guns. Several attempts were made to reach the Italian positions, but all were thwarted by prompt defensive fire. But despite the inability of the Red Army to take those positions, its infantry had at least achieved one major goal. They had worn down the Italians, forcing them to deploy some of their divisional reserves such as the three remaining Blackshirt groups, one of the Valle Scrivia and two of the Leonessa.

The Russian plan appeared clear aiming essentially at wearing down the defenders until all the reserve forces had been deployed. During the night of 11–12 December, in order to halt any further attacks by the Russians, the Italian artillery units of the Ravenna and the contiguous Cosseria Division shelled the frontline positions of the enemy in an attempt to stifle the attackers and hit them hard near their assembly points. The barrage had its desired effects since the Red Army troops were forced to retreat further back from their start lines. Meanwhile, the temperature during the night had dropped to -24, forcing the soldiers not only to battle against the enemy but also against the weather. Both sides were affected by extremely bitter temperatures and many soldiers suffering from frostbite had to be evacuated to the rear.

At 6 a.m. on 12 December, the Soviets renewed their attacks in the Krassno Orechowo sector, engaging in the struggle the fresh reserve forces of the *Raggruppamento* CCNN M 23 Marzo. Once again, however, the already depleted ranks of V Assault Battalion took the brunt of the Soviet attack since they were charged with holding the most advanced positions 8, 9, 9/A, and 10. In the afternoon, faced with massive Soviet pressure, V Battalion was forced to hastily evacuate two advanced machine-gun positions. But a little later in a swift counterattack, the same unit was able to regain possession of the two positions and retake the two guns. To stem the growing tide of Russian forces, at 7 p.m., the 3rd Company of XXXIV Assault Battalion was also deployed alongside V Battalion, on the Krassno Orechowo ridge. The two units swept the field of battle with flanking machine-gun fire breaking up several enemy attempts to reach their strongpoints. Undeterred, the Russians continued to attack and the fighting raged throughout the night, but at dawn, command of V Battalion was still firmly stationed in Krassno Orechowo, while the other companies still held on to positions 8, 9, 9/A, and 10. It is interesting to note that on 12 December, the Germans still believed that a major offensive against the Italian 8th Army was unlikely. At the time, German General Tippelskirch maintained that the Russian attacks were to be considered as small-scale raids rather than full-scale attacks. Moreover, Tippelskirch asserted that the battle was going well for the Axis since the Italian counterattack was repelled by the Soviets, but only after they had called in all the reserves of the 127th Rifle Division.[68]

On the 13th, the Soviet infantry came forward again against the positions held by the Ravenna and the Cosseria infantry, with the main thrust effectuated by two battalions of the 127th Rifle Division. But this attack was also broken up by the prompt response of the artillery, and by 10 a.m., none of the frontline positions had been ceded to the Russians.

At 11 a.m., the positions held by the 38th Infantry at Krassno Orechowo were subjected to a Soviet mass attack with the deployment of three infantry battalions. Strong fire from trench mortars began half an hour prior to the main assault and shortly thereafter the infantry attacked supported by fire from artillery of all sizes, which blanketed all positions held by the 38th Infantry. Shortly after the preparatory barrage, the Russian shock troops deftly penetrated the main position. The attack was so fierce that the entire V Assault Battalion, including its command platoon, had to be hastily dispatched to parry the blow. The main garrison had taken shelter from the barrage in the dugouts and trenches and did not realise that the Russians were within a few feet of their positions. As soon as they realised that the troops were almost upon them, they opened fire. The remnants of the infantry fought stubbornly, together with the Blackshirt Battalion, which contributed to parry the main blow, seeking to push back the enemy in repeated counterattacks. The infantry were still holding out in the main position, while the determined thrusts of the Blackshirts with hand grenades and bayonets were instrumental in pushing the enemy off the hill position.

Although the unit was successful in repelling the attack, its losses of men and equipment were heavy. The commander of the unit, for instance, was one of those killed along with several *legionaries*.

By midday, heavy fighting was flaring all over the frontline positions held by II Army Corps, forcing the commander General Zanghieri to move further up the line the Leonessa. By this time, all reserve units had been deployed.

Up to that point, the Blackshirts had been deployed in a haphazard fashion by the commander of the Ravenna Division, who had split up the troops often at the company or platoon level and therefore Blackshirts platoons were often deployed side to side with the standard infantry. In order to use these troops more effectively, the commander of the *Raggruppamento* CCNN M 23 Marzo, intervened and forced the commander of the Ravenna Division to assign to the Blackshirts a sector of the frontline to hold by deploying all of its troops on a continuous section of the line. As a result of this intervention, the units were then placed under the command of *Console* Bertoni, the commander of the Valle Scrivia M Battalion Group and tasked with defending a number of contiguous strongholds within the positions held by the Ravenna.

During the night the 3rd Company of XXXIV Assault Battalion was tasked with retaking possession of post 7, which had been lost to the enemy during the morning attack. Despite losing in the action all of its three officers (one died and two were wounded) and half of the *legionaries*, the unit was able to recover the position after attacking it with bayonets and hand grenades. During the operation, the Italian infantry stormed forward five times, but the defenders refused to budge from their positions, while inflicting heavy casualties on their opponents. Finally, on the sixth attempt and while fighting with hand grenades, the Italians managed to wrest post 7 from the Russians. On the same night, the Soviets moved against another key position, Hill 192, which was defended by two battalions of the 90th Infantry. A unit of the Leonessa consisting of the unit's command platoon, XV Assault Battalion, half a company of 81-mm mortars, and half a company of 47/32-mm guns of XXXV Heavy Weapons Battalion promptly intervened. The combined machine-gun and mortar fire of *legionaries* and infantrymen not only preserved the positions of Hill 192, but also caused the enemy huge casualties. In fact, huge gaps in the enemy line were made when the Soviet infantry came forward in great numbers only to be mercilessly targeted by the combination of mortar and machine-gun fire. The Blackshirt unit was then deployed at 8:45 a.m. on the 14th to clear out Hill 192 of any enemy presence and then by rounding up several stragglers.

Already on the morning of 14 December, the unit was called again to defend Hill 192 from successive enemy attacks put forth by two battalions of the 747th Fusiliers Regiment of the 172nd Division. Despite attempting to attack three times, the Italians were able to check the Soviet infantry offensive and remain in possession of the much contested hill.

In the afternoon, the much-depleted frontline troops were finally relieved. Some units of the Leonessa, for instance, were moved from Filoon to Orobinsky, while the V Assault Battalion of the Valle Scrivia had to be withdrawn from the line altogether due to excessive losses.

At 3:30 a.m. on 15 December, a new Soviet attack was able to surround and separate one of the focal centres of the 38th Infantry, thus threatening the meeting point between the Ravenna and the Cosseria. The remnants of these Italian infantry unit fought stubbornly and, together with the Blackshirts, which hurried to the scene, they sought to recover the lost ground in repeated counterattacks. The Russian garrison initially checked these counters while still holding out in the main captured strongpoints. But after several hours of stubborn fighting, they were finally forced to surrender. Both the defenders and the attackers had suffered heavy losses. But while the Russians could deploy more reserves, the Italians at that point had little or no reserves left to deploy.

The war diary of the *Raggruppamento* CCNN M 23 Marzo Group states:

> On the 15th the legionnaires of the Valle Scrivia and of the Leonessa were scattered almost everywhere, fractionated in small platoons throughout the line trying to fend off numerous offensive attempts put forth by the Russians. In order to ward off the numerous attacks, the Blackshirts repeatedly counter-attacked with hand grenades together with their comrades in the infantry units. By night-time the situation was restored and even the much contested Hill 192 was still held by the Axis forces. By this date, the 23 Marzo Group had suffered the loss of 699 men, of whom 39 were officers. The soldiers that were still able to fight were exhausted by the lack of rest and the extremely cold temperatures that were seriously impacting the Soviet units as well, even though they were operating in their own surroundings. The only respite from the cold weather was the time the troops spent resting in the dugouts underground and below the trenches. It was here that they could recuperate their strength, rest and shelter from the cold.[69]

Two days before the start of Operation Little Saturn, General Von Tippelskirch had maintained that according to German field intelligence reports, the Russians were conducting local attacks to tie down Axis forces on the Don and that a major Russian counteroffensive was unlikely because there were not enough troops amassed on the Don to force a major offensive.

On 15 December, Tippelskirch reported that the Italian infantry had counterattacked to recapture lost positions but had suffered heavy losses. He noted 'the Italians were conducting themselves well and were decisively defending at all costs'.[70]

On the morning of 16 December, an unprecedented artillery barrage from both the standpoint of the volume of fire and its duration invested the Italian positions with great force. The barrage from mortars, artillery, rocket launchers, and aircraft lasted from 6 a.m. to 10 a.m., causing widespread losses within the ranks of the Ravenna Division. This was just the preliminary start of the major offensive. Soon after 10 a.m., the Soviet Army came forward in great numbers and each battalion was accompanied by tanks. It is in fact estimated that more than 300 tanks (mostly T-34s) were deployed against the Ravenna positions on that day. The aim of the tanks was to break the defensive line and then manoeuvre into the rear positions in order to capture the main artillery pieces and then the supply depots. It was a deep penetration manoeuvre put forth by armoured units accompanied by special shock troops, and it was something the Italian troops had not experienced before. Even in the first offensive of the Don River during the summer of 1942, the Soviets had come forward in large numbers, but had never before deployed so many tanks and so many aircraft bombing the frontline positions.

Initially, the attack stalled as up to thirty Russian tanks were put out of action either because they crossed minefields or because they were the target of the anti-tank guns. But as the battle wore on, some of the advanced strongpoints were quickly submerged and the few survivors were forced to head backward. The lack of reinforcements made it impossible for any of the Italian officers to react promptly to this unprecedented, large-scale attack by sending in much-needed fresh reserves to plug holes in the defensive perimeter.

By 11 a.m., a full squadron of tanks attacked head on against the positions defended by Ravenna and its Blackshirt reinforcements. Resistance was stubborn even though in certain cases it was futile. A 47/32-mm anti-tank gun unit of XLI Battalion, for instance, fired at close range against several T-34s. But the latter bravely disregarding the fire continued to advance and eventually mowed down the unit including the gun and its three servers who sacrificed their life rather than abandon the position.

In the afternoon, the troops of the *Raggruppamento* CCNN M 23 Marzo, German grenadiers of the 318th, supported by few tanks of the 27th Armoured Division, attempted to restore the frontline positions of the Ravenna. With some of the troops riding on the tanks while others operating German truck-mounted guns, the Axis units fired a barrage of fire against the enemy tanks with all the anti-tank guns, rifles, and *panzerfaust* weapons they could muster. The attack, sudden and hitting the enemy from the flanks, initially achieved the desired result, forcing the Soviet forces into a retreat. However, by night-time, the Soviet forces had already regrouped and were once again being organised for a new foray into the Italian lines.

> The Germans sent an armoured division to help, but they were not close enough to immediately seal the enemy penetration. The German armoured division confronted the Russian 195th Rifle Division, but the Soviets had already set up an anti-tank screen, forcing the German Panzers and their accompanying Italian infantry to break contact.[71]

Frustrated by the lack of substantial progress, the next day, Soviet General Nikolai Vatutin committed three armoured units (17th, 18th, and 25th Tank Corps) to achieve a decisive breakthrough against the Italian II Army Corps.

The Italian defence put forth by both the infantry and the Blackshirts was again stubborn and determined. The two Heavy Weapons Battalions of the *Raggruppamento* CCNN M 23 Marzo, which were bolstered by several German *panzerfausts*, initially held their ground and together with the divisional artillery were able to knock out twenty-one enemy tanks. But in order to achieve the breakthrough, General Vatutin committed all three tank units to the battle and this move finally proved successful. The great number of tanks could not be stopped by the artillery and the frontline positions were first surrounded by the enemy and then subjected to mortar fire. Shortly after, the positions were levelled by the tanks, which in essence smashed their way through the strongholds destroying everything that stood in their way. By late afternoon, some of them had even reached the field artillery positions, forcing many Italian artillery units to abandon their weapons.

In the sector held by the 385th German Division, the resistance lasted until the evening of 17 December. But at 7:30 p.m., General Eibl, cognisant of the fact that his troops had been encircled, ordered his men and the Italian units that were fighting alongside them to retreat west to Mitrofanowka.

With regards to the hard fighting that took place along the frontline sector held by the Ravenna, *Legionary* Roberto Maluberti of the Valle Scrivia recalled:

> For five days we were deployed in the frontline strongpoints which were mercifully targeted by enemy guns and mortars repeatedly to the point that many of our brave comrades fell under this continuous fire. Despite the enemy's best efforts and the virulent way in which we were attacked, we held our positions and inflicted grave losses on the enemy. For five days under snow and ice we fought in very precarious conditions taking only a small break from time to time to eat our food from the storage tins. We had to eat the food in storage because there was no way for us to receive our warm meal from the rear due to the enemy siege. In the meantime the enemy kept coming at us with great force. On the fifth day the enemy even launched the tanks against us but our rifles and machine guns kept the enemy at bay. The trenches were full of cadavers. Our dead were taken away by sleds while our wounded soldiers were treated on the spot. But many had suffered grave injuries and they were also taken by sleds to the rear. Now I can't write to you anymore about this. Hopefully the military intelligence will not censor my letter. What followed after the battle was a march that lasted two months to return to safer positions in the rear. After two months we finally arrived at a safe position. But I will never forget what I experienced. All of us from Serravalle Scrivia have managed to survive the battle, while the *legionaries* from Parma were not as

fortunate. Many of them will not return home. But enough now I don't want to talk about this anymore.[72]

On 16 December, General Von Tippelskirch had recorded in his diary that the Soviets were able to break into the positions held by the Ravenna and Cosseria divisions. The next day, he recorded that a major breakthrough had been achieved by the Russians and mainly by the armoured units.

On the 18th, the Blackshirts together with the standard infantry troops began to retreat. After a prolonged march in the bitter winter weather, the remnants of the Leonessa and the Valle Scivia arrived to the village of Zapkovo, which had already been occupied by the Soviet Army. Here the Blackshirts, intermingled with the German units, were surrounded and took heavy mortar and artillery fire. As the unit's war diary asserts:

> The fight raged on for many hours with hand grenades, rifles and even daggers. The German units thanks to their trucks and their self propelled guns were able to disengage. But they were forced to leave approximately 300 Blackshirts which were not motorised to resist the Russian onslaught. The commander of the Leonessa *Console* Sardu, who had been wounded, was given the chance to be brought to safety by riding on a German tank. But he instead opted to remain with his men stating: 'My place is here until there will be at least one of my Blackshirts that is still fighting.' During the subsequent Soviet attack he was first wounded on one arm and then on the abdomen. He would die shortly thereafter in a field hospital. Only some of the Leonessa soldiers managed to escape the encirclement managing to march west to Mitrofanowka, while the majority died or were captured by the enemy.[73]

By this stage, the Leonessa was reduced to just over 400 men, from the 1,792 who had begun the campaign in the summer of 1942. The Valle Scivia had also suffered casualties but its three battalions could still count upon over 1,000 soldiers. After the remnants of the Blackshirts and the infantry had reached Mitrofanowka, the commander of the II Army Corps dispatched General Martensian to try to reorganise these troops. But after a speedy review of the physical status of the men and a headcount, the latter reported that the physical conditions of most soldiers were extremely poor since they had been fighting non-stop since the beginning of the month and that their morale was also very poor after having retreated back in the cold, bitter weather. In his view, it was not possible at the time to reorganise these troops under smaller companies and platoons.

The situation was made even worse when on the evening of the 19th when the Soviet tanks suddenly irrupted into the assembly point of the Italian units causing widespread havoc with their quick forays. The men were forced to fall further back to the west reaching Woroschilowgrad on 21 December. Here the remnants of the *Raggruppamento* CCNN M 23 Marzo were assembled and deployed along the Donets River in defence of Wesselaja Gora bridge.

At that time, the total number of survivors of the Group consisted of 1,536 soldiers, many of whom were injured or suffered from frostbite. The losses were 1,861 in total. Of these, 125 (of which nineteen officers) were dead, 389 wounded (including twenty-three officers), 1,328 (twenty-six officers) were missing, and nineteen (one officer) were affected by serious frostbite. The missing were, for the most part, considered to be dead, having fallen on the battlefield or fallen to their death during the retreat on foot or captured.

Meanwhile, on the bridgehead held by the Pasubio on 19 December, the units there deployed were still firmly holding on to their positions, but by then they were virtually isolated on both flanks as the Russians had broken through. It was evident that if they remained in their frontline positions, they would be totally encircled by the enemy. Moreover, the weather was once again causing frostbite among the soldiers while the frozen ground had slowed to a halt the motor vehicles.

Regarding the Russian winter, *Legionary* Pietro Calamai recalls:

> We had to wear the so-called three-fourth coats since the heavier leather jackets were still being held in the depot in Verona. We were also wearing helmets wrapped by small blankets for extra protection from the cold since the balaclavas had also been left by the army in Verona. We also had no gloves.... We were forced to be very careful with the rifle holding it on the wooden side only without touching the steel as the skin would stick to it given the bitter temperatures.[74]

As a result, the troops were ordered to withdraw by the commander of XXXV Army Corps. So the troops began to move west on foot trying to escape the fast moving Red Army in temperatures that dropped to -35 degrees centigrade at night. At 4:20 p.m., a long column of soldiers flanked by a few German tanks began to slowly retreat. The front of the column was led by the two assault battalions of the Tagliamento along with LXIII Heavy Weapons Battalion, while the rearguard was comprised of two Blackshirt platoons, which were incessantly attacked by enemy infantry. Both were virtually destroyed by the fast-paced raids of the Soviets, which never relented in the pursuit and their multiple attempts of cutting off large chunks of the Pasubio. To break out of the encirclement, the soldiers continued to march west. During the night, the troops reached the town of Medovo:

> The houses were enflamed having been hit by the enemy artillery and by the incendiary shells of the tanks. We heard that the enemy encirclement was now

> complete and that countless of scattered troops were retreating toward the town. *Consoli* Vianini and Galardo (who at that point had assumed command of the Tagliamento), the latter which had been injured, maintained order in their depleted ranks. Flanking the German self-propelled guns, the infantry troops attacked Popovka where the armour cleared the streets and allowed the column to proceed.[75]

The next day (21 December), the march west was resumed. But after having marched for a further 14 miles west to the town of Arbuzovka, the Axis forces were forced into a corner and thus into the first set-piece battle of the retreat. The engagement lasted two days and saw the Italian infantry together with a number of German self-propelled guns and tanks attempting several times to punch a hole in the Soviet deployment in order to break free. The Red Army had created a *cordon sanitaire* around the town, hoping to capture the entire Axis contingent in one fell swoop. On the first day of battle, the Russian artillery limited itself to pour in tremendous fire into the Axis positions. On the second day of battle, cognisant that their troops could not take another day of heavy pounding by the enemy artillery, the Axis commanders attempted to evade the pincer. At 8 a.m., the German armour led the way, followed closely by 30,000 infantrymen. The armour, though heavily outnumbered, confronted head on the Soviet tanks, while the self-propelled guns concentrated fire against them from the flank.

After knocking several tanks out of action, both the armour and the infantry charged the Russian soldiers and eventually managed to escape. The battle, however successful for the Axis, was very costly. It is estimated that 9,000 men were captured and 7,000 killed. Some soldiers, including the commander of XIV Battalion of the Leonessa (Mario Bianchi), was also captured.

On 22 December, the Blackshirts were once again called upon to break up the pressing enemy encirclement, but even though the operation was successful, it led once again to heavy casualties. Tagliamento officers Vianini and Galardo, the latter severely injured, maintained order in the ranks of their depleted units, by marching at the head of their men. In contrast, scattered groups of Italian infantry soldiers marched in a disorganised fashion. These troops no longer comprised a viable fighting force, but a disorganised, leaderless mass of soldiers. Together with German infantry and tanks, the Blackshirts then opened up the way to the town of Popovka enabling the mass of the infantry to continue their retreat.[76]

The Montebello, for instance, had lost in these clashes another 115 dead, 380 wounded, and sixty-six afflicted by frostbite. The Tagliamento also suffered heavy casualties. Despite the heavy casualties, the Blackshirts and the Germans continued the phased withdrawal without panicking. As an eyewitness, certainly not sympathetic to the Blackshirts, admitted:

> Moving forward the Germans, which were great organisers, decided to have us march alongside their troops. But they did not want those soldiers that had abandoned or lost their weapons. The only units that were still effective were the Blackshirts that advanced at the head of the column alongside the Germans.[77]

During the night of 22 December, the temperatures dropped even further, causing several casualties among the retreating troops—many of whom were unable to continue and died after laying down to rest a few minutes in the snow. Many of the wounded or suffering from frostbite had to be abandoned even though it was known that their fate was sealed as the soldiers of the Red Army like their German counterparts in many cases killed the enemy wounded that fell in their hands.

On 24 December, the Axis troops reached the town of Bukarevskij. A Blackshirt recalls:

> After a few hours we passed a village and then approached a frozen river. As we crossed the river we could observe on the banks the cadavers of three dead German soldiers and of two Russian civilians. Then shortly after we passed another empty village. We continued to march in a western direction but found ourselves in the middle of nowhere. On the side of the road there were several destroyed Russian tanks and the corps of several Russian soldiers. It was a trail of death and destruction and safety was nowhere in sight.[78]

Then, after many more hours of marching in the sub-zero temperatures, the troops reached Septuchovka. Here on the 25th, the German armoured units were once again instrumental in clearing the main road of enemy tanks that were attempting to block the progress of the Axis units. During the same day, both the German units and the Blackshirts had to intervene by attacking several times when Red Army troops attempted to isolate group of soldiers by cutting them off from the bulk of the retreating columns. The soldiers of the *Raggruppamento* CC.NN M 3 Gennaio were tasked to fend off these raids and lost several casualties in the close quarter combat that periodically erupted during the day. As eyewitness Italian officer Eugenio Corti asserts:

> My prejudice against the Blackshirts of the M Battalions, whom before the retreat regular army men hadn't been able to abide and even despised, had vanished since I had seen them fight. Now too, while our own generals were nowhere to be seen, their consul was trying somehow to keep at the head of the Italian column.[79]

Corti's account is similar to those of other eyewitnesses of the retreat such as Mario Rigoni Stern and Giulio Bedeschi. All compared the disorganisation within the ranks of the standard infantry and the fact that many of their units with no weapons were no longer to be considered viable fighting units to the Blackshirts or the *alpini* of the Tridentina, for instance, which despite the great reversal of fortune experienced on the Don frontline, had retained their capability to fight. Higher morale and their desperate willingness to continue fighting characterised these units and distinguished them from the disorganisation and demoralisation that was prevalent in the other ranks.

The Blackshirts willingness to continue the fight against the Red Army was recognised with the post humorous award of the gold medal to *Capomanipolo* Guerriero Battistini of LXIII Battalion Tagliamento. The motivation describes the tough, determined resistance put up by the Blackshirts despite the desperate conditions in which the retreating Axis forces found themselves in.

> During an extremely long and harsh operational cycle, the *capomanipolo* distinguished himself for his disdain of the grave danger his unit was in. Being part of a stronghold that was attacked by superior forces, he contributed to its defence with great courage. In the subsequent retreat, although suffering from frostbite and while having been wounded, he kept up the morale of his troops and led them into fierce counterattacks to contain the pressure exerted by the enemy. When his troops were surrounded, were short of ammunition and were exhausted by the constant fighting and lack of rest, he led them in a counterattack to tear a gap in the enemy deployment. He fell in battle while fighting to break out of the encirclement. Don–Tscherkowo Front (Russia), December 15, 1942–January 5, 1943.[80]

On 26 December, approximately 8,000 soldiers of the initial force that had left Arbuzovka finally reached the Axis assembly point of Chertkovo, where the troops would station for several days in order to regroup and prepare for the final battle to disengage from the Russian encirclement. In the next few days, scattered units from the Valle Scrivia and the Leonessa also managed to reach the position. The town was a large industrial hub near the border with Ukraine that was divided into two sections by the railroad. Its main advantage was that it was fairly close to the new Axis defensive lines and it was large enough to house the troops and protect them from the cold temperatures. Having been forced to abandon the heavy weapons on the Don River once the Russians had broken through, the remnants of these broken armies were forced to face tanks with few guns, hand grenades, and bayonets. Their only saving grace was that the German armoured units were still accompanying the troops and would be in the lead in the attempt to breakout from Chertkovo. The soldiers that had managed to escape were all commingled and they included: the remnants of *Raggruppamento* CCNN M 3 Gennaio, few soldiers from the second Blackshirt group, 298th German Infantry Division, and scattered elements of the Pasubio, Torino, and Cosseria Divisions.

In the words of historian Heinz Magenheimer:

> After the devastating defeat of the Romanian Third and Fourth Armies, the collapse of the Italian Eight Army on the Don, and the Soviet breakthrough south of the Voronezh in the sector of the extremely combat weak Hungarian Second Army after 12 January 1943, it was clear that these four armies no longer existed as operational units.[81]

Instead, the German account of the Second Battle of the Don River states:

> Considering the fact that the Italians were not used to the Russian winter and greatly suffered from the cold weather, the Soviet Army opted initially for a series of small raids rather than a major set piece battle against the 8th Army. It attempted to weaken the enemy resolve by deploying special assault units and by executing multiple attacks that were conducted by various battalion groups. Specifically targeting the Italian II Army Corps and the German units that were supporting it, the Soviets managed to weaken it to the point that by the time the major attack began on 16–17 December these troops were already greatly fatigued. For this reason the rupture of the frontline was sudden and the armoured units were able to advance to the rear of the XXIX German Army Corps (Sforzesca, Celere, Torino) and of the XXXV Italian Army Corps (Pasubio, 298th German Infantry Division) and reach Belovodsk near Millerovo. In light of the fact that the right flank of the Italian deployment was at risk of being encircled, the divisions received the retreat order from the Don River positions and then to open up the way toward the new lines in order to avoid being encircled.[82]

The retreat was extremely costly, with tremendous losses to all the units both German and Italian that were positioned on the Don River. The Red Army had dealt a deadly blow against the Axis troops and was now in a position to completely encircle General von Paulus 6th Army. The advance against the Romanians and the Italians on the Don River and the following destruction of the German 6th Army in Stalingrad were the key two turning points on the Eastern Front.

Breakout

After retreating for many miles in sub-zero temperatures, the remnants of the Tagliamento along with other Italian and German troops had arrived at Chertkovo on the 26th from where, a few weeks later, they would attempt to break out of the enemy encirclement to reach the Axis frontline. Chertkovo was located approximately 100 km south of the area where the Soviet had broken through. The retreat through the snow and ice had been exhausting since the few heavy weapons left and the ammunition were transported by mule drawn carts or hand towed by the soldiers themselves. At times, the snow had come down in abundance and the icy wind had accompanied the soldiers throughout their ordeal. The soldiers needed some time to rest to recover their strength. The Chertkovo garrison in December 1942 was comprised of approximately 10,000 troops, of which 700 were deployed around the defensive perimeter on the frontline. According to the testimony of a *legionary* of the Tagliamento on 29 December, the commander of the ARMIR ordered all available troops to take turns in defending the garrison. 'We began to organise our defensive positions by deploying troops along the perimeter of the town. We staggered the machine gun positions and built several pillboxes. Finally, we set up several teams to provide sentry duty'.[83]

These troops were charged with carrying out sentry patrols around the perimeter of the town, as well as manning the garrison's defences. As Italian officer, Eugenio Corti, asserts: 'all the Blackshirts from the Montenello and Tagliamento Battalions who were not wounded or afflicted by frostbite joined the line: the meagre, haggard remains of great assault units, who still seemed to have preserved something of the fighting spirit'.[84]

For many days, these troops, alongside German infantry soldiers especially those of the 19th Panzer Division's 73rd Panzer Grenadier Regiment, sent as reinforcements, repulsed several Soviet combined arms attempts by three different divisions of the 4th Guards Rifle Corps to break their defensive lines and capture the entire garrison. One day, supported by German Stukas, the defenders were not only able to stop but also to deal a severe blow to the Russians. On 9 January 1943 at 7 a.m., after a very intense artillery barrage that was in turn followed by the strafing attacks of the fighter planes, two Soviet infantry battalions along with nine T-34 tanks attacked the defensive positions of the Axis forces. In more than two hours of heavy fighting, Blackshirts and German soldiers were able to knock out eight out of nine Soviet tanks and mow down an entire enemy battalion. At first, the troops began to target the enemy shock units travelling on the tanks with machine-gun and rifle fire. Many were prevented by even setting foot on the ground by the strong and persistent machine-gun fire. Then the defenders set forth to stop the tanks from invading their position. One of the tanks was put out of action by a team of Blackshirts armed with two Solothurn anti-tank rifles. The tank in question was advancing quickly and menacing their position with machine-gun fire. As it was fast approaching the anti-tank ditch, the Blackshirts had the fortitude of standing firm against the hulk and fire several shots, two of which were direct hits into the front and side of the tank. The main hit against the tank came from the rifle of *Camicia Nera* Dino Betti. The *legionary* showed considerable nerve while lying in wait in a ditch and firing his weapon at the most opportune moment when the enemy tank was only 15–20 metres away from his position. In more than two hours of heavy fighting, an entire Red Army battalion had been practically annihilated and eight tanks knocked out of action.

As eyewitness Eugenio Corti asserts:

> The Russians didn't get through this time either. When Thor tanks came into the range of the anti-tank guns, they were all annihilated ... the Blackshirts distinguished themselves admirably in this action. A tank was knocked out by a large antitank rifle of a Blackshirt, a certain Dino Betti. I was also told by M that they had even climbed up onto tanks to slip hand grenades down through the embrasures.[85]

Total losses among the Blackshirts were two dead, eleven wounded, and seventeen affected by frostbite. German losses are unknown while Soviet losses, also unknown, were likely to be considerably higher. As a result of the Blackshirts efforts, an officer of the 298th German Infantry Division, Captain Lewandosky, bestowed to ten *legionaries* the Iron Cross Second Class.

During the next few days, the Russians refrained from attacking Certkovo head on, but continued to barrage the Axis garrison especially with the deadly Katyusha rocket launchers, which caused several casualties.

On the night of 15 January 1943, the commander of the garrison, having received a handful of German tanks in support, decided to attempt the breakout. All able troops (5,000 in total), with the exception of the injured and the ones physically unfit to continue the retreat, were assembled in the main square and shortly thereafter began to advance in a single column. At the head of the column were five German tanks and overhead the troops were supported by five German Stukas and three Italian Fiat CR.42 planes. At the back where the remaining troops of the Blackshirts (Tagliamento and Montebello), which could only muster two infantry battalions. These proud troops had lost more than two-thirds of their original strength and there were no reserves left to take the place of the dead and wounded and replenish their much-depleted ranks. From the onset, the Soviet Army attempted to interfere with the retreat by continuously attacking the rearguard, which suffered several casualties. The fighting took the form of continuous raids by the Russians which led to bitter and chaotic clashes between the opposing forces.

Those that were more fatigued, thus walking slower, were positioned at the very rear of the column and were continuously assaulted by the Russians soldiers, the tanks, and partisan units. Many of them were taken prisoner or killed.

As Eugenio Corti describes the Axis troops soon after leaving the town began to clash with the enemy:

> When the German vanguard, with most of the village behind them, had opened fire with their tanks in an attempt to break through the line, the Russian tanks behind them had hurled themselves on the column, levelling away all and everybody. The German troops up at the front scattered but not before they had relayed news of the attack rapidly down the column ... three of their

> tanks, including one or two small ones, French war trophies, had immediately returned. Crushing their own infantry in the wake, they hurled themselves at the Russian tanks.[86]

An intensive fight between opposing tanks soon materialised, but the Axis forces were eventually able to gain the upper hand and continue breakout operations. The German motorised anti-tank guns were instrumental in knocking out Soviet tanks and opening up a passage for the soldiers travelling on foot. During the rest of the day, the troops continued to march west. The next day, the Russians attacked the retreating column again. The Blackshirts took the brunt of the enemy thrust this time, but fought tooth and nail in repulsing both tanks and infantry. The troops travelling on foot were plagued by the freezing temperatures and by the enemy fire. But they were pushed on by desperation and by the knowledge that there was now a short distance that separated them from the Axis line. Some did not make it and fell to their death exhausted in the darkness of the night, while a majority continued to carry on. On the 16th, the Soviet Army and several tanks attempted a flanking attack against the retreating column. But a unit of German Stukas promptly intervened to bomb the Soviet tanks, which were forced to disperse. On the night of 17 January, the column finally reached Novaja Strel'covka, which hosted a large garrison of Italian troops. The wounded were then picked up by several trucks and were taken back to hospitals in the rear. The rest of the troops were fed and later brought back to the rear for a period of rest. On 17 March, what remained of the Italian 8th Army was taken back to Italy.

By the end of the retreat, the Tagliamento could count upon nineteen officers, eight NCOs, and 184 soldiers. The Montebello was down to 400 men. The CC. NN. 23 Marzo Group had also lost half its strength. Initially, the Italian High Command had hoped to reconstitute a Blackshirt unit in order to continue deploying it in Russia, but the dire conditions of the men forced a reconsideration and the soldiers were taken back to Italy.

As Battistelli and Crociani assert: 'As the Blackshirt combat elite, the M Battalions would suffer the most from the setbacks on the Eastern front in Winter 1942–43'.[87]

Most units in fact could not be fully reconstituted due to the tremendous losses and had to be merged into one infantry and armoured division that was constituted in May 1943.

The post-campaign report of the M Battalions Groups states that 'given their light constitution with little anti-tank support and no tank support, the M Battalions provided a good account of themselves on the Eastern Front. The troops could always be relied upon to conduct quick offensive actions and to bolster infantry defences'.[88]

The Blackshirts likely performed better in the Eastern Front as opposed to Greece or North Africa for two reasons. First, the Blackshirt units deployed in

Russia represented the elite of the legions and of the M Battalions of the MVSN. Accordingly, they were comprised by trained and experienced soldiers that had already taken part to several campaigns. The training allowed them to fight more effectively and their mostly defensive and counterattacking deployment exalted the defensive qualities of the Italian soldiers given the mostly static nature of the fighting throughout the campaign. In contrast, the last two days of the Second Don Offensive evidenced that even well-trained and motivated troops could do little while facing a massive tank attack with shoddy and light anti-tank weapons. Second, their morale never wavered as much as that of the standard infantry, despite the huge reversal of fortune in the winter of 1942–43, which was greatly compounded by the harsh weather and the poor conditions of service. This is attested by the post-war memoirs of writers of the calibre of Eugenio Corti and Mario Rigoni Stern and from some of the war diaries of the German units that fought alongside the Blackshirts. The reasons for the higher morale of the Blackshirts and their continuing to be viable fighting units despite the major enemy breakthrough are not easily identifiable. One reason can be surmised by reading the war diaries of those who served in the Eastern Front. Their morale and fighting efficiency remained high because the Blackshirts knew that they were facing the implacable Red Army foe. To be captured meant that one was likely to get shot on the spot for wearing the Blackshirt or be taken to a gulag with its primitive living conditions. This thought likely urged the soldiers to carry on fighting. Another factor as to do with their *raison d'être* being units that were originally assembled to fight an anti-Communist crusade. Hence the ideological component of the Eastern Front campaign was another motivating factor urging some of the Blackshirts to fight effectively against the Red Army.

Although the Blackshirts had been beaten by an enemy that enjoyed superior numbers and weapons, they had given a good account of themselves on the Russian front. The enormous losses were a testament to their fighting capabilities. Upon their return to Italy, most of them would not receive a warm welcome as Tagliamento volunteer Carlo Mazzantini stated:

> Referring to the murder of two Blackshirt Eastern Front veterans at the hand of the partisans in Italy, he commented bitterly that this was a poor reward they had been given after valiantly serving their country overseas. Having survived the experience of the war in Russia, they ended up being killed in one of the streets of one of those cities from whence they had departed feted by songs and flags, girls and flowers.[89]

An officer of the Tagliamento (Silvio Margini of LXXIX Battalion) receiving a decoration from the commander of the 3 Gennaio Filippo Diamanti during the Eastern Front campaign in September 1942. (*Legione Tagliamento*)

Soldiers of the Tagliamento resting somewhere in Ukraine in the summer of 1942. Note how the soldiers typically wore the fez hat rather than the helmet while away from the frontline. (*Legione Tagliamento*)

General Italo Gariboldi, commander of the Italian 8th Army reviews the soldiers of the Tagliamento in the summer of 1942. (*Legione Tagliamento*)

Luogotenente Generale della Milizia for Sicily Enrico Francisci, commander of the *Raggruppamento* CCNN M 23 Marzo during the campaign in the Eastern Front. He was to die in July 1943 during the Allied invasion of Sicily where he held the position of *Luogotenente Generale della Milizia* of Sicily. (*Archivio Centrale dello stato*)

A Blackshirt somewhere on the Eastern Front pictured with a few OTO (Odero Terni Orlando) hand grenades. Along with the Model 91 rifle and a dagger, the OTO hand grenades were the standard weapons of the Blackshirts units. (*Archivio Centrale dello stato*)

Right: A Blackshirt crew of a Breda Model 30 6.5-mm machine gun. (*Archivio Centrale dello stato*)

Below: Blackshirts advancing against soviet troops under the cover of a 6.5-mm Breda Model 30 machine gun. The Blackshirt on the right is carrying on his back an ammunition case and two spare barrels for the machine gun. (*Archivio Centrale dello stato*)

An *alpini* officer reviews a Blackshirt unit in the Eastern Front in the summer of 1942. (*Archivio Centrale dello stato*)

An *alpini* officer greeting Blackshirts in the rear area of the Eastern Front in the summer of 1942. (*Archivio Centrale dello stato*)

Blackshirts marching on the Eastern Front. The soldier is carrying a Breda Model 37 heavy machine gun. (*Archivio Centrale dello stato*)

Luogotenente Generale della Milizia Enzo Galbiati meets Italian and German troops during his visit to the Don River frontline in September 1942. (*Archivio Centrale dello stato*)

The photo captures an Italian anti-tank crew that has just debilitated a Soviet tank during the First Battle of the Don River in August 1942. (*Ufficio Storico*)

German tank hunter manual showing how to immobilise Soviet tanks. It was distributed to Italian troops fighting against the Soviet Union. (*Ufficio Storico*)

5

The M Armoured Division

Introduction: *Divisione* M

By the spring of 1943, the soldiers of the Tagliamento, Leonessa, Valle Scrivia, and Montebello M Battalions that had survived the vicissitudes of the Eastern Front campaign had returned to Italy and after a month of authorised leave from service had been assembled under the newly formed 1. *Divisione Corazzata Camicie Nere* M (1st Blackshirt Armoured M Division) in May 1943. This unit was formed as Mussolini's personal protection unit after the defeat of the Axis forces in North Africa in May 1943. The unit was the brainchild of several personalities, but the German leadership had actually been instrumental in making the M Division possible. Hitler, fearful of a potential *putsch* against Mussolini and the Fascist Party by the Italian monarchy and the highest-ranking officers of the Royal Army, had urged its creation. He not only had advocated the constitution of an armoured division of the militia, but also supplied it with weapons and equipment. Historian Renzo de Felice details one of Hitler's statements made to the German High Command in the spring of 1943 regarding aiding and propping up the faltering Italian regime:

> I could support the *Duce* with a conditional proposition. If he is willing to provide a unit comprised of battle hardened soldiers drawn from the militia, I would be willing to dispatch the necessary weapons and equipment. This unit would then have to be organised, equipped and trained in Germany. I am willing and ready to support the *Duce* by sending to Italy the most modern German equipment such as tanks, self-propelled guns, anti-tank guns, etc. to allow for the creation of an Italian panzer grenadier division. The latter should be constituted by militia soldiers and trained by German officers. It should be comprised of soldiers that are fully committed to the war effort and the Axis

> cause. The unit can then be used as a tactical reserve at the disposal of the Italian government.[1]

It is very significant, especially in the light of the events that would shortly thereafter follow in the fall of 1943, that one of the first proponents of the M Division was the German leadership itself. Most likely this attempt to arm the Blackshirts was seen by Germany as an attempt to keep Italy in the war by propping up its much weakened leader and his faltering regime after the defeats in Russia and North Africa. In Russia, the Italian 8th Army had been defeated by the Soviet offensive of Operation Little Saturn, which caused tremendous losses and the total destruction of the entire Italian Army on the Eastern Front. The total losses included almost 50 per cent of the strength of the ARMIR/8th Army with 84,930 dead during combat operations and 29,690 injured. As a result of these tremendous losses, the ARMIR was disbanded and even the II Army Corps, which originally was supposed to be reorganised and re-equipped in order to be once again be redeployed in Russia, had to be disbanded as well due to the huge losses. To make matters worse for the Axis, a few months later, the 1st Army, a joint Italian and German force under Erwin Rommel (first) and Giovanni Messe (during the tail end of the campaign), was forced to surrender to the Allies in Tunisia. Thus another 200,000 Axis soldiers were taken into captivity along with artillery pieces of all kinds, tanks, trucks, and hundreds of machine guns. With the loss of Tunisia, the Axis no longer had a military presence in North Africa and this defeat dangerously exposed Italy to an Allied invasion.

While Germany was clearly alarmed that the Allies could attack Italy from their bases in North Africa, the Italian proposal to initiate peace talks with the Soviet Union to then focus the Axis war effort against the British and the American forces was clearly rejected by Hitler. But the continuation of a two-front war did not bode well for the Axis and especially for its weaker partner, Italy, which was now threatened directly. These considerations were probably the strategic underpinnings that forced Germany to expedite and facilitate the creation of the M Division. Although it is pretty clear that even if such a unit had been constituted in record time, the situation remained dire and there was little such a unit could do to reserve the military course. Germany had provided support before, but this time it was different since there was an entire Italian division that was being fully equipped with German weapons and equipment. In the past, Germany had supplied mostly captured Soviet or French Army equipment to its allies, while in some cases its military had also furnished German equipment such as the Flak 88-mm guns to Italian troops in North Africa and the 75-mm artillery units supplied to the Italians in late 1942. What is striking about this supply of weapons in mid-1943 was that the M Division was equipped with such modern equipment in so little time. Most likely this was the result of the precipitous situation that Italy found itself after defeat in Tunisia in May 1943. The equipment that was shipped from Germany to Italy was of the highest quality and the most advanced from a technological standpoint. It was for sure the most advanced equipment ever placed at the disposal of the Italian Army during the war. Not only was the equipment furnished very quickly but it was also accompanied by an exceedingly high number of German officers, trainers, and NCOs who had been assigned the task of training the M Division.

Origins of the M Division

Originally in the winter of 1942, Enzo Galbiati, the *Luogotenente Generale* of the MVSN, had first broached the subject of the creation of an armoured division within the MVSN. The unit was seen by Galbiati as another effort to further specialise the MVSN, which a year earlier had constituted the M Battalions in order to deploy better trained and prepared assault infantry and light artillery units. In the fall of 1942, Galbiati travelled to the frontline to carry out a series of inspections to determine the state of readiness of the troops on the Eastern Front in bracing for major Soviet counterattacks. After wrapping up his visit to the front, Galbiati had also conducted a number of interviews with members of the German High Command that had expressed negative opinions on the effectiveness of the Italian troops, including the Blackshirts on the Eastern Front. Upon returning to Italy, Galbiati issued a report highlighting his findings and recommending further training and specialisation for the M Battalions to counteract the negative perceptions.[2]

Increased training was seen as a way to improve the combat readiness of the troops, while a higher degree of specialisation was deemed as a way to increase overall combat effectiveness. For example, an area where improvements could be made through training was in refining attack plans and raids through improved intelligence of enemy strength. Thus, newly made Blackshirt officers and NCOs were to undergo specific training on how to more fully conduct the reconnaissance and surveillance functions of enemy units with the aid of improved tools and maps. Whereas an example of specialisation was the creation within the M Battalions of fully motorised command platoons. In addition, the officers and NCOs of such platoons were to be furnished with automatic weapons.

The creation of the armoured division was to address two specific needs: to provide a unit that could guarantee internal peace and order and one that also could be deployed in battle against the Allies that threatened southern Europe.

The *Duce* and the leader of the party Carlo Scorza had also been contemplating for some time the creation of an armoured division to be used for both political tasks and military ones.[3] Both were of the opinion that the unit could play a dual role—one that was political, and mainly to underpin the regime, and one that was purely military. As far as the political tasks were concerned, it was envisioned that the unit could be deployed to put down local rebellions or to confront general discontent about the war. With regards to a strictly military role, the unit was to defend key Italian military installations or bases on the mainland which was now threatened directly by the Allies. The problem for both was that the army did not possess advanced modern tank units and, moreover, what little new resources were available, these were typically placed at the disposal of the Royal Army that was in also dire need of new equipment. There was also another problem that was tied to the lack of specialists within the MVSN such as drivers, tank operators, artillery specialists, etc. Without such specialists, it was not possible to create an armoured division. Thus in order to achieve the objective of creating a modern panzer division, securing German assistance in training the unit and equipping it with modern weapons was of uttermost importance. In addition, another critical issue was to find drivers, sappers, combat engineers, and other specialists within the Italian Royal Army since these specialists could not be recruited within the MVSN. By 1943, even the Royal Army was having difficulty filling the specialists' ranks since many of the most experienced soldiers had either been captured or killed/wounded during the campaigns in 1942.

Mussolini was also cognisant of the fact that he had a bigger problem. In fact, the creation of such a division could further deteriorate his relationship with the king and the *Comando Supremo*, which obviously saw a well-trained and armed militia unit as a threat to the integrity of the Royal Army. In fact, if the division was to be fully supplied with German weapons, its capabilities and firepower would exceed anything that the Italian Army had at its disposal. In essence, on paper, the unit armed with German weapons would become the most powerful division within the Italian Army. At the time, the Royal Army had only one armoured division, the reconstituted Ariete, which was armed with MI15/42 tanks that were clearly inferior to the German armoured units. For this reason alone and for the fear of creating a widening split within the regime, the *Duce* did not urge its creation until mid-1943 when the political-military situation had become dire and the need to take action became more necessary than ever.

During the first half of 1943, deep divisions began to emerge within the political class. On one hand, as the war effort took a downward spiral, top military officers and the king began to distance themselves from the regime as they planned a potential *putsch* or takeover of the reins of government to distance Italy from Germany and seek a negotiated peace with the Allies. For both the king and his advisers, the war was lost and there was a need to extricate Italy from a burdensome alliance with Germany. On the other hand, the loyalists of the regime, which continued to side with the *Duce*, made efforts to rally the population behind the war effort with propaganda in the face of defeat in both North Africa and in Russia. Overall, the MVSN was still fully behind the war effort, although as Battistelli and Crociani assert, among the ranks (by mid-1943) there was also considerable war weariness. Fatigue about the war was clearly in evidence during the Allied landing in Sicily and the corresponding reaction of the Italian units. In fact, while some units of the MVSN, and the armoured units fought effectively against superior forces, other units did not fight well and some even melted away after just a few hours of fighting.

As a result of the negative turn of the war, the socio-political situation in the mainland became very dire as well. The population was deeply demoralised being subjected to daily bombardments from the Allies and facing huge shortages of food and other primary goods. The working classes were more and more beginning to heed the message for peace of the socialist and communist organisations by participating in work stoppages and unrest in the major cities. Meanwhile, the leaders of the major industries were also beginning to distance themselves from the regime by urging the king and his entourage to take action to end the war. Their opinions reflected not only the downturn in the Italian economy but also the dire prospect of facing another year of Allied bombardments and economic embargo. The war had not only taken a turn for the worse, but also it appeared that the industrial military effort had reached a standstill. While the Germans and the Japanese had introduced new, powerful weapons between 1942 and 1943, the Italians continued to rely for the most part, on obsolete equipment. In 1943, the Germans, for instance, were producing record numbers of 88-mm and 90-mm artillery guns and had jettisoned their small anti-tank guns, while the Italians were forced to rely on the obsolete and much less powerful 47/32-mm unit. In fact, no new weapon had been developed to take the place of the 47/32-mm gun and as a result of the absence of an effective anti-tank unit the Italian Army had become more reliant on the Semovente self-propelled gun. But unfortunately not enough of these units could reach the front due to low production rates and shortages of raw materials. Thus the troops had nothing but the obsolete 47/32-mm gun to fight against enemy armour. The Breda machine guns were also for the most part obsolete, with a low volume of fire and negligible production numbers. The Breda 45 and 81-mm mortars were still single-fire weapons, while the Russians and the Germans had developed much more menacing mortars, howitzers, and even rocket launchers. Italy's few armoured divisions were also a negligible force armed with light to medium tanks compared to the British or the Soviet Army, which could deploy many more armoured units and with much more efficient tanks. The Russian T-34 tank, for instance, was much more powerful than any Italian tank, while the British Army was receiving record numbers of Sherman and Grant tanks from the United States. Not even the German war machine could keep up with the exceedingly high production rates of the Soviet Union and the United States.

The internal social unrest that emerged in early 1943 and the final outcome of the campaign in Tunisia in May 1943 were the two turning points that forced Mussolini and Scorza to break the *impasse* and take action. Despite the objections of the king and his entourage, they approached the German ambassador in Rome Hans Georg von Mackensen and lodged a formal request for military assistance. The request included the supply of German armoured units, anti-tank guns, and self-propelled guns. Within a matter of weeks, the requested equipment was shipped by train from Germany accompanied by a team of armoured and artillery officers and specialists whose task was to train and whip into shape the armoured division. Hitler's direct involvement in the matter assured the timely supply to the MVSN of a number of modern weapons to make possible the constitution of an advanced mechanised division. The basic concept was to create an Italian version of the standard German Panzer Grenadier division armed with the most technologically advanced tanks, anti-tank and anti-aircraft guns, self-propelled guns, and several small crew served arms such as flamethrowers and mortars. The unit was to be comprised of only experienced soldiers and it was to be trained by the best training specialists that Germany could offer.

The unit was assembled in the area near Chiusi (Siena) during the first two weeks of May 1943, and according to the guidelines issued by its leadership, the recruits had to be carefully selected. They had to be selected from the most experienced and battle hardened soldiers of the militia. Moreover, another prerequisite was prior combat expertise gained in campaigns in Albania, Greece, or Russia. These soldiers were to be complemented by a number of younger recruits, all volunteers, while the artillery crews were to be selected primarily from the units of the coastal and the anti-aircraft artillery militia. The drivers of the tanks and the trucks were to be recruited from experienced armoured or motorised units of the Royal Army. The leader of the unit was going to be designated as the *console* of the division, and he had to have had extensive prior experience in leading one or more M Battalions groups in either the Balkans or Russia. Similarly, the heads of operations and of security and intelligence were to be drawn from the best and most experienced officers of the MVSN. A tank armoured specialist was also highly sought after, together with a high-level officer from the artillery branch. All the officers had to have completed training at the war school in Turin for at least three years and had to have prior significant combat experience. Since the majority of the soldiers had little or no prior experience in operating tanks or such heavy guns, the *Divisione* M was not expected to be combat ready for many months.

The training began in earnest in mid-May. Some soldiers were sent to Germany to train on German tanks, while others began extensive training in Chiusi with the armour that had been dispatched by the Germans. German armour and artillery instructors were based in Chiusi as well to initiate an extensive training period for the units of the M Division.

The day in the training camp of the division was typically split into several sessions. The morning was dedicated to live fire exercises with the individual and crew served weapons, while the afternoon was dedicated to rehearsing manoeuvres where soldiers advanced riding or advancing behind the armoured units against makeshift enemy positions. The expenditure of ammunition was considerable during these training exercises and an incredible amount of equipment and supply was put at the disposal of the M Division. At least for Italian standards during the Second World War, the Blackshirts received above-average training with unusually high numbers of weapons and ammunition. The level of training and the large availability of weapons and ammunition constituted a definite break with the past.

After almost two months of training, the M Division was thus officially constituted on 25 June 1943 and had been transferred to Bracciano near Rome, but at the time it was not deemed battle ready. According to *Luogotenente Generale* Galbiati, for instance, the unit was to be deemed battle ready only by the late summer or early fall of 1943. Its initial strength was comprised by 5,800 soldiers that were subdivided in the following units: four infantry battalions, two artillery battalions, a combat engineer battalion, a sapper and a signals company, and several small teams of medical staff, cooks, etc. The four infantry battalions were LXIII Udine Assault Battalion, LXXIX Reggio Emilia Assault Battalion (Ex-Tagliamento), VI Vigevano Assault Battalion, and XXX Novara Assault Battalion from the Montebello. These units were considered as *fanteria legionaria motorizzata* (motorised legionary infantry units) since they were each comprised of three infantry companies and one machine-gun company and were endowed with a number of trucks to transport equipment as well as soldiers. The former Tagliamento units had at their disposal XLI Trento Heavy Weapons Battalion with six *Sturmgeschutz* III 75/48-mm German guns. In addition, it had some logistics units such as *Milizia della Strada* (motorised militia), a Blackshirt *Genio* (sapper) unit, a medical unit, and the 228th motorised unit. The Montebello had also its own artillery unit: XII Aosta Heavy Weapons Battalion with six *Sturmgeschutz* III 75/48-mm artillery pieces. The armoured component of the M Division was comprised by the *Gruppo Carri* Leonessa (Armoured Group Leonessa), which operated the German tanks, and the *Gruppo Artiglieria* Valle Scrivia, which was armed primarily with twenty-four Flak 88-mm guns. Thus the unit not only had approximately 5,800 soldiers but with the addition of German officers and NCOs, the drivers and armoured specialists drawn from the Royal Army, its total strength exceeded 6,000 soldiers.

Its order of battle was as follows:

1a. *Divisione Corazzata Camicie Nere* M: *Console Generale* Alessandro Lusana
- -*Comando e compagnia commando* (Command Company).
- -*Compagnia Carabinieri.*
- -*Nucleo Movimento Stradale* (Mobile Unit).
- -306 *ufficio Posta Militare* (Postal unit).
- -*Autoreparto Divisionale* (Mobile unit).

-*Gruppo carri* M Leonessa: *Primo Seniore* Ferdinando Tesi
- -1a. *Compagnia*, twelve Panzer Kpfw IV Ausf. H with 75-mm gun.
- -2a. *Compagnia*, twelve Panzer Kpfw III Ausf. N with 75-mm gun.
- -3a. *Compagnia*, twelve StuG III Ausf. N. with 75-mm gun.

-*Gruppo Battaglioni* CCNN M Tagliamento: *Console* Ermacora Zuliani
- -LXIII *Battaglione d'assalto* M (Udine Assault Battalion).
- -LXXIX *Battaglione d'assalto* M (Reggio Emilia assault Battalion).
- -XLI *Battaglione d'armi d'accompagnamento* M (Trento Heavy Weapons Group)

-*Gruppo Battaglioni* CCNN M Montebello: *Console* Roberto Gloria
- -VI *Battaglione d'assalto* M (Vigevano Assault Battalion).
- -XXX *Battaglione d'assalto* M (Novara Assault Battalion).
- -XII *Battaglione d'armi d'accompagnamento* M (XII Aosta Heavy Weapons Battalion).

-*Reggimento Artiglieria* Valle Scrivia (Valle Scrivia Artillery Regiment): *Primo Seniore* Franco Gallerani
- -I *Gruppo* (First Artillery Group), three batteries each with four Flak 37 88/56-mm guns, twenty 47/32-mm guns, thirty-six 45-mm mortars, and 81-mm mortars.
- -II *Gruppo* (Second Artillery Group), three batteries each with four Flak 37 88/56-mm guns, twenty 47/32-mm guns, thirty-six 45-mm mortars, and 81-mm mortars.
- -*Battaglione Guastatori* (Engineer Battalion)
- -*Reparto Misto Genio* (Sappers Mixed Group):
- -*Compagnia artieri.*
- -*Compagnia Telegrafisti.*
- -1. *Compagnia Radio Telegrafisti* (Radio Transmission Company).
- -2. *Compagnia Radio Telegrafisti* (Radio Transmission Company).
- -*Nucleo Sanita'* (Medical Services).
- -*Nucleo Sussistenza* (Provisions unit).
- -*Ufficio Commissariato* (Administrative unit).

On 3 July 1943, the M Division participated in a large-scale training exercise that was observed by the most senior officers of the High Command. Then on 10 July 1943, the unit carried out another full-scale rehearsal, which was observed by the *Duce*, the head of the *Comando Supremo*, and several other high-ranking officers of the Royal Army and the head of the MVSN. The war diary of the unit states: 'On the day the Allies landed in Sicily the unit carried out a very impressive training session with live fire exercises. The latter was exemplary demonstrating the great firepower that the M Division was able to unleash. Such firepower was so great with the new weapons and unprecedented and never seen before by any unit of the Italian Army'.[4]

Palace Intrigues

The fact that the division was slowly coming together into a cohesive fighting unit was a matter of extreme worry to Badoglio and his followers and to the heads of the Royal Army, Navy, and Air Force. These entities saw in the M Division a potential competitor for their monopoly on military matters. They were especially fearful of its size, weapons, and capabilities. As a result of this fear, they began to plot on how to limit its power and how to take it away from the control of the MVSN. These plots were predicated on the understanding that in order to sign a peace treaty with the Allies, it was necessary to disarm all units that could stand in the way of such a switch in alliances. One of the early schemes to weaken it, for example, was the proposal to cut it up into many little units and deploy it to defend airports in southern Italy.

On 14 July, the *Comando Supremo* with the intent to dismantle it ordered the division to be dispatched to the Salento region of southern Italy, while Mussolini, who was still unaware of the plans of the king and the *Comando Supremo*, wanted to dispatch the unit to Sicily as fast as possible in order to use it to contrast the Allied landing of 10 July. Both decisions, however, were opposed by the German training officers that maintained the unit was not ready and needed to train more, and by *Luogotenente Generale* Galbiati, who wanted to keep the unit near Rome. Ultimately, the latter won the day and the M Division was kept near Rome, in Campagnaro, to continue its training.

The military and the political situation then quickly precipitated. A few days later, there was an Axis meeting in Feltre where General Ambrosio made an urgent request for military aid from Germany to help Italy against the Allies. Another request that was made was to recall all Italian troops deployed in the Balkans to Italy to be deployed against the Allies. On the day that the meeting was taking place, over 400 Allied planes bombed Rome, killing 3,000 civilians and injuring 10,000. It was then apparent that the Allies were determined to hit hard the Axis forces in Italy as well as key infrastructure to force Italy to exit the war. In addition to the bombing raids, the combined German Italian counterattack to push back the Allies from Sicily that was attempted on 11 July had failed forcing the Axis forces to give up even more terrain on the island.

Even though the situation at the front was dire and called for emergency measures, the results of the meeting were inconclusive since the German High Command did not agree to dispatch additional military aid to Italy. In addition, no decision was made to seek a negotiated peace with the Soviet Union.

Facing a desperate situation at the front and with no additional aid forthcoming, the king and his advisers fast tracked a strategy to disengage Italy from the Axis alliance. The key to their plans was to overthrow the party and the regime and to disarm the militia. The attempt by the High Command to dismantle the militia in general, but the M Division in particular can be gleaned from the memoirs of Marshal Badoglio, which were written in 1946. In one of the passages, Badoglio states:

> General Ambrosio had succeeded Marshal Cavallero in the position of Chief of Staff of *Comando Supremo*. Together we examined the situation and agreed that it was no longer possible to continue the war with Germany. We agreed that two were the goals to be achieved with extreme speed: the arrest of Mussolini and half a dozen of the most important party leaders and the neutralisation of the Militia forces, especially the Armoured Division that was training near Rome.[5]

On the night of 24–25 July 1943, all the issues came to a head during the meeting of the Grand Council where Dino Grandi proposed an order of the day to overthrow Mussolini. The Grand Council had not met for a few years, but Grandi, who was working closely with the king and his entourage, had asked for an emergency meeting. The meeting was granted by Mussolini and began on the early evening of 24 July. After a heated discussion, a majority (nineteen *versus* eight, with one abstention) voted in favour of the motion and the following day Mussolini was dismissed by the king who nominated Pietro Badoglio as the prime minister. The latter vowed publicly that Italy would continue to fight with the Axis, but behind the scenes there was an attempt almost immediately to arrive at a negotiated peace with the Allies.

In order to depoliticise the M Division, the king and Badoglio took several pre-emptive measures prior to the dismissal of Mussolini. In fact, the coup against the regime was planned with great detail and nothing was left to chance. The first initiative that was taken on 23 July was to move an armoured division (Ariete) of the Royal Army near the base of the M Division and specifically stationed on the main road outside the barracks to block it inside its headquarters. This measure was taken to ensure that the M Division would not be able to leave the barracks in case it reacted to Mussolini's dismissal. A second initiative involved the moving away from Rome of some of the assault battalions such as the Tagliamento in order to break up the M Division. For instance, the plan was to move the two assault battalions of the Tagliamento to Puglia to guard military bases and airports from potential enemy paratrooper attacks. The third initiative involved the decapitation of the leadership of the M Division. In fact, Galbiati was arrested a few days after Mussolini was deposed and the other officers of the M Division were promoted and co-opted into the Royal Army. The fourth initiative was to rename the M Division and place it under the command of military officers loyal to the king.

The plans of the king and Badoglio to depoliticise the M Division and the MVSN were facilitated by the very cautious and prudent manner with which the heads of the MVSN reacted to the political change. When they heard the news that a new government had been installed, they pledged their allegiance to it, vowing that the militia's charter was to serve both the regime and the monarchy.

As a result of an agreement between Galbiati and Badoglio, on 26 July, the commander of the M Division issued the following guidelines to his troops:

> First, all personnel of the M Division is required to stay in the barracks and at all costs should avoid clashing with civilians or with units of the Royal Army. Second, if any personnel is to leave the barracks to pick up supplies or for an emergency situation, it is preferable that they be accompanied by two or more soldiers. The soldiers should be armed with their rifle and well equipped with plenty of ammunition. Third, inside the barracks the soldiers are expected to behave as soldiers by keeping their composure in the face of such a grave situation and they should remain loyal to their officers. Discipline within the barracks must be maintained at all costs. Forth, the commanders, the officers and even the NCOs must persuade the soldiers to remain calm at all costs. Officers are to exert a firm degree of control over their troops.

These guidelines, which essentially called on the soldiers of the M Division to stay put, were aimed to avoid any confrontation with the Royal Army or with civilians. The intent was to remain loyal to the new government and the rationale for this was that the latter had vowed to continue the war alongside the Axis partners and secondly because the militia had sworn a pledge of loyalty to both the regime and the monarchy in 1924. A secondary intent was to avoid any blood from being spilled avoiding a major confrontation between the MVSN and the Royal Army. A third motivation was that the unit had not terminated its training process. The three reasons that were given at the time to avoid a confrontation between the militia and the Royal Army were also reiterated during the post-war when Galbiati published his memoirs. In this book, he reiterated that the M Division in July 1943 was not combat ready and that he had ordered it to remain in the barracks to avoid a confrontation or worse a civil war with the Royal Army.

The rank and file, however, reacted less cautiously to the news of the change of the government. Once the soldiers of the militia became aware of the political developments, they immediately made contact with the Germans of the 3rd *Panzergrenadier* Division, which was also stationed near Rome. Both wanted to invade the capital and take over key buildings and block main roads. The 16th Blackshirt Battalion, for instance, came out of its barracks located north of Rome and headed for city. But its attempt to alter the latest political development by way of a military intervention was short-lived because it was shortly thereafter dissuaded from continuing on by the intervention of the head of the MVSN. The latter justified his intervention by stating that it wanted to avoid Italian troops fighting against each other. Galbiati's orders were enough to force the unit back to its barracks. During the night of the 26th, there were exchanges of rifle fire between the *Granatieri di Sardegna* and Blackshirts units around the headquarters of the MVSN in Rome. Then, the next day, civilians tried to storm the headquarters of the MVSN in Rome and some of the party's local branches. Meanwhile, in major cities, many civilians had taken to the streets to overturn statues of the regime and torch party branches. During the rioting, several individuals lost their life due to these street fights as the Blackshirts fired at the demonstrators. The army was then called to the streets to re-establish order. Throughout these street riots, the M Division remained in the barracks outside Rome.

Conclusion

Its lack of reaction of the militia after the fall of the regime has baffled military historians. Despite the fact that the unit's *raison d'être* was to defend and rally support for the *Duce*, it failed to act on the day of the overthrow. There are several reasons why the unit failed to act. First, while Mussolini was deposed, the king and the army chief of staff stated that Italy would continue to fight alongside the German Army. The heads of the militia understood this to mean that there was no change in alliances despite the change in government. Second, on that day (25 July), there was considerable confusion and even the German forces and the ambassador were unable to determine exactly what had happened. The lack of information and the chaos and street protests that ensued showed that the M Division and the remnants of the regime had only some popular support left. Third, the regime melted away completely on that day as most of the senior leaders still loyal to Mussolini sought to seek shelter at the German embassy in Rome rather than attempt to rally their supporters. As Morgan asserts, the rank and file also did not immediately react, but afterwards took up arms once again with the Germans:

> According to Grandi, Galbiati had ordered mobilisation of the Militia a few hours before Mussolini's audience with the king on the afternoon of 25 July. There was a newly formed M Division, trained by the Germans for internal security, stationed quite near Rome, though it was unclear whether it could concentrate its forces quickly enough for another 'March on Rome'. Galbiati's orders, anyway, were intercepted by the Interior Ministry and never arrived. Lacking any initial incentive or order to react, both Party and Militia now found it impossible to act. Whether the Fascist Party and Militia would have reacted to any call to arms is a moot point; 25 July was a Sunday, after all. Hitler later derisively condemned a Fascist Party which had melted away like

> snow in the sun at the time of Mussolini's fall. This was probably unfair, since even he anticipated that the Fascists would 'come over to us' once the Germans had intervened quickly and decisively, which he expected and wanted.[6]

Fourth, many party branches were abandoned and some local party leaders fled to Germany. In fact, only a minority of party branches rallied on behalf of the fallen leader. Finally as Battistelli and Crociani assert:

> On 25 July 1943 the division had not yet reached operational status, which may explain why it did not react to these events. Nevertheless the Italian Army staff naturally considered it completely unreliable, and took precautionary measures. Since, during the hiatus between Mussolini's downfall and the announcement of Italy's capitulation to the Allies, the units could not be disbanded without alarming the Germans, they were reorganised, with many MVSN officers being replaced by army ones.[7]

One can argue also that another factor that influenced the soldiers of the M Division not to take action against the Badoglio government was the grave morale and military crisis that pervaded all soldiers of the Royal Army and the militia in July 1943. This was the result of the military defeats, the fact that the war had lasted for so many months, and the disappearance of Mussolini from the political scene. However, according to historian Stefano Fabei, the greatest responsibility for this crisis of the militia should be attributed to its leadership, which failed to take any actions once the new government took power. As MVSN historian Carlo Rastrelli asserts: 'In 1950, Galbiati printed his memoirs where he repeatedly argued that the "M" Division was not ready on 25 July, 1943, since it was only at the beginning of a complex training program. Moreover, the fact that the MVSN failed to react to the new government of Badoglio had in fact avoided a civil war'.[8]

In contrast, many historians have argued that the reasons listed above appear to be excuses for not acting on the part of the leadership of the MVSN rather than actual motivations.

One of the few leaders to react to Mussolini's downfall and take the political initiative was ex-secretary of the party and decorated war pilot Ettore Muti. It appears from intelligence files and police reports that Muti, after 25 July, had participated in meetings with other leaders of the regime to try to resurrect and refund the party. At one of the meetings, it appears that Muti had hatched a plan to free Mussolini in order to reinstall him as leader of the government.

According to the police chief loyal to Badoglio:

> After 25 July Ettore Muti had not abandoned his plans to rebel against the new government and he had been seen walking in Rome dressed with his

> uniform, with a huge pistol and a very menacing pace. We knew that he kept contact with the disbanded M Battalions and with Kesselring. On the day of my appointment as leader of the intelligence service I had been ordered to keep an eye on him since Badoglio considered him to be extremely dangerous. One day it must have been the 21 or 22 August Badoglio called me and without any preamble he ordered me to arrest him for spying and plotting against the state.[9]

On the night of 23–24 August 1943, the *Carabinieri* broke into his house in Fregene in the outskirts of Rome and after a brief pursuit in the beach Muti was killed. The Badoglio government denied any wrongdoing but on 26 September the Salo government explicitly accused of Muti's killing the police forces loyal to Badoglio and the crown. The most recent reconstruction of Muti's death accuses the *Carabinieri* of shooting him from the back while he was being taken into custody.

In August, the M Division unit was reorganised and renamed as the Centauro Division. Its MVSN officers assigned to other tasks, while a close relative of the king was placed at its head. By that time, its training had also been halted.

On 8 September 1943, the Badoglio government surrendered to the Allies and this precipitated major changes. Many of the Blackshirts units, including a majority of soldiers from the old M Division, joined the German Army and also took with them most of the equipment. The old MVSN garrisons, weapons, and ammunition depots were reopened in Northern and Central Italy and most of the Blackshirt units were rearmed and deployed against the Allies and the partisans. While the MVSN units attempted to reorganise, the units of the Royal Army and the police forces, especially in the north, disintegrated due to the lack of directives from the Badoglio government and the king. Not only were Royal Army units forced to bear the brunt of the German Army without any warning or direction, but they were also left leaderless given the flight of the king and the government to the south of Italy following the Armistice of 8 September. As a result, many units disbanded and the soldiers fled the barracks, while many other units were captured in their entirety by the Germans and dispatched to Germany to labour camps.

The Tagliamento Legion standard being paraded in the streets of Udine in the spring of 1943 at the conclusion of the Eastern Front campaign. (*Legione Tagliamento*)

The Tagliamento Legion standard being paraded in the streets of Udine in the spring of 1943 at the conclusion of the Eastern Front campaign. (*Legione Tagliamento*)

Above left: The Tagliamento Legion standard being paraded in the streets of Udine in the spring of 1943 at the conclusion of the Eastern Front campaign. (*Legione Tagliamento*)

Above right: A tank of the 1.a *Divisione Corazzata* M in the spring or summer of 1943 whose insignia can be seen on the turret of the German supplied Panzer IV Ausf. G. (*Archivio Centrale dello stato*)

Below: A flamethrower team from the 1a *Divisione Corazzata* M training outside Rome in the spring of 1943. The flamethrower is a German Model 41 *Flammenwerfer*, which was part of the supply of weapons provided by the Germans to arm the fledgling Blackshirt armoured division. (*Archivio Centrale dello stato*)

Above left: An artillery crew of the 1a *Divisione Corazzata* M training outside Rome in the summer of 1943 with a German 88-mm Flak 36/37. The artillery ranks of the division were filled primarily with soldiers coming from the coastal and anti-aircraft militia. (*Archivio Centrale dello stato*)

Above right: Italian soldiers training with a 47/32-mm anti-tank gun. The weapon was very ineffective lacking firepower against medium-sized Soviet tanks such as the T-34. (*Ufficio Storico*)

Below: Blackshirts of the 1a *Divisione Corazzata* riding on a German Sdkfz 7 halftrack prime mover towing a Flak 36 (88-mm) anti-tank gun. (*Archivio Centrale dello stato*)

Above: Blackshirt crew from the *Reggimento Corazzato* Leonessa of the 1a *Divisione Corazzata* M during training near Rome in the summer of 1943. The tank the crew is riding on is a German Pzkw III Ausf N armed with a 75-mm gun. (*Archivio Centrale dello stato*)

Below: A recent photo of the old garrison of the MVSN in Cremona.

Conclusion: Final Assessment

Introduction

An overall assessment regarding the combat performance of the Blackshirts on the Eastern Front should focus on four levels of analysis. First, it should compare the M Assault Battalions to other standard Italian infantry troops of the CSIR and the ARMIR that also fought on the Eastern Front. This level of analysis would compare the Blackshirts to say the Sforzesca Infantry Division or the Pasubio or any other standard division of the army to determine any major difference in combat effectiveness. Since both Royal Army and Blackshirts were armed with similar weapons, any difference in combat effectiveness would be dependent on such things as basic training, morale, and troop cohesion.

Second, it should compare the performance of the Blackshirt M Battalions that fought on the Eastern Front *versus* similar units that fought in other campaigns during the Second World War. This level of analysis should evaluate the Blackshirts from the Tagliamento or Montebello units, for instance, compared to the Blackshirt legions that were deployed in North Africa and Greece and later with the remaining Blackshirt M Battalions that were deployed in North Africa, France, and Yugoslavia in 1942–43. The latter comparison should be especially enlightening since it would essentially compare troops that were similarly trained and equipped but that fought in different theatres of operation.

Third, it should compare the M Assault Battalions to other volunteer units that also fought on the Eastern Front, such as the Spanish Blue Division, the Belgian volunteer units, and the Legion of French Volunteers Against Bolshevism (LFV). Both the Italian and the Spanish unit, for instance, were comprised of volunteers and by a majority of soldiers that was ideologically motivated to fight against the Soviet Union. Therefore, such a comparison would be enlightening, specifically if it could reveal some key differences in combat efficiency or power.

Fourth, a true comparative analysis should seek to glean from the opinions of the German Army liaison officers for clues as to how the German Army valued the overall combat effectiveness of the Axis volunteer units. The Germans rightly believed that their weapons, organisational skills, and tactics were superior and their views on the Axis allies were typically critical and focused on highlighting their training, tactical, or equipment shortcomings. Although the Germans were critical of their allies, some allies came under stronger criticism than others. Therefore, it is important to highlight how the Blackshirts ranked overall in the German view *versus* the other European volunteer units. The German view is thus instrumental not only to determine how well-prepared the volunteer units were for the Eastern Front campaign, but also to gain valuable insights on their overall combat effectiveness during the campaign.

For each level of analysis, such factors as training, availability and type of weapons, and type of combat deployment will be considered to determine the overall effectiveness of the Blackshirt units in relation to other Axis allies, standard Italian troops, and other MVSN units deployed elsewhere.

Blackshirts and Royal Army

The first level of analysis concerns the comparison between the Blackshirts to the units of the standard Royal Army during the Eastern Front campaign. The standard Blackshirt units of the MVSN were typically subordinated to the units of the Royal Army since they did not have their own independent source of funding, they relied on the Royal Army to fill the leadership and senior officer ranks, and finally relied on the Royal Army for artillery, sapper/engineering, and other support functions. Most importantly, in the vast majority of cases, the Blackshirts were typically under the command of a Royal Army divisional or army corps general at any one time during the Eastern Front campaign. At the start of the war, the standard Italian infantry division had approximately 10,000 to 12,000 soldiers and 100 trucks. The division was composed by two infantry regiments, one artillery regiment, and support services. Each regiment consisted of three infantry battalions. Each infantry battalion was composed of three infantry rifle companies and one machine-gun company with eight heavy machine guns and eighteen 45-mm mortars. Each regiment also had a heavy mortar company with six 81-mm units and an infantry gun company with four 65-mm guns, while the artillery arm consisted of an artillery regiment, a mortar battalion, and an anti-tank company. The artillery regiment was structured on three battalions with three batteries (each battery had four weapons). One battalion was equipped with twelve Skoda Model 1914 howitzers (100-mm), the second with twelve Model 1912 field guns (75-mm), and the third with twelve Skoda Model 1918 howitzer (75-mm). The regiment also included an anti-aircraft company with eight Breda Model 35 cannons (20-mm) and an anti-tank company with eight 47/32-mm guns. The division support services typically included an engineer battalion, with one engineer company, and a telecommunications service unit, medical unit, and various other services such as a motorised unit attached to each regiment. Thus unlike the British, German or Soviet infantry divisions, the Italian standard infantry division was not only smaller in size (the typical Soviet or British division, for example, had 18,000 soldiers), but it was also much less mobile unit and its troops primarily moved on foot. It lacked a real effective set of anti-tank weapons such as automatic rifles and rocket launchers that could pierce modern tanks since its only viable anti-tank weapons was the 65-mm gun. The latter was effective on the Eastern Front, although it was vastly outdated being a vintage First World War weapon. Its anti-aircraft units could only target low-flying, low-speed planes, while being totally ineffective against planes that were developed after 1940. It also lacked heavy artillery especially since by 1941 Soviet infantry regiments were armed with powerful 200-mm and 220-mm guns and howitzers. In contrast, most Italian units still relied on many First World War vintage field guns and howitzers. Finally it had a binary as opposed to a triangular structure with only two infantry regiments (as opposed to three as in most armies of the time) and one artillery regiment. This organisation was in sharp contrast to pre-Second World War military best practices and knowhow, which had shown that a triangular structure with three infantry regiments 'was much more flexible, resilient and self-supporting in prolonged combat'.[1]

The original strength of the Tagliamento in 1941 was not comparable to an Italian infantry division since it was still based on the legion (regiment) structure. Only with the development of the M Battalions and the M Battalion Groups in 1942 did the Blackshirts assume an organisational structure that more closely resembled the standard infantry division. At the time, their organisational structure was still fairly light since the two M Battalion Groups combined deployed in Russia were still smaller than an infantry division but at least it had acquired a greater degree of capacity and organisational autonomy. In mid-1942, the two standard M Battalion Groups deployed in Eastern Europe had, collectively, 6,500 to 7,500 soldiers of all ranks, 144 motorcycles, sixteen cars, and 496 trucks. Each M Battalion Group such as the Tagliamento or the Montebello had two infantry battalions and one heavy weapons/artillery battalion. Similarly to standard infantry, the two Blackshirt infantry battalions were structured on three rifle companies and one machine-gun company. The weapons of each group consisted of forty-eight assault rifles, twenty-four machine guns, eighteen 45-mm mortars, six 81-mm mortars, and eight 47/32-mm anti-tank guns. Thus, the Blackshirts lacked the 65-mm guns that were older but nonetheless more effective than the 47/32-mm guns against enemy tanks. Moreover, the Blackshirt units still had no heavy field artillery under their Heavy Weapons battalions and had to rely upon the Royal Army artillery for other support services as well. Even though it was smaller, the Blackshirt unit, however, was structured along similar lines of the standard infantry division with two infantry brigades and one artillery brigade. In addition, with regards to organisation the Blackshirt units had the same light, binary type of structure that characterised the standard infantry. Their infantry were armed, for the most part, with the same weapons of the standard infantry division, thus shared the same combat limitations especially with regards to the anti-tank defence. Thus, as a result of their organisation not only were the Blackshirts frequently outnumbered during battle engagements by Soviet Red Army units endowed with larger cohorts, but in addition the M Battalions also found themselves fighting with inferior firepower. They also did not, for the most part, unlike the Soviets or the Russians, have any tank or anti-tank support from self-propelled guns and lacked heavy artillery thus were often outgunned by larger Soviet units. Critically, the Blackshirts and the Italian infantry divisions enjoyed little or no air support.

The general of the Torino Division wrote a report after the retreat in 1943, which was very critical of the weapons used by his troops during the Eastern Front campaign. General Roberto Lerici stated:

> Our automatic guns given the extremely cold temperature and the low-quality of the antifreeze frequently did not work. Other weapons such as the hand grenades and the machine guns also did not work properly. The machine guns had to be kept near a fireplace during the night to keep them warm, while the hand grenades often did not explode. In contrast most automatic guns available to the Germans and the Russians worked fine most of the time and even under dire weather conditions. Such a disparity in the performance of the equipment created a lot of discontent among my troops to the point that during the retreat many weapons were abandoned because they were too heavy and the soldiers thought they were useless.[2]

Field Marshal Kesselring, who collaborated extensively with the Italian Supreme Command and knew the Italian Army inside and out, asserted in relation to Italian infantry weapons:

> It was expecting too much of the individual soldier to ask him to stop a heavy tank attack with inadequate weapons, for example with 4-cm anti-tank guns and dummy tanks, or to deliver an assault with tanks too thinly armoured and with insufficient firepower against a modernised enemy.[3]

The same weapons limitations outlined above would apply to the Blackshirt units since they had similar weaponry. The only exception was that by 1942 Blackshirt M Battalion Groups officers and NCOs were armed with Beretta light machine guns, which the Royal Army officers, for the most part, did not have. But this weapon, even though very effective, could do little to help the Blackshirt units in the anti-tank defence.

Kesselring's opinion in regard to the ineffective and outdated weapons of the Italian infantry should also be interpreted as a favourable view of the fighting abilities of the Italian infantry soldier, which often fought an unequal fight with great limitations both in the quality of the weapons and the ammunition.

Most of the weapons available to the Italian soldiers were very ineffective compared to the weapons of the German or Soviet soldiers. Italian anti-tank guns were very light and with little firepower capable of piercing only light tanks and armoured vehicles, while both the Germans and the Soviet Armies were endowed with more durable and powerful guns for their anti-tank defence. For example, as the number and quality of Soviet armoured vehicles increased, Nazi Germany decided that a multiplicity of weapons was needed by the infantry to counter the threat. Initially the Germans had a similar anti-tank gun to the Italian 47/32-mm gun. Their first gun was the Pak 37 (37-mm) deployed during the campaign against France in 1940. Due to its low firepower at the time of the Battle of France, the gun was superseded by the Pak 38 (50-mm). The Pak 38 could fire both high explosive and solid armour-piercing shots at a range of 1,000 metres or less and it was able to penetrate 84-mm of armour. This weapon, which was already superior to the Italian gun, was gradually replaced by an even more effective weapon, the Pak 40 (75-mm), which was capable of penetrating 99 mm of armour plate at 2,000 metres or less. These three guns also had a large protective shield, while they remained fairly light and hence highly mobile. The Italians on the other hand never developed an anti-tank gun that represented an improvement over the 47/32-mm model during the course of the war and the penetrative power of the Italian gun did not compare well to the Pak 40. In fact, the Italian gun could only pierce a 45-mm armoured plate at a distance of 150 to 200 metres or less.

The Solothurn 20-mm anti-tank rifle was also used by the Italian soldiers as an anti-tank weapon during the Second World War. It was used primarily against light vehicles and tanks and it was effective at a range of 120 metres or less.

The Germans also had similar types of rifles but also developed other weapons such as the *panzerfaust*. With an effective range of 100 metres, the weapon could fire a projectile and penetrate up to 200 mm of tank armoured plate. The Italians had no comparable weapon.

Thus as the German Army began to develop effective anti-tank weapons to deal with the growing threat of enemy tank attacks against static infantry defences, the Italians on the other hand, even in 1943, failed to develop additional effective anti-tank weapons. This largely explains why their line infantry experienced tremendous difficulties in facing large scale Soviet tank attacks. During the Second Don River Offensive, for instance, both the Blackshirts and the standard infantry defences were blown away by the Soviet tank attack and their lack of effective anti-tank weapons or mechanised reserves to plug holes largely explains their inability to stop the enemy attack. By that time, the Soviet Army not only had great numbers of tanks and larger anti-tank guns but could also count upon more effective rifles and machine guns. Italian rifles, for instance, were capable of firing eight bullets per minute, while comparable Soviet automatic light rifles by 1942 could fire 100 bullets per minute.

Although the Blackshirt M Battalion Groups remained lighter than the Royal Army divisions due to the absence of heavy artillery, the one diverging factor between the Blackshirts and the standard infantry was that by 1942 some slight improvements were made to some of the former's infantry weapons and equipment. In 1942, largely thanks to organisational changes and reforms to the training and structure of the Blackshirts, both the number of weapons and the quality of some of the new weapons and equipment was slightly improved *versus* 1941. The standard assault battalion of the M Battalions Group, for instance, was endowed with the same number of anti-tank guns and mortars of the legion but was armed with new armoured piercing ammunition such as the Effetto Pronto shells. Officers and NCOs were armed with Beretta light machine-gun pistols that were comparable to similar automatic weapons of the Soviet Army, while special Blackshirt platoons were supplied with a variety of special ammunition pouches such as the so-called samurai pouch, which could accommodate up to ten cartridge magazines. Although these were for the most part marginal improvements, they did slightly improve the fighting effectiveness of the Blackshirts of 1942.

Another factor that set apart the Blackshirts from the standard infantry was the higher degree of motorisation. While the standard remained low for the infantry even in 1942, the Blackshirt M Battalions Group were equipped with enough trucks to at least move their bulkier weapons by motor vehicles and also to dispatch on a speedier basis select infantry platoons to either prop up defensive positions or to carry out surprise counterattacks or raids. While the degree of motorisation of the Blackshirt units was still low compared to German and Russian infantry units, it was definitively higher than the standard Italian infantry division.

In conclusion, it can be argued that although the Blackshirt units (especially the M Battalion Groups) had a fairly light organisation and inferior weapons they made up for these deficiencies by deploying trained troops that were also experienced and to a certain degree highly motivated:

> Few crew served weapons and their light battalion structure made the Blackshirts clearly inferior to the battalions of the Royal Army and to call them assault battalions was clearly an exaggeration. On the other hand, the deficiencies in their equipment and the small size of their units were counterbalanced by the fact that the soldiers were motivated and well aware of the task that was ahead of them when the campaign began. In addition, many of them were more experienced than the typical conscript of the Royal Army and were better at handling weapons having used them previously in Ethiopia, Spain and Albania.[4]

Thus, while the Blackshirt units were smaller than comparable standard infantry units, they had other advantages. The soldiers deployed on the Eastern Front represented the elite of the Blackshirts, while their enhanced mobility, solid training, and their slightly improved weapons gave them an elite status that the Royal Army units lacked. Despite this enhanced status, the Blackshirts continued to have the same difficulties experienced by the Royal Army when fighting against enemy armoured units, especially due to the lack of effective anti-tank weapons. During the campaign, the Blackshirts often were used to prop up the standard infantry and their fighting effectiveness during the First and Second Offensive of the Don River, in many cases contributed to shoring up the Italian lines. In August 1942, for instance, the Tagliamento Blackshirts were instrumental in stopping the Soviet attack, while many soldiers of the Sforzesca experienced great difficulties in resisting the enemy onslaught. But the Second Battle of the Don River revealed that even well-motivated Blackshirt units could do little to stop a well-planned and co-ordinated mass tank attack put forth not only by entire tank brigades but also by special infantry shock troops.

In addition to the deficiencies related to ineffective weapons and lack of mobility, both the standard infantry division and the Blackshirts lacked some of the special units that were essential in set-piece battles of the Eastern Front. The retreat following the Second Offensive of the Don River, for instance, would not have been possible without the aid of key special German units. These few German units that were typically attached to the standard Wehrmacht infantry division, that either marched alongside, or that accompanied the Italian troops headed for ⊠ertkovo were instrumental in allowing the column to escape the Russian encirclement. German motorised and aerial reconnaissance, for instance, was critical in identifying a path that was as clear as possible of Russian troops. Scout cars, trucks, and Luftwaffe aircraft were deployed ahead of the column to anticipate enemy troops movements and guide the Axis units out of the encirclement. In addition, the dropping of much-needed supplies of fuel, ammunition, and food from the Luftwaffe was also decisive and kept the column going at critical times. While the presence of German self-propelled guns and tanks within the column allowed the troops to properly engage the Russian armoured units at critical junctures during the retreat. The most advanced German infantry divisions of the time comprised a mixture of armour, anti-tank, and infantry units with the key addition of self-propelled guns and truck-mounted Flak 88-mm guns to aid the anti-tank defence. Time and time again during the retreat, these guns were called upon to engage the Soviet tanks and to open a path for the Axis foot soldiers and motorised columns to escape the entrapment. Without these three elements, it can be argued that the retreating Axis column would have been most likely captured or destroyed in its entirety by the enemy. The Soviet tanks, in fact, would have had an easy time in chasing the footsoldiers that had abandoned most of the anti-tank weapons on the line. Both Blackshirts and Royal Army units would have been powerless against the Soviet tanks.

Blackshirts on the Eastern Front *versus* Blackshirts Active in Other Theatres

How did the Blackshirt units deployed on the Eastern Front such as the Tagliamento and the Montebello compare to other similar units deployed in Greece, North Africa, or Yugoslavia? In 1940, many Blackshirt legions or battalions were hastily sent to the frontline without proper training and with a very lightweight organisation that was very weak in support services (artillery, anti-tank, medical, and signal). Moreover, both the Blackshirt units deployed in North Africa and in Greece suffered large casualties and, for the most part, performed poorly because of a host of factors but mainly because they were not properly deployed by Royal Army commanders unfamiliar with mechanised warfare. The Blackshirt units in North Africa, for instance, were assembled and mobilised a few weeks prior to the start of the war and received very little training. With regards to the latter, the units did conduct 'desert marches to acquaint them with the environment and climate,' but no field exercises were conducted with tanks or with anti-tank weapons.[5]

In addition, when in December 1940 they were deployed in North Africa, they were tasked with defending very static defensive strongholds against enemy units that in contrast were highly mobile and enjoyed armoured support. The lack of effective anti-tank weapons and the inexperience of the Blackshirt units in fighting against well-co-ordinated tank attacks ensured the virtual destruction of not only the volunteer units but also of the Royal Army infantry and artillery units that fought alongside them. Each North African Blackshirt division, for example, could not muster more than 100 light or medium-sized trucks. Without proper motorisation the units could not, for instance, implement anti-amour reconnaissance patrols or transport troops and guns during battle engagements in the sectors where they were most needed. As a result of these huge limitations, the three Blackshirt divisions deployed in North Africa were destroyed by the British counteroffensive of late 1940. In Greece, the Blackshirts units were also deployed in battle after having received very little training. XCIII Battalion, for instance, was deployed in frontline combat 'after a single live fire exercise'.[6] Meanwhile, 'IV Battaglione had last done military service some five or six years previously'.[7]

Although conceived as assault battalions, these units were hastily deployed to stem the offensive tide of the Greek Army, which launched a surprise counterattack against the Italian Army in November 1941. Frontline commanders faced with a very difficult situation threw unto the field of battle every unit they could muster, including the Blackshirts, which, given their light weaponry and their training, were not particularly suited for the defensive function. Hence these units, although they fought valiantly, suffered huge casualties, and as a result were either captured/destroyed by the enemy or had to ultimately be withdrawn due to high losses. What characterised their experience was that until the start of the Second World War, Blackshirt units were only mobilised for brief periods of time and lacked the training and cohesiveness of regular infantry units. Once deployed, they lacked adequate services and their weaponry was fairly light being assault units, hence not particularly suited for the defensive or to fight against enemy armoured units. Finally, their specific deployment in operations where mobile warfare prevailed or where heavy artillery and infantry strongpoints were more suited in stemming enemy attacks rather than light infantry largely determined their overall combat effectiveness. These factors explain the overall poor performance of the Blackshirt units against the British in 1940 and the Greeks in 1940–41. The experience of the Tagliamento initially and then of the M Battalions Groups later on the Eastern Front, however, tell a different story. First, the Tagliamento was dispatched to the front after having received more thorough training. Although the training was marred by the lack of ammunition with limited opportunities for shooting practice and live fire exercises, its greater duration allowed the troops to develop *esprit de corps* and an overall combat cohesiveness that the earlier Blackshirt units clearly lacked. Moreover, the Tagliamento was initially (between September 1941 and June 1942) deployed in offensive operations aimed at capturing large swaths of territory and in pursuing retreating Soviet Army units that were well-suited to its initial training with soldiers having been prepared as shock troops and organised into assault battalions. The Tagliamento was also one of the few legions that in 1941 had been reinforced with the attachment of one heavy weapons/artillery battalion. In contrast, most other Blackshirt legions in 1940 did not have such an artillery battalion. Even though the guns were largely inadequate, they did provide some degree of defence against enemy tank attacks especially in close-range combat operations. Finally, although the Tagliamento was also like other Blackshirt units armed with ineffective weapons and with obsolete anti-tank guns, it fought surprisingly well during its first defensive battle during the week of Christmas 1941. As the war went on, the MVSN selected the best Blackshirts to form elite M Battalion Groups, which were slightly better equipped and motorised, decidedly better trained and had also could rely upon improved support services. In fact, by mid-1942, the MVSN had completed the selective reorganisation process that distinguished the Blackshirt units into standard and elite. Whereas by then the legions took on a secondary role supporting the army in garrison and anti-partisan duties, the M Battalions, constituted as the elite of the MVSN, took on a much more important role and were deployed on the frontline or in very troubled regions in anti-partisan, garrison duties. The majority of the M Battalions (eleven out of twenty-three) were dispatched to the Eastern Front to fight against the Soviet Union, while some were dispatched to France, Yugoslavia, and Tunisia. The fact that half of the M Battalions force was dispatched to the Soviet Union demonstrates how important this campaign was for the MVSN and the Blackshirts. How did their battlefield performance compare to the remaining M Battalions which were deployed in other theatres of operation?

In the spring of 1942, four M Battalions (XLII, XLIII, L, and LX, the so-called *Gruppo Battaglioni* CC.NN da Sbarco) were trained to conduct the seaborne invasion of Malta. Although the unit was perhaps the most well-trained of all the M Battalions, it was ultimately deployed for other combat roles once the invasion of Malta was cancelled in the summer of 1942. In November 1942, this unit landed unopposed on the island of Corsica in order to occupy it as a reprisal against Vichy France. Then, in 1943, it performed garrison duty in southern France (Toulon) near harbour and naval installations but saw very little combat.

Six other M Battalions fought against Tito's partisans in Yugoslavia (VIII, XVI, XXIX, LXXI, LXXXI, and LXXXV), where they were engaged for the most part in irregular warfare involving such actions as setting up checkpoints, performing sentry duty over key installations and bases, fighting insurgents in localised, small-scale clashes, and in identifying and rounding up bands of partisans. Finally, the X M Battalion fought a mostly defensive battle in Tunisia against the British 8th Army between January and May 1943. Thus it was the only unit that fought a comparable campaign to the M Battalions deployed in Russia as it was deployed first on the Mareth and then on the Enfidaville defensive line in a defensive and counterattacking capacity. It experienced similar widespread losses and was ultimately wiped out by the final Allied assault against the Enfidaville line in April–May 1943. The units deployed in France and the ones deployed in Yugoslavia thus played a much inferior role to the M Battalions units deployed in Russia and definitively experienced secondary combat roles. In contrast, the units deployed in Russia: 'As the Blackshirts' combat elite, the M Battalions would suffer the most from the setbacks on the Eastern Front in winter 1942–43'.[8]

The fact that they were always and uninterruptedly deployed on the frontline to either contest enemy attacks or to conduct offensive raids or actions against the Soviet Army implies several things. First, these M Battalions carried out more sophisticated, and tactically relevant combat roles than simply performing rear garrison duty, which in most cases the German Army typically assigned to reserve or secondary units unfit for frontline service. Second, the fact that these troops were never rotated out of service to perform other duties indicates that they were considered highly effective by both the Italian and the German High Command. In many instances, they were considered irreplaceable especially when they were deployed to solidity the Axis defences against major Soviet attacks. In the winter of 1941–42, the Tagliamento Blackshirts took centre stage during the Christmas Battle. The Blackshirts were again to play a central role during the First Offensive of the Don River and were used to forcefully push back enemy infiltrations during the Second Offensive of the Don River. Third, often deployed as tactical reserves to the Italian standard infantry corps these units were often called in to perform sensitive and highly critical combat missions such as propping up infantry defensive positions during critical moments of the battle or to forcefully counterattack to re-establish key positions and outposts.

Blackshirts and the Other Axis Volunteer Units

The Blackshirt units fought on the Eastern Front alongside other volunteer units from Spain, Belgium, Holland, and France. Spain was represented by the 18,000-strong Blue Division, while Belgium was represented by the Légion Wallonie and its Flemish counterpart, the Legion Flandern. Finally, Vichy France was represented by the LFV. Throughout the campaign, the Blue Division was deployed more akin to the Blackshirts since it saw extensive combat in both a defensive and offensive capacity on the frontline, while the Belgian and French soldiers were for the most part deployed in anti-partisan, rear area garrison duties rather than frontline action.

What distinguished these politicised units *versus* the standard army was the fact that they were purely volunteer units, although when they were deployed in the Soviet Union they had different degrees of training and combat expertise. These differences dictated the type of combat engagement that volunteer units were involved in, as well as how they were perceived by the German armed forces.

The Belgian Legion, for instance, committed a total of 4,000 soldiers to the Eastern Front campaign, but from the onset, its volunteers performed mainly rear area security duties in the Ukraine at the disposal of Army Group South.

Their training and preparation prior to the dispatch to the Eastern Front was fairly limited, although their equipment and weapons were first rate being furnished by the German Army. Given the scarce preparations and the fact that many of the volunteers were not experienced, the Belgian Legion was initially deployed exclusively for rear area tasks during the fall and winter of 1941. Because of its specific deployment, during this period the unit's heavy weapons were taken back by the Germans and redistributed to frontline Wehrmacht troops. At the time, a German officer from the 17th Army Corps wrote:

> We are having some difficulties with the Walloon Battalion. Members of the battalion complain about unfair treatment by our command to OKW, while IV Corps reports that the behaviour and non co-operation of the Belgian troops borders on treason. The only use we can see is to transfer them to the rear areas of LII Corps.[9]

On 28 February 1942, although it sustained heavy losses, the unit contributed in repulsing an attack put forth by two Soviet infantry regiments. During the operation, it was supported by a German machine-gun company. During the German offensive in the summer of 1942 in the Caucasus, the unit was tasked again with guarding the supply lines and saw no frontline combat. In June 1943, the Belgians were placed under the command of the German SS and renamed the SS Volunteer *Sturmbrigade* Wallonien. On 24 December 1943, the unit experienced its first major battle engagement when it defended the western bank of the Dnieper River against a major Soviet offensive. In this capacity, the Belgian forces acted as the rearguard of the Axis defence and suffered considerable losses. From then onwards, the unit was reorganised but performed mostly rear area garrison duties until the end of the war.

Similarly, the two-battalion, 2,461-strong LFV was formed in 1941 and participated with Army Group Centre to the siege against Moscow. The unit was not fully trained but based on political considerations was hurriedly assembled and dispatched to the Eastern Front by the French authorities. The LFV's main weapons included German Mauser rifles, Maxim light and heavy machine guns, and PAK 35 anti-tank units. However, although sharing similar weapons, the LFV, unlike the advanced German infantry units, was not a very mobile force, having to rely on horse-drawn carts to transport the heavy machine guns and the artillery. As a result, it moved very slowly and its approach to the frontline was slow and costly, due to the loss of valuable equipment. Its main combat action of the Eastern Front campaign was the assault against Diutkovo on 1 December 1941, which was successful but was also the cause of several losses among the French troops, which were forced to eventually hand over its defence to the Germans. Following this battle, the unit was reorganised in the spring of 1942 and later was deployed to fight partisans in Belarus.

A German artillery officer who witnessed the one and only French offensive operation wrote of 'a courageous, but absolutely idiotic attack by the French volunteers as in the times of Frederick the Great!'[10]

As Beyda asserts:

> Undertrained, poorly equipped, and torn by inside political rivalries, the regiment still marched to the front and fought the Red Army in December 1941. Being almost destroyed, the formation was then withdrawn and thoroughly purged and reshaped by the Germans, who wanted to gain more from the collaboration with the Frenchmen.[11]

Thus, although the French unit was furnished with better equipment and weapons by the Germans, it never matched the Blackshirts combat effectiveness and its mostly rear area deployment demonstrated that the Germans had low esteem of the LFV fighting abilities.

The Blue Division, on the other hand, participated to the initial German offensive aimed against Leningrad in the fall of 1941. This was after it had spent several months conducting rigorous training in Germany under the tutelage of German training officers. But then in the winter of 1941, it fought a large-scale defensive action that was very similar to the battle engagements experienced by the Italian 8th Army during the first and second offensives on the Don River, or the Christmas Battle of the Tagliamento in 1941. The Blue Division was tasked with defending the Krasny Bor sector from a major enemy counterattack put forth by the Soviet 55th Army. This combat unit was able to deploy considerable infantry forces and firepower to attempt to break through the Spanish defences including the 72nd Rifle Division, 43rd Rifle Division, 63rd Guards Rifle Division, 45th Rifle Division, a tank battalion of twenty tanks, an armoured brigade of sixty tanks, and 800 artillery pieces.[12]

To fight off this major enemy counter, the Blue Division had 18,000 soldiers armed with bolt-action, K98 7.92-mm Mauser rifles, MG34 machine guns, and 81-mm mortars. Its anti-tank companies had twenty-four PAK 37 anti-tank guns and could also count upon a German detachment with three PAK 40 anti-tank guns. Fire support was provided by Blue Division's own field artillery, consisting of two 75-mm guns, thirty-two 105-mm howitzers and twelve 150-mm howitzers.

While the Blue Division faced similar odds as the Italian Blackshirts on the Don River being outnumbered nine to one in infantry and fifteen to one in artillery, the former could rely on a larger and more effective artillery support while facing only eighty enemy tanks. These are the two critical differences between the two Russian operations. The Soviet operation against the Blue Division also still relied on more primitive combined arms tactics deploying the armour in a piecemeal fashion, while the Italians, at least during the Second Offensive of the Don River, faced a massive Soviet tank attack and with more obsolete anti-tank and artillery weapons.

The Blue Division fought valiantly against overwhelming enemy troops, and after this major engagement, it continued to be deployed in the frontline and was never utilised by the Germans to perform anti-partisan duty in the rear. It was ultimately withdrawn from the front and returned back to Spain only after Franco began to distance his regime from the Axis alliance in 1943.

Like the soldiers of the Blue Division, the Blackshirts were never sent to the rear for long periods of time and were always deployed defensively on the line. They also did not participate to anti-partisan patrols in the rear. Both facts are indicative of the fact that these troops were considered by the Axis commanders to be reliable and effective especially when fighting in a defensive capacity as line infantry.

It can be argued that, unlike the French and Belgian units, from the onset of the Blue Division's and the Blackshirts' arrival on the Eastern Front, both volunteer units acquitted themselves well in frontline engagements and were particularly effective when fighting on the defensive. In contrast, both the French and Belgian units while armed with German equipment and weapons, largely due to their lack of training and their organisational deficiencies could not be held on the frontline positions for extended periods of time. Most of their tasks were thus relegated to rear area security duties, which required less combat effectiveness and readiness than troops deployed for frontline assignments.

The German View

Like most European armies of the 1930s and '40s, the Italian Army followed the tactics of what then was considered the most effective and largest army of Europe, the French Army. The German doctrine of rapid, highly mobile, manoeuvres with tanks and motorised infantry supported by Stuka planes above was very foreign to the Italians as it was very foreign to the French infantry as well that fought the Germans in 1940. Like the French, the Italians believed on large infantry-based armies and on the strength of field fortifications such as bunkers, pillboxes, and Maginot Line-type structures to confront enemy armoured units. At the beginning of the war, for instance, the Italians had many infantry divisions but only three armoured divisions, and most infantry units were not motorised.

In fact, when the Italians took up defensive positions in Ukraine in the winter of 1941, they adopted a rigid defensive fortification system grounded on machine-gun and artillery strongpoints that was very foreign to the more flexible German defence system. Then when the German advance in Ukraine resumed, there were problems between the Italians and the Wehrmacht since the former advanced at a much slower pace and in the German view, the Italians were too preoccupied with defensive tasks such as setting up strongpoints and covering their flanks. There was also another difficulty given that the Germans had more advanced communication systems and hence moved much more quickly than the Italians because orders from central command to field units could be delivered more rapidly.

However, the most critical issue between the two Axis countries remained the defensive system and the tactics that should have been adopted to counter Soviet Army offensives. In this regard, the Blackshirts used the same tactics of the standard Italian infantry units by huddling one or more platoons into fortified strongholds. With regards to this defensive system, the war diary of General von Tippelskirch states:

> In discussing this theme raised many times before, General Tippelskirch once again emphasised with the aid of the situation map of the Alpine Corps, the importance of the abandonment by the Italians of their fortress tactic and its replacement by a flexible line of fire. The impression was given that General Malaguti wanted to evade the tactical discussion. He admitted that he had not submitted the previous memorandum of General von Tippelskirch, which dealt with the same theme to the G.O.C. He had written on it 'has discovered America', whereupon the discussion became very heated.[13]

Thus the differences between Germans and Italians persisted even in late 1942, but a more mobile, more scattered defensive positioning by the Italian troops was probably not viable even at that time since they lacked key equipment to implement it.

The Germans levelled the same critiques to the Spanish Blue Division and to the Italians, especially with regards to defensive deployments were both tended to amass soldiers in strongholds and failure to make proper use of the terrain. The Spanish units, for instance, were criticised by Wehrmacht Colonel Hoppe for their lack of mobility and firepower when attacking against superior enemy forces: 'Military development are wholly unsatisfactory. The officers do not control their men, and do not follow sound military or tactical principles. Also the men have totally insufficient basic training. Thoughtlessness and carelessness lead to their shocking casualties'.[14]

The same officer stated that the Blue Division defensive tactics based on mutually supporting strongholds were costly and that Spanish troops incurred higher losses than German infantry.

Despite the perceived lack of defensive tactical acumen and the inability of deploying advanced weapons and more mobile strategies during offensive combat operations, the Germans did single out the Italian and Spanish volunteer units for their high fighting spirit and their ability to maintain and hold defensive positions despite sufferings above average losses. In Chapter 3, for instance, the German paratroopers that fought alongside the Tagliamento during the tail end of the Christmas Battle were very impressed by its ability to halt the advance of larger Soviet cohorts. While in Chapter 4, for example, the German 8th Army *attaché* was quoted stating how the Blackshirts had been instrumental in propping up and hardening Italian defences during the First Offensive of the Don River. Similarly, the Blue Division was praised by the Germans during the defensive battle of 1941 at Krasny Bor. Hitler, for instance, was so impressed by the Spanish troops that he issued a special decoration for some of its volunteers. Ultimately, the German view stressed that the Italian and Spanish volunteer units had shown themselves capable in conducting limited offences and in performing static defensive tasks, while the LVF and the Belgian volunteers on the other hand, could not be relied upon to cover frontline positions or to take part in manoeuvre warfare. Thanks to experienced officers, well-motivated soldiers, and well-situated machine-gun strongpoints, the former were often able to have the better against superior Soviet forces. On the other, the latter could only be deployed for rear area duties.[15]

The major differences observed by the Germans were that the Spanish division was better organised with a more common structure comprised of three infantry regiments and one artillery regiment as compared to the Italian Blackshirts, which were structured on a binary, hence a weaker organisation. Moreover, the Germans observed that the Spanish volunteer units were fully armed with German weapons, while the Blackshirts fought with inferior Italian weapons.

Spanish historian Carlos Caballero Jurado has also underlined the notable difference between the Blue Division and Germany's Axis allies such as the Blackshirts by highlighting that the former were completely equipped with German weapons.[16]

However, Jurado argues that personal motivation and morale were the two critical factors that enabled the Blue Division to fight more effectively than the conscript troops supplied by the other Axis allies. I partially disagree with his statement and believe that weapons and troop selection, and most importantly training, were more important factors explaining why these elite units fought more effectively.

Unlike the Italians, the Spanish troops also did not experience the reversal and retreat of the Don River. German senior officers such as General von Tippelskirch and Lieutenant Salazer were eyewitnesses to the retreat of the combined German and Italian armies from the Don, and these officers did not refrain from criticising aspects of the retreat. The distinguished German officer, for example, reported on 18 March 1943 on several aspects of the retreat. His report, which summarised events that followed Operation Little Saturn, contained mixed opinions regarding the 8th Army. The overall view was that the Italians, especially the *alpini* and the Blackshirts, had fought a spirited defensive battle against superior Russian forces. Although, the units fought effectively on the defensive line, there were clearly flaws in their deployment. First and foremost, the report accused the Italians of deploying a strongpoint cantered defence rather than a more mobile defensive organisation. The report underlies how the Italian troops had not been properly trained in fighting the Russian armour at close range, and how they suffered huge losses due to the deep infiltrations of the enemy tanks. Once the rout was underway, the German officer pointed out that the Italian retreating columns lacked proper motorised reconnaissance units to stay clear of the Russians and how many troops were lost or captured during the retreat because the flanks of the column were not well protected. But generally, the German officer outlined how the *alpini* and the militia fought more effectively than the standard infantry units of the Cosseria Division. It also highlights that even these more combative troops would not have escaped the encirclement without the key aid provided by the German self-propelled guns and tanks.[17]

Ultimately, the German High Command blamed the Hungarians, Romanians, and the Italians for the defeat holding them responsible for not being able to stop the Russian counteroffensive. On the other hand, the Axis allies pointed out in their post campaign reports that the Germans too, especially XXIV Army Corps, were responsible for the downturn since they too were beaten on the line by the Russians and forced to retreat from the Don River.[18]

Thus, while the battalions of the Blackshirt units lacked effective weapons and were deployed for the most part as standard line infantry units, they ultimately demonstrated that well-trained and drilled infantry units could perform adequately even if vastly outnumbered and outgunned by the Soviet Army. Their most striking feature was the way in which in the Soviet Union they redeemed the Blackshirt volunteer units from the early debacles of 1940–41 in North Africa and Greece. Specifically, how improved training, slight improvements to weapons and ammunition, and, most importantly, more sound tactical dispositions helped these units gain greater combat efficiency.

Above: Reconstituted militia unit after the fall of the regime somewhere in northern Italy in 1944. (*Archivio Centrale dello stato*)

Right: A soldier of the M *Battaglione* IX *Settembre* in the winter of 1943 in the Abruzzo region. Note the M insignia badge on the collar and the samurai vest used to hold weapons or equipment such as grenades. The soldier is most likely an ex-member of the Blackshirt seaborne unit, which was supplied with the samurai vests. (*Archivio Centrale dello stato*)

Appendix

Camicie Nere Medals of Military Valour by *Gruppo di Battaglione* during the Eastern Front Campaign (1941–43)

MOVM (Italian Gold Medal of Military Valor)
MAVM (Italian Silver Medal of Military Valor)
MBVM (Italian Bronze Medal of Military Valor)
CGVM (Cross of War Medal of Military Valor)

Raggruppamento CCNN M 23 Marzo—Valle Scrivia

MBVM *Generale* FRANCISCI Enrico
CGVM *Seniore* MARINETTI Emilio
CGVM *Centurione* TOSO Giuseppe
MAVM *Console* BERTONI Mario
MAVM *Seniore* MASPER Giuseppe
MAVM M *Seniore* MASPER Giuseppe
MAVM *Centurione* ASNICAR Giovanni
MAVM *Centurione* BATTISTELLA Aldo
MAVM *Centurione* NASCIMBENE Giorgio
MAVM M *Centurione* ORIANI Angelo
MAVM *Capomanipolo* MALAVASI Felice
MAVM *camicia nera* CASSULO Vincenzo
MAVM *camicia nera* GIACOMINI Carlo
MAVM *camicia nera* SALDARINI Attilio
MBVM *Console* BERTONI Mario
MBVM *Seniore* ABRILE Enzo

MBVM *Centurione* ANDREINI Renzo
MBVM *Centurione* POLVANI Fortunato
MBVM *Centurione* SOCINO Giuseppe
MBVM M *Capomanipolo* BERNACCHI Tommaso
MBVM M *Capomanipolo* SAPORITI Francesco
MBVM *Sotto Capomanipolo* LEONE Luigi
MBVM M *capo squadra* AVIGO Giuseppe
MBVM M *capo squadra* BRUMAT Giuseppe
MBVM M *capo squadra* GUIDO Ernesto
MBVM *vice capo squadra* BINDA Silvio
MBVM M *vice capo squadra* BUNI Gino
MBVM *vice capo squadra* CAVAGNI Rino
MBVM *vice capo squadra* CHIESA Giovanni
MBVM *vice capo squadra* RIZZOGLIO Alessandro
MBVM M *camicia nera* ANDREONI Celestino
MBVM M *camicia nera* BALBI Armando
MBVM M *camicia nera* BELLINI Cesare
MBVM *camicia nera* BRECCIOLOTTI Costantino
MBVM *camicia nera* CAMPANA Massimo
MBVM *camicia nera* CHIAVAZZA Matteo
MBVM *camicia nera* FILADELFI Albo
MBVM *camicia nera* GIORDANO Aldo
MBVM *camicia nera* GOTTA Paolo
MBVM M *camicia nera* GUARNIERI Ugo
MBVM *camicia nera* LAZZARONI Serafino
MBVM *camicia nera* MANFRIN Virginio
MBVM M *camicia nera* MOLINO Carlo
MBVM *camicia nera* NOVELLO Giovanni
MBVM *camicia nera* NOVERO Giuseppe
MBVM *camicia nera* RAULE Romolo
MBVM *camicia nera* RICCI Domenico
MBVM *camicia nera* TOME' Giov.Battista
CGVM *Centurione* PELLEGRINI Bruno
CGVM *Centurione cappellano* SANGIORGIO Leandro
CGVM *Centurione* SCIANCA Carlo
CGVM M *Capomanipolo* BUSATTI Oscar
CGVM M *capo squadra* FIORINESCHI Giuseppe
CGVM M *capo squadra* PERTUSI Giovanni
CGVM M *capo squadra* ROCCO Arcangelo
CGVM M *capo squadra* SOARDO Alcide
CGVM *vice capo squadra* CARLOTTI Mario
CGVM *vice capo squadra* FEDELI Mario

CGVM *vice capo squadra* POLLINI Giuseppe
CGVM M *camicia nera* BARONCI Armando
CGVM M *camicia nera* BIANI Carlo
CGVM M *camicia nera* CAROSIO Aldo
CGVM M *camicia nera* CARTASEGNA Giovanni
CGVM M *camicia nera* CECCHINI Giuseppe
CGVM M *camicia nera* CIVERCHIA Dino
CGVM M *camicia nera* DANI Rinaldo
CGVM M *camicia nera* ESPOSITO Vincenzo
CGVM *camicia nera* FELICE Umberto
CGVM *camicia nera* GIRAUDO Chiaffredo
CGVM *camicia nera* GROSSI Renzo
CGVM *camicia nera* MAZZI Pietro
CGVM *camicia nera* MORACCHIOLI Annunzio
CGVM *camicia nera* PASQUALE Alessandro
CGVM *camicia nera* PIARDI DEBORMIDA Giac.
CGVM *camicia nera* PIROTTO Giovanni
CGVM *camicia nera* RENZI Alfredo
CGVM *camicia nera* SALA Pietro
CGVM *camicia nera* SERENA Agostino
CGVM *camicia nera* SIANO Luigi
CGVM *camicia nera* SIANO Luigi
CGVM *camicia nera* TARCHI Rodolfo
CGVM *camicia nera* VALLI Amelio
CGVM *camicia nera* VIANELLO Silvestro

Raggruppamento CCNN M 23 Marzo–Leonessa

MAVM M *Console* SARDU Graziano
MAVM *Seniore* ALBONETTI Fortunato
MAVM M *Seniore* COMINCIOLI Giacomo
MAVM M *Capomanipolo* MERINGHI Giorgio
MAVM *Capomanipolo* QUADRELLI Marcello
MAVM *capo squadra* BONCUORE Renato
MAVM *capo squadra* PIAZZETTI Vittorio
MBVM *Centurione* DE GIOVANNI Piero
MBVM M *Capomanipolo* ARLOTTI Antonio
MBVM *vice capo squadra* BORTOLOTTI Bruno
MBVM *vice capo squadra* ODARDA Davide
MBVM *vice capo squadra* REBUZZINI Lorenzo
MBVM *camicia nera* GHIGLIA Enrico

MBVM *camicia nera* MAZZOLA Carlo
MBVM M *camicia nera* NICOLA Giuseppe
CGVM *capo squadra* BANFI Luigi
CGVM M *capo squadra* ZAUSA Umberto
CGVM *vice capo squadra* CIOFFI Pasquale
CGVM *vice capo squadra* COSCIA Giuseppe
CGVM M *camicia nera* BREVIARIO Vincenzo
CGVM *camicia nera* PITAMORSI Mario
CGVM *camicia nera* PROSIO Pietro

Ragguppamento CCNN M 23 Marzo (but no group battalion identified)

MAVM *Centurione* BALDERI Alberto
MAVM *Centurione* CHELOTTI Giorgio
MAVM *Centurione* LORENZA Francesco
MAVM M *Capomanipolo* CIRONI Manlio
MAVM *capo squadra* BONACCIN Ettore
MAVM *capo squadra* MANNINI Alfredo
MAVM *capo squadra* SORAGNI Renzo
MAVM *camicia nera* MODUGNO Settimio
MBVM *Capomanipolo* CUCCODORO Camillo
MBVM *vice capo squadra* ZANDO' Gino
MBVM *camicia nera* BONI Dante
MBVM *camicia nera* VITALI Antonio

Raggruppamento CCNN M 3 Gennaio

MAVM *Generale milizia* DIAMANTI Filippo
MAVM *Console* VIANINI Italo
MAVM *Tenente Colonnello* DE FRANCO Vittorio
MAVM M *Centurione* CANTE G. Maria
MAVM *Capomanipolo* TADDEI Rinaldo
MBVM *Seniore* MEZZETTI Nazzareno
MBVM M *camicia nera* GUIZZARDI Gino
MBVM *camicia nera* TEDESCO Italo
CGVM *Centurione* PESSINA Carlo
CGVM M *camicia nera* CAPPELLETTI Ercole
CGVM *camicia nera* DONE' Giuseppe
CGVM *camicia nera* EDERLE Antonio

Raggruppamento CCNN M 3 Gennaio–Tagliamento

MOVM M *Capomanipolo* BATTISTINI Guerriero
MOVM M *Capomanipolo* VELLANI DIONISI Fr.
MOVM M *camicia nera* PAOLUCCI Mario
MAVM *Console* GALARDO Antonio
MAVM *Console* GALARDO Antonio
MAVM *Console* MITTICA Domenico
MAVM *Console* NICCHIARELLI Nicolo’
MAVM *Seniore* CANGEMI Giosuè
MAVM *Seniore* MARGINI Silvio
MAVM M *Seniore* MEZZETTI Nazzareno
MAVM *Primo Seniore* ZULIANI Ermacora
MAVM *Centurione* DE APOLLONIA Leonello
MAVM M *Centurione* GENTILE Mario
MAVM *Centurione* MINGIARDI Alberto
MAVM M *Centurione* MUTTI Luigi
MAVM *Centurione* ROTA Mario
MAVM *Centurione* TRENTINI Alessandro
MAVM *Tenente cappellano* BIASUTTI Guglielmo
MAVM M *Capomanipolo* CANCIANI Italo
MAVM M *Capomanipolo* GALEAZZI Alessandro
MAVM *Capomanipolo* LIMOLI Vito
MAVM *Capomanipolo* LIMOLI Vito
MAVM M *Capomanipolo* MAZZOCCHI Amilcare
MAVM M *Capomanipolo* SANDRIGO Luca
MAVM M *Capomanipolo* ZAGO Mario
MAVM *Sotto Capomanipolo* GLEYSER Federico
MAVM M *capo squadra* ARIOSI Mario
MAVM M *capo squadra* AZZONI Giuseppe
MAVM M *capo squadra* BERNI Aldo
MAVM M *capo squadra* CARLET Luigi
MAVM *capo squadra* CHEMELLO Giuseppe
MAVM *capo squadra* CHEMELLO Giuseppe
MAVM *capo squadra* COZZARIN Luigi
MAVM M *capo squadra* DEL PICCOLO Giovanni
MAVM M *capo squadra* MARZI Umberto
MAVM M *capo squadra* MAZZOLINI Osvaldo
MAVM M *capo squadra* PELATI Erio
MAVM *vice capo squadra* DAVOLI Cesare
MAVM *vice capo squadra* DAVOLI Pietro
MAVM *vice capo squadra* MOLINO Primo

MAVM *camicia nera* BASEGGIO Gualtiero
MAVM *camicia nera* BREDEON Ferruccio
MAVM M *camicia nera* CARLETTI Amelio
MAVM M *camicia nera* CHIARAMONTI Egidio
MAVM M *camicia nera* FERRI Carlo
MAVM *camicia nera* GARNERI Pietro
MAVM *camicia nera* INAUDI Clemente
MAVM *camicia nera* MARGARIA Angelo
MAVM *camicia nera* MERLO Emerio
MAVM M *camicia nera* MONTASI Telesforo
MAVM M *camicia nera* MONTORSI
MAVM *camicia nera* PARENTI Raffaele
MAVM *camicia nera* RICCI Filippo
MAVM M *camicia nera* SANCANDI Domenico
MAVM *camicia nera* SCHIAVI Orazio
MAVM *camicia nera* SIMONAZZI Giovanni
MAVM *camicia nera* TOMATIS Mateo
MAVM *camicia nera* VANZO Giovanni
MBVM *Seniore* MARGINI Silvio
MBVM *Centurione* ARMANI Bruno
MBVM *Centurione* CALBI Giorgio
MBVM *Centurione* MARCHETTI Giancarlo
MBVM *Centurione* MINGIARDI Alberto
MBVM *Centurione* PESSINA Carlo
MBVM *Centurione* PLISCA Gualtiero
MBVM *Centurione* VIGORITI Luigi
MBVM *Centurione* VIGORITI Luigi
MBVM *Centurione* ZANOTTI Garibaldi
MBVM M *Capomanipolo* ANDREUSSI Francesco
MBVM M *Capomanipolo* BERGOMI Franco
MBVM M *Capomanipolo* BONARDI Mario
MBVM M *Capomanipolo* CANCIANI Italo
MBVM M *Capomanipolo* COGO Aldo
MBVM *Tenente cappellano* CONTE Gius. Maria
MBVM *Tenente cappellano* CONTE Gius. Maria
MBVM *Tenente cappellano* DROETTO Ferdinando
MBVM M *Capomanipolo* ERONZAGLIA Umberto
MBVM M *Capomanipolo* MAGNATI Giacinto
MBVM M *Capomanipolo* MENEGOZZO Oreste
MBVM M *Capomanipolo* MENEGOZZO Oreste
MBVM M *Capomanipolo* MEOLI Luigi
MBVM M *Capomanipolo* MINGIARDI Alberto

MBVM M *Capomanipolo* MURAGLIA Santo
MBVM M *Capomanipolo* PIGNOTTI Luigi
MBVM M *Capomanipolo* POLVEROSI Giuseppe
MBVM M *Capomanipolo* STAFFUZZA Bruno
MBVM M *Capomanipolo* TONOLINI Vittorio
MBVM *Capomanipolo* ZUELLI Tullio
MBVM M *capo squadra* BORTOLIN Luigi
MBVM M *capo squadra* CASOLI Vasco
MBVM M *capo squadra* IETRI Umberto
MBVM M *capo squadra* MASSEROTTO Renato
MBVM M *capo squadra* TAGLIAVINI Otello
MBVM *capo squadra* TUMBURUS Francesco
MBVM *vice capo squadra* FERRIN Pompilio
MBVM *vice capo squadra* GIACOMETTI Rosolino
MBVM *vice capo squadra* MARIANO Giovanni
MBVM *vice capo squadra* MERLINI Mario
MBVM *vice capo squadra* SPAZIANI Giovanni
MBVM *camicia nera* ANFOSSI Giov.Batt.
MBVM M *camicia nera* BENZI Natale
MBVM *camicia nera* BERTOGNA Eugenio
MBVM *camicia nera* BIGI Oscar
MBVM *camicia nera* BIGI Vittorio
MBVM *camicia nera* CATTELANI Prospero
MBVM *camicia nera* CAVALLETTI Gino
MBVM M *camicia nera* COLLI Pellegrino
MBVM *camicia nera* COLUCCIA Carlo
MBVM M *camicia nera* CONTI Giuseppe
MBVM *camicia nera* COSSU Giovanni
MBVM *camicia nera* FINARDI Giuseppe
MBVM *camicia nera* GRILLO Vincenzo
MBVM *camicia nera* LUSENTI William
MBVM *camicia nera* MANCINI Gino
MBVM *camicia nera* MARGINI Silvio
MBVM *camicia nera* MASSANI Leardo
MBVM *camicia nera* POLMONIERI Italo
MBVM M *camicia nera* RIZZI Renato
MBVM *camicia nera* ROSSI Ovidio
MBVM *camicia nera* RUSSO Giuseppe
MBVM M *camicia nera* SIMONETTO Vincenzo
MBVM *camicia nera* TASSILE Duilio
MBVM *camicia nera* VITTORINO Angelo
MBVM M *camicia nera* ZOPPI Vittorio

CGVM *Console* MITTICA Domenico
CGVM *Seniore* FORMICA Luigi
CGVM *Primo Seniore* GAMBONI Vincenzo
CGVM *Centurione* BERTRANDI Nicola
CGVM *Centurione* CHELOTTI Vittorio
CGVM *Centurione* ENGOLI Rinaldo
CGVM *Centurione* GIORDANO Nicola
CGVM *Centurione* MARGINI Silvio
CGVM *Centurione* MENNA Federigo
CGVM *Centurione* TRENTINI Alessandro
CGVM M *Capomanipolo* ANDREUSSI Francesco
CGVM M *Capomanipolo* AZZOLINI Pietro
CGVM M *Capomanipolo* AZZOLINI Pietro
CGVM M *Capomanipolo* BIASUTTI Guglielmo
CGVM M *Capomanipolo* BORTOLOZZI Edmiro
CGVM M *Capomanipolo* CRISTOFOLI Angelo
CGVM M *Capomanipolo* MENEGOZZO Oreste
CGVM M *Capomanipolo* MINGIARDI Alberto
CGVM *Capomanipolo* ONOLINI Vittorio
CGVM *Capomanipolo* PAGLIA Edmondo
CGVM *Capomanipolo* RAFFAELLI Giacomo
CGVM *Capomanipolo* STURLA Alessandro
CGVM *capo squadra* ANGELINI Giuseppe
CGVM *capo squadra* BINDA Silvio
CGVM *capo squadra* BONDIOLI Luigi
CGVM *capo squadra* COMAR Viscardo
CGVM *capo squadra* CONTI Giuseppe
CGVM *capo squadra* DEL BIANCO Secondo
CGVM *capo squadra* DEL PICCOLO Egone
CGVM M *capo squadra* EBECCHI Paolo
CGVM M *capo squadra* ERRANA Michele
CGVM *capo squadra* FERRO Mario
CGVM *capo squadra* GALLI Leopoldo
CGVM *capo squadra* GASPAROTTO Felice
CGVM *capo squadra* MASTRANGELO Domenico
CGVM *capo squadra* PARMISAN Antonio
CGVM *capo squadra* PELLI Gino
CGVM *capo squadra* PICCIOTTI Angelo
CGVM M *capo squadra* SPIGHI Antonio
CGVM M *capo squadra* ZATTI Alessandro
CGVM *vice capo squadra* CROCI Natale
CGVM *vice capo squadra* CROCI Natale

CGVM *vice capo squadra* DEGANO Sergio
CGVM M *vice capo squadra* DEL PONTE Luigi
CGVM *vice capo squadra* EGESTE Enrico
CGVM *vice capo squadra* GALEAZZI Admiro
CGVM *vice capo squadra* GIUA Federico
CGVM *vice capo squadra* GRANDO Giovanni
CGVM *vice capo squadra* PICCA Martino
CGVM M *vice capo squadra* PLATE' Pacifico
CGVM M *vice capo squadra* SBAIZ Francesco
CGVM *vice capo squadra* ZIN Bruno
CGVM M *camicia nera* ARDORI Napoleone
CGVM M *camicia nera* ASPARAGI Mario
CGVM M *camicia nera* ASTOLFO Luigi
CGVM M *camicia nera* ATENASIO Antonio
CGVM M *camicia nera* AVANZI Severino
CGVM M *camicia nera* AVENATI Carlo
CGVM M *camicia nera* BANELLI Guido
CGVM M *camicia nera* BASSO Amadio
CGVM M *camicia nera* BEGGI Luigi
CGVM M *camicia nera* BENATTI Bruno
CGVM M *camicia nera* BIANCO Francesco
CGVM M *camicia nera* BIGI Oscar
CGVM M *camicia nera* BIZZOLI Umberto
CGVM M *camicia nera* BOMBARDA Angelo
CGVM M *camicia nera* BREZIL Guido
CGVM M *camicia nera* BRUNINI Guido
CGVM M *camicia nera* C1NEDELLA Pietro
CGVM M *camicia nera* CANESTRI Gioacchino
CGVM M *camicia nera* CAVANDOLI Marino
CGVM M *camicia nera* CERRI Gino
CGVM M *camicia nera* CERVINI Vittorio
CGVM M *camicia nera* CHIAPPONI Oreste
CGVM M *camicia nera* CORTESI Gino
CGVM M *camicia nera* COSTA Arsenio
CGVM M *camicia nera* DE GOBBI Arturo
CGVM M *camicia nera* DEL PIN Attilio
CGVM M *camicia nera* DI NARDO Biagio
CGVM M *camicia nera* FERRI Carlo
CGVM M *camicia nera* FERRI Giuseppe
CGVM M *camicia nera* FOCACCI Lino
CGVM M *camicia nera* FOCARDI Oscar
CGVM M *camicia nera* FORNACIARI Mario

CGVM *camicia nera* FRACCHIA Serafino
CGVM *camicia nera* FRANCI Florestano
CGVM *camicia nera* FURLAN Giovanni
CGVM *camicia nera* GAROFALO Umberto
CGVM *camicia nera* GHISLOTTI Giovanni
CGVM *camicia nera* GHISLOTTI Giovanni
CGVM *camicia nera* GIANI Ezio
CGVM *camicia nera* GIORGIONE Abelardo
CGVM *camicia nera* GOVI Romeo
CGVM *camicia nera* LANZANO Voncenzo
CGVM *camicia nera* LANZILLOTTI Pietro
CGVM *camicia nera* MANAZZONE Francesco
CGVM M *camicia nera* MANFREDI Pierino
CGVM *camicia nera* MARINELLO Mario
CGVM *camicia nera* MARTINI Agostino
CGVM *camicia nera* MEZZETTI Ruggero
CGVM *camicia nera* MUNNARI Rolando
CGVM *camicia nera* MUSSI Pietro
CGVM *camicia nera* NOVELLI Valentino
CGVM *camicia nera* ORLANDI Ferdinando
CGVM *camicia nera* PAIANO Tommaso
CGVM *camicia nera* PAVONE Giuseppe
CGVM *camicia nera* PERESSON Leonardo
CGVM *camicia nera* PETTINELLA Amedeo
CGVM *camicia nera* PICA Settimio
CGVM *camicia nera* PINOTTI Giuseppe
CGVM *camicia nera* PRAMPOLINI Guerrino
CGVM *camicia nera* PRAMPOLINI Guerrino
CGVM *camicia nera* QUAGLIA Carmelo
CGVM *camicia nera* REOLON Gino
CGVM *camicia nera* ROMANO Nicola
CGVM *camicia nera* RUSSO Giuseppe
CGVM *camicia nera* RUSTICANI Fioravante
CGVM *camicia nera* SCAGLIONE Felice
CGVM *camicia nera* SEBENELLO Antonio
CGVM *camicia nera* SECCHIONI Emilio
CGVM *camicia nera* SOLIANI Dino
CGVM *camicia nera* SOLIANI Sante
CGVM *camicia nera* STRACCIARI Gino
CGVM *camicia nera* TASSILE Duilio
CGVM *camicia nera* TORRENTI Roberto
CGVM *camicia nera* TOSCAN Giuseppe

CGVM M *camicia nera* TOSELLO Luigi
CGVM *camicia nera* ZANCHETTIN Sante
CGVM *camicia nera* ZANUSSI Alfredo
CGVM *camicia nera* ZOLA Giovanni

Tagliamento 63rd Heavy Weapons Battalion

MAVM *Tenente Colonnello* DE FRANCO Vittorio
MAVM *Tenente* EMANUELE Antonio
MAVM *Tenente* SUPPA Domenico
MAVM *Sottotenente* ALVISI Lucio
MAVM *Sottotenente* MOSCA Carlo
MAVM *aiutante di battaglia* ARADELLO Ferdinando
MAVM *sergente* ZANNINI Francesco
MAVM M *caporal maggiore* ERRI Antonio
MBVM *Maggiore* CASTELBARCO VISCONTI P.
MBVM *Capitano* CARUSO Francesco
MBVM *Sottotenente* CLEVA Marino
MBVM *Sottotenente* DE DONNO Nicola
MBVM M *Sottotenente* ORGANO Dario
MBVM *Sottotenente* PEDANI Adelmo
MBVM M *Sottotenente* PREGELLIO Ezio
MBVM *Sottotenente* ZANGRANDE Girolamo
MBVM *sergente* FACCHINI Michele
MBVM *sergente* GALLO Carlo
MBVM *sergente* MARINOZZI Zeno
MBVM M *caporale* AIELLO Francesco
MBVM *caporale* GIANNELLI Andrea
MBVM *caporale* LO IACONO Salvatore
MBVM *caporale* ORTUNATO Bruno
MBVM *soldato* BARADELLO Luigi
MBVM *soldato* BERTINI Elio
MBVM *soldato* BIANCHI Mario
MBVM *soldato* GIANNELLI Anrea
MBVM *soldato* MILANDRI Werter
MBVM M *soldato* PAULETIC Marcello
MBVM *soldato* TUBIANA Arturo
CGVM *Tenente* MASIA Giovanni
CGVM *Sottotenente* CHIAROTTO Francesco
CGVM *Sottotenente* MARINI Mario
CGVM *Sottotenente* MEREU Giuseppe

CGVM *Sottotenente* NICOLELLA Tonino
CGVM *Sottotenente* PAPPALEPORE Nicola
CGVM *Sottotenente* RESMINI Aldo
CGVM *sergente* NIEDDU Giovanni
CGVM *caporal maggiore* IOLO Guerrino
CGVM *caporale* CONFICONI Aurelio
CGVM *caporale* ZANNIER Giovanni
CGVM *soldato* BOLOGNINI Sulpizio
CGVM *soldato* CONTU Antonio
CGVM *soldato* GEMIN Guido
CGVM *soldato* MORO Nicolò
CGVM *soldato* PREDA Girolamo
CGVM *soldato* ROSSO Emilio
CGVM *soldato* SIMONETTO Remo
CGVM *soldato* ZAPPATA Mario

Raggruppamento CCNN M 3 Gennaio–*Gruppo* Montebello

MOVM M *Centurione* DI PASQUALE Ettore
MOVM M *Capomanipolo* CREMISI Giorgio
MOVM M *aiutante di battaglia* IAGI Oreste
MOVM M *camicia nera* BRACCINI Gianfilippo
MAVM *Seniore* ARIANI Vittorio
MAVM M *Seniore* UPERTI Stefano
MAVM M *Centurione* BARON Amos
MAVM *Centurione* CALBO Luigi
MAVM *Centurione* COMOGLIO Anselmo
MAVM M *Centurione* GRIGNAFFINI Lucedio
MAVM *Centurione* SANCHINI Eugenio
MAVM M *Capomanipolo* LOISI Alvise
MAVM M *Capomanipolo* MALTINTI Paolo
MAVM M *Capomanipolo* OVATO Oscar
MAVM M *Capomanipolo* VALLERANI Achille
MAVM M *Capomanipolo* VANNUTELLI Alberto
MAVM *capo squadra* CEOLIN Nello
MAVM M *capo squadra* RICOTTI Luigi
MAVM M *vice capo squadra* COMMITTERI Giuseppe
MAVM *vice capo squadra* FARINELLI Emilio
MAVM *camicia nera* AMBROSIO Fortunato
MAVM *camicia nera* BERNI Garibaldi

MAVM *camicia nera* CHIAROTTO Luciano
MAVM *camicia nera* DELLA ROSA Vero
MAVM *camicia nera* FRANZO' Giovanni
MAVM *camicia nera* MANGIAVACCHIN Stefano
MAVM *camicia nera* PERRI Domenico
MAVM *camicia nera* PIERI Giulio
MBVM *Seniore* OLLINI Giovanni
MBVM *Centurione* DI PINO Antonio
MBVM *Centurione* DOTTI Stefano
MBVM *Centurione* QUATRARO Manfredi
MBVM M *Capomanipolo* CAVAGNA Sandro
MBVM M *Capomanipolo* GIONERIDA Gaetano
MBVM M *Capomanipolo* ROVIDA Alberto
MBVM M *Capomanipolo* ZAPPI Ezio
MBVM M *capo squadra* ANZA Giorgio
MBVM M *capo squadra* ANZA Giorgio
MBVM *vice capo squadra* D'EUGENIO Antonio
MBVM *vice capo squadra* PIAZZI Giuseppe
MBVM *camicia nera* ACRISTO Teodoro
MBVM M *camicia nera* AVIGNONE Giuseppe
MBVM *camicia nera* CREMA Francesco
MBVM *camicia nera* DONA' Alessandro
MBVM *camicia nera* GUIDI Vinicio
MBVM *camicia nera* MATTACCHINI Pietro
MBVM *camicia nera* OTTAVIANI Aldo
MBVM *camicia nera* RAMPINELLI Pietro
MBVM *camicia nera* SICHERI Candido
MBVM *camicia nera* VERGA Luigi
CGVM *Centurione* CALBO Luigi
CGVM *Centurione* DOTTI Stefano
CGVM *Centurione* JANNICELLI Vittorio
CGVM *Centurione* MICHELANGELI Ennio
CGVM M *Capomanipolo* IGNORATO Luigi
CGVM M *Capomanipolo* TERZO Agostino
CGVM M *capo squadra* ALAMINI Guido
CGVM M *capo squadra* ESTI Giovanni
CGVM M *capo squadra* ONNA Antonio
CGVM M *capo squadra* UANTARO Sabino
CGVM *vice capo squadra* CALABRISE Quirino
CGVM *vice capo squadra* CANTONI Mario
CGVM *vice capo squadra* CARLI Aldo
CGVM *vice capo squadra* CASADIO Angelo

CGVM *vice capo squadra* CORNO Antonio
CGVM *vice capo squadra* JULITA Alessandro
CGVM *vice capo squadra* RIZZATO Antonio
CGVM M *camicia nera* BARDUCCI Romeo
CGVM *camicia nera* BATTAGLIA Aroldo
CGVM *camicia nera* BETTI Silverio
CGVM *camicia nera* BIAGI Oreste
CGVM *camicia nera* BIGHIGNOLI Ettore
CGVM *camicia nera* BORGHETTI Savino
CGVM *camicia nera* BUSCEMI Serafino
CGVM *camicia nera* CARNIELLI Guido
CGVM *camicia nera* DE MARTIN Adamo
CGVM *camicia nera* DI NATALE Vincenzo
CGVM *camicia nera* DI PASQUALE Domenico
CGVM *camicia nera* FASANI Giuseppe
CGVM *camicia nera* FODARO Giuseppe
CGVM *camicia nera* GRANCIA Armando
CGVM *camicia nera* MAGGI Mario
CGVM *camicia nera* MANZINI Angelo
CGVM *camicia nera* MASSIMI Paride
CGVM M *camicia nera* MOGAVERO Antonino
CGVM M *camicia nera* NASINI Vincenzo
CGVM M *camicia nera* NERI Medardo
CGVM M *camicia nera* PAPPINI Secondo
CGVM M *camicia nera* PETRARCA Gino
CGVM M *camicia nera* PEZZINI Celestino
CGVM M *camicia nera* PIRACCINI Augusto
CGVM M *camicia nera* PRAVETTONI Ambrogio
CGVM M *camicia nera* PROLI Francesco
CGVM *camicia nera* PUGLIESE Antonio
CGVM *camicia nera* RAMPI Pietro
CGVM *camicia nera* RANIERI Pietro
CGVM *camicia nera* RIGHINI Vittorio
CGVM M *camicia nera* SCACCHETTI Ottorino
CGVM *camicia nera* SPERONI Enrico
CGVM *camicia nera* TORNOTTI Battista
CGVM *camicia nera* VALLINI Giuseppe
CGVM *camicia nera* ZAMPETTI Giovanni

Anthem of the M Battalions

'*Battaglioni* "M"'
Text written by: Auro D'Alba
Music written by: Francesco Pellegrino

Battaglioni del DUCE, battaglioni
della morte, creati per la vita:
a primavera s'apre la partita,
i continenti fanno fiamme e fior.
Per vincere ci vogliono i leoni
di Mussolini armati di valor.

Battaglioni
della morte,
battaglioni
della vita,
rincomincia la partita,
senza l'odio non c'è amor.

Emme rossa
uguale sorte,
fiocco nero alla squadrista,
noi la morte
l'abbiam vista,
con due bombe e in bocca un fior.

Contro l'oro c'è il sangue—e fa la storia,
contro i ghetti profumano i giardini,
sul mondo batte il cuor di Mussolini:
a Marizai il buon seme germogliò.
Nel clima di battaglia e di Vittoria
la fiamma nera a ottobre divampò.

Contro Giuda, contro l'oro,
sarà il sangue a far la storia,
ti daremo la vittoria,
DUCE, o l'ultimo respir.
Battaglioni del lavoro,
battaglioni della fede,
vince sempre chi più crede,
chi più a lungo sa patir.

Endnotes

Chapter One

1 Glantz, *Barbarossa: Hitler's Invasion of Russia 1941* (Stroud: Tempus, 2001), p. 23.
2 Campbell, *Winter War 1939–40* (Oxford: Osprey, 2016), p. 11.
3 Forczyk, *Tank Warfare on the Eastern Front 1941–1942* (Barnsley: Pen & Sword, 2014), p. 10.
4 Campbell, *Winter War (2016)*, p. 74.
5 Glantz, *Barbarossa* (2001), p. 24.
6 Rottman, *Soviet Rifleman 1941–45* (Oxford: Osprey, 2007), pp. 16-17.
7 Giusti, *La Campagna di Russia* (Bologna: Il Mulino, 2016), p. 223.
8 Ufficio Storico, 'Addestramento delle unita' destinate alla fronte russa', n. 5000, 20 March 1942.
9 Ufficio Storico, Ufficio Addestramento Stato Maggiore Regio Esercito: "Addestramento dei minori reparti di fanteria destinati alla fronte russa," n. 18400, 21 October 1942.
10 *Tactical and Technical Trends*, "Russian Employment of Tanks," No. 18, 11 February, 1943.
11 Cappellano and Pignato, *Andare contro i carri armati* (Udine: Gaspari Editore, 2007), p. 175.
12 *Ibid.*, p. 176.
13 Ufficio Storico, 'Relazione sull'attivita' svolta dal corpo d'armata alpino in Russia,' Generale Nasci, March 1943.
14 *Tactical and Technical Trends*, "Some Principles from the War on the Russian Front," No. 22, April 8, 1943.
15 Glantz, *Barbarossa* (2001), p. 27.
16 Cavallero, *Diario* (Rome: Ciarrapico Editore, 1984), p. 132.
17 Burgwyn, *Mussolini Warlord* (New York: Enigma Books, 2012), p. 115.
18 de Felice, *Mussolini l'alleato*, tomo 1 (Turin: Einaudi, 1990), p. 391.
19 Giovanni Messe (10 December 1883 to 18 December 1968) fought during the Great War as a major of the *arditi*, the elite assault units that like the German and Austro-Hungarian storm troopers introduced new tactics to break the stalemate of positional warfare. Messe at the time was the commander of IX *Reparto d'Assalto*, which distinguished itself in the summer of 1918 when it took from the Austrians the peak of Col. Moschin capturing over 500 enemy troops.

In the Second World War, Messe commanded an army corps during the Greek Campaign in 1940 and early 1941. He was subsequently nominated as the head of the CSIR. In February 1943, Messe was appointed as the new commander of the Italian-German Army, formerly commanded by Erwin Rommel, in North Africa. On 12 May 1943, Messe was promoted to the rank of marshal of Italy (*Maresciallo d'Italia*). Shortly thereafter, the Axis forces in North Africa were forced to surrender to the Allies on the line at Enfidaville. When the Badoglio government signed a peace agreement with the Allies, Messe opted to fight for the Italian troops that remained loyal to King Victor Emmanuel of Italy. In September 1943, Messe became the chief of staff of the *Esercito Cobelligerante Italiano*. He retired from the military in 1947.

20 Messe, *La Guerra al fronte russo* (Milan: Mursia, 1964), pp. 215-16.
21 MacGregor Knox, *Mussolini Unleashed, 1939–1941* (Cambridge: Cambridge University Press, 1982), p. 23.
22 *Ibid.*, p. 23.
23 Burgwyn, *Mussolini Warlord* (2012), p. 119.
24 Apostolo and Massimello, *Italian Aces of World War Two* (Oxford: Osprey, 2000), p. 22.
25 Ceva, *La condotta italiana nella Guerra—Cavallero e il Comando Supremo 1941–1942* (Milan: Feltrinelli, 1975).

Chapter Two

1 Battistelli and Crociani, *Italian Blackshirt 1935–45* (Oxford: Osprey, 2014), p. 9.
2 Greene and Massignani, *Rommel's North Africa Campaign: September 1940–November 1942* (New York: Da Capo Press, 1999), p. 41.
3 Rastrelli, "Un Esercito in Camicia Nera", *Storia Militare,* June 2004 carlorastrelli.it/un-esercito-in-camicia-nera/.
4 Greene and Massignani, *Rommel's North Africa Campaign* (1999), p. 41.
5 *Ibid.*
6 Carlo Rastrelli, "Un Esercito in Camicia Nera," (2004).
7 Greene and Massignani, *Rommel's North Africa Campaign* (1999), p. 41.
8 Kaufmann, Kaufmann, Potocnik, Lang, *The Maginot Line* (Barnsley: Pen & Sword Military, 2017), p. 154.
9 *Ibid.*, p. 154.
10 Lucas, *Storia delle unita' combattenti della MVSN* (Rome: Volpe, 1976), p. 91.
11 *Ibid.*, p. 90.
12 Kaufmann, Kaufmann, Potocnik, and Lang, *The Maginot Line* (2017), p.163.
13 Pier Paolo Battistelli and Piero Crociani, *Italian Blackshirt (2014),* p. 11.
14 Ufficio Storico, *Bollettini del Comando Supremo*, 1941.
15 Bedeschi, *Fronte Greco-albanese; c'ero anch'io* (Milan: Mursia Editore, 1977), p. 647.
16 Guerrazzi, *The Italian Army in Slovenia: Strategies of Antipartisan Repression, 1941–1943* (London: Palgrave MacMillan, 2013.).
17 *Ibid.*, p. 121.
18 *Ibid.*
19 Oliva, Foibe. *Le stragi negate degli italiani della Venezia Giulia e dell'Istria* (Milan: Mondadori, 2003).
20 Battistelli and Crociani, *Italian Blackshirt* (2014), pp. 11-12.
21 Griffith, *World War II Desert Tactics* (Oxford: Osprey, 2008).
22 Greene and Massigani, *Rommel's North Africa Campaign* (1999), p. 124.

23 Gooch (ed.), *Decisive Campaigns of the Second World War* (London: Frank Cass, 2004), p. 101.
24 *Ibid.*
25 *Ibid.*
26 Rastrelli. "Enzo Galbiati," *Storia Militare,* no. 161, February, 2007, p. 36.
27 Enzo Galbiati (1897–1982). During the First World War, he fought as a junior officer with the *Bersaglieri* and then the *arditi* in the Carso. He was wounded during an assault in 1917. In 1919, Galbiati joined Mussolini's party and became the leader of the *fascio* of Monza. He then fought in Africa during the colonial campaign and was later nominated inspector general of the university militia. In 1941, he led the so-called *Raggruppamento Galbiati* during the Greek campaign. He was then promoted to the rank of *Luogotenente Generale* of the MVSN in mid 1941. In 1943 Galbiati, as head of the MVSN, played a leading role in the creation of the *Divisione* M, the armoured division of Blackshirts armed with the most advanced German tanks and artillery guns. When a majority of the Grand Council of Fascism voted against Mussolini in July 1943, Galbiati was one of the few that remained loyal to the *Duce* and proposed to Mussolini the arrest of the nineteen Fascist leaders headed by Dino Grandi that had voted the dismissal motion. After the change in government, Galbiati was dismissed as head of the MVSN and the organisation was dissolved. Following Italy's exit from the war, Galbiati joined the Italian Social Republic in the north. He survived the war and subsequently spent eleven months in prison. Apart from writing his memoirs in the 1950s, he kept a low profile in post-war Italy.
28 di Colloredo, *Emme rossa!: Le camicie nere sul fronte russo 1941–1943* (Genoa: Ass. Culturale Italia, 2008), p. 57.
29 *Ibid.*
30 Battistelli and Crociani, *Italian Blackshirt* (2014), p. 56.
31 *Ibid.*, p. 40.
32 *Ibid.*, p. 57.
33 *Ibid.*, p. 15.
34 *Ibid.*, p. 40.
35 Aga Rossi, A *Nation Collapses: The Italian Surrender of September 1943* (Cambridge: Cambridge University Press, 2000), p. 45.
36 'This highly valued officer, who was assigned a key command during a particularly critical battle against overwhelming enemy forces, reached the frontline the night prior to the planned counter-attack. The next day at dawn, while the battle flared up again between enemy tanks and Italian self-propelled units, he personally led the counter-attack. While standing beside a self propelled gun he was hit by a grenade and died instantly. His soldiers, both bersaglieri and artillerymen, animated by his sublime example fought on stubbornly to repel the enemy attack'. Favarotta-Campobello di Licata, 11 July, 1943. www.quirinale.it/elementi/DettaglioOnorificenze.aspx?decorato=45467, accessed 21 September 2017.
37 Mitcham, Jr., and von Stauffenberg, *The Battle of Sicily* (Mechanicsburg: Stackpole, 2012), p. 194.
38 Rossi, 'Le Camicie Nere passano ai tedeschi,' anpi.it/media/uploads/patria/2003/4-5/31_33_Rossi.pdf.
39 *Ibid.*
40 Avigliano and Palmentieri, *L'Italia di Salo': 1943–45* (Bologna: Il Mulino, 2016), p. 218.
41 Rossi, 'Le Camicie Nere passano ai tedeschi'.
42 Fabei, *Tagliamento* (2004), p. 242.

43 Gatti: 'The Blackshirts in the Militia, the Military Soul of the Fascist Regime,' Paper given at the Association for the Study of Modern Italy Annual Conference 2005.
44 Phoebus Athanassiou, *Armies of the Greek-Italian War 1940–41* (Oxford: Osprey, 2017), p. 22.
45 Greene and Massignani, *Rommel's North Africa Campaign* (1999), p. 42.
46 Battistelli and Crociani, *Italian Blackshirt* (2014), p. 24.
47 Sullivan, 'The Italian Armed Forces, 1918–40', in Williamson Murray, Allan R. Millett, *Military Effectiveness, vol. 2* (Cambridge, Cambridge University Press, 2010), pp. 169-217.
48 Griffith, *World War II Desert Tactics* (2008), p. 21.
49 *Ibid*, p. 21.
50 Battistelli and Crociani, *Italian Blackshirt* (2014), p. 32.
51 *Ibid*.
52 Ufficio Storico: Francesco Andreussi, 'Relazione sui fatti d'arme delle CC.NN in Russia', Legione Tagliamento, August 1941.
53 Niccolo' Nicchiarelli (1898–1969). At sixteen years old, Nicchiarelli joined a Granatieri Regiment during the Great War and fought his first encounter battle on Mount Sabotino. He was then assigned to the 37th Infantry Regiment (Ravenna Brigade) and in this capacity was severely injured during an assault on Mount Seluggio in July 1916. The following year, he was assigned to the lieutenant to the 261st Infantry Regiment (Elba Brigade) where he fought during the Italian offensive that resulted in the capture of the Bainsizza. On 27 October 1917, he was captured, along with his men, while fighting in a trench near San Pietro al Natisone after the Central Powers had broken through at Caporetto. He spent the rest of the war at the Cellelager concentration camp. After the war, he joined the fascist movement and participated to the March on Rome. He then joined the MVSN as a *seniore*. He then fought in Libya. At the outbreak of the Second World War, Nicchiarelli was deployed in North Africa and fought against the British Army during several military operations including at Buq Buq and Sidi el Barrani from June 1940 to January 1941. At the time, he was the commander of the 233rd Legion. In July 1941, he was appointed commander of the 63rd Legion. In early 1942, he assumed command of the 21 April M Battalion Group, which was deployed in Yugoslavia. After the armistice of 1943, he joined the Italian Social Republic and was nominated as the general and chief of staff of the *Guardia Nazionale Repubblicana*.
54 Fabei, *Tagliamento* (2004), p. 99.
55 Giusti, *La Campagna di Russia* (2016), p. 165.
56 *Ibid*., 121.
57 Rottman, *Panzerfaust and Panzerschreck* (Oxford: Osprey, 2016), p. 1.
58 Ufficio Storico, *Le operazioni delle unita' italiane al fronte russo (1941–43)* (Rome: Ufficio Storico, 2000), p. 330.
59 *Ibid*.
60. Ufficio Storico, R. Lerici, 'All'eccellenza il gen. d'armata Italo Gariboldi, comandante 8. armata', 28 January 1943.
61 *Ibid*.
62 Vicentini, *Il sacrificio della Julia in Russia* (Udine, Gaspari Editore, 2011), p. 14.
63 Battistelli and Crociani, *Italian Blackshirt* (2014), p. 37.
64 Sangster and Battistelli, *Myths, Amnesia and Reality in Military Conflicts, 1935–1945* (Cambridge: Scholars Publishing, 2017), p. 66.
65 *Ibid*., p. 67.
66 Sweet, *Iron Arm: The Mechanization of Mussolini's Army* (Mechanicsburg: Stackpole, 2011), p. 130.

67 Fugate, *Operation Barbarossa: Strategy and Tactics on the Eastern Front, 1941* (Novato: Presidio, 1984), p. 300.
68 Ufficio Storico, 'Principi della difesa anticarro', no. 4141, 12 September 1943.

Chapter Three

1 Giusti, *La campagna di Russia* (2016), p. 87.
2 Ufficio Storico: Gruppo Camicie Nere Leonessa, Comando XIV Battaglione M, 'Varie', no. 3720/4/4, 6 December 1942.
3 Battistelli and Crociani, *Italian Blackshirt* (2014), p. 12.
4 Cecini, 'Il giallo e il nero: le Medaglie d'Oro al Valor Militare della MVSN', *Uniformi*, n. 6 2015, pp. 40-61.
5 Giusti, *La Campagna di Russia* (2016), p 92.
6 *Ibid.*, p. 92
7 *Ibid.*, p. 93.
8 Weinberg, *A World at Arms* (Cambridge: Cambridge University Press, 1994), p. 221.
9 Hamilton, *Sacrifice on the Steppe* (Mechanicsburg: Stackpole, 2014).
10 Rigoni Stern, *Il sergente nella neve* (Turin: Einaudi, 1967), p. 162.
11 Giusti, *La Campagna di Russia* (2016), p. 208.
12 *Ibid.*, p. 208.
13 *Ibid.*
14 Ufficio Storico: Gruppo Camicie Nere Leonessa, Comando XIV Battaglione M, 'Rilievi fatti in occassione della rivista dell'eccellenza il comandante del II C.D.A.', no. 3021/1/3, 1 October 1942.
15 Ufficio Storico: Gruppo Camicie Nere Leonessa, Comando XIV Battaglione M, 'Contegno legionari', no. 2203:1, 23 July 1942.
16 Ufficio Storico: Gruppo Camicie Nere Leonessa, Comando XIV Battaglione M, 'Illecito Baratto', no. 2329/1/3, 6 August, 1942.
17 Malatesta, 'La Milizia nella campagna di Russia', *Storia Militare*, no. 225, 2012, pp. 24-36.
18 Giusti, *La Campagna di Russia* (2016), p. 208.
19 *Ibid.*, p. 212.
20 Miller, *Fighting Men of World War II: Uniforms, Equipment and Weapons* (Mechanicsburg: Stackpole, 2012), p. 365.
21 Lucas and De Vecchi, *Storia delle unità combattenti della M.V.S.N. 1923–1943* (Rome: Giovanni Volpe Editore, 1976), p. 121.
22 Fabei, *Tagliamento*, (2004) p. 71.
23 *Ibid.*, p. 77.
24 Malatesta, *Storia della Legione Tagliamento dalla fondazione alla guerra di Russia* (Varese: Pietro Macchione Editore, 2001), p. 178.
25 Fabei, *Tagliamento*, (2004), p. 81.
26 Leonardo Malatesta, *Storia della legione* (2001), p. 199.
27 *Ibid.*, p. 200.
28 Messe, *La Guerra al fronte russo* (Milan: Rizzoli, 1964), p. 108.
29 *Ibid.*
30 McCarthy, *Panzerkrieg: The Rise and Fall of Hitler's Tank Divisions* (New York: Carroll and Graf, 2002,), p. 167.
31 Messe, *La Guerra* (1964), p. 169.
32 di Colloredo, *Emme Rossa* (Genoa: Associazione Culturale, 2008), pp. 56-57.

33 Messe, *La guerra* (1964), p. 172.
34 Fabei, *Tagliamento* (2004), p. 108.
35 Ufficio Storico: 'Relazione del generale Mario Marazzani sulla divisione Celere Principe Amedeo d'Aosta nella campagnia di Russia', August 1941 to October 1942.
36 Malatesta, *Storia della Legione* (2001), pp. 282-83.
37 Bedeschi, *Fronte russo: c'ero anch'io* (Milan: Mursia, 1983), p. 158.
38 Crespi, *La battaglia di Natale dal diario storico di un ufficiale del Corpo di spedizione italiano in Russia* (Milan: Longanesi, 1965), p. 159.
39 *Ibid.*
40 *Ibid.*
41 *Ibid.*, p. 164.
42 www.quirinale.it/elementi/DettaglioOnorificenze.aspx?decorato=13260.
43 Ufficio Storico: 'Protocollo 2/3469,' Comando della 3a Divisione Celere, P.A.D.A.', 27 December 1941.
44 Malatesta, *Storia della Legione* (2001), pp. 316-7.
45 *Ibid.*, p. 318.
46 Valori, *Gli Italiani in Russia* (Milan: Betti, 1967), p. 66.
47 Ufficio Storico: 'Relazione del generale Mario Marazzani sulla divisione Celere Principe Amedeo d'Aosta nella campagnia di Russia', August 1941 to October 1942.
48 Kurowski, *Infantry Aces: The German Soldier in Combat in World War II* (Mechanigsburg: Stackpole, 2010), p. 75.
49 *Ibid.*, p. 76.
50 Vasta, 'Battaglioni M', *Coorte*, vol. 1, issue no. 7, 2000.
51 Giusti, *La Campagna di Russia* (2016), p. 127.
52 Schlemmer, Die Italiener an der Ostfront 1942/43. Dokumente zu Mussolinis Krieg gegen die Sowjetunion, hrsg. und eingeleitet von Thomas Schlemmer, München 2005. The Italian edition: *Invasori non vittime: La Campagna Italiana in Russia* (Bari: Laterza, 2008).
53 Messe, *La Guerra* (1964), p. 178.
54 *Ibid.*, p. 179.
55 Giusti, *La Campagna di Russia* (2016), p. 117.

Chapter Four

1 Messe, *La Guerra* (1964), p. 215.
2 Battistelli and Crociani, *Italian Blackshirt*, (2014), p. 38.
3 Pierluigi Romeo di Colloredo, *Emme Rossa* (Genoa: Associazione Culturale, 2008), p. 81.
4 *Ibid.*, p. 75.
5 Battistelli and Crociani, *Italian Blackshirt* (2014), p. 21.
6 Lucas, *Storia delle unita' combattenti della MVSN* (Rome: Volpe, 1976), p. 524.
7 Una Memoria negata: 'Storia di un volontario della seconda guerra mondiale', Novitate, no. 42, 2006.
8 The motivation for Paolucci's goal medal reads. Despite being on official leave at the start of Barbarossa, he opted to enlist. Always volunteering for the most risky actions, and despite the gravity of the situation, he threw himself at the enemy position hurling hand grenades. Severely wounded during the charge to his right arm, he continued to fight with great courage. After having reached the enemy position and after withstanding a violent counterattack, he volunteered to cross

an area under heavy enemy fire in order to retrieve ammunition. During this action, he was injured once again this time on the left arm. After he witnessed his officer fall to ground after having been shot, he willingly aided him. He was then struck by machine-gun fire, which further tore into his left arm. Despite the injuries, he dragged back the wounded officer with all the strength that he could muster. Shortly thereafter, he was killed by another enemy round. He gave his life for his comrade showing indomitable heroism. www.quirinale.it/elementi/DettaglioOnorificenze.aspx?decorato=45569, accessed 27 August 2017.

9 Lucas, *Storia delle unita' combattenti della MVSN* (Rome: Volpe, 1976), p. 497.
10 Giusti, *La Campagna di Russia* (2016), p. 225.
11 *Ibid.*, p. 225.
12 Giusti, *La Campagna di Russia* (2016), p. 215.
13 Cited in: Fabei, *Tagliamento* (2004), pp. 170-71.
14 Lenzi, *Dal Dnieper al Don. La 63a legione CC. NN. Tagliamento nella Campagna di Russia. Rievocazione di Egisto Laldi, documentazione del Gruppo reduci della Legione* (Rome: Volpe Editore, 1968), p. 318.
15 Burgwyn, *Mussolini Warlord* (New York: Enigma Books, 2012), p. 123.
16 Lenzi, *Dal Dnieper and Don* (1968), p. 319.
17 Malatesta, *Storia della legione Tagliamento*, vol. 1, (2001), p. 521.
18 *Ibid.*, p. 521.
19 Fabei, *Tagliamento* (2004), p. 171.
20 Ufficio Storico, Gruppo Autocarrato CC.NN. Tagliamento—Comando 79. Battaglione, 'Relazione del seniore Silvio Margini sui fatti d'arme del 20-23 Agosto e dal 23 al 25 Agosto', 5 September 1942, p. 5.
21 Burgwyn, *Mussolini Warlord* (2012), p. 126.
22 Lucas, *Storia delle unita' combattenti della MVSN* (1968), p. 505.
23 Una Memoria negata: 'Storia di un volontario della seconda guerra mondiale', Novitate, n. 42, 2006.
24 'Sintesi delle relazioni sui combattimenti dei nuclei di collegamento tedeschi presso le divisioni dell 8. armata italiana e le conclusioni comuni del 12 novembre 1943', signed by German Wehrmacht Lieutenant Salazer, cited in Thomas Schlemmer, *Invasori non vittime. La Campagna italiana di Russia 1941–43* (Rome: Laterza, 2009), p. 190.
25 Giusti, La *campagna di Russia* (2016) pp.217-18.
26 'Sintesi delle relazioni sui combattimenti dei nuclei di collegamento tedeschi presso le divisioni dell 8. armata italiana e le conclusioni comuni del 12 novembre 1943'.
27 Lenzi, *Dal Dnieper al Don* (1977), p. 324.
28 'Una Memoria negata: Storia di un volontario della seconda guerra mondiale', Novitate, no. 42, 2006.
29 Ufficio Storico, Comando Divisione di fanteria Ravenna, 'Prot. n. 1344', 13 September 1942.
30 Lucas, *Storia delle unita' combattenti della MVSN*, (1968), p. 532.
31 Ufficio Storico: Comando Raggruppamento Camicie Nere 23 Marzo, 'Idee Chiare', no. 652/02/lb, 16 September 1942.
32 di Colloredo, *Emme Rossa* (Genoa: Associazione Culturale, 2008), p. 88.
33 *Ibid.*, p. 91.
34 *Ibid.*, p. 90.
35 Messe, *La Guerra sulla fronte* (1964), p. 269.
36 Maria Teresa Giusti, *La campagna di Russia* (2016), p. 221.
37 Ufficio Storico: Servizio Informazioni Esercito: 'Schacciere germanico-sovietico', 6 September 1942.

38 Burgwyn, *Mussolini Warlord* (2012), p. 202.
39 Rastrelli, L' ultimo comandante delle camicie nere. Enzo Emilio Galbiati (Milan: Mursia, 2008), p. 121.
40 Burgwyn, *Mussolini Warlord* (2012) p. 203.
41 Syron and McCarty, *Panzerkrieg: The Rise and Fall of Hitler's Tank Divisions* (London: Constable Publication, 2002), p. 123.
42 West Point History of World War Two (New York: Simon and Schuster, 2015), p. 187.
43 *Ibid.*
44 Forczyk, *Tank Warfare on the Eastern Front 1941-1942* (Barnsley: Pen & Sword, 2014), p. 243.
45 Magenheimer, *Hitler's War* (1998), p. 158-59.
46 *Ibid.*, p. 159.
47 Griffith, *World War II Desert Tactics* (2009), p. 32.
48 Magenheimer, *Hitler's War* (1998), p. 168.
49 Burgwyn, *Mussolini Warlord* (2012), p. 204.
50 Lucas, *Storia delle unita' combattenti della MVSN* (1976), pp. 508-09.
51 Ufficio Storico: Comando 8a Armata, Stato Maggiore, Ufficio Operazioni, 'Addestramento della difesa anticarro', no. 02/5395, 13 November 1942.
52 Forczyk, *Tank Warfare on the Eastern Front 1941–1942* (2014), p. 244.
53 Giusti, *La Campagna di Russia* (2016), p. 244.
54 *Ibid.*, p. 244.
55 Leonardo Malatesta, *Storia della Legione Tagliamento*, vol. 1, (2001), p. 565.
56 di Colloredo, *Emme Rossa* (2008), p. 129.
57 Lucas, *Storia delle unita' combattenti della MVSN* (1976), p. 512.
58 Luoni, *La Pasubio sul fronte russo* (Roma: Edizioni dell'Ateneo & Bizzarri, 1977), p. 264.
59 *Ibid.*, p. 566.
60 *Ibid.*, p. 567.
61 Diario del Raggruppamento 3 Gennaio, 11 December 1942 cited in Leonardo Malatesta, *Storia della legione Tagliamento*, vol. 1, p. 633.
62 *Ibid.*
63 *Ibid.*
64 Ufficio Storico: Gruppo Camicie Nere Leonessa, Comando XIV Battaglione M, 'Servizio di sicurezza del campo', no. 3614/8/3, 28 November 1942.
65 Ufficio Storico: Gruppo Camicie Nere Leonessa, Comando XIV Battaglione M, 'Consegne per i servizi di sicurezza', no. 3613/1/3, 28 November 1942.
66 *Ibid.*
67 Paolo Zanlucchi, *La milizia del Duce muore sul Don–La 41ª Legione 'Cesare Battisti': memorie dal fronte russo 1942–1943*, (Rovereto: Egon Edizioni, 2014), p. 24.
68 Giusti, *La Campagna di Russia* (2016), p. 249.
69 Lucas, *Storia delle unita' combattenti della MVSN*, (1976), p. 571.
70 Giusti, *La Campagna di Russia* (2016), p. 249.
71 Patrick, *Panzerkrieg*, (2002), p. 155
72 'Una Memoria negata: Storia di un volontario della seconda guerra mondiale', Novitate, n. 42, 2006
73 Lucas, *Storia delle unita' combattenti della MVSN*, (1976), p. 587.
74 di Colloredo, *Emme Rossa*, (2008), p. 135.
75 Lenzi, *Dal Dnieper and Don*, (1968), p. 374.
76 *Ibid.*, p. 68.
77 Rigoni Stern and Hieddeger, *Ritorno sul Don* (Milan: Transeruropa, 2008), p. 61.

78 Lenzi, *Dal Dnieper and Don*, (1968), p. 374.
79 Corti, *Few Returned Twenty-eight Days on the Russian Front, Winter 1942–1943* (Columbia: University of Missouri Press, 1997), p. 110.
80 www.quirinale.it/elementi/DettaglioOnorificenze.aspx?decorato=45329, accessed 12 July, 2017>
81 Heinz Magenheimer, *Hitler's War*, (2004), p. 167.
82 Sintesi delle relazioni sui combattimenti dei nuclei di collegamento tedeschi presso le divisioni dell 8. armata italiana e le conclusioni comuni del 12 novembre 1943, signed by German Wehrmacht Lieutenant Salazer, cited in Thomas Schlemmer, Invasori non vittime. La Campagna italiana di Russia 1941–43 (Rome: Laterza, 2009), p. 191-92.
83 Lenzi, *Dal Dnieper and Don*, (1968), p. 379.
84 Corti, *Few Returned*, (1997), p. 148.
85 *Ibid.*, 151.
86 *Ibid.*, p. 174.
87 Pier Paolo Battistelli and Piero Crociani, *Italian Blackshirt*, p. 55.
88 Diario del Raggruppamento 3 Gennaio, 30 March 1943 cited in Leonardo Malatesta, *Storia della legione Tagliamento*, vol. 1, p. 669.
89 Battistelli and Crociani, *Italian Blackshirt*, (2014), p. 55.

Chapter Five

1 de Felice, *Mussolini l'alleato* (Turin: Einaudi, 1990), p. 432.
2 Rastrelli, *L'ultimo comandante delle camicie nere. Enzo Emilio Galbiati* (Milan: Ugo Mursia Editore, 2016).
3 Carlo Scorza (1897–1988) was a leading member of the Fascist Party during the Second World War. He was originally a member of the Blackshirts and later rose to the position of party secretary, second only to Benito Mussolini. His brief tenure as party leader began on 19 April 1943 and ended in July of 1943 after the Grand Council voted for Dino Grandi's motion to dismiss Mussolini. After being nominated party secretary, Scorza attempted to revitalise the party but despite his best efforts little could be done to improve morale while Italy was facing defeat on almost all fronts. Scorza voted against Dino Grandi's motion, but the latter's order of the day received majority support within the Grand Council and Mussolini was dismissed from office. After July 1943, Scorza fled north and later joined the Italian Social Republic.
4 Fabei, *Tagliamento*, (2004), p. 191.
5 Badoglio, *L' Italia nella seconda guerra mondiale. Memorie e documenti* (Milan: Mondadori, 1946), p. 167.
6 Morgan, *The Fall of Mussolini* (Oxford: Oxford University Press, 2007), p. 30.
7 Battistelli and Crociani, *Italian Elite Units & Special Forces 1940–43* (Oxford: Osprey, 2011), p. 60.
8 carlorastrelli.it/il-generale-enzo-galbiati/, accessed 21 September 2017.
9 Giusti, *La Campagna di Russia*, (2016), p. 156.

Conclusion

1 Askey, *Operation Barbarossa: The Complete Organizational and Statistical Analysis* (New York: Lulu Publishing, 2013), p. 121.
2 Giusti, *La Campagna di Russia*, (2016), p. 145.

3 Kesserling, *The Memoirs of Field-Marshal Kesselring* (New York: Skyhorse Publishing, 2016), p. 107.
4 Fabei, *Tagliamento*, (2004), p. 21.
5 Battistelli and Crociani, *Italian Blackshirt 1935–45*, (2014), p. 36.
6 *Ibid.*, p. 37.
7 *Ibid.*
8 *Ibid.*
9 Bishop, *SS Hitler's Foreign Divisions: Foreign Volunteers in the Waffen-SS 1940–45* (London: Amber books, 2013), p. 117.
10 Beyda, 'La Grande Armeé in Field Gray: The Legion of French Volunteers Against Bolshevism, 1941', *The Journal of Slavic Military Studies*, Vol. 29, Issue 3, 2016, pp. 513.
11 *Ibid.*, p. 500.
12 Kleinfeld and Tambs, *Hitler's Spanish Legion: The Blue Division in Russia in WWII* (Mechanicsburg: Stackpole, 2014).
13 Steinberg, *All or Nothing: The Axis and the Holocaust 1941–43*, (1994), p. 208.
14 Estes, *A European Anabasis: Western European Volunteers in the German Army and SS* (Solihull: Helion and Co., 2014), p. 108.
15 *Ibid.*, p. 109.
16 Jurado, *Blue Division Soldier 1941–45: Spanish Volunteer on the Eastern Front* (Oxford: Osprey, 2014).
17 Massignani, *Alpini e tedeschi sul Don* (Valdagno: Rossato, 1994).
18 *Ibid.*

Bibliography

Archive Documents

Ufficio Storico: Francesco Andreussi, 'Relazione sui fatti d'arme delle CC.NN in Russia', Legione Tagliamento, August 1941.
Ufficio Storico: 'Protocollo 2/3469,' Comando della 3a Divisione Celere, P.A.D.A., 27 December 1941.
Ufficio Storico: Legione Tagliamento, 'Il Comandante la Legione al Capo si S. M. Della MVSN', n.1834, 25 December 1941.
Ufficio Storico: 'Addestramento delle unita' destinate alla fronte russa', n. 5000, 20 March 1942.
Ufficio Storico: Gruppo Autocarrato CC.NN. Tagliamento–Comando 79. Battaglione, 'Relazione del seniore Silvio Margini sui fatti d'arme del 20-23 Agosto e dal 23 al 25 Agosto', 5 September 1942.
Ufficio Storico: Servizio Informazioni Esercito: 'Schacciere germanico-sovietico,' 6 September 1942.
Ufficio Storico: Ufficio Addestramento Stato Maggiore Regio Esercito: 'Addestramento dei minori reparti di fanteria destinati alla fronte russa', n. 18400, 21 October 1942.
Ufficio Storico: Gruppo Camicie Nere Leonessa, Comando XIV Battaglione M, 'Rilievi fatti in occassione della rivista dell'eccellenza il comandante del II C.D.A.', n.3021/1/3, 1 October 1942.
Ufficio Storico: Gruppo Camicie Nere Leonessa, Comando XIV Battaglione M, 'Contegno legionari', n.2203:1, 23 July 1942.
Ufficio Storico: Gruppo Camicie Nere Leonessa, Comando XIV Battaglione M, 'Illecito Baratto', n.2329/1/3, 6 August, 1942.
Ufficio Storico, Comando Raggruppamento CCNN 3 Gennaio, 'Relazione del Console generale Filippo Diamanti al Comando del XXXV Corpo d'armata sui fatti d'armi 20-26 agosto 1942', .577/op.6, 12 September 1942.
Ufficio Storico: Comando Raggruppamento Camicie Nere 23 Marzo, 'Idee Chiare', n. 652/02/lb, 16 September, 1942.
Ufficio Storico: Gruppo Camicie Nere Leonessa, Comando XIV Battaglione M, 'Varie', n.3720/4/4, 6 December 1942.
Ufficio Storico: Comando 8a Armata, Stato Maggiore, Ufficio Operazioni, 'Addestramento della difesa anticarro', n. 02/5395, 13 November 1942.

Ufficio Storico: 'Relazione sull'attivita' svolta dal corpo d'armata alpino in Russia', Generale Nasci, March 1943.

Ufficio Storico: 'Relazione del generale Mario Marazzani sulla divisione Celere Principe Amedeo d'Aosta nella campagnia di Russia', August 1941 to October 1942.

Ufficio Storico: Comando Divisione di fanteria Ravenna, 'Prot. n. 1344', 13 September 1942.

German Wehrmacht: 'Sintesi delle relazioni sui combattimenti dei nuclei di collegamento tedeschi presso le divisioni dell 8. armata italiana e le conclusioni comuni del 12 novembre 1943', signed by German Wehrmacht Lieutenant Salazer, cited in Thomas Schlemmer, *Invasori non vittime. La Campagna italiana di Russia 1941–43* (Rome: Laterza, 2009).

Ufficio Storico: R. Lerici, 'All'eccellenza il gen. d'armata Italo Gariboldi, comandante 8. Armata', 28 January 1943.

Ufficio Storico: 'Principi della difesa anticarro', n. 4141, 12 September 1943.

Ufficio Storico: 'Diario Storico della 1a Divisione Corazzata CCNN M', 1943.

(Note: Ufficio storico stands for Ufficio Storico dello Stato Maggiore in Rome.)

Magazine and Journal Articles

Una Memoria negata: 'Storia di un volontario della seconda guerra mondiale', *Novitate*, n. 42, 2006.

Oleg Beyda, '"La Grande Armeé in Field Gray": The Legion of French Volunteers Against Bolshevism, 1941', The *Journal of Slavic Military Studies*, Vol. 29, Issue 3, 2016.

Giovanni Cecini, 'Il giallo e il nero: le Medaglie d'Oro al Valor Militare della MVSN', *Uniformi*, n. 6 2015, pp. 40-61.

Gian Luigi Gatti: 'The Blackshirts in the Militia, the Military Soul of the Fascist Regime', 'Italy at War', Paper given at the Association for the Study of Modern Italy Annual Conference 2005.

Leonardo Malatesta, 'La Milizia nella campagna di Russia', *Storia Militare*, n. 225, 2012, pp. 24-36.

Tactical and Technical Trends, 'Russian Employment of Tanks', No. 18, 11 February, 1943.

Tactical and Technical Trends, 'Some Principles from the War on the Russian Front', No. 22, April 8, 1943.

Carlo Rastrelli, 'Un Esercito in Camicia Nera', *Storia Militare,* June 2004.

Salvatore Vasta, 'Battaglioni M', *Coorte*, vol. 1, issue n.7, 2000.

Books

Apostolo, G., and Massimello, G., *Italian Aces of World War Two* (Oxford: Osprey, 2000).

Askey, N., *Operation Barbarossa: The Complete Organizational and Statistical Analysis* (New York: Lulu Publishing, 2013).

Avigliano, M., and Palmentieri, M., *L'Italia di Salo': 1943–45* (Bologna: Il Mulino, 2016).

Badoglio, P., *L' Italia nella seconda guerra mondiale. Memorie e documenti* (Milan: Mondadori, 1946).

Battistelli, P. P., and Crociani, P., Italian Elite Units & Special Forces 1940–43 (Oxford: Osprey, 2011).

Bedeschi, G., *Fronte russo: c'ero anch'io* (Milan: Mursia, 1983).

Bishop, C., *SS Hitler's Foreign Divisions: Foreign Volunteers in the Waffen-SS 1940–45* (London: Amber books, 2013).

Burgwyn, H. J., *Mussolini Warlord* (New York: Enigma Books, 2012).
Campbell, D., *Winter War 1939–40* (Oxford: Osprey, 2016).
Cappellano, F., and Pignato, N., *Andare contro i carri armati* (Udine: Gaspari Editore, 2009).
Cavallero, U., *Diario* (Rome: Ciarrapico Editore, 1984).
Ceva, L., *La condotta italiana nella guerra–Cavallero e il Comando Supremo 1941–1942* (Milan: Feltrinelli, 1975).
Corti, E., Few *Returned Twenty-eight Days on the Russian Front, Winter 1942–1943* (Columbia: University of Missouri Press, 1997).
Crespi, B., *La battaglia di Natale dal diario storico di un ufficiale del Corpo di spedizione italiano in Russia* (Milan: Longanesi ,1965).
de Felice, R., *Mussolini l'alleato*, tomo *1* (Turin: Einaudi, 1990).
di Colloredo, P. R., *Emme rossa* (Genoa: Associazione Culturale, 2008).
Estes, K., *A European Anabasis: Western European Volunteers in the German Army and SS* (Solihull: Helion and Co., 2014).
Fabei, S., *Tagliamento: La legione delle camicie nere in Russia 1941–1943* (Rome: Edibus, 2014).
Forczyk, R., *Tank Warfare on the Eastern Front 1941–1942* (Barnsley: Pen & Sword, 2014).
Fugate, B. I., *Operation Barbarossa: Strategy and Tactics on the Eastern Front, 1941* (Novato: Presidio, 1984).
Giusti, M. T., *La Campagna di Russia* (Bologna: Il Mulino, 2016).
Glantz, D. M., *Barbarossa: Hitler's Invasion of Russia 1941* (Stroud: Tempus, 2001).
Gooch, J., (ed.) *Decisive Campaigns of the Second World War* (London: Frank Cass, 2004).
Greene, J., and Massignani, A., Rommel's *North Africa Campaign: September 1940–November 1942*(New York: Da Capo Press, 1999).
Griffith, P., *World War II Desert Tactics* (Oxford: Osprey, 2009).
Guerrazzi, A. O., *The Italian Army in Slovenia: Strategies of Antipartisan Repression, 1941–1943* (London: Palgrave MacMillan, 2013).
Hamilton, H., *Sacrifice on the Steppe* (Mechanicsburg: Stackpole, 2014).
Jurado, C. C., *Blue Division Soldier 1941–45: Spanish Volunteer on the Eastern Front* (Oxford: Osprey, 2014).
Kaufmann, J. E., Kaufmann, H. W., Potocnik, A. J., and Lang, P., *The Maginot Line* (Barnsley: Pen & Sword Military, 2017).
Kesserling, A., *The Memoirs of Field-Marshal Kesselring* (New York: Skyhorse Publishing, 2016).
Kleinfeld, G. R., and Tambs, L. A., *Hitler's Spanish Legion: The Blue Division in Russia in WWII* (Mechanicsburg: Stackpole, 2014).
Knox, M., *Mussolini Unleashed, 1939–1941* (Cambridge: Cambridge University Press, 1982).
Kurowski, F., *Infantry Aces: The German Soldier in Combat in World War II* (Mechanigsburg: Stackpole, 2010).
Lenzi, L., *Dal Dnieper al Don. La 63a legione CC. NN. Tagliamento nella Campagna di Russia. Rievocazione di Egisto Laldi, documentazione del Gruppo reduci della Legione* (Rome: Volpe Editore, 1968).
Lucas, E., *Storia delle unita' combattenti della MVSN* (Rome: Volpe, 1976).
Luoni, V., *La Pasubio sul fronte russo* (Roma: Edizioni dell'Ateneo & Bizzarri, 1977).
Magenheimer, H., *Hitler's War* (London: Arms and Armour, 1998).
Malatesta, L., *Storia della Legione Tagliamento dalla fondazione alla guerra di Russia* (Varese: Pietro Macchione Editore, 2001).
Massignani, A., *Alpini e tedeschi sul Don. Documenti e testimonianze sulla ritirata del Corpo d'armata alpino e del XXIV Panzerkorps germanico in Russia nel gennaio 1943* (Valdagno: Rossato Ed., 1991).

McCarthy, P., *Panzerkrieg: The Rise and Fall of Hitler's Tank Divisions* (New York: Carroll and Graf, 2002).
Messe, G., *La Guerra al fronte russo* (Milan: Rizzoli, 1964).
Miller, D., Fighting *Men of World War II: Uniforms, Equipment and Weapons* (Mechanicsburg: Stackpole, 2012), p. 365.
Mitcham, Jr., S. W., and von Stauffenberg, F., *The Battle of Sicily* (Mechanicsburg: Stackpole, 2012).
Morgan, P., *The Fall of Mussolini* (Oxford: Oxford University Press, 2007).
Oliva, G., *Foibe. Le stragi negate degli italiani della Venezia Giulia e dell'Istria* (Milan: Mondadori, 2003).
Rastrelli, C., *L'ultimo comandante delle camicie nere. Enzo Emilio Galbiati* (Milan: Ugo Mursia Editore, 2016).
Rossi, E. A., *A Nation Collapses: The Italian Surrender of September 1943* (Cambridge: Cambridge University Press, 2000).
Rottman, G. L., *Panzerfaust and Panzerschreck* (Oxford: Osprey, 2016).
Rottman, P., *Soviet Rifleman 1941-45* (Oxford: Osprey, 2007).
Safronov, V., *Italyanskie vojska na Vostochnom fronte. 1941–1943* (Moscow, 1990).
Sangster, A., and Battistelli, P. P., *Myths, Amnesia and Reality in Military Conflicts, 1935–1945* (Cambridge Scholars Publishing, 2017).
Schlemmer, T., Die Italiener an der Ostfront 1942/43. Dokumente zu Mussolinis Krieg gegen die Sowjetunion, hrsg. und eingeleitet von Thomas Schlemmer, München 2005. The Italian edition: *Invasori non vittime: La Campagna Italiana in Russia* (Bari: Laterza, 2008).
Stern, M. R., and Hieddeger, H., *Ritorno sul Don* (Milan: Transeruropa, 2008).
Stern, M. R., *Il sergente nella neve* (Turin: Einaudi, 1967).
Sullivan, B. R., 'The Italian Armed Forces, 1918–40', in Williamson Murray, Allan R. Millett, *Military Effectiveness, vol. 2* (Cambridge, Cambridge University Press, 2010).
Sweet, J., *Iron Arm: The Mechanization of Mussolini's Army* (Mechanicsburg: Stackpole, 2011).
Syron, M., and McCarty, P., *Panzerkrieg: The Rise and Fall of Hitler's Tank Divisions* (London: Constable Publication, 2002).
Ufficio Storico, *Le operazioni delle unita' italiane al fronte russo (1941–43)* (Rome: Ufficio Storico, 2000).
Valori, A., *Gli Italiani in Russia* (Milan: Betti, 1967).
Vicentini, C., *Il sacrificio della Julia in Russia* (Udine, Gaspari Editore, 2011).
Weinberg, G., *A World at Arms* (Cambridge: Cambridge University Press, 1994).
West Point History of World War Two (New York: Simon and Schuster, 2015).
Zanlucchi, P., *La milizia del Duce muore sul Don—La 41ª Legione 'Cesare Battisti': memorie dal fronte russo 1942–1943*, (Rovereto: Egon Edizioni, 2014).

Internet

carlorastrelli.it/distintivi-di-grado-degli-ufficiali-della-mvsn-4/
carlorastrelli.it/il-generale-enzo-galbiati/
carlorastrelli.it/un-esercito-in-camicia-nera/
Rossi, A., 'Le Camicie Nere passano ai tedeschi', anpi.it/media/uploads/patria/2003/4-5/31_33_Rossi.pdf
www.quirinale.it/elementi/DettaglioOnorificenze.aspx?decorato=13260
www.quirinale.it/elementi/DettaglioOnorificenze.aspx?decorato=45329